Thackray's 2016 Investor's Guide

THACKRAY'S
2016
INVESTOR'S
GUIDE

Brooke Thackray MBA, CIM, CFP

Published in 2015 by: MountAlpha Media:
alphamountain.com

ISBN13: 978-0-9918735-4-8

Printed and Bound by Webcom Inc.
10 9 8 7 6 5 4 3 2 1

To my wife Jane

Acknowledgments

This book is the product of many years of research and could not have been written without the help of many people. I would like to thank my wife, Jane Steer-Thackray, and my children Justin, Megan, Carly and Madeleine, for the help they have given me and their patience during the many hours that I have devoted to writing this book. Thanks must be given to Wade Guenther for helping me source and filter a lot of the data in this book. Special mention goes to Jane Stiegler, my proofreader and editor, for the countless hours she spent helping with formatting and editing this book.

INTRODUCTION

2016 THACKRAY'S INVESTOR'S GUIDE
Technical Commentary

The seasonal strategies that I have included in my previous books have proven to be very successful. The buy and sell dates are based upon iterative comparisons of different time periods measured by gain and frequency of success. Although the buy and sell dates are the optimal dates on which seasonal investors should focus on making their investment decisions, the markets have different dynamics from year to year, shifting the optimal buy and sell dates. Combining technical analysis with seasonal trends helps to adjust the decision process, allowing seasonal investors to enter and exit trades early or late, depending on market conditions.

The universe of technical indicators and techniques is huge. It is impossible to use all of the indicators. Only a small number of indicators and techniques that suit an investment style should be used. In the case of seasonal investing, a lot of long-term indicators provide very little benefit. For example, the standard Moving Average Convergence Divergence (MACD), is far too slow to be of any use in shorter term seasonal strategies. In this book I have chosen to illustrate the use of three technical indicators that have provided a lot of value in fine-tuning the dates for seasonal investing: Full Stochastic Oscillator (FSO), Relative Strength Index (RSI) and Relative Strength. The indicators are used in conjunction with the price pattern and moving averages of the security being considered. Investors must remember that technical analysis is not absolute and there will be exceptions when utilizing indicators and price patterns.

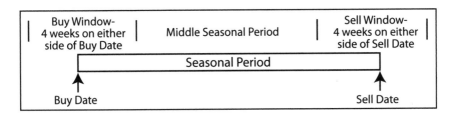

To combine technical indicators with seasonal trends, the indicators should only be used within the windows of the buy and sell dates. The indicators should be ignored outside the seasonal buy/sell windows. The only exception to this occurs when an indicator gives a signal during its middle seasonal period, which is in the seasonal period, but after the buy window and before the sell window. In this case a technical signal can support selling a full position based upon a fundamental breakdown in the price action of a security. By itself, a FSO or RSI indicator showing weakness in a security during its middle seasonal period, does not warrant action, it can only be used to support a decision being made in conjunction with underperformance relative to the broad market, or a major price action break.

Below are short descriptions of the three technical indicators that are used in this book and the metrics of how they are used with seasonal analysis. Full evaluation of the indicators and their uses with seasonal analysis is beyond the scope of this book.

Full Stochastic Oscillator (FSO)

A stochastic oscillator is a range bound momentum indicator that tracks the location of the close price relative to the high-low range, over a set number of periods. It tracks the momentum of price change and helps to indicate the strength and direction of price movement.

I have found that generally the best method to combine the FSO with seasonal trends is to buy an early partial position when the FSO turns up above 20 within four weeks of the seasonal buy date. Additionally, the best time to sell an early partial position occurs when the FSO turns below 80, within four weeks of the seasonal exit date.

For practical purposes in this book, %D, a 3 period smoothed %K, has been omitted. The standard variables are used in the FSO calculation (14 day look back period, and a 3 day simple moving average smoothing constant).

Relative Strength Index (RSI)

The RSI is a momentum oscillator that measures the speed and change of price movements. I have found that the best method to combine the RSI with seasonal trends is to buy an early partial position when the RSI turns up above 30 within four weeks of the seasonal buy date. The best time to sell an early partial position occurs when the RSI turns below 70, within four weeks of the seasonal exit date. Compared with the FSO, the RSI is less useful as it is slower and gives too few signals in the buy/sell windows.

Relative Strength

Relative strength calculates the performance of one security versus another security. When the relative strength is increasing, it indicates the seasonal security is outperforming. When the relative strength is declining, the seasonal security is underperforming. When a downward trend line is broken to the upside by the performance of the seasonal security, relative to the benchmark, this is a positive signal. This action carries a lot of weight and can justify a full early entry into a position if other technical evidence is positive. Likewise, if an upward trend line is broken to the downside, a negative technical signal is given and can justify a full early exit from a position if other technical evidence is negative.

THACKRAY'S 2016 INVESTOR'S GUIDE

You can choose great companies to invest in and still underperform the market. Unless you are in the market at the right time and in the best sectors, your investment expertise can be all for naught.

Successful investors know when they should be in the market. Very successful investors know when they should be in the market, and the best sectors in which to invest. *Thackray's 2016 Investor's Guide* is designed to provide investors with the knowledge of when and what to buy, and when to sell.

The goal of this book is to help investors capture extra profits by taking advantage of the seasonal trends in the markets. This book is straightforward. There are no complicated rules and there are no complex algorithms. The strategies put forward are intuitive and easy to understand.

It does not matter if you are a short-term or long-term investor, this book can be used to help establish entry and exit points. For the short-term investor, specific periods are identified that can provide profitable opportunities. For the long-term investor best buy dates are identified to launch new investments on a sound footing.

The stock market has its seasonal rhythms. Historically, the broad markets, such as the S&P 500, have a seasonal trend of outperforming during certain times of the year. Likewise, different sectors of the market have their own seasonal trends of outperformance. When oil stocks tend to do well in the springtime before "driving season," health care stocks tend to underperform the market. When utilities do well in the summertime, industrials do not. With different markets and different sectors having a tendency to outperform at different times of the year, there is always a place to invest.

Until recently, investors did not have access to the information necessary to analyse and create sector strategies. In recent years there have been a great number of sector Exchange Traded Funds (ETFs) and sector indexes introduced into the market. For the first time, investors are now able to easily implement a sector rotation strategy. This book provides a seasonal road map of what sectors tend to do well at different times of the year. It is a first of its kind, revealing new sector-based strategies that have never before been published.

In terms of market timing there are ample strategies in this book to help determine the times when equities should be over or underweight. During a favorable time for the market, investments can be purchased to overweight equities relative to their target weight in a portfolio (staying within risk tolerances). During an unfavorable time, investments can be sold to underweight equities relative to their target.

A large part of the book is devoted to sector seasonality – the underpinnings for a sector rotation strategy. The most practical rotation strategy is to create a core part of a portfolio that represents the broad market and then set aside an allocation to be rotated between favored sectors from one time period to the next.

It does not makes sense to apply any investment strategy only once with a large investment. Seasonal strategies are no exception. The best way to apply an investment strategy is to use a disciplined methodology that allows for diversification and a large enough number of investments to help remove the anomalies of the market. This reduces risk and increases the probability of a long term gain.

Following the specific buy and sell dates put forth in this book would have netted an investor large, above market returns. To "turbo-charge" gains, an investor can combine seasonality with technical analysis. As the seasonal periods are never exactly the same, technical analysis can help investors capture the extra gains when a sector turns up early, or momentum extends the trend.

IMPORTANT: Strategy Buy and Sell Dates

The beginning date of every strategy period in this book represents a full day in the market; therefore, investors should buy at the end of the preceding market day. For example the *Biotech Summer Solstice* seasonal period of strength is from June 23rd to September 13th. To be in the sector for the full seasonal period, an investor would enter the market before the closing bell on June 22nd. If the buy date landed on a weekend or holiday, then the buy would occur at the end of the preceding trading day.

The last day of a trading strategy is the sell date. For example, the Biotech sector investment would be sold at the end of the day on September 13th. If the sell date is a holiday or weekend, then the investment would be sold at the close on the preceding trading day.

What is Seasonal Investing?

In order to properly understand seasonal investing in the stock market, it is important to look briefly at its evolution. It may surprise investors to know that seasonal investing at the broad market level, i.e. Dow Jones or S&P 500, has been around for a long time. The initial seasonal strategies were written by Fields (1931, 1934) and Watchel (1942), who focused on the *January Effect*. Coincidentally, this strategy is still bantered about in the press every year.

Yale Yirsch Senior has been largely responsible for the next stage in the evolution, producing the *Stock Trader's Almanac* for more than forty years. This publication focuses on broad market trends such as the best six months of the year and tendencies of the market to do well depending on the political party in power and holiday trades.

In 1999, Brooke Thackray and Bruce Lindsay wrote, *Time In Time Out: Outsmart the Market Using Calendar Investment Strategies*. This work focused on a comprehensive analysis of the six month seasonal cycle and other shorter seasonal cycles in the broad markets such as the S&P 500.

Seasonal investing has changed over time. The focus has shifted from broad market strategies to taking advantage of sector rotation opportunities – investing in different sectors at different times of the year, depending on their seasonal strength. This has created a whole new set of investment opportunities. Rather than just being "in or out" of the market, investors can now always be invested by shifting between different sectors and asset classes, taking advantage of both up and down markets.

Definition – Seasonal investing is a method of investing in the market at the time of the year when it typically does well, or investing in a sector of the market when it typically outperforms the broad market such as the S&P 500.

The term seasonal investing is somewhat of a misnomer, and it is easy to see why some investors might believe that the discipline relates to investing based upon the seasons of the year – winter, spring, summer and autumn. Other than some agricultural commodities where the price is often correlated to growing seasons, generally seasonal investment strategies use the calendar as a reference for buy and sell dates. It is usually a specific event, i.e. Christmas sales, that occurs on a recurring annual basis that creates the seasonal opportunity.

The discipline of seasonal investing is not restricted to the stock market. It has been used successfully for a number of years in the commodities market. The opportunities in this market tend to be based upon changes in supply and/or demand that occur on a yearly basis. Most commodities, especially the agricultural commodities, tend to have cyclical supply cycles, i.e., crops are harvested only at certain times of the year. The supply bulge that occurs at the same time every year provides seasonal investors with profit opportunities. Recurring increased seasonal demand for commodities also plays a major part in providing opportunities for seasonal investors. This applies to most metals and many other commodities, whether the end-product is industrial or consumer based.

Seasonal investment strategies can be used with a lot of different types of investments. The premise is the same, outperformance during a certain period of the year based upon a repeating event in the markets or economy. In my past writings I have developed seasonal strategies that have been used successfully in the stock, commodity, bond and foreign exchange markets. Seasonal investing is still relatively new for most markets with a lot of new opportunities waiting to be discovered.

How Does Seasonal Investing Work?

Most stock market sector seasonal trends are the result of a recurring annual catalyst: an event that affects the sector positively. These events can range from a seasonal spike in demand, seasonal inventory lows, weather effects, conferences and other events. Mainstream investors very often anticipate a move in a sector and incorrectly try to take a position just before an event takes place that is supposed to drive a sector higher. A good example of this would be investors buying oil just before the cold weather sets in. Unfortunately, their efforts are usually unsuccessful as they are too late to the party and the opportunity has already passed.

By the time the anticipated event occurs, a substantial amount of investors have bought into the sector – fully pricing in the expected benefit. At this time there is little potential left in the short-term. Unless there is a strong positive surprise, the sector's outperformance tends to slowly roll over. If the event produces less than its desired result, the sector can be severely punished.

So how does the seasonal investor take advantage of this opportunity? "Be there" before the mainstream investors, and get out before they do. Seasonal investors usually enter a sector two or three months before an event is anticipated to have a positive effect on a sector and get out before the actual event takes place. In essence, seasonal investors are benefiting from the mainstream investor's tendency to "buy in" too late.

Seasonality in the markets occurs because of three major reasons: money flow, changing market analyst expectations and the *Anticipation-Realization Cycle*. First, money flows vary throughout the year and at different times of the month. Generally, money flows increase at the end of the year and into the start of the next year. This is a result of year end bonuses and tax related investments. In addition, money flows increase at month end from money managers "window dressing" their portfolios. As a result of these money flows, the months around the end of the year and the days around the end of the month, tend to have a stronger performance than the other times of the year.

Second, the analyst expectations cycle tends to push markets up at the end of the year and the beginning of the next year. Stock market analysts tend to be a positive bunch – the large investment houses pay them to be positive. They start the year with aggressive earnings for all of their favorite companies. As the year progresses, they generally back off their earnings forecast, which decreases their support for the market. After a lull in the summer and early autumn months, they start to focus on the next year with another rosy forecast. As a result, the stock market tends to rise once again at the end of the year.

Third, at the sector level, sectors of the market tend to be greatly influenced by the *Anticipation-Realization Cycle*. Although some investors may not be familiar with the term "anticipation-realization," they probably are familiar with the concept of "buy the rumor – sell the fact," or in the famous words of Lord Rothschild "Buy on the sound of the war-cannons; sell on the sound of the victory trumpets."

The *Anticipation-Realization Cycle* as it applies to human behavior has been much studied in psychology journals. In the investment world, the premise of this cycle rests on investors anticipating a positive event in the market to drive prices higher and buying in ahead of the event. When the event takes place, or is realized, upward pressure on prices decreases as there is very little impetus for further outperformance.

A good example of the *Anticipation-Realization Cycle* takes place with the "conference effect." Very often large industries have major conferences that occur at approximately the same time every year. Major companies in the industry often hold back positive announce-

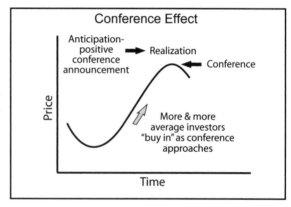

ments and product introductions to be released during the conference.

Two to three months prior to the conference, seasonal investors tend to buy into the sector. Shortly afterwards, the mainstream investors anticipate "good news" from the conference and start to buy in. As a result, prices are pushed up. Just before the conference starts, seasonal investors capture their profits by exiting their positions. As the conference unfolds, company announcements are made (realized), but as the potential good news has already been priced into the sector, there is little to push prices higher and the sector typically starts to rolls over.

The same *Anticipation-Realization Cycle* takes place with increased demand for oil to meet the "summer driving season", increased sales of goods at Christmas time, increased demand for gold jewellery to meet the autumn and winter demand, and many other events that tend to drive the outperformance of different sectors.

Does Seasonal Investing ALWAYS Work?

The simple answer to the above question is "No." There is not any investment system in the world that works all of the time. When following any investment system, it is probability of success that counts. It has often been said that "being correct in the markets 60% of the time will make you rich." Investors tend to forget this and become too emotionally attached to their losses. Just about every investment trading book states that investors typically fail to let their profits run and cut their losses quickly. I concur. In my many years in the investment industry, the biggest mistake that I have found with investors is not being able to cut their losses. Everyone wants to be right, that is how we have been raised. Investors feel that if they sell at a loss they have failed, and as a result, often suffer bigger losses by waiting for their position to trade at profit.

With any investment system, investors should let probability work for them. This means that investors should be able to enter and exit positions capturing both gains and losses without becoming emotionally attached to any positions. Emotional attachment clouds judgement, which leads to errors. When all of the trades are put together, the goal is for profits to be larger than losses in a way that minimizes risks and beats the market.

If we examine the winter oil stock trade, we can see how probability has worked in an investor's favor. This trade is based upon the premise that at the tail end of winter, the refineries drive up demand for oil in order to produce enough gas for the approaching "driving season" that starts in the spring. As a result, oil stocks tend to increase and outperform the market (from February 25th to May 9th). The oil stock sector, represented by the Amex Oil Index (XOI), has been very successful at

XOI vs S&P 500 1984 to 2015			
Feb 25 to May 9	S&P 500	positive XOI	Diff
1984	1.7 %	5.6 %	3.9 %
1985	1.4	4.9	3.5
1986	6.0	7.7	1.7
1987	3.7	25.5	21.8
1988	-3.0	5.6	8.6
1989	6.3	8.1	1.8
1990	5.8	-0.6	-6.3
1991	4.8	6.8	2.0
1992	0.9	5.8	4.9
1993	0.3	6.3	6.0
1994	-4.7	3.2	7.9
1995	7.3	10.3	3.1
1996	-2.1	2.2	4.3
1997	1.8	4.7	2.9
1998	7.5	9.8	2.3
1999	7.3	35.4	28.1
2000	4.3	22.2	17.9
2001	0.8	10.2	9.4
2002	-1.5	5.3	6.9
2003	12.1	5.7	-6.4
2004	-3.5	4.0	7.5
2005	-1.8	-1.0	0.8
2006	2.8	9.4	6.6
2007	4.2	10.1	5.8
2008	2.6	7.6	5.0
2009	20.2	15.8	-4.4
2010	0.5	-2.3	-2.8
2011	3.1	-0.6	-3.7
2012	-0.8	-13.4	-12.5
2013	7.3	3.8	-3.5
2014	1.7	9.1	7.4
2015	0.3	1.2	1.1
Avg	3.0 %	7.1 %	4.1 %
Fq > 0	78 %	84 %	78 %

this time of year, producing an average return of 7.1% and beating the S&P 500 by 4.1%, from 1984 to 2015. In addition it has been positive 27 out of

32 times. Investors should always evaluate the strength of seasonal trades before applying them to their own portfolios.

If an investor started using the seasonal investment discipline in 1984 and chose to invest in the winter-oil trade, they would have been very happy with the results. Over the last few years, the fact that the trade did not produce a gain in 2010, 2011 and 2012, does not mean that the seasonal trade no longer works. All seasonal trades go through periods, sometimes multiple years where they do not work. An investor can start any methodology of trading at the "wrong time," and be unsuccessful in a particular trade. In fact, if an investor started the oil-winter trade in 1990 and had given up in the same year, they would have missed the following successful twelve years. Investors have to remember that it is the final score that counts, after all of the gains have been weighed against the losses.

In practical terms, investors should not put all of their investment strategies in one basket. If one or two large investments were made based upon seasonal strategies, it is possible that the seasonal methodology might be inappropriately evaluated and its use discontinued. A much more prudent strategy is to use a larger number of strategic seasonal investments with smaller investments. The end result will be to put the seasonal probability to work with a much greater chance of success.

Measuring Seasonal Performance

How do you determine if a seasonal strategy has been successful? Many people feel that ten years of data is a good sample size, others feel that fifteen years is better, and yet others feel that the more data the better. I tend to fall into the camp that, if possible, it is best to use fifteen or twenty years of data for sectors and more data for the broad markets, such as the S&P 500. Although the most recent data in almost any analytical framework is the most relevant, it is important to get enough data to reflect a sector's performance across different economic conditions. Given that historically the economy has performed on an eight year cycle, four years of expansion and then four years of contraction, using a short data set does not provide for enough exposure to different economic conditions.

A data set that is too long can run into the problem of older data having too much of an influence on the numbers when fundamental factors affecting a sector have changed. It is important to look at trends over time and assess if there has been a change that should be considered in determining the dates for a seasonal cycle. Each sector should be judged on its own merit. The analysis tables in this book illustrate the performance level for each year in order to provide the opportunity for readers to determine any relevant changes.

In order to determine if a seasonal strategy is effective there are two possible benchmarks, absolute and relative performance. Absolute performance measures if a profit is made and relative performance measures the performance of a sector in relationship to a major market. Both measurements have their merits and depending on your investment style, one measurement may be more valuable than another. This book provides both sets of measurement in tables and graphs.

It is not just the average percent gain of a sector over a certain time period that determines success. It is possible that one or two spectacular years of performance skew the results substantially (particularly with a small data set). The frequency of success is also very important: the higher the percentage of success the better. Also, the fewer large drawdowns the better. There is no magic number (percent success rate) per se of what constitutes a successful strategy. The success rate should be above fifty percent, otherwise it would be better to just invest in the broad market. Ideally speaking a strategy should have a high percentage success rate on both an absolute and relative basis. Some strategies are stronger than others, but that does not mean that the weaker strategies should not be used. Prudence should be used in determining the ideal portfolio allocation.

Illustrating the strength of a sector's seasonal performance can be accomplished through either an absolute yearly average performance graph, or a relative yearly average performance graph. The absolute graph shows the average yearly cumulative gain for a set number of years. It lets a reader visually identify the strong periods during the year. The relative graph shows the average yearly cumulative gain for the sector relative to the benchmark index.

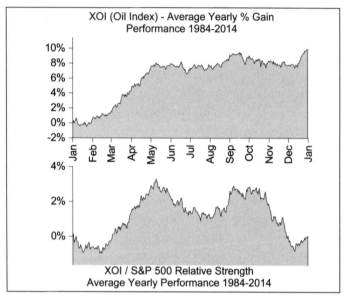

Both graphs are useful in determining the strength of a particular seasonal strategy. In the above diagram, the top graph illustrates the average year for the NYSE Arca Oil & Gas Index (XOI) from 1984 to 2014. Essentially it illustrates the cumulative average gain if an investment were made in the index. The steep rising line starting in January/February shows the overall price rise that typically occurs in this sector at this time of year. In May the line flattens out and then rises very modestly starting in July.

The bottom graph is a ratio graph, illustrating the strength of the XOI Index relative to the S&P 500. It is derived by dividing the average year of the XOI by the average year of the S&P 500. When the line in the graph is rising, the XOI is outperforming the S&P 500, and vise versa when it is declining. This is an important graph and should be used in considering seasonal investments because the S&P 500 is a viable alternative to the energy sector. If both markets are increasing, but the S&P 500 is increasing at a faster rate, the S&P 500 represents a more attractive opportunity. This is particularly true when measuring the risk of a volatile sector relative to the broad market. If both investments were expected to produce the same rate of return, generally the broad market is a better investment because of its diversification.

Who Can Use Seasonal Investing?

Any investor from novice to expert, from short-term trader to long-term investor can benefit from using seasonal analysis. Seasonal investing is unique because it is an easy to understand system that can be used by itself or as a complement to another investment discipline. For the novice it provides an easy to follow strategy that makes intuitive sense. For the expert it can be used as a stand-alone system or as a complement to an existing system.

Seasonal investing is easily understood by all levels of investors, which allows investors to make rational decisions. This may seem obvious, but it is very common for investors to listen to a "guru of the market", be impressed and blindly follow his advice. When the advice works there is no problem. When the advice does not work investors wonder why they made the investment in the first place. When investors do not understand their investments it causes stress, bad decisions and a lack of "stick-to-it ness" with any investment discipline. Even expert investors realize the importance of understanding your investments. Peter Lynch of Fidelity Investments used to say "Never invest in any idea that you can't illustrate with a crayon." Investors do not need to go that far, but they should understand their investments.

Novice investors find seasonal strategies very easy to understand because they are intuitive. They do not have to be investing for years to understand why seasonal strategies work. They understand that an increase in demand for gold every year at the same time causes a ripple effect in the stock market pushing up gold stocks at the same time every year.

Most expert investors use information from a variety of sources in making their decisions. Even experts that primarily use fundamental analysis can benefit from using seasonal trends to get an edge in the market. Fundamental analysis is a very crude tool and provides very little in the way of timing an investment. Using seasonal trends can help with the timing of the buy and sell decisions and produce extra profit.

Seasonal investing can be used by both short-term and long-term investors, but in different ways. For short-term investors it provides a complete trade – buy and sell dates. For long-term investors it can provide a buy date for a sector of interest.

Combining Seasonal Analysis with other Investment Disciplines

Seasonal investing used by itself has historically produced above average market returns. Depending on an investor's particular style, it can be combined with one of the other three investment disciplines: fundamental, quantitative and technical analysis. There are two basic ways to combine seasonal analysis with other investment methodologies – as the primary or secondary method. If it is used as a primary method, seasonally strong time periods are established for a number of sectors and then appropriate sectors are chosen based upon fundamental, quantitative or technical screens. If it is used as a secondary method, sector selections are first made based upon one of three methods and then final sectors are chosen based upon which ones are in their seasonally strong period.

Technical analysis is an ideal mate for seasonal analysis. Unlike fundamental and quantitative analysis, which are very blunt timing tools at best, seasonal and technical analysis can provide specific trigger points to buy and sell. The combination can turbo-charge investment strategies, adding extra profits by fine-tuning entry and exit dates.

Seasonal analysis provides both buy and sell dates. Although a sector in the market can sometimes bottom on the exact seasonal buy date, it more often bottoms a bit early or a bit late. After all, the seasonal buy date is based upon an average of historical performance. Depending on the sector, buying opportunities start to develop approximately one month before and after the seasonal buy date. Using technical analysis gives an investor the advantage of buying into a sector when it turns up early or waiting when it turns up late. Likewise, technical analysis can be used to trigger a sell signal when the market turns down before or after the sell date.

The sell decision can be extended with the help of a trailing stop-loss order. If a sector has strong momentum and the technical tools do not provide a sell signal, it is possible to let the sector "run." When a trailing stop-loss is used, a profitable sell point is established. If the price continues to run, then the selling point is raised. If, on the other hand, the price falls through the stop-loss point, the position is sold.

Sectors of the Market

Standard & Poor's has done an excellent job in categorizing the U.S. stock market into its different parts. Although the demand for this service initially came from institutional investors, many individual investors now seek the same information. Knowing the sector breakdown in the market allows investors to see how different their portfolio is relative to the market. As a result, they are able to make conscious decisions on what parts of the stock market to overweight based upon their beliefs of which sectors will outperform. It also helps control the amount of desired risk.

Standard & Poor's uses four levels of detail in its Global Industry Classification Standard (GICS©) to categorize stock markets around the world. From the most specific, it classifies companies into sub-industries, industries, industry groups and finally economic sectors. All companies in the Standard & Poor's global family of indices are classified according to the GICS structure.

This book focuses on the U.S. market, analysing the trends of the venerable S&P 500 index and its economic sectors and industry groups. The following diagram illustrates the index classified according to its economic sectors.

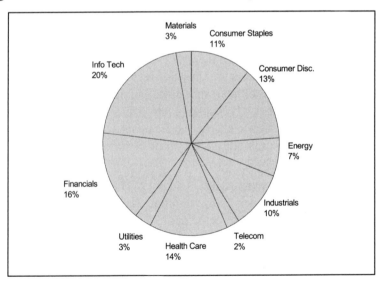

Standard and Poor's, Understanding Sectors, June 30, 2015

For more information on Standard and Poor's Global Industry Classification Standard (GICS©), refer to www.standardandpoors.com

Investment Products – Which One Is The Right One?

There are many ways to take advantage of the seasonal trends at the broad stock market and sector levels. Regardless of the investment products that you currently use, whether exchange traded funds, mutual funds, stocks or options, all can be used with the strategies in this book. Different investments offer different risk-reward relationships and return potential.

Exchange Traded Funds (ETFs)

Exchange Traded Funds (ETFs) offer the purest method of seasonal investment. The broad market ETFs are designed to track the major indices and the sector ETFs are designed to track specific sectors without using active management. Relatively new, ETFs are a great way to capture both market and sector trends. They were originally introduced into the Canadian market in 1993 to represent the Toronto stock market index. Shortly afterward they were introduced to the U.S. market and there are now hundreds of ETFs to represent almost every market, sector, style of investing and company capitalization. Originally ETFs were mainly of interest to institutional investors, but individual investors have fast realized the merits of ETF investing and have made some of the broad market ETFs the most heavily traded securities in the world.

An ETF is a single security that represents a market, such as the S&P 500; a sector of the market, such as the financial sector; or a commodity, such as gold. In the case of the S&P 500, an investor buying one security is buying all 500 stocks in the index. By investing into a financial ETF, an investor is buying the companies that make up the financial sector of the market. By investing into a gold commodity ETF, an investor is buying a security that represents the price of gold.

ETFs trade on the open market just like stocks. They have a bid and an ask, can be shorted and many are option eligible. They are a very low cost, tax efficient method of targeting specific parts of the market.

Mutual Funds

Mutual funds are a good way to combine market or sector investing with active management. In recent years, many mutual fund companies have added sector funds to accommodate an increasing appetite in this area.

As the seasonal strategies put forward in this book have a short-term nature, it is important to make sure that there are no fees (or a nominal charge) for getting into and out of a position in the market.

Stocks

Stocks provide an opportunity to make better returns than the market or sector. If the market increases during its seasonal period, some stocks will increase dramatically more than the index. Choosing one of the outperforming stocks will greatly enhance returns; choosing one of the underperforming stocks can create substantial loses. Using stocks requires increased attention to diversification and security selection.

Options

Disclaimer: Options involve risk and are not suitable for every investor. Because they are cash-settled, investors should be aware of the special risks associated with index options and should consult a tax advisor. Prior to buying or selling options, a person must receive a copy of Characteristics and Risks of Standardized Options and should thoroughly understand the risks involved in any use of options. Copies may be obtained from The Options Clearing Corporation, 440 S. LaSalle Street, Chicago, IL 60605.

Options, for more sophisticated investors, are a good tool to take advantage of both market and sector opportunities. An option position can be established with either stocks or ETFs. There are many different ways to use options for seasonal trends: establish a long position on the market during its seasonally strong period, establish a short position during its seasonally weak period, or create a spread trade to capture the superior gains of a sector over the market.

THACKRAY'S 2016
INVESTOR'S GUIDE

CONTENTS

JANUARY

	MONDAY	TUESDAY	WEDNESDAY
WEEK 01	28	29	30
WEEK 02	**4** 27	**5** 26	**6** 25
WEEK 03	**11** 20	**12** 19	**13** 18
WEEK 04	**18** 13 USA Market Closed- Martin Luther King Jr. Day	**19** 12	**20** 11
WEEK 05	**25** 6	**26** 5	**27** 4

THURSDAY	FRIDAY
31	**1** 30
	CAN Market Closed - New Year's Day
	USA Market Closed - New Year's Day
7 24	**8** 23
14 17	**15** 16
21 10	**22** 9
28 3	**29** 2

FEBRUARY

M	T	W	T	F	S	S
1	2	3	4	5	6	7
8	9	10	11	12	13	14
15	16	17	18	19	20	21
22	23	24	24	26	27	28
29						

MARCH

M	T	W	T	F	S	S
	1	2	3	4	5	6
7	8	9	10	11	12	13
14	15	16	17	18	19	20
21	22	23	24	25	26	27
28	29	30	31			

APRIL

M	T	W	T	F	S	S
				1	2	3
4	5	6	7	8	9	10
11	12	13	14	15	16	17
18	19	20	21	22	23	24
25	26	27	28	29	30	

MAY

M	T	W	T	F	S	S
						1
2	3	4	5	6	7	8
9	10	11	12	13	14	15
16	17	18	19	20	21	22
23	24	25	26	27	28	29
30	31					

JANUARY
SUMMARY

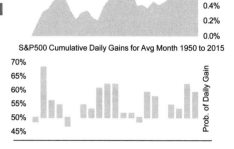

S&P500 Cumulative Daily Gains for Avg Month 1950 to 2015

	Dow Jones	S&P 500	Nasdaq	TSX Comp
Month Rank	6	5	1	3
# Up	42	40	28	19
# Down	23	25	14	11
% Pos	65	62	65	63
% Avg. Gain	1.0	1.1	2.7	1.2

Dow & S&P 1950-2014, Nasdaq 1972-2014, TSX 1985-2014

♦ From the lows in October 2013 and October 2014, the S&P 500 rallied strongly into the respective year-ends. In both cases, investors questioned stock valuations and pushed the S&P 500 down in January. ♦ Defensive sectors tend to perform poorly in January and in 2015, after a brief rally higher at the beginning of January, the utilities sector started a multi-month correction. ♦ Small cap stocks tend to perform well in January and outperform the S&P 500. This was true in 2015 as small caps received support from a stronger U.S. dollar.

BEST / WORST JANUARY BROAD MKTS. 2006-2015

BEST JANUARY MARKETS
♦ Russell 2000 (2006) 8.9%
♦ Nasdaq (2012) 8.0%
♦ Nikkei 225 (2013) 7.2%

WORST JANUARY MARKETS
♦ Nikkei (2008) -11.2%
♦ Russell 2000 (2009) -11.2%
♦ Nasdaq (2008) -9.9%

Index Values End of Month

	2006	2007	2008	2009	2010	2011	2012	2013	2014	2015
Dow	10,865	12,622	12,650	8,001	10,067	11,892	12,633	13,861	15,699	17,165
S&P 500	1,280	1,438	1,379	826	1,074	1,286	1,312	1,498	1,783	1,995
Nasdaq	2,306	2,464	2,390	1,476	2,147	2,700	2,814	3,142	4,104	4,635
TSX Comp.	11,946	13,034	13,155	8,695	11,094	13,552	12,452	12,685	13,695	14,674
Russell 1000	1,341	1,507	1,444	860	1,133	1,371	1,396	1,599	1,916	2,137
Russell 2000	1,822	1,989	1,773	1,102	1,496	1,942	1,970	2,242	2,811	2,896
FTSE 100	5,760	6,203	5,880	4,150	5,189	5,863	5,682	6,277	6,510	6,749
Nikkei 225	16,650	17,383	13,592	7,994	10,198	10,238	8,803	11,139	14,915	17,674

Percent Gain for January

	2006	2007	2008	2009	2010	2011	2012	2013	2014	2015
Dow	1.4	1.3	-4.6	-8.8	-3.5	2.7	3.4	5.8	-5.3	-3.7
S&P 500	2.5	1.4	-6.1	-8.6	-3.7	2.3	4.4	5.0	-3.6	-3.1
Nasdaq	4.6	2.0	-9.9	-6.4	-5.4	1.8	8.0	4.1	-1.7	-2.1
TSX Comp.	6.0	1.0	-4.9	-3.3	-5.5	0.8	4.2	2.0	0.5	0.3
Russell 1000	2.7	1.8	-6.1	-8.3	-3.7	2.3	4.8	5.3	-3.3	-2.8
Russell 2000	8.9	1.6	-6.9	-11.2	-3.7	-0.3	7.0	6.2	-2.8	-3.3
FTSE 100	2.5	-0.3	-8.9	-6.4	-4.1	-0.6	2.0	6.4	-3.5	2.8
Nikkei 225	3.3	0.9	-11.2	-9.8	-3.3	0.1	4.1	7.2	-8.5	1.3

January Market Avg. Performance 2006 to 2015[1]

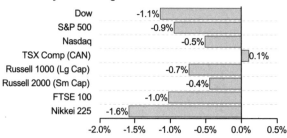

Dow	-1.1%
S&P 500	-0.9%
Nasdaq	-0.5%
TSX Comp (CAN)	0.1%
Russell 1000 (Lg Cap)	-0.7%
Russell 2000 (Sm Cap)	-0.4%
FTSE 100	-1.0%
Nikkei 225	-1.6%

Interest Corner Jan[2]

	Fed Funds % [3]	3 Mo. T-Bill % [4]	10 Yr % [5]	20 Yr % [6]
2015	0.25	0.02	1.68	2.04
2014	0.25	0.02	2.67	3.35
2013	0.25	0.07	2.02	2.79
2012	0.25	0.06	1.83	2.59
2011	0.25	0.15	3.42	4.33

(1) Russell Data provided by Russell (2) Federal Reserve Bank of St. Louis- end of month values (3) Target rate set by FOMC (4)(5)(6) Constant yield maturities.

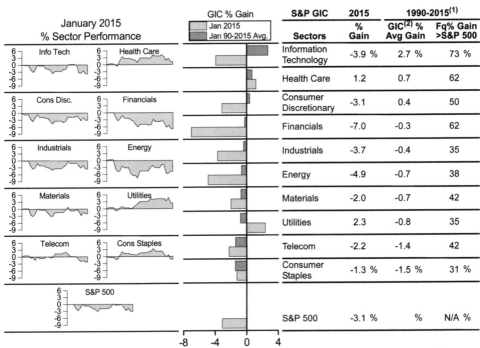

S&P GIC Sectors	2015 % Gain	1990-2015[1]	
		GIC[2] % Avg Gain	Fq% Gain >S&P 500
Information Technology	-3.9 %	2.7 %	73 %
Health Care	1.2	0.7	62
Consumer Discretionary	-3.1	0.4	50
Financials	-7.0	-0.3	62
Industrials	-3.7	-0.4	35
Energy	-4.9	-0.7	38
Materials	-2.0	-0.7	42
Utilities	2.3	-0.8	35
Telecom	-2.2	-1.4	42
Consumer Staples	-1.3 %	-1.5 %	31 %
S&P 500	-3.1 %	%	N/A %

Sector Commentary

♦ After a sharp drop at the beginning of December 2014 and then a sharp rally in the later half of the month, the S&P 500 was set for a breather in January 2015. ♦ The commodity complex continued to struggle. ♦ The financial sector was the worst performing sector, with a loss of 7.0%. Typically, the financial sector should be performing well to support an advancing market. In January, the poorly performing financial sector was indicating that the S&P 500 lacked the power to advance strongly past its previous high level. ♦ Investors were concerned with the valuation of the market and were attracted to the utilities sector, which produced a gain of 2.3% for the month. As investors became more comfortable with the markets towards the end of month, the utilities sector started a multi-month correction.

Sub-Sector Commentary

♦ In some respects, January 2015 was very much like January 2014, as the cyclical sub-sectors, especially the commodity sub-sectors, were the big losers of the month. ♦ Precious metals performed well with gold bullion producing a gain of 4.5%. ♦ Biotech produced a large gain of 5.0%, as mergers and acquisitions helped to boost the sub-sector.

SELECTED SUB-SECTORS[3]

SOX (1995-2015)	-4.9 %	3.8 %	57 %
Home-builders	-2.2	3.1	62
Silver	5.9	3.0	69
Biotech (1993-2015)	5.0	2.4	57
Software & Services	-5.0	2.1	69
Gold (London PM)	4.5	1.4	58
Railroads	-4.4	1.2	58
Steel	-12.4	0.5	50
Pharma	-0.2	0.0	58
Transportation	-4.7	0.0	50
Retail	-0.2	-0.1	54
Banks	-10.7	-0.1	50
Agriculture (1994-2015)	-10.3	-0.6	36
Chemicals	-1.1	-0.7	42
Metals & Mining	-8.7	-1.1	42

(1) Sector data provided by Standard and Poors (2) GIC is short form for Global Industry Classification (3) Sub Sector data provided by Standard and Poors, except where marked by symbol.

U.S. Dollar vs. Euro – "V" Trade
①SELL SHORT (Nov17-Dec31)
②LONG (Jan1-Feb7)

The U.S. dollar tends to underperform the euro from November 17th to December 31st, and then outperform it from January 1st to February 7th.

This down-and-up pattern, creates an opportunistic double-trade strategy. The first leg is a short sell trade for USD/EUR and the second leg is a long position. Both trades are contiguous and create a combination "V" shaped trade.

Most times, the transition between the trades will not take place precisely at the end of the year and technical analysis should be used to help with the appropriate timing.

88% of the time positive

What makes the "V" trade a success is that the sum of its parts is greater than the individual pieces. The first leg of the "V," represents U.S. dollar weakness. Short selling the U.S. dollar from November 17th to December 31st, during the period 1999 to 2014, has produced an average gain of 1.7% with a 62% success rate. The second leg, from January 1st to February 7th, has produced an average gain of 1.4% with a 63% success rate. Combining both legs of the trade has produced an average gain of 3.1%, but the real benefit of the combination trade is the 88% success rate, which is much higher than both individual legs by themselves.

In the first part of the "V" trade, the U.S. dollar tends to weaken at the tail end of the year as U.S. dollars flow to foreign countries at this time. The year-end outward flow is the result of two factors.

First, foreign companies repatriate their profits back to their home countries in order to settle their books.

Source data: Federal Reserve Bank of St. Louis. Noon buying rates in New York City for cable transfers payable in foreign currencies.

USD/EUR vs S&P500 1999/00 to 2014/15*

	Nov 17 to Dec 31		Jan 1 to Feb 7		Compound Growth
Year	S&P 500	USD/ EUR	S&P 500	USD/ EUR	USD/ EUR
1999/00	3.5 %	2.4 %	0.8 %	4.7 %	2.2 %
2000/01	-3.8	-9.1	-3.1	2.9	12.3
2001/02	0.8	-0.6	1.6	0.6	1.2
2002/03	-3.3	-3.8	-5.9	2.4	6.4
2003/04	5.9	-6.8	-5.7	-2.9	3.7
2004/05	3.1	-4.1	2.8	-0.8	3.3
2005/06	1.4	-1.4	-0.8	6.0	7.5
2006/07	1.3	-3.0	0.5	-1.1	1.8
2007/08	0.7	0.3	2.2	1.4	1.0
2008/09	3.4	-8.5	-9.0	0.8	9.4
2009/10	0.5	4.5	-3.8	8.1	3.3
2010/11	6.7	1.9	-4.4	5.3	3.4
2011/12	1.7	4.1	4.9	-2.1	-6.1
2012/13	4.9	-3.6	7.1	-2.1	1.4
2013/14	2.8	-2.2	5.8	-1.5	0.7
2014/15	0.9	3.3	-2.8	1.2	-2.1
Avg.	1.9 %	-1.7 %	-0.6 %	1.4 %	3.1 %
Fq>0	88 %	38 %	50 %	63 %	88 %

Negative Short ☐   Positive Long ☐

Second, migrants remit funds back to their home countries, an activity that happens mainly at year-end. In 2014, U.S. migrants remitted $131 billion back to their home countries versus the U.S. citizens receiving $7 billion (World Bank 2014 Annual Remittance Data). The U.S. is by far the largest net remitter compared to all other countries. Although this would not have a large impact boosting the euro, the large remittances would be a factor in exerting downward pressure on the U.S. dollar.

The second part of the "V" trade, the upwards leg of the U.S. dollar outperforming the euro, occurs in the New Year as foreign companies demand U.S. dollars to enact their transactions at the start of the year.

USD/EUR - Avg. Year 1999 to 2014

- 5 -

USD/EUR Performance

USD/EUR Monthly Performance (1999-2014)

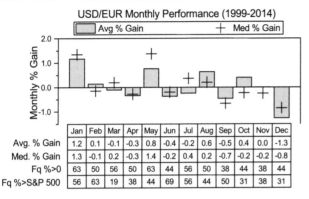

	Jan	Feb	Mar	Apr	May	Jun	Jul	Aug	Sep	Oct	Nov	Dec
Avg. % Gain	1.2	0.1	-0.1	-0.3	0.8	-0.4	-0.2	0.6	-0.5	0.4	0.0	-1.3
Med. % Gain	1.3	-0.1	0.2	-0.3	1.4	-0.2	0.4	0.2	-0.7	-0.2	-0.2	-0.8
Fq %>0	63	50	56	50	63	44	56	50	38	44	38	44
Fq %>S&P 500	56	63	19	38	44	69	56	44	50	31	38	31

USD/EUR 5 Year (2010-2014) % Gain

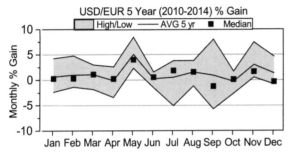

USD/EUR Performance 2014-2015

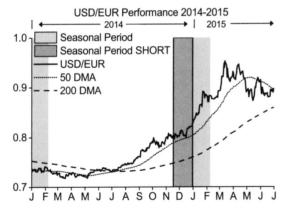

Market Indices & Rates
Weekly Values**

Stock Markets	2014	2015
Dow	16,498	17,919
S&P500	1,838	2,072
Nasdaq	4,151	4,762
TSX	13,586	14,673
FTSE	6,732	6,574
DAX	9,462	9,832
Nikkei	16,291	17,590
Hang Seng	23,177	23,684
Commodities	**2014**	**2015**
Oil	96.78	53.42
Gold	1,221.3	1187.8
Bond Yields	**2014**	**2015**
USA 5 Yr Treasury	1.73	1.67
USA 10 Yr T	3.01	2.18
USA 20 Yr T	3.69	2.47
Moody's Aaa	4.55	3.72
Moody's Baa	5.35	4.68
CAN 5 Yr T	1.94	1.34
CAN 10 Yr T	2.75	1.79
Money Market	**2014**	**2015**
USA Fed Funds	0.25	0.25
USA 3 Mo T-B	0.07	0.03
CAN tgt overnight rate	1.00	0.80
CAN 3 Mo T-B	0.90	0.92
Foreign Exchange	**2014**	**2015**
EUR/USD	1.37	1.21
GBP/USD	1.65	1.55
USD/CAD	1.06	1.17
USD/JPY	105.08	120.03

JANUARY

M	T	W	T	F	S	S
				1	2	3
4	5	6	7	8	9	10
11	12	13	14	15	16	17
18	19	20	21	22	23	24
25	26	27	28	29	30	31

FEBRUARY

M	T	W	T	F	S	S
1	2	3	4	5	6	7
8	9	10	11	12	13	14
15	16	17	18	19	20	21
22	23	24	25	26	27	28
29						

MARCH

M	T	W	T	F	S	S
	1	2	3	4	5	6
7	8	9	10	11	12	13
14	15	16	17	18	19	20
21	22	23	24	25	26	27
28	29	30	31			

The USD/EUR tends to perform poorly in the second half of November into the end of the year and then rebound at the start of the year. From 1999 to 2014, on average, the USD/EUR declined in the last few months of the year and then rebounded in January. On average, over the last five years, the seasonal trend of USD/EUR performing well in May (the second strongest month over the long-term) remained intact, as well as the seasonal trend of January being a stronger month than December.

In 2014, the loss on the short USD/EUR position at the end of the year was more than offset by the strong gain of the long USD/EUR position at the beginning of the next year.

CLX CLOROX— CLEAN PROFITS
①LONG (Jan14-Mar2) ②LONG (Sep22-Nov17)
③SELL SHORT (Nov18-Jan13)

Clorox tends to clean up twice a year with strong gains, once at the beginning of the year from January 14th to March 2nd and the second time from September 22nd to November 17th.

14% gain & positive 80% of the time

The strongest seasonal period for Clorox occurs from September 22nd to November 17th, when it has produced an average gain of 7.3% and has been positive 80% of the time from 1990 to 2014.

Clorox is part of the consumer staples sector which has been one of the top performing major S&P GIC sectors of the market in October since 1990. The sector typically performs well at this time of the year as investors act cautiously in the transition time between the unfavorable and favorable six month periods that occurs in October.

The one major difference between Clorox and the consumer staples sector is that the consumer staples sector derives most of its revenues from foreign operations, compared to Clorox's 21%. (www.thecloroxcompany.com). This can be a benefit in an environment of a rising U.S. dollar.

(i) *CLX - stock symbol for Clorox Inc. which trades on the NYSE, adjusted for splits.*

Clorox vs. S&P 500 1990 to 2014

Negative Short [ ]   Positive Long [ ]

Year	Jan 14 to Mar 02 S&P 500	CLX	Sep 22 to Nov 17 S&P 500	CLX	Nov 18 to Jan 13 S&P 500	CLX	Compound Growth S&P 500	CLX
1990	-1.3 %	-5.0 %	1.9 %	2.6 %	-0.6	3.9 %	-0.1 %	-6.4 %
1991	17.5	9.3	-1.4	-1.2	8.3	2.5	25.5	5.2
1992	-0.5	18.0	-0.7	0.9	3.3	1.1	2.1	17.7
1993	3.4	6.1	2.6	2.6	1.7	-2.1	7.9	11.1
1994	-1.6	-0.2	0.5	10.1	0.5	0.0	-0.7	9.8
1995	4.1	9.6	2.9	7.0	0.3	-6.7	7.5	25.2
1996	7.1	20.6	7.4	13.3	3.0	-7.2	18.4	46.4
1997	4.1	19.4	-0.5	3.5	0.6	1.8	4.3	21.3
1998	10.0	13.7	11.3	42.7	8.4	-3.5	32.7	68.0
1999	-0.7	12.4	7.9	17.4	2.8	11.5	10.1	16.7
2000	-4.7	-26.1	-5.6	26.0	-3.6	-27.3	-13.3	18.4
2001	-6.4	5.0	17.9	13.2	0.6	-1.4	11.0	20.5
2002	-1.2	14.0	7.6	5.8	1.8	-12.8	8.2	35.9
2003	-9.2	6.7	0.7	3.8	7.4	-1.8	-1.8	12.8
2004	2.5	4.1	4.7	7.5	-0.4	0.9	6.9	10.8
2005	2.8	4.3	2.7	-2.8	3.6	8.2	9.3	-6.9
2006	0.1	4.8	6.3	3.0	2.1	-1.6	8.7	9.7
2007	-3.0	-2.3	-4.4	8.4	-4.0	-7.0	-11.0	13.4
2008	-5.0	-5.5	-32.2	-4.4	2.5	-12.5	-34.0	1.7
2009	-19.6	-9.9	4.3	4.4	3.2	2.9	-13.5	-8.6
2010	-2.4		3.4	-5.9	8.9	1.0	9.9	-7.4
2011	1.9	6.8	4.2	-2.7	6.0	4.7	12.6	-1.0
2012	6.3	-0.7	-6.9	4.1	8.3	1.9	7.1	1.4
2013	3.1	11.0	5.2	13.3	1.2	-4.8	9.7	31.8
2014	2.2	-2.0	1.5	11.5	-0.9	5.7	2.8	3.0
Avg.	0.4 %	4.5 %	1.7 %	7.3 %	2.6 %	-1.7 %	4.8 %	13.9 %
Fq>0	52 %	64 %	72	80 %	80 %	48 %	72 %	80 %

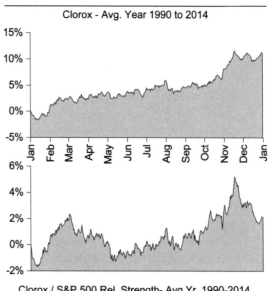

Clorox - Avg. Year 1990 to 2014

Clorox / S&P 500 Rel. Strength- Avg Yr. 1990-2014

Clorox Performance

Clorox Monthly Performance (1990-2014)

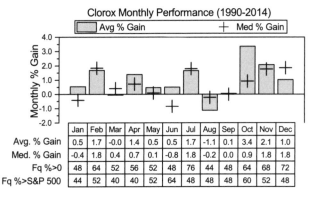

	Jan	Feb	Mar	Apr	May	Jun	Jul	Aug	Sep	Oct	Nov	Dec
Avg. % Gain	0.5	1.7	-0.0	1.4	0.5	0.5	1.7	-1.1	0.1	3.4	2.1	1.0
Med. % Gain	-0.4	1.8	0.4	0.7	0.1	-0.8	1.8	-0.2	0.0	0.9	1.8	1.8
Fq %>0	48	64	52	56	52	48	76	44	48	64	68	72
Fq %>S&P 500	44	52	40	40	52	64	48	48	48	60	52	48

Clorox 5 Year (2010-2014) % Gain

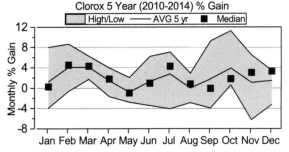

Clorox Performance 2014-2015

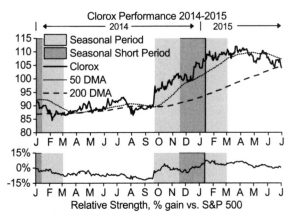

Relative Strength, % gain vs. S&P 500

Market Indices & Rates
Weekly Values**

Stock Markets	2014	2015
Dow	16,460	17,621
S&P500	1,837	2,031
Nasdaq	4,153	4,667
TSX	13,617	14,353
FTSE	6,728	6,455
DAX	9,465	9,589
Nikkei	15,927	17,108
Hang Seng	22,805	23,729

Commodities	2014	2015
Oil	92.76	48.75
Gold	1,233.0	1210.8

Bond Yields	2014	2015
USA 5 Yr Treasury	1.71	1.50
USA 10 Yr T	2.96	2.00
USA 20 Yr T	3.63	2.29
Moody's Aaa	4.53	3.54
Moody's Baa	5.28	4.53
CAN 5 Yr T	1.86	1.24
CAN 10 Yr T	2.67	1.67

Money Market	2014	2015
USA Fed Funds	0.25	0.25
USA 3 Mo T-B	0.05	0.03
CAN tgt overnight rate	1.00	1.00
CAN 3 Mo T-B	0.89	0.92

Foreign Exchange	2014	2015
EUR/USD	1.36	1.19
GBP/USD	1.64	1.52
USD/CAD	1.08	1.18
USD/JPY	104.54	119.09

JANUARY

M	T	W	T	F	S	S
				1	2	3
4	5	6	7	8	9	10
11	12	13	14	15	16	17
18	19	20	21	22	23	24
25	26	27	28	29	30	31

FEBRUARY

M	T	W	T	F	S	S
1	2	3	4	5	6	7
8	9	10	11	12	13	14
15	16	17	18	19	20	21
22	23	24	24	26	27	28
29						

MARCH

M	T	W	T	F	S	S
	1	2	3	4	5	6
7	8	9	10	11	12	13
14	15	16	17	18	19	20
21	22	23	24	25	26	27
28	29	30	31			

From 1990 to 2014, on average, the strongest month of the year for Clorox was October. This trend is consistent with the consumer staples sector outperforming the S&P 500 in October since 1990. It should be noted that Clorox's median performance in October is well below the average. In other words, a few strong months dominated the results from 1990 to 2014. Over the last 5 years, on average, October's maximum return was much higher than the other months of the year.

In 2014 and 2015, the overall combination of seasonal long and short positions provided a gain and outperformed the S&P 500.

RETAIL – POST HOLIDAY BARGAIN
Ist of II Retail Strategies for the Year
SHOP Jan 21st and RETURN Your Investment Apr 12th

Consumer spending continued to be strong in 2014 and 2015. Investors have been attracted to the retail sector due to the relative strength of the U.S. economy.

Historically, the retail sector has outperformed from January 21st until April 12th - the start of the next earnings season. From 1990 to 2015, during its seasonally strong period, the retail sector produced an average gain of 8.5%, compared with the S&P 500's average gain of 2.3%. Not only has the retail sector had greater gains than the broad market, but it has also outperformed it on a fairly regular basis: 81% of the time.

> *6.2% extra & 81% of the time*
> *better than the S&P 500*

Retail Sector vs. S&P 500 1990 to 2015			
Jan 21 to Apr 12	S&P 500	Positive Retail	Diff
1990	1.5 %	9.7 %	8.1 %
1991	14.5	29.9	15.4
1992	-2.9	-2.7	0.2
1993	3.5	-0.6	-4.0
1994	-5.8	2.0	7.8
1995	9.1	7.4	-1.8
1996	4.1	19.7	15.7
1997	-5.0	6.0	11.0
1998	13.5	20.1	6.6
1999	8.1	23.4	15.2
2000	1.5	5.8	4.3
2001	-11.8	-0.5	11.3
2002	-1.5	6.7	8.2
2003	-3.7	6.5	10.3
2004	0.6	6.7	6.1
2005	1.1	-1.6	-2.7
2006	2.1	3.4	1.3
2007	1.2	-0.7	-1.9
2008	0.6	3.5	3.0
2009	6.4	25.1	18.7
2010	5.1	15.5	10.4
2011	2.7	4.4	1.7
2012	5.5	12.1	6.6
2013	6.9	10.1	3.2
2014	-1.3	-7.1	-5.8
2015	3.9	15.5	11.5
Avg.	2.3 %	8.5 %	6.2 %
Fq > 0	73 %	77 %	81 %

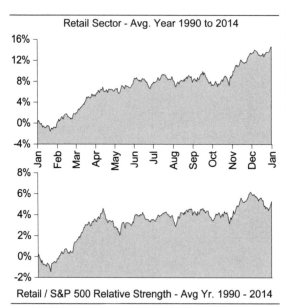

Retail Sector - Avg. Year 1990 to 2014

Retail / S&P 500 Relative Strength - Avg Yr. 1990 - 2014

the beginning of the year. These forecasts generally rely on healthy consumer spending which makes up approximately 2/3 of the GDP. The retail sector benefits from the optimistic forecasts and tends to outperform the S&P 500.

From a seasonal basis, investors have been best served by exiting the retail sector in April and then returning to it later at the end of October (see *Retail Shop Early* strategy).

Most investors think that the best time to invest in retail stocks is before Black Friday in November. Yes, there is a positive seasonal cycle at this time, but it is not as strong as the cycle from January to April.

The January retail bounce coincides with the "rosy" stock market analysts' forecasts that tend to occur at

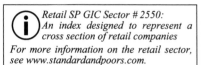

Retail SP GIC Sector # 2550:
An index designed to represent a cross section of retail companies
For more information on the retail sector, see www.standardandpoors.com.

Retail Performance

Retail Monthly Performance (1990-2014)

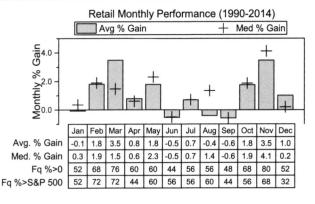

	Jan	Feb	Mar	Apr	May	Jun	Jul	Aug	Sep	Oct	Nov	Dec
Avg. % Gain	-0.1	1.8	3.5	0.8	1.8	-0.5	0.7	-0.4	-0.6	1.8	3.5	1.0
Med. % Gain	0.3	1.9	1.5	0.6	2.3	-0.5	0.7	1.4	-0.6	1.9	4.1	0.2
Fq %>0	52	68	76	60	60	44	56	56	48	68	80	52
Fq %>S&P 500	52	72	72	44	60	56	56	60	44	56	68	32

Retail 5 Year (2010-2014) % Gain

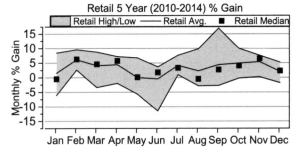

Retail Performance 2014-2015

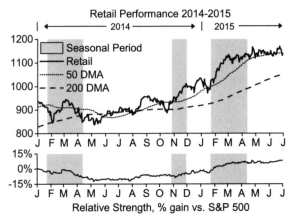

Relative Strength, % gain vs. S&P 500

From 1990 to 2014, the two best months for the retail sector were March and November, on an average basis. November is the core part of the autumn retail seasonal trade and has the highest median performance. Over the last five years, on average the retail sector has followed its general seasonal pattern: with the strongest months being February, April and November. These months are part of either the spring seasonal trade or the autumn seasonal trade. In 2014, the retail sector outperformed the S&P 500 in its autumn seasonal period and in 2015 it outperformed in its spring seasonal period.

WEEK 03

Market Indices & Rates
Weekly Values**

Stock Markets	2014	2015
Dow	16,398	17,503
S&P500	1,838	2,015
Nasdaq	4,185	4,634
TSX	13,773	14,178
FTSE	6,798	6,496
DAX	9,649	9,948
Nikkei	15,678	16,964
Hang Seng	22,940	24,162

Commodities	2014	2015
Oil	93.38	47.08
Gold	1,245.4	1245.9

Bond Yields	2014	2015
USA 5 Yr Treasury	1.65	1.32
USA 10 Yr T	2.86	1.86
USA 20 Yr T	3.53	2.19
Moody's Aaa	4.48	3.46
Moody's Baa	5.19	4.45
CAN 5 Yr T	1.74	1.11
CAN 10 Yr T	2.55	1.56

Money Market	2014	2015
USA Fed Funds	0.25	0.25
USA 3 Mo T-B	0.04	0.03
CAN tgt overnight rate	1.00	1.00
CAN 3 Mo T-B	0.89	0.91

Foreign Exchange	2014	2015
EUR/USD	1.36	1.17
GBP/USD	1.64	1.52
USD/CAD	1.09	1.20
USD/JPY	104.09	117.46

JANUARY

M	T	W	T	F	S	S
				1	2	3
4	5	6	7	8	9	10
11	12	13	14	15	16	17
18	19	20	21	22	23	24
25	26	27	28	29	30	31

FEBRUARY

M	T	W	T	F	S	S
1	2	3	4	5	6	7
8	9	10	11	12	13	14
15	16	17	18	19	20	21
22	23	24	24	26	27	28
29						

MARCH

M	T	W	T	F	S	S
	1	2	3	4	5	6
7	8	9	10	11	12	13
14	15	16	17	18	19	20
21	22	23	24	25	26	27
28	29	30	31			

TJX COMPANIES INC.
January 22nd to March 30th

In 2015, TJX during its seasonally strong period, underperformed the retail sector, but outperformed the S&P 500. Over the long-term, TJX has typically outperformed the retail sector when the sector has been positive, making it an excellent complement to a retail sector investment during its seasonal period.

TJX is an off-price apparel and home fashions retailer that typically reports its fourth quarter earnings in approximately the third week of February. The company, like the retail sector, benefits from investors expecting positive results from the Christmas season.

TJX's period of seasonal strength is similar to the seasonal period for the retail sector. The best time to invest in TJX has been from January 22nd to March 30th. From 1990 to 2015, investing in this period has produced an average gain of 12.5%, which is substantially better than the 1.8% performance of the S&P 500. It is also important to note that the stock has been positive 73% of the time during this period.

12.5% gain & positive 73% of the time

Equally impressive is the amount of times TJX has produced a large gain, versus a large loss in its seasonal period. In the last twenty-five years, TJX has only had one loss of 10% or greater. In the same time period, TJX had gains of 10% or greater, twelve times.

TJX* vs. Retail vs. S&P 500 1990 to 2015			
			Positive
Jan 22 to Mar 30	S&P 500	Retail	TJX
1990	0.2%	6.3%	6.7%
1991	13.3	21.7	61.9
1992	-2.3	1.7	17.0
1993	3.8	3.0	21.7
1994	-6.1	-0.1	-2.8
1995	8.1	9.7	-6.9
1996	5.5	19.7	43.6
1997	-1.1	10.4	-0.3
1998	12.6	19.7	25.4
1999	5.3	16.5	18.9
2000	3.2	5.1	35.4
2001	-13.6	1.7	16.4
2002	1.8	4.7	2.9
2003	-2.7	6.6	-6.7
2004	-1.8	5.4	3.5
2005	1.2	-0.6	-1.6
2006	3.1	4.5	3.8
2007	-0.7	-2.7	-10.2
2008	-0.8	1.4	13.1
2009	-6.3	8.1	29.0
2010	5.1	12.5	17.2
2011	3.5	3.5	6.1
2012	7.1	12.9	19.3
2013	5.6	6.2	4.5
2014	0.8	-2.7	-0.2
2015	2.7	12.5	6.8
Avg	1.8%	7.2%	12.5%
Fq > 0	65%	85%	73%

It is interesting to note that the seasonally strong period for TJX ends before April, one of the strongest months of the year for the stock market. It is possible that by the end of March, after a typically strong run for TJX, the full value of TJX's first quarter earnings report has already been priced into the stock and investors look to other companies in which to invest. This is particularly true if the economy and the stock market are in good shape.

On the other hand, in a soft economy, consumers favor off-price apparel companies such as TJX. In this scenario, TJX is more likely to perform strongly past the end of its seasonal period in March, allowing seasonal investors to continue to hold TJX until it shows signs of weakness.

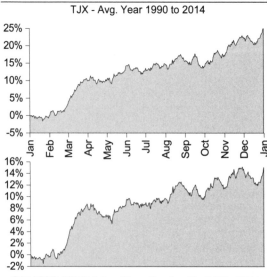

TJX - Avg. Year 1990 to 2014

TJX / S&P 500 Relative Strength - Avg Yr. 1990 - 2014

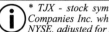
(i) * TJX - stock symbol for The TJX Companies Inc. which trades on the NYSE, adjusted for stock splits.

TJX Performance

TJX Monthly Performance (1990-2014)

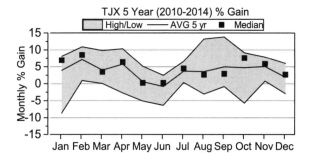

	Jan	Feb	Mar	Apr	May	Jun	Jul	Aug	Sep	Oct	Nov	Dec
Avg. % Gain	-0.1	3.3	6.8	-0.5	3.6	-1.1	1.7	1.1	-1.2	2.5	4.3	1.8
Med. % Gain	1.9	2.4	4.3	-2.0	1.6	-1.7	3.1	3.2	-2.1	3.3	3.4	3.3
Fq %>0	52	60	76	48	68	36	60	56	44	68	60	60
Fq %>S&P 500	60	60	80	40	64	48	64	72	48	60	60	60

TJX 5 Year (2010-2014) % Gain

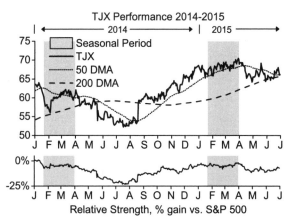

TJX Performance 2014-2015

Market Indices & Rates
Weekly Values**

Stock Markets	2014	2015
Dow	16,216	17,639
S&P500	1,827	2,042
Nasdaq	4,204	4,708
TSX	13,916	14,545
FTSE	6,787	6,713
DAX	9,638	10,377
Nikkei	15,669	17,300
Hang Seng	22,846	24,283

Commodities	2014	2015
Oil	96.46	46.22
Gold	1253.0	1289.3

Bond Yields	2014	2015
USA 5 Yr Treasury	1.65	1.35
USA 10 Yr T	2.82	1.85
USA 20 Yr T	3.47	2.17
Moody's Aaa	4.46	3.45
Moody's Baa	5.13	4.45
CAN 5 Yr T	1.65	0.93
CAN 10 Yr T	2.46	1.46

Money Market	2014	2015
USA Fed Funds	0.25	0.25
USA 3 Mo T-B	0.04	0.03
CAN tgt overnight rate	1.00	0.85
CAN 3 Mo T-B	0.90	0.73

Foreign Exchange	2014	2015
EUR/USD	1.36	1.15
GBP/USD	1.65	1.51
USD/CAD	1.10	1.22
USD/JPY	103.71	118.12

JANUARY

M	T	W	T	F	S	S
				1	2	3
4	5	6	7	8	9	10
11	12	13	14	15	16	17
18	19	20	21	22	23	24
25	26	27	28	29	30	31

FEBRUARY

M	T	W	T	F	S	S
1	2	3	4	5	6	7
8	9	10	11	12	13	14
15	16	17	18	19	20	21
22	23	24	24	26	27	28
29						

MARCH

M	T	W	T	F	S	S
	1	2	3	4	5	6
7	8	9	10	11	12	13
14	15	16	17	18	19	20
21	22	23	24	25	26	27
28	29	30	31			

From 1990 to 2014, March has been the best month for TJX on an average, median and frequency basis. March is the core part of the seasonal period for TJX which lasts from January 22nd to March 30. The seasonal trade falls off sharply in April and investors should consider exiting early if weakness is evident. Over the last five years, March has been an average month for TJX. The best performing month has been February, making the complete trade successful. In 2014, TJX corrected at the beginning and the end of its seasonal period, underperforming the S&P 500 slightly. In 2015, TJX outperformed the S&P 500 in its seasonal period and then corrected sharply in April.

ROYAL BANK— A TRADE TO BANK ON
①Oct10-Nov28 ②Jan23-Apr13

Canadians love their banks and tend to hold large amounts of the banking sector in their portfolios. Their love for the sector has remained strong, as international accolades have supported a positive viewpoint of Canadian banks. In a 2012 Bloomberg report, the Canadian banks dominated the top ten strongest banks in the world, with four banks in the top ten.

For years, Royal Bank was considered one of the most conservative banks and often attracted investors during tough times. After a few mis-steps in their expansion into the U.S., Royal Bank seems to be getting back on track.

Through its ups and downs, Royal Bank has followed the same general pattern as the banking sector: rising in autumn and then once again in the new year.

11.8% gain & positive 77% of the time

In the period from October 10th to November 28th, from 1989 to 2014, Royal Bank has produced an average gain of 5.1% and has been positive 88% of the time. The bank tends to perform well at this time, as Canadians tend to increase their bank holdings before the year-end earnings reports are released in late November. It is not a coincidence that Royal Bank's seasonally strong period ends at approximately the same time as their year-end earnings announcements. Seasonal investors benefit from buying Royal Bank before the "masses," whom are also trying to take advantage of the possibility of positive earnings.

In the second seasonal period from January 23rd to April 13, Canadian banks tend to outperform the TSX Composite, as they benefit from the typically strong economic forecasts at the beginning of the year. In addition, they "echo," or get a boost from the strong seasonal performance of the U.S banks at this time.

Royal Bank* vs. TSX Comp 1989/90 to 2014/15 Positive ▢

Year	Oct 10 to Nov 28 TSX Comp	RY	Jan 23 to Apr 13 TSX Comp	RY	Compound Growth TSX Comp	RY
1989/90	-2.8 %	2.4 %	-6.3 %	-10.0 %	-8.9 %	-7.8 %
1990/91	0.2	3.5	9.8	11.6	10.0	15.5
1991/92	2.9	3.3	-6.8	-14.5	-4.1	-11.6
1992/93	1.8	5.0	10.7	17.6	12.6	23.4
1993/94	3.8	0.0	-5.6	-13.1	-2.1	-13.1
1994/95	-4.7	2.2	5.0	13.2	0.0	15.7
1995/96	4.0	3.3	3.6	0.0	7.7	3.3
1996/97	10.7	23.3	-6.2	1.3	3.9	24.9
1997/98	-8.7	7.6	19.9	24.0	9.4	33.4
1998/99	18.0	20.9	4.8	0.6	23.7	21.6
1999/00	10.9	8.6	3.8	34.5	15.1	46.0
2000/01	-14.5	5.1	-14.1	-12.0	-26.5	-7.5
2001/02	7.1	3.2	2.3	11.8	9.6	15.4
2002/03	16.4	18.1	-4.3	1.8	11.4	20.2
2003/04	3.4	0.3	2.0	1.8	5.4	2.1
2004/05	2.8	4.0	4.5	17.6	7.3	22.3
2005/06	3.1	7.3	5.5	7.0	8.8	14.8
2006/07	7.2	8.5	6.9	7.1	14.5	16.2
2007/08	-4.4	-5.1	8.2	-4.9	3.5	-9.8
2008/09	-3.4	4.3	9.4	35.0	5.7	40.8
2009/10	0.2	1.3	6.7	12.6	6.9	14.1
2010/11	2.9	0.4	4.3	12.4	7.3	12.8
2011/12	0.5	-6.3	-2.9	3.8	-2.4	-2.8
2012/13	-1.1	2.1	-3.8	-0.3	-4.8	1.9
2013/14	5.0	6.0	1.9	-0.5	7.1	5.5
2014/15	2.0	3.0	4.2	7.3	6.2	10.5
Avg.	2.4 %	5.1 %	2.4 %	6.4 %	4.9 %	11.8 %
Fq > 0	73 %	88 %	69 %	69 %	77 %	77 %

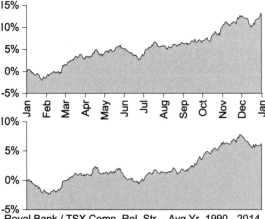

Royal Bank* Avg. Year 1990 to 2014

Royal Bank / TSX Comp. Rel. Str. - Avg Yr. 1990 - 2014

Ⓨ *Alternate Strategy—*
Investors can bridge the gap between the two positive seasonal trends for the bank sector by holding from October 10th to April 13th. Longer term investors may prefer this strategy, shorter term investors can use technical tools to determine the appropriate strategy.

ⓘ ** Royal Bank of Canada (RBC) is a diversified financial services company that trades on both the Toronto and NYSE exchanges under the symbol RY. Data from TSX Exchange, includes stock splits only.*

Royal Bank Performance

Royal Bank Monthly Performance (1990-2014)

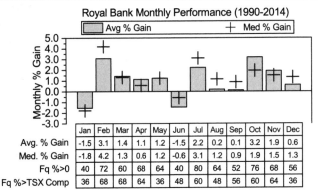

	Jan	Feb	Mar	Apr	May	Jun	Jul	Aug	Sep	Oct	Nov	Dec
Avg. % Gain	-1.5	3.1	1.4	1.1	1.2	-1.5	2.2	0.2	0.1	3.2	1.9	0.6
Med. % Gain	-1.8	4.2	1.3	0.6	1.2	-0.6	3.1	1.2	0.9	1.9	1.5	1.3
Fq %>0	40	72	60	68	64	40	80	64	52	76	68	56
Fq %>TSX Comp	36	68	68	64	36	48	60	48	56	60	64	36

Royal Bank 5 Year (2010-2014) % Gain

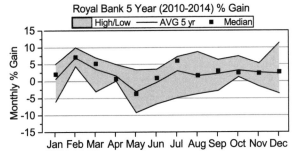

Royal Bank Performance 2014-2015

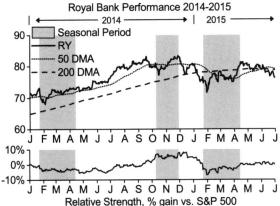

Relative Strength, % gain vs. S&P 500

Market Indices & Rates
Weekly Values**

Stock Markets	2014	2015
Dow	15,811	17,368
S&P500	1,785	2,021
Nasdaq	4,092	4,682
TSX	13,669	14,709
FTSE	6,543	6,810
DAX	9,355	10,714
Nikkei	15,058	17,663
Hang Seng	22,028	24,736

Commodities	2014	2015
Oil	97.24	45.72
Gold	1253.9	1277.4

Bond Yields	2014	2015
USA 5 Yr Treasury	1.55	1.28
USA 10 Yr T	2.73	1.77
USA 20 Yr T	3.39	2.10
Moody's Aaa	4.45	3.36
Moody's Baa	5.10	4.36
CAN 5 Yr T	1.59	0.71
CAN 10 Yr T	2.39	1.37

Money Market	2014	2015
USA Fed Funds	0.25	0.25
USA 3 Mo T-B	0.04	0.02
CAN tgt overnight rate	1.00	0.75
CAN 3 Mo T-B	0.89	0.60

Foreign Exchange	2014	2015
EUR/USD	1.36	1.13
GBP/USD	1.65	1.51
USD/CAD	1.11	1.26
USD/JPY	102.51	117.93

JANUARY

M	T	W	T	F	S	S
				1	2	3
4	5	6	7	8	9	10
11	12	13	14	15	16	17
18	19	20	21	22	23	24
25	26	27	28	29	30	31

FEBRUARY

M	T	W	T	F	S	S
1	2	3	4	5	6	7
8	9	10	11	12	13	14
15	16	17	18	19	20	21
22	23	24	24	26	27	28
29						

MARCH

M	T	W	T	F	S	S
	1	2	3	4	5	6
7	8	9	10	11	12	13
14	15	16	17	18	19	20
21	22	23	24	25	26	27
28	29	30	31			

From 1990 to 2014, February has been the best month for Royal Bank on an average and median basis and January has been the worst month. Given that the second leg of the seasonal strategy starts in late January, investors should use technical analysis in choosing the best entry date for Royal Bank at this time.

Over the last five years, on average, Royal bank has followed its general seasonal trend with February being the strongest month of the year and May being the weakest month.

In the 2014 October to November seasonal period, Royal Bank outperformed the TSX Composite and then declined, only to outperform once again in its January to April seasonal period.

FEBRUARY

MONDAY	TUESDAY	WEDNESDAY

| **1** 28 | **2** 27 | **3** 26 |

WEEK 06

| **8** 21 | **9** 20 | **10** 19 |

WEEK 07

| **15** 14 | **16** 13 | **17** 12 |

CAN Market Closed - Family Day

USA Market Closed - Presidents' Day

WEEK 08

| **22** 7 | **23** 6 | **24** 5 |

WEEK 09

| **29** | 1 | 2 |

WEEK 10

THURSDAY		FRIDAY	
4	25	**5**	24
11	18	**12**	17
18	11	**19**	10
25	4	**26**	3
3		4	

MARCH

M	T	W	T	F	S	S
	1	2	3	4	5	6
7	8	9	10	11	12	13
14	15	16	17	18	19	20
21	22	23	24	25	26	27
28	29	30	31			

APRIL

M	T	W	T	F	S	S
				1	2	3
4	5	6	7	8	9	10
11	12	13	14	15	16	17
18	19	20	21	22	23	24
25	26	27	28	29	30	

MAY

M	T	W	T	F	S	S
						1
2	3	4	5	6	7	8
9	10	11	12	13	14	15
16	17	18	19	20	21	22
23	24	25	26	27	28	29
30	31					

JUNE

M	T	W	T	F	S	S
		1	2	3	4	5
6	7	8	9	10	11	12
13	14	15	16	17	18	19
20	21	22	23	24	25	26
27	28	29	30			

FEBRUARY
SUMMARY

S&P500 Cumulative Daily Gains for Avg Month 1950 to 2015

	Dow Jones	S&P 500	Nasdaq	TSX Comp
Month Rank	8	11	9	5
# Up	37	36	23	18
# Down	28	29	20	12
% Pos	57	55	53	60
% Avg. Gain	0.2	0.0	0.5	1.0

Dow & S&P 1950-2014, Nasdaq 1972-2014, TSX 1985-2014

♦ Historically over the long-term, February has been one of the weaker months of the year, but in 2014 and 2015, after strong corrections in January, the S&P 500 rallied strongly in February. ♦ Small caps tend to outperform in February, which was once again the case in 2015. ♦ The energy sector typically starts to outperform in late February, which helps to boost the S&P/TSX Composite. Over the last ten years, the S&P/TSX Composite has produced an average gain of 1.4% in February.

BEST / WORST FEBRUARY BROAD MKTS. 2006-2015

BEST FEBRUARY MARKETS
- ♦ Nikkei 225 (2012) 10.5%
- ♦ Nasdaq (2015) 7.1%
- ♦ Nikkei (2015) 6.4%

WORST FEBRUARY MARKETS
- ♦ Russell 2000 (2009) -12.3%
- ♦ Dow (2009) -11.7%
- ♦ S&P 500 (2009) -11.0%

Index Values End of Month

	2006	2007	2008	2009	2010	2011	2012	2013	2014	2015
Dow	10,993	12,269	12,266	7,063	10,325	12,226	12,952	14,054	16,322	18,133
S&P 500	1,281	1,407	1,331	735	1,104	1,327	1,366	1,515	1,859	2,105
Nasdaq	2,281	2,416	2,271	1,378	2,238	2,782	2,967	3,160	4,308	4,964
TSX Comp.	11,688	13,045	13,583	8,123	11,630	14,137	12,644	12,822	14,210	15,234
Russell 1000	1,341	1,478	1,396	768	1,168	1,415	1,454	1,617	2,002	2,256
Russell 2000	1,816	1,972	1,705	967	1,562	2,046	2,015	2,264	2,940	3,065
FTSE 100	5,792	6,172	5,884	3,830	5,355	5,994	5,872	6,361	6,810	6,947
Nikkei 225	16,205	17,604	13,603	7,568	10,126	10,624	9,723	11,559	14,841	18,798

Percent Gain for February

	2006	2007	2008	2009	2010	2011	2012	2013	2014	2015
Dow	1.2	-2.8	-3.0	-11.7	2.6	2.8	2.5	1.4	4.0	5.6
S&P 500	0.0	-2.2	-3.5	-11.0	2.9	3.2	4.1	1.1	4.3	5.5
Nasdaq	-1.1	-1.9	-5.0	-6.7	4.2	3.0	5.4	0.6	5.0	7.1
TSX Comp.	-2.2	0.1	3.3	-6.6	4.8	4.3	1.5	1.1	3.8	3.8
Russell 1000	0.0	-1.9	-3.3	-10.7	3.1	3.3	4.1	1.1	4.5	5.5
Russell 2000	-0.3	-0.9	-3.8	-12.3	4.4	5.4	2.3	1.0	4.6	5.8
FTSE 100	0.5	-0.5	0.1	-7.7	3.2	2.2	3.3	1.3	4.6	2.9
Nikkei 225	-2.7	1.3	0.1	-5.3	-0.7	3.8	10.5	3.8	-0.5	6.4

February Market Avg. Performance 2006 to 2015[1]

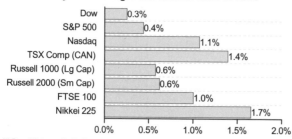

	Dow	0.3%
	S&P 500	0.4%
	Nasdaq	1.1%
	TSX Comp (CAN)	1.4%
	Russell 1000 (Lg Cap)	0.6%
	Russell 2000 (Sm Cap)	0.6%
	FTSE 100	1.0%
	Nikkei 225	1.7%

Interest Corner Feb[2]

	Fed Funds %[3]	3 Mo. T-Bill %[4]	10 Yr %[5]	20 Yr %[6]
2015	0.25	0.02	2.00	2.38
2014	0.25	0.05	2.66	3.31
2013	0.25	0.11	1.89	2.71
2012	0.25	0.08	1.98	2.73
2011	0.25	0.15	3.42	4.25

(1) Russell Data provided by Russell (2) Federal Reserve Bank of St. Louis- end of month values (3) Target rate set by FOMC (4)(5)(6) Constant yield maturities.

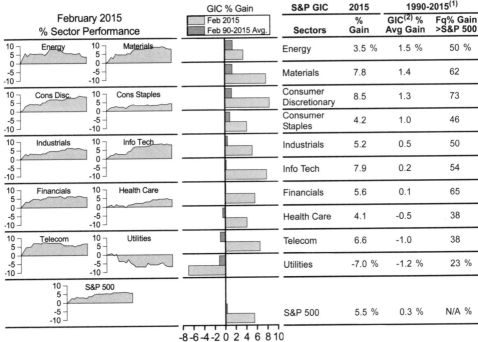

S&P GIC	2015	1990-2015[1]	
Sectors	% Gain	GIC[2] % Avg Gain	Fq% Gain >S&P 500
Energy	3.5 %	1.5 %	50 %
Materials	7.8	1.4	62
Consumer Discretionary	8.5	1.3	73
Consumer Staples	4.2	1.0	46
Industrials	5.2	0.5	50
Info Tech	7.9	0.2	54
Financials	5.6	0.1	65
Health Care	4.1	-0.5	38
Telecom	6.6	-1.0	38
Utilities	-7.0 %	-1.2 %	23 %
S&P 500	5.5 %	0.3 %	N/A %

SELECTED SUB-SECTORS[3]			
SOX (1995-2015)	9.4 %	3.0 %	62 %
Silver	-2.3	2.6	50
Retail	8.8	2.1	73
Chemicals	6.8	1.7	73
Metals & Mining	9.5	1.4	54
Gold (London PM)	-3.7	0.8	46
Agriculture (1994-2015)	2.7	0.8	50
Steel	9.6	0.7	50
Transportation	2.3	0.4	54
Banks	8.3	0.4	58
Homebuilders	11.0	0.2	62
Railroads	3.6	0.2	46
Software & Services	7.1	0.2	50
Pharma	3.6	-0.6	38
Biotech (1993-2015)	1.9	-1.0	52

Sector Commentary

♦ In February 2015, the market showed its strength as all of the major sectors except utilities, increased in value. ♦ The top performing sector in February was consumer discretionary, as retail sales remained strong and investors concentrated on sectors that that were more focused on U.S. domestic operations. ♦ After having a strong run at the beginning of January, the utilities sector started to correct at the end of the month and then carried its correction into February. The sector lost 7% in February, mainly driven by investor concern that the Federal Reserve was going to raise interest rates shortly.

Sub-Sector Commentary

♦ Homebuilders bounced off a loss in January and in February produced an 11% gain. The sub-sectors outperformance carried well past the beginning of February when its seasonal period ends.♦ Similarly, the steel sub-sector also bounced after a large loss in January and produced a large gain of 9.6% in February. ♦ The metals and mining sub-sector produced a large gain of 9.5%.♦ Overall, the cyclical sub-sectors performed well in February. ♦ The precious metals, gold and silver, both produced losses for the month as investors feared the impact of the Federal Reserve possibly raising interest rates.

DUPONT
January 28th to May 5th

In 2015, Dupont broke its long-term fourteen year positive streak and produced a small loss in its strong seasonal period. Dupont's loss during its seasonal period was consistent with the cyclical sectors of the market that started to underperform in the spring due to concerns of a global growth slowdown.

DuPont is a diversified chemicals company that operates in seven segments: Agriculture & Nutrition, Electronics & Communications, Performance Chemicals, Performance Coatings, Performance Materials, Safety & Protection, and Pharmaceuticals.

The chemicals sub-sector is a large part of the U.S. materials sector, which has a seasonally strong period from January 23rd to May 5th. DuPont has a similar seasonal trend that starts a few days later on January 28th. Investors can use technical analysis to determine if an earlier position in DuPont should be taken.

10.5% gain & positive 92% of the time

The DuPont seasonal trade has worked very well since 1990, producing an average gain of 10.5% with a very high 92% frequency rate of being positive.

DuPont* vs. S&P 500
1990 to 2015

Jan 28 to May 5	S&P 500	DD	Diff
			Positive
1990	3.9%	0.3%	-3.5%
1991	13.3	19.6	6.3
1992	0.5	11.2	10.7
1993	1.5	15.2	13.8
1994	-5.4	6.6	12.0
1995	10.6	21.8	11.2
1996	3.2	6.1	2.9
1997	8.5	4.4	-4.2
1998	15.1	35.2	20.0
1999	8.4	33.6	25.2
2000	2.4	-16.7	-19.1
2001	-6.5	12.8	19.3
2002	-5.3	3.2	8.4
2003	9.3	11.3	2.0
2004	-2.0	2.5	4.5
2005	-0.2	2.6	2.8
2006	3.3	13.4	10.1
2007	5.9	4.2	-1.7
2008	5.8	11.1	5.4
2009	6.9	24.9	18.1
2010	6.2	15.3	9.0
2011	2.7	7.2	4.4
2012	4.0	4.3	0.3
2013	7.4	11.6	4.2
2014	5.8	11.9	6.1
2015	3.0	-0.5	-3.5
Avg	4.2%	10.5%	6.3%
Fq > 0	81%	92%	81%

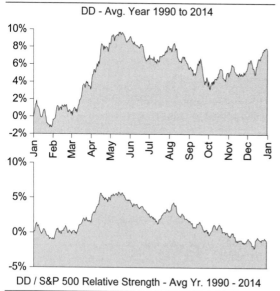

DD - Avg. Year 1990 to 2014

DD / S&P 500 Relative Strength - Avg Yr. 1990 - 2014

1.6% and has only been positive 44% of the time.

This compares to the S&P 500, which has produced an average gain of 4.4% and has been positive 72% of the time, during the same time period.

If investors are interested in purchasing DuPont on a seasonal basis, it is clear that they should concentrate their efforts from the end of January to the beginning of May.

Investors should be aware that DuPont does not perform as well as the broad market from May 6th to the end of the year. In fact, during this period, from 1990 to 2014, DuPont has generated an average loss of

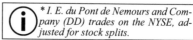

*I. E. du Pont de Nemours and Company (DD) trades on the NYSE, adjusted for stock splits.

Dupont Performance

Dupont Monthly Performance (1990-2014)

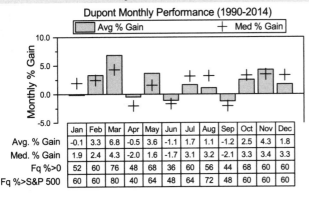

	Jan	Feb	Mar	Apr	May	Jun	Jul	Aug	Sep	Oct	Nov	Dec
Avg. % Gain	-0.1	3.3	6.8	-0.5	3.6	-1.1	1.7	1.1	-1.2	2.5	4.3	1.8
Med. % Gain	1.9	2.4	4.3	-2.0	1.6	-1.7	3.1	3.2	-2.1	3.3	3.4	3.3
Fq %>0	52	60	76	48	68	36	60	56	44	68	60	60
Fq %>S&P 500	60	60	80	40	64	48	64	72	48	60	60	60

Dupont 5 Year (2010-2014) % Gain

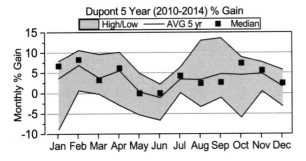

Dupont Performance 2014-2015

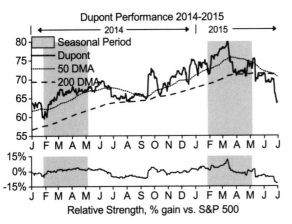

Relative Strength, % gain vs. S&P 500

Market Indices & Rates
Weekly Values**

Stock Markets	2014	2015
Dow	15,536	17,682
S&P500	1,764	2,046
Nasdaq	4,045	4,726
TSX	13,610	15,034
FTSE	6,501	6,847
DAX	9,198	10,876
Nikkei	14,285	17,545
Hang Seng	21,432	24,633

Commodities	2014	2015
Oil	97.74	50.65
Gold	1256.5	1261.1

Bond Yields	2014	2015
USA 5 Yr Treasury	1.48	1.31
USA 10 Yr T	2.68	1.81
USA 20 Yr T	3.37	2.18
Moody's Aaa	4.45	3.42
Moody's Baa	5.09	4.41
CAN 5 Yr T	1.57	0.67
CAN 10 Yr T	2.38	1.33

Money Market	2014	2015
USA Fed Funds	0.25	0.25
USA 3 Mo T-B	0.07	0.02
CAN tgt overnight rate	1.00	0.75
CAN 3 Mo T-B	0.88	0.55

Foreign Exchange	2014	2015
EUR/USD	1.36	1.14
GBP/USD	1.63	1.52
USD/CAD	1.11	1.25
USD/JPY	101.70	117.81

FEBRUARY

M	T	W	T	F	S	S
1	2	3	4	5	6	7
8	9	10	11	12	13	14
15	16	17	18	19	20	21
22	23	24	24	26	27	28
29						

MARCH

M	T	W	T	F	S	S
	1	2	3	4	5	6
7	8	9	10	11	12	13
14	15	16	17	18	19	20
21	22	23	24	25	26	27
28	29	30	31			

APRIL

M	T	W	T	F	S	S
				1	2	3
4	5	6	7	8	9	10
11	12	13	14	15	16	17
18	19	20	21	22	23	24
25	26	27	28	29	30	

From 1990 to 2014, March has been the strongest month for Dupont on an average, median and frequency basis. Although April is part of the seasonal trade that lasts from January 28th to May 5th, investors should consider exiting the seasonal trade early if it is showing weakness. Over the last five years, Dupont has generally performed well in the first few months and then faded into the summer months (not part of the seasonal period). In 2014, the seasonal trade worked well, outperforming the S&P 500. In 2015, Dupont performed well for the first part of the trade into March and then underperformed for the rest of its seasonal period.

EASTMAN CHEMICAL COMPANY—
①LONG (Jan28-May5)
②SELL SHORT (May30-Oct27)

EMN (NEW)

In 2014, Eastman Chemical performed according to its seasonal trends, outperforming from January 28th to May 5th and underperforming from May 30th to October 27th. So far in 2015, Eastman Chemical has once again outperformed in its upward seasonal leg.

In its positive seasonal period from January 28th to May 5th, Eastman Chemical during the period from 1994 to 2014, has produced an average 12.9% gain and has been positive 86% of the time. In its short sell seasonal period from May 30th to October 27th, in the same yearly period, Eastman Chemical has produced an average loss of 6.2% and has been positive 38% of the time. The short sell seasonal period has not been as successful as the long seasonal period, especially in recent years. Nevertheless, investors should still be aware of the weaker period for Eastman Chemical in the summer months.

Eastman Chemical* vs. S&P 500 1994 to 2014
Positive Long   Negative Short

	LONG Jan 28 to May 5		SHORT May 30 to Oct 27		Compound Growth	
Year	S&P 500	EMN	S&P 500	EMN	S&P 500	EMN
1994	-4.9 %	6.9 %	1.9 %	8.7 %	-3.2 %	-2.4 %
1995	11.9	8.1	10.7	2.6	23.9	5.3
1996	4.6	10.0	4.9	-21.8	9.8	34.0
1997	5.6	-0.2	3.9	2.7	9.7	-2.9
1998	15.8	17.2	-2.3	-15.3	13.1	35.1
1999	10.0	30.7	-0.4	-24.5	9.5	62.6
2000	-0.6	19.5	0.1	-19.3	-0.5	42.5
2001	-5.7	18.9	-12.9	-33.1	-17.8	58.1
2002	-4.1	19.1	-15.9	-21.2	-19.4	44.3
2003	5.5	-15.0	8.6	-0.6	14.5	-14.6
2004	-2.0	12.6	0.4	-1.9	-1.5	14.8
2005	0.4	11.2	-1.7	-15.7	-1.3	28.6
2006	5.1	13.7	7.6	5.5	13.1	7.5
2007	5.8	6.0	1.1	-0.1	7.0	6.1
2008	7.4	26.8	-39.3	-55.6	-34.8	97.3
2009	9.2	44.9	15.7	34.3	26.4	-4.8
2010	6.8	13.7	8.5	33.0	15.9	-23.8
2011	4.0	12.0	-3.5	-23.1	0.4	37.9
2012	4.1	10.3	6.0	21.6	10.3	-13.6
2013	8.2	-5.0	6.8	8.4	15.5	-13.0
2014	2.2	10.3	2.2	-15.6	4.4	27.5
Avg.	4.3 %	12.9 %	-0.1 %	-6.2 %	4.5 %	20.3 %
Fq>0	76 %	86 %	67 %	38 %	67 %	67 %

20% growth & positive 14 times out of 21

Eastman Chemical, in its 10-K report filed with regulators in 2013, outlines the seasonal trends in its business. "The Company's earnings are typically greater in second and third quarters." This is a bit different than many other cyclical companies, that tend to have weaker earnings over the summer months. The net result is for Eastman Chemical to outperform into May and then underperform at the tail end of Q2, and Q3, as investors anticipate a weaker Q4 earnings report. In Q4, Eastman tends to perform at market.

ⓘ *Eastman Chemical Company manufactures and sells chemicals, fibers, and plastics, globally. Its stock symbol is EMN. which trades on the NYSE, adjusted for splits.*

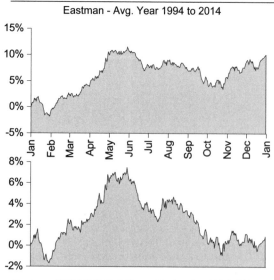

Eastman - Avg. Year 1994 to 2014

Eastman / S&P 500 Rel. Strength- Avg Yr. 1994-2014

Eastman Chemical Performance

EMN Monthly Performance (1994-2014)

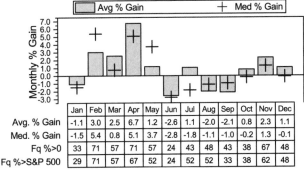

	Jan	Feb	Mar	Apr	May	Jun	Jul	Aug	Sep	Oct	Nov	Dec
Avg. % Gain	-1.1	3.0	2.5	6.7	1.2	-2.6	1.1	-2.0	-2.1	0.8	2.3	1.1
Med. % Gain	-1.5	5.4	0.8	5.1	3.7	-2.8	-1.8	-1.1	-1.0	-0.2	1.3	-0.1
Fq %>0	33	71	57	71	57	24	43	48	43	38	67	48
Fq %>S&P 500	29	71	57	67	52	24	52	52	33	38	62	48

EMN 5 Year (2010-2014) % Gain

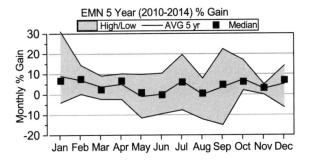

EMN Performance 2014-2015

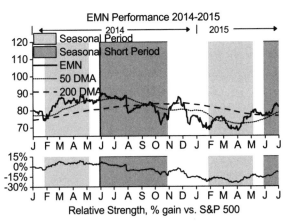

Relative Strength, % gain vs. S&P 500

WEEK 07

Market Indices & Rates
Weekly Values**

Stock Markets	2014	2015
Dow	15,988	17,890
S&P500	1,821	2,074
Nasdaq	4,205	4,813
TSX	13,926	15,172
FTSE	6,652	6,837
DAX	9,514	10,811
Nikkei	14,592	17,814
Hang Seng	22,058	24,494

Commodities	2014	2015
Oil	100.20	51.14
Gold	1292.9	1230.4

Bond Yields	2014	2015
USA 5 Yr Treasury	1.53	1.51
USA 10 Yr T	2.75	2.00
USA 20 Yr T	3.41	2.33
Moody's Aaa	4.50	3.62
Moody's Baa	5.13	4.53
CAN 5 Yr T	1.64	0.74
CAN 10 Yr T	2.45	1.43

Money Market	2014	2015
USA Fed Funds	0.25	0.25
USA 3 Mo T-B	0.04	0.01
CAN tgt overnight rate	1.00	0.75
CAN 3 Mo T-B	0.88	0.53

Foreign Exchange	2014	2015
EUR/USD	1.37	1.14
GBP/USD	1.66	1.53
USD/CAD	1.10	1.25
USD/JPY	102.28	119.28

FEBRUARY

M	T	W	T	F	S	S
1	2	3	4	5	6	7
8	9	10	11	12	13	14
15	16	17	18	19	20	21
22	23	24	24	26	27	28
29						

MARCH

M	T	W	T	F	S	S
	1	2	3	4	5	6
7	8	9	10	11	12	13
14	15	16	17	18	19	20
21	22	23	24	25	26	27
28	29	30	31			

APRIL

M	T	W	T	F	S	S
				1	2	3
4	5	6	7	8	9	10
11	12	13	14	15	16	17
18	19	20	21	22	23	24
25	26	27	28	29	30	

From 1994 to 2014, the best performing months for Eastman Chemical are February and April on an average, median and frequency basis. These months are the cornerstones of the long seasonal trade. On a median basis, the worst performing contiguous months are June through October, as all five months have negative medians. These months make up the bulk of the ideal time to short Eastman Chemical. Over the last five years, Eastman Chemical has performed well in its seasonally strong period, but has not made a good short sell in its seasonally weak period. In 2014 and 2015, the combination of the long and short seasonal legs worked well.

AUTOMOTIVE & COMPONENTS
①LONG (Dec14-Jan7) ②LONG (Feb24-Apr24)
③SELL SHORT (Aug3-Oct3)

Note: The automotive short sell seasonal period start date has been adjusted to August 3rd to better reflect the negative seasonal trend opportunity at this time.

The automotive and components sector (auto sector) has its main seasonal period from February 24th to April 24. In this time period, from 1990 to 2014, the sector has produced an average gain of 8.5% and has been positive 76% of the time. The total seasonal strategy of investing in the auto sector on December 14th, exiting on January 7th, reinvesting on February 24th, exiting on April 24th and shorting the sector from August 3rd to October 3rd, has produced an average gain of 22.3%.

22% gain

The auto sector tends to rise in the spring, as investors look to benefit from being in this sector ahead of the peak in auto sales in May. After the peak, auto sales generally decline from May until November (1975-2013, source: BEA). As a result, shorting the sector from August 3rd to October 3rd has proven to be profitable. The trend changes as auto sales increase in December, creating a positive seasonal period from December 14th to January 7th.

The SP GICS Automotive and Components Sector encompasses a wide range of automotive based companies. For more information, see www.standardandpoors.com

Automotive & Components* vs. S&P 500 1990 to 2014

Negative Short ☐   Positive Long ▢

Year	Dec 14 to Jan 07 S&P 500	Auto	Feb 24 to Apr 24 S&P 500	Auto	Aug 3 to Oct 3 S&P 500	Auto	Compound Growth S&P 500	Auto
1990	-4.2 %	-4.0 %	1.9 %	4.4 %	-11.4	-19.3 %	-13.5 %	19.6 %
1991	8.6	15.7	4.7	6.9	-0.7	-6.3	12.9	31.5
1992	-0.7	3.6	-0.6	9.1	-3.2	-16.4	-4.5	31.5
1993	0.9	1.5	0.5	11.2	2.5	-1.8	3.9	14.9
1994	2.3	10.9	-4.9	-11.1	0.3	-9.5	-2.4	7.9
1995	-0.8	1.1	5.3	2.7	4.2	-0.5	8.9	4.3
1996	3.4	4.3	-1.4	11.4	4.6	-2.1	6.6	18.7
1997	1.1	0.1	-3.8	-4.0	1.9	6.9	-0.9	-10.6
1998	8.9	10.0	6.7	10.4	-10.5	-23.0	3.9	49.3
1999	1.9	8.5	6.7	5.8	-3.4	-2.8	5.0	18.0
2000	-4.5	8.7	5.1	22.9	-0.9	1.8	-0.5	31.2
2001	4.1	4.6	-2.9	4.0	-12.2	-27.9	-11.3	39.3
2002	3.8	5.2	0.3	12.2	-5.2	-12.1	-1.4	32.2
2003	4.9	12.8	7.5	10.1	5.1	7.2	18.4	15.3
2004	-1.0	0.7	0.0	7.0	2.3	-2.8	1.2	10.7
2005	1.4	0.8	-3.3	-22.4	-1.4	-10.5	-3.2	-13.6
2006	-0.3	5.1	1.6	-0.8	4.4	7.9	5.8	-4.0
2007	-4.9	-9.6	2.0	-2.5	4.6	2.0	1.5	-13.6
2008	3.1	1.0	2.6	6.1	-12.8	-15.1	-7.7	23.3
2009	3.2	16.3	16.5	102.4	3.8	-11.4	24.8	162.3
2010	2.5	9.8	11.2	21.3	1.8	-3.1	16.1	37.2
2011	4.3	10.3	2.3	2.7	-12.4	-24.0	-6.5	40.4
2012	3.0	13.6	0.6	-5.8	6.3	10.8	10.2	-4.5
2013	3.5	-1.4	4.2	6.9	-1.8	-0.3	5.9	5.7
2014	1.2	3.5	2.3	1.0	2.2	-6.8	5.8	11.6
Avg.	1.8 %	5.3 %	2.6 %	8.5 %	-1.3 %	6.4 %	3.2 %	22.3 %
Fq>0	72 %	88 %	72	76 %	52 %	24 %	60 %	80 %

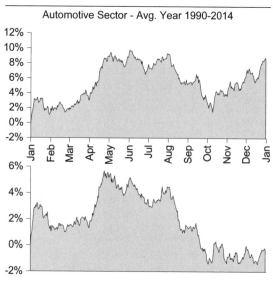

Automotive Sector - Avg. Year 1990-2014

Automotive / S&P 500 Rel. Strength- Avg Yr. 1990-2014

Automotive Performance

Auto Monthly Performance (1990-2014)

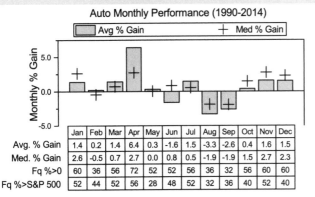

Legend: ☐ Avg % Gain   + Med % Gain

	Jan	Feb	Mar	Apr	May	Jun	Jul	Aug	Sep	Oct	Nov	Dec
Avg. % Gain	1.4	0.2	1.4	6.4	0.3	-1.6	1.5	-3.3	-2.6	0.4	1.6	1.5
Med. % Gain	2.6	-0.5	0.7	2.7	0.0	0.8	0.5	-1.9	-1.9	1.5	2.7	2.3
Fq %>0	60	36	56	72	52	52	56	36	32	56	60	60
Fq %>S&P 500	52	44	52	56	28	48	52	32	36	40	52	40

Auto 5 Year (2010-2014) % Gain

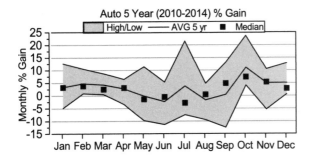

Legend: ☐ High/Low — AVG 5 yr ■ Median

Auto Performance 2014-2015

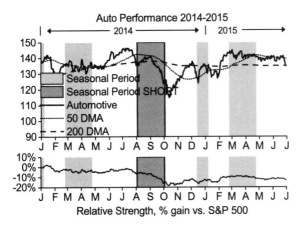

Legend: Seasonal Period / Seasonal Period SHORT / Automotive / 50 DMA / 200 DMA

Relative Strength, % gain vs. S&P 500

WEEK 08

Market Indices & Rates
Weekly Values*

Stock Markets	2014	2015
Dow	16,102	18,051
S&P500	1,836	2,102
Nasdaq	4,260	4,922
TSX	14,153	15,212
FTSE	6,796	6,891
DAX	9,650	10,966
Nikkei	14,664	18,158
Hang Seng	22,550	24,781

Commodities	2014	2015
Oil	102.79	51.79
Gold	1321.7	1212.5

Bond Yields	2014	2015
USA 5 Yr Treasury	1.54	1.58
USA 10 Yr T	2.73	2.11
USA 20 Yr T	3.42	2.49
Moody's Aaa	4.48	3.77
Moody's Baa	5.13	4.64
CAN 5 Yr T	1.66	0.79
CAN 10 Yr T	2.48	1.46

Money Market	2014	2015
USA Fed Funds	0.25	0.25
USA 3 Mo T-B	0.05	0.02
CAN tgt overnight rate	1.00	0.75
CAN 3 Mo T-B	0.87	0.50

Foreign Exchange	2014	2015
EUR/USD	1.37	1.14
GBP/USD	1.67	1.54
USD/CAD	1.10	1.25
USD/JPY	102.28	118.90

FEBRUARY

M	T	W	T	F	S	S
1	2	3	4	5	6	7
8	9	10	11	12	13	14
15	16	17	18	19	20	21
22	23	24	24	26	27	28
29						

MARCH

M	T	W	T	F	S	S
	1	2	3	4	5	6
7	8	9	10	11	12	13
14	15	16	17	18	19	20
21	22	23	24	25	26	27
28	29	30	31			

From 1990 to 2014, April has been the best month of the year for the auto sector on an average, median and frequency basis. April is the core of the spring seasonal strategy.

Over the last five years, the auto sector has generally followed its seasonal trend of weakening into the summer months and strengthening into autumn. October has been uncharacteristically strong, especially given that the auto sector underperforms the S&P 500 at this time of the year. In 2014 and 2015, the combination of long and short trades was successful as it produced a gain of 11.6% and outperformed the S&P 500.

APRIL

M	T	W	T	F	S	S
				1	2	3
4	5	6	7	8	9	10
11	12	13	14	15	16	17
18	19	20	21	22	23	24
25	26	27	28	29	30	

OIL STOCKS– WINTER/SPRING STRATEGY
Ist of II Oil Stock Strategies for the Year
February 25th to May 9th

In 2015, the *Energy- Winter/Spring Strategy* outperformed the S&P 500 during its winter-spring seasonal period, despite a long downtrend that started in 2014. The *Energy- Winter/Spring Strategy* is a strong seasonal performer over the long-term. From 1984 to 2015, for the two and half months starting on February 25th and ending May 9th, the energy sector (XOI) has outperformed the S&P 500 by an average 4.1%.

What is even more impressive are the positive returns, 27 out of 32 times, and the outperformance of the S&P 500, 25 out of 32 times.

4.1% extra and 27 out of 32 times positive, in just over two months

XOI* vs S&P 500 1984 to 2015			
Feb 25 to May 9		positive	
S&P 500	XOI		Diff
1984	1.7 %	5.6 %	3.9 %
1985	1.4	4.9	3.5
1986	6.0	7.7	1.7
1987	3.7	25.5	21.8
1988	-3.0	5.6	8.6
1989	6.3	8.1	1.8
1990	5.8	-0.6	-6.3
1991	4.8	6.8	2.0
1992	0.9	5.8	4.9
1993	0.3	6.3	6.0
1994	-4.7	3.2	7.9
1995	7.3	10.3	3.1
1996	-2.1	2.2	4.3
1997	1.8	4.7	2.9
1998	7.5	9.8	2.3
1999	7.3	35.4	28.1
2000	4.3	22.2	17.9
2001	0.8	10.2	9.4
2002	-1.5	5.3	6.9
2003	12.1	5.7	-6.4
2004	-3.5	4.0	7.5
2005	-1.8	-1.0	0.8
2006	2.8	9.4	6.6
2007	4.2	10.1	5.8
2008	2.6	7.6	5.0
2009	20.2	15.8	-4.4
2010	0.5	-2.3	-2.8
2011	3.1	-0.6	-3.7
2012	-0.8	-13.4	-12.5
2013	7.3	3.8	-3.5
2014	1.7	9.1	7.4
2015	0.3	1.2	1.1
Avg	3.0 %	7.1 %	4.1 %
Fq > 0	78 %	84 %	78 %

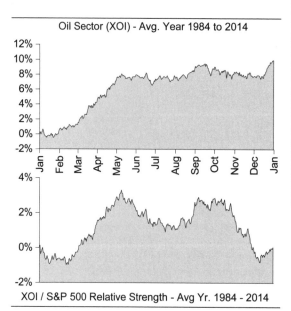

Oil Sector (XOI) - Avg. Year 1984 to 2014

XOI / S&P 500 Relative Strength - Avg Yr. 1984 - 2014

A lot of investors assume that the time to buy oil stocks is just before the winter cold sets in. The rationale is that oil will climb in price as the temperature drops.

The results in the market have not supported this assumption. The price for a barrel of oil has more to do with oil inventory. Refineries have a choice: they can produce either gasoline or heating oil. As the winter progresses, refineries start to convert their operations from heating oil to gasoline.

In late winter and early spring, as refineries start coming off their conversion and winter maintenance programs, they increase their demand for oil, putting upward pressure on its price. In addition, later in the spring, in April and early May, investors increase their holdings in the oil sector before the kick-off of the driving season (Memorial Day in May), helping to drive up the price of oil stocks.

ⓘ *NYSE Arca Oil Index (XOI):*
An index designed to represent a cross section of widely held oil corporations involved in various phases of the oil industry.

For more information on the XOI index, see www.cboe.com

NYSE Arca Oil Index (XOI) Performance

XOI Monthly Performance (1984-2014)

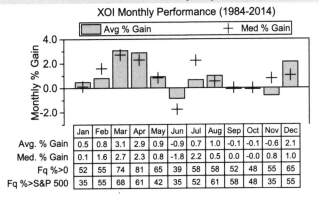

	Jan	Feb	Mar	Apr	May	Jun	Jul	Aug	Sep	Oct	Nov	Dec
Avg. % Gain	0.5	0.8	3.1	2.9	0.9	-0.9	0.7	1.0	-0.1	-0.1	-0.6	2.1
Med. % Gain	0.1	1.6	2.7	2.3	0.8	-1.8	2.2	0.5	0.0	-0.0	0.8	1.0
Fq %>0	52	55	74	81	65	39	58	58	52	48	55	65
Fq %>S&P 500	35	55	68	61	42	35	52	61	58	48	35	55

XOI 5 Year (2010-2014) % Gain

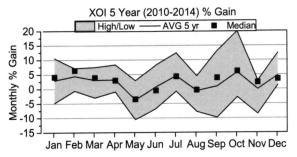

XOI Performance 2014-2015

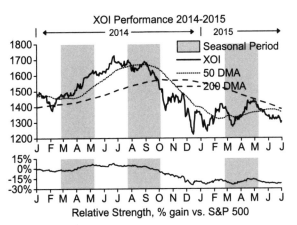

Relative Strength, % gain vs. S&P 500

Market Indices & Rates
Weekly Values**

Stock Markets	2014	2015
Dow	16,236	18,180
S&P500	1,850	2,111
Nasdaq	4,300	4,970
TSX	14,206	15,214
FTSE	6,823	6,939
DAX	9,670	11,255
Nikkei	14,925	18,648
Hang Seng	22,562	24,818

Commodities	2014	2015
Oil	102.58	49.09
Gold	1332.9	1204.8

Bond Yields	2014	2015
USA 5 Yr Treasury	1.52	1.51
USA 10 Yr T	2.69	2.01
USA 20 Yr T	3.35	2.39
Moody's Aaa	4.37	3.65
Moody's Baa	5.06	4.48
CAN 5 Yr T	1.65	0.75
CAN 10 Yr T	2.46	1.33

Money Market	2014	2015
USA Fed Funds	0.25	0.25
USA 3 Mo T-B	0.05	0.02
CAN tgt overnight rate	1.00	0.75
CAN 3 Mo T-B	0.85	0.54

Foreign Exchange	2014	2015
EUR/USD	1.37	1.13
GBP/USD	1.67	1.55
USD/CAD	1.11	1.25
USD/JPY	102.21	119.14

FEBRUARY

M	T	W	T	F	S	S
1	2	3	4	5	6	7
8	9	10	11	12	13	14
15	16	17	18	19	20	21
22	23	24	24	26	27	28
29						

MARCH

M	T	W	T	F	S	S
	1	2	3	4	5	6
7	8	9	10	11	12	13
14	15	16	17	18	19	20
21	22	23	24	25	26	27
28	29	30	31			

APRIL

M	T	W	T	F	S	S
				1	2	3
4	5	6	7	8	9	10
11	12	13	14	15	16	17
18	19	20	21	22	23	24
25	26	27	28	29	30	

From 1984 to 2014, March and April have been the best performing months for the energy sector on an average, median and frequency basis. Over the last five years, the energy sector has generally followed its seasonal pattern of positive performance in the early winter and weaker performance in the summer. The outlier to the trend was October's positive performance. In 2014, the energy sector performed well in its February to May seasonal period, but in its secondary seasonal period from July to October global oversupply of oil hurt the sector. In its 2015 winter seasonal period, the energy sector, once again performed well.

MARCH

	MONDAY	TUESDAY	WEDNESDAY
WEEK 10	29	1 30	2 29
WEEK 11	7 24	8 23	9 22
WEEK 12	14 17	15 16	16 15
WEEK 13	21 10	22 9	23 8
WEEK 14	28 3	29 2	30 1

THURSDAY	FRIDAY
3 28	**4** 27
10 21	**11** 20
17 14	**18** 13
24 7	**25** 6
	USA Market Closed- Good Friday
	CAN Market Closed- Good Friday
31	1

APRIL

M	T	W	T	F	S	S
				1	2	3
4	5	6	7	8	9	10
11	12	13	14	15	16	17
18	19	20	21	22	23	24
25	26	27	28	29	30	

MAY

M	T	W	T	F	S	S
						1
2	3	4	5	6	7	8
9	10	11	12	13	14	15
16	17	18	19	20	21	22
23	24	25	26	27	28	29
30	31					

JUNE

M	T	W	T	F	S	S
		1	2	3	4	5
6	7	8	9	10	11	12
13	14	15	16	17	18	19
20	21	22	23	24	25	26
27	28	29	30			

JULY

M	T	W	T	F	S	S
				1	2	3
4	5	6	7	8	9	10
11	12	13	14	15	16	17
18	19	20	21	22	23	24
25	26	27	28	29	30	31

MARCH
S U M M A R Y

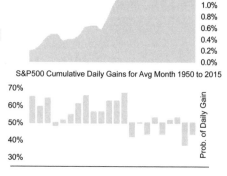

S&P500 Cumulative Daily Gains for Avg Month 1950 to 2015

	Dow Jones	S&P 500	Nasdaq	TSX Comp
Month Rank	5	4	7	4
# Up	43	43	27	18
# Down	22	22	16	12
% Pos	66	66	63	60
% Avg. Gain	1.1	1.2	0.7	1.1

Dow & S&P 1950-2014, Nasdaq 1972-2014, TSX 1985-2014

♦ March tends to be a strong month for stocks. From 1990 to 2015, the S&P 500 has produced an average gain of 1.3%. ♦ Typically, it is the cyclicals that perform well and the defensive sectors that underperform. ♦ In March 2015, the health care sector was the top performing sector. ♦ Silver can perform well in March, given its industrial uses, but its success is not reflected in gold. Since 1990, silver has produced an average gain of 1.7% and gold has produced a loss of 1.1%. In 2015, silver produced a gain of 0.4% and gold a loss of 2.2%.

BEST / WORST MARCH BROAD MKTS. 2006-2015

BEST MARCH MARKETS
♦ Nasdaq (2009) 10.9%
♦ Nikkei 225 (2010) 9.5%
♦ Russell 2000 (2009) 8.7%

WORST MARCH MARKETS
♦ Nikkei 225 (2011) -8.2%
♦ Nikkei 225 (2008) -7.9%
♦ FTSE 100 (2014) -3.1%

Index Values End of Month

	2006	2007	2008	2009	2010	2011	2012	2013	2014	2015
Dow	11,109	12,354	12,263	7,609	10,857	12,320	13,212	14,579	16,458	17,776
S&P 500	1,295	1,421	1,323	798	1,169	1,326	1,408	1,569	1,872	2,068
Nasdaq	2,340	2,422	2,279	1,529	2,398	2,781	3,092	3,268	4,199	4,901
TSX	12,111	13,166	13,350	8,720	12,038	14,116	12,392	12,750	14,335	14,902
Russell 1000	1,359	1,492	1,385	834	1,238	1,417	1,497	1,676	2,012	2,224
Russell 2000	1,902	1,990	1,710	1,051	1,687	2,096	2,064	2,365	2,915	3,113
FTSE 100	5,965	6,308	5,702	3,926	5,680	5,909	5,769	6,412	6,598	6,773
Nikkei 225	17,060	17,288	12,526	8,110	11,090	9,755	10,084	12,398	14,828	19,207

Percent Gain for March

	2006	2007	2008	2009	2010	2011	2012	2013	2014	2015
Dow	1.1	0.7	0.0	7.7	5.1	0.8	2.0	3.7	0.8	-2.0
S&P 500	1.1	1.0	-0.6	8.5	5.9	-0.1	3.1	3.6	0.7	-1.7
Nasdaq	2.6	0.2	0.3	10.9	7.1	0.0	4.2	3.4	-2.5	-1.3
TSX	3.6	0.9	-1.7	7.4	3.5	-0.1	-2.0	-0.6	0.9	-2.2
Russell 1000	1.3	0.9	-0.8	8.5	6.0	0.1	3.0	3.7	0.5	-1.4
Russell 2000	4.7	0.9	0.3	8.7	8.0	2.4	2.4	4.4	-0.8	1.6
FTSE 100	3.0	2.2	-3.1	2.5	6.1	-1.4	-1.8	0.8	-3.1	-2.5
Nikkei 225	5.3	-1.8	-7.9	7.1	9.5	-8.2	3.7	7.3	-0.1	2.2

March Market Avg. Performance 2006 to 2015[1]

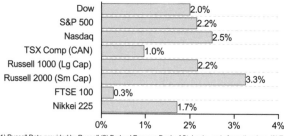

Dow	2.0%
S&P 500	2.2%
Nasdaq	2.5%
TSX Comp (CAN)	1.0%
Russell 1000 (Lg Cap)	2.2%
Russell 2000 (Sm Cap)	3.3%
FTSE 100	0.3%
Nikkei 225	1.7%

Interest Corner Mar[2]

	Fed Funds %[3]	3 Mo. T-Bill %[4]	10 Yr %[5]	20 Yr %[6]
2015	0.25	0.03	1.94	2.31
2014	0.25	0.05	2.73	3.31
2013	0.25	0.07	1.87	2.71
2012	0.25	0.07	2.23	3.00
2011	0.25	0.09	3.47	4.29

(1) Russell Data provided by Russell (2) Federal Reserve Bank of St. Louis- end of month values (3) Target rate set by FOMC (4)(5)(6) Constant yield maturities.

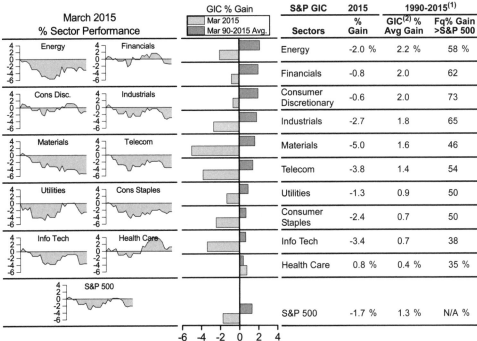

S&P GIC Sectors	2015 % Gain	1990-2015[1] GIC[2] % Avg Gain	1990-2015[1] Fq% Gain >S&P 500
Energy	-2.0 %	2.2 %	58 %
Financials	-0.8	2.0	62
Consumer Discretionary	-0.6	2.0	73
Industrials	-2.7	1.8	65
Materials	-5.0	1.6	46
Telecom	-3.8	1.4	54
Utilities	-1.3	0.9	50
Consumer Staples	-2.4	0.7	50
Info Tech	-3.4	0.7	38
Health Care	0.8 %	0.4 %	35 %
S&P 500	-1.7 %	1.3 %	N/A %

Sector Commentary

♦ After producing a large gain of 7.8% in February, the materials sector lost 5.0%. ♦ The financial sector is typically one of the better sectors in the market during March. Although the sector produced a loss of 0.8%, it outperformed the S&P 500 which produced a loss of 1.7%. ♦ The energy sector continued its multi-month decline and produced a 2.0% loss. ♦ Information technology, typically one of the weaker performing sectors, produced a loss of 3.4%

Sub-Sector Commentary

♦ For the first part of the year, the commodity based sectors of the stock market tended to oscillate back and forth looking for direction. After producing a large gain in February 2015, the metals and mining sector corrected sharply in March, producing a loss of 10.5%. ♦ After outperforming the S&P 500 in 2014, the railroads underperformed at the beginning of 2015, including a large loss of 8.1%. Falling commodity prices and the global slowing economy were starting to take their toll on the sector. ♦ Based upon positive trending home starts, homebuilders were one of the few positive sub-sectors with a gain of 2.2%.

SELECTED SUB-SECTORS[3]

	% Gain	% Avg Gain	Fq% Gain
Retail	-0.2 %	3.3 %	73 %
Steel	-1.3	2.4	62
Chemicals	-4.6	2.1	54
Transportation	-5.2	2.1	65
Railroads	-8.1	1.9	58
Silver	0.4	1.7	50
Banks	-1.0	1.6	54
Software & Services	-2.1	1.4	54
SOX (1995-2015)	-2.7	1.4	43
Metals & Mining	-10.5	0.7	42
Agriculture (1994-2015)	-1.0	0.6	36
Homebuilders	2.2	0.6	46
Pharma	0.5	0.5	35
Biotech (1993-2015)	-1.3	-0.3	39
Gold (London PM)	-2.2	-1.1	35

NKE NIKE RUNS INTO EARNINGS
①Mar1-Mar20 ②Sep1-Sep25 ③Dec12-Dec24

Nike has had a strong run in the stock market since it went public in 1980. More recently, from 1990 to 2014, it has produced an average annual gain of 22.6%. A lot of the gains in the stock price can be accounted for in the two to three week periods leading up to its first, second and third quarters earnings reports.

Nike's year-end is May 31st, and although from year to year the actual report dates for Nike's earnings changes, generally speaking, Nike reports its earnings in the third or fourth week in the months of March, June, September and December.

It is interesting to note that Nike has strong seasonal runs at different times of the year. Stocks typically have similar seasonal patterns as the sector to which they belong. Nike belongs to the consumer discretionary sector and it would be expected that Nike would have a similar seasonal pattern.

There are large differences in Nike's pattern of seasonal strength compared with the consumer discretionary's seasonal pattern. First, Nike has a period of seasonal strength that includes September, a month that is not favorable to consumer discretionary stocks. Second, Nike's outperformance is focused on very short periods in the weeks leading up to three of its earnings periods. In contrast, the consumer discretionary sector has a much longer seasonal period and has a more gradual transition from its favorable seasonal period to its unfavorable seasonal period and vice versa.

From 1990 to 2014, Nike produced an average annual gain of 22.6%. In comparison, its three short seasonal periods within the year have produced an average compound gain of 16.0%. The seasonal periods in total are approximately eight weeks and yet, they have produced most of the average annual gains of Nike. Investors have been well served investing in Nike in its seasonal periods and then running to another investment during its "off-season."

Nike Inc*. Seasonal Gains 1990 to 2014

Positive ▢

| Year | Mar 1 | Sep 1 | Dec 12 | Compound |
%	to Mar 20	to Sep 25	to Dec 24	Growth
1990	51.8 %	14.7 %	1.0 %	11.7 %	29.3 %
1991	79.4	-5.7	9.3	12.7	16.2
1992	14.8	-8.3	6.2	-2.8	-5.3
1993	-44.3	5.8	-13.7	0.7	-8.0
1994	61.3	10.5	-7.0	14.7	17.9
1995	86.7	5.4	18.8	10.7	38.6
1996	72.4	22.2	13.6	13.0	56.9
1997	-34.9	-6.1	1.0	-14.1	-18.5
1998	3.8	1.0	18.0	14.8	36.8
1999	22.2	15.6	15.1	18.2	57.2
2000	12.6	16.0	1.6	16.4	37.2
2001	0.8	-2.7	-8.7	3.7	-7.9
2002	-20.9	8.7	2.7	2.0	13.9
2003	54.0	14.0	6.0	4.4	26.2
2004	32.4	5.0	5.8	5.1	16.7
2005	-4.3	-1.8	3.0	1.3	2.4
2006	14.1	-1.5	7.1	2.6	8.2
2007	29.7	4.6	3.7	4.2	13.0
2008	-20.6	11.8	7.3	0.8	20.9
2009	29.6	8.4	5.9	2.2	17.3
2010	29.3	8.8	13.5	-2.0	20.9
2011	12.8	-12.9	2.3	-0.8	-11.6
2012	7.1	3.5	-2.3	6.2	7.4
2013	52.4	0.7	9.7	1.1	11.6
2014	22.3	1.2	1.5	-0.7	2.1
Avg.	19.0 %	4.8 %	4.9 %	5.0 %	16.0 %

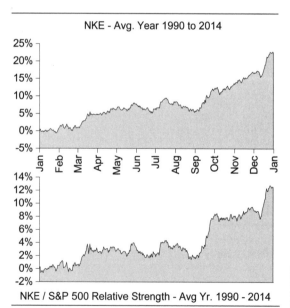

NKE - Avg. Year 1990 to 2014

NKE / S&P 500 Relative Strength - Avg Yr. 1990 - 2014

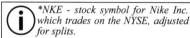

(i) *NKE - stock symbol for Nike Inc. which trades on the NYSE, adjusted for splits.*

- 31 -

Nike Performance

Nike Monthly Performance (1990-2014)

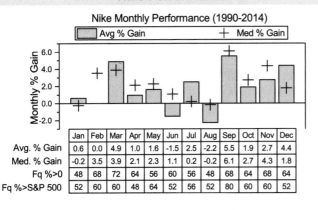

	Jan	Feb	Mar	Apr	May	Jun	Jul	Aug	Sep	Oct	Nov	Dec
Avg. % Gain	0.6	0.0	4.9	1.0	1.6	-1.5	2.5	-2.2	5.5	1.9	2.7	4.4
Med. % Gain	-0.2	3.5	3.9	2.1	2.3	1.1	0.2	-0.2	6.1	2.7	4.3	1.8
Fq %>0	48	68	72	64	56	60	56	48	68	64	68	64
Fq %>S&P 500	52	60	60	48	64	52	56	52	80	60	60	52

Nike 5 Year (2010-2014) % Gain

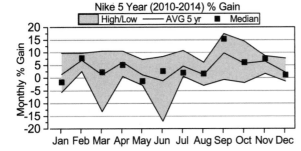

Nike Performance 2014-2015

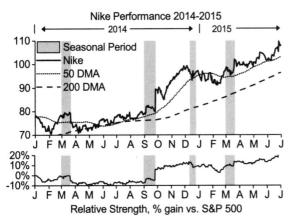

Relative Strength, % gain vs. S&P 500

Market Indices & Rates
Weekly Values**

Stock Markets	2014	2015
Dow	16,360	18,116
S&P500	1,870	2,099
Nasdaq	4,335	4,973
TSX	14,276	15,107
FTSE	6,762	6,924
DAX	9,477	11,427
Nikkei	14,936	18,814
Hang Seng	22,620	24,483

Commodities	2014	2015
Oil	102.77	50.40
Gold	1340.4	1200.5

Bond Yields	2014	2015
USA 5 Yr Treasury	1.55	1.61
USA 10 Yr T	2.71	2.13
USA 20 Yr T	3.37	2.51
Moody's Aaa	4.38	3.74
Moody's Baa	5.07	4.60
CAN 5 Yr T	1.68	0.90
CAN 10 Yr T	2.48	1.49

Money Market	2014	2015
USA Fed Funds	0.25	0.25
USA 3 Mo T-B	0.05	0.02
CAN tgt overnight rate	1.00	0.75
CAN 3 Mo T-B	0.83	0.59

Foreign Exchange	2014	2015
EUR/USD	1.38	1.11
GBP/USD	1.67	1.53
USD/CAD	1.11	1.25
USD/JPY	102.46	120.10

MARCH

M	T	W	T	F	S	S
	1	2	3	4	5	6
7	8	9	10	11	12	13
14	15	16	17	18	19	20
21	22	23	24	25	26	27
28	29	30	31			

APRIL

M	T	W	T	F	S	S
				1	2	3
4	5	6	7	8	9	10
11	12	13	14	15	16	17
18	19	20	21	22	23	24
25	26	27	28	29	30	

MAY

M	T	W	T	F	S	S
						1
2	3	4	5	6	7	8
9	10	11	12	13	14	15
16	17	18	19	20	21	22
18	19	25	26	27	28	29
30	31					

From 1990 to 2014, on average, the three best months for Nike were March, September and December, which are all part of the *Nike Runs Into Earnings* strategy. September was the best month of the three as it has a higher average and median than the other two months. Performing well in September is particularly valuable as the S&P 500 tends not to perform well in this month. On average, over the last five years, Nike has performed extremely well in the month of September.

In 2014 and 2015, the Nike combination strategy was positive and outperformed the S&P 500.

LNR LINAMAR
February 24th to May 12th

Linamar is a parts supplier to the automotive business and as a result is largely affected by its seasonal cycle. The automotive segment is not the only division in Linamar, but it is a major driving force.

The automotive sector has its main strong seasonal period from February 24th to April 24th (see *Automotive & Components* strategy). If the auto sector is performing well in its seasonal period, then ceterius paribus (everything else being equal), it would be expected that Linamar should also perform well. As expected, Linamar has a similar strong seasonal period as the auto sector and outperforms the TSX Composite from February 24th to May 12th.

17.7% gain & positive 85% of the time

In its seasonal period, from 1996 to 2015, Linamar has produced an average rate of return of 20.8% and has been positive 75% of the time. Even more impressive is the 85% frequency that Linamar has outperformed the TSX Composite in its seasonal period. During its seasonal period in 2009, Linamar performed extremely well, as did many other automotive companies, after the 2008 financial crisis.

LNR* vs. TSX Composite 1996 to 2014			
			Positive
Feb 24 to May 12	TSX Comp	LNR	Diff
1996	4.3%	23.1%	18.8%
1997	0.7	29.5	28.8
1998	11.2	-4.3	-15.5
1999	8.5	-12.4	-20.9
2000	-1.1	24.4	25.5
2001	-0.1	13.6	13.6
2002	2.3	6.0	3.7
2003	2.4	-4.7	-7.1
2004	-4.9	1.8	6.7
2005	-3.6	-0.7	2.8
2006	2.6	13.0	10.4
2007	5.0	26.9	22.0
2008	8.0	14.4	6.5
2009	31.8	178.5	146.7
2010	5.8	43.5	37.7
2011	-4.1	-0.2	3.8
2012	-8.1	18.2	26.3
2013	-0.9	8.1	9.0
2014	3.2	33.0	29.8
2015	-1.0	4.6	5.7
Avg	3.1%	20.8%	17.7%
Fq > 0	60%	75%	85%

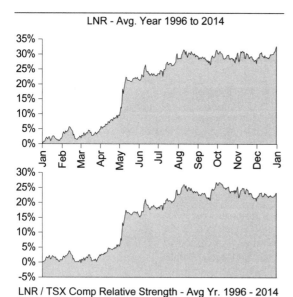

LNR - Avg. Year 1996 to 2014

LNR / TSX Comp Relative Strength - Avg Yr. 1996 - 2014

There is no question that the exceptionally strong results in 2009 skew the seasonal results, but even with the 2009 results removed, Linamar has performed extremely well in its seasonal period.

In its 2014 annual report, Linamar acknowledged a seasonally weak period for its business: "The third and fourth quarters are generally negatively impacted by the scheduled shutdowns at automotive customers and seasonal slowdowns in the aerial work platform and agricultural businesses."

The third and fourth quarter seasonal weakness for business shows up in Linamar's stock price. From 1996 to 2014, for all of the months from August to November, Linamar both underperformed the TSX Composite more than half of the time and was positive less than half of the time.

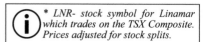

* LNR- stock symbol for Linamar which trades on the TSX Composite. Prices adjusted for stock splits.

Linamar Performance

Linamar Monthly Performance (1996-2014)

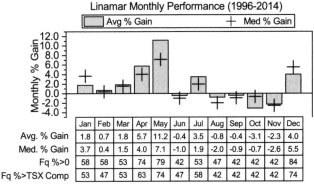

	Jan	Feb	Mar	Apr	May	Jun	Jul	Aug	Sep	Oct	Nov	Dec
Avg. % Gain	1.8	0.7	1.8	5.7	11.2	-0.4	3.5	-0.8	-0.4	-3.1	-2.3	4.0
Med. % Gain	3.7	0.4	1.5	4.0	7.1	-1.0	1.9	-2.0	-0.9	-0.7	-2.6	5.5
Fq %>0	58	58	53	74	79	42	53	47	42	42	42	84
Fq %>TSX Comp	53	47	53	63	74	47	58	42	42	42	42	74

Linamar 5 Year (2010-2014) % Gain

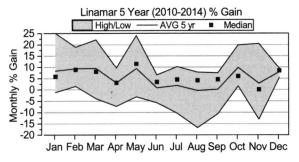

Linamar Performance 2014-2015

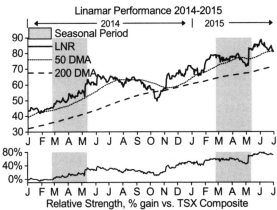

Relative Strength, % gain vs. TSX Composite

Market Indices & Rates
Weekly Values**

Stock Markets	2014	2015
Dow	16,257	17,788
S&P500	1,860	2,057
Nasdaq	4,294	4,883
TSX	14,272	14,748
FTSE	6,616	6,760
DAX	9,167	11,718
Nikkei	14,864	18,885
Hang Seng	21,946	23,872

Commodities	2014	2015
Oil	99.25	47.67
Gold	1362.0	1157.0

Bond Yields	2014	2015
USA 5 Yr Treasury	1.59	1.61
USA 10 Yr T	2.72	2.14
USA 20 Yr T	3.37	2.50
Moody's Aaa	4.41	3.70
Moody's Baa	5.10	4.59
CAN 5 Yr T	1.64	0.91
CAN 10 Yr T	2.44	1.52

Money Market	2014	2015
USA Fed Funds	0.25	0.25
USA 3 Mo T-B	0.05	0.03
CAN tgt overnight rate	1.00	0.75
CAN 3 Mo T-B	0.82	0.56

Foreign Exchange	2014	2015
EUR/USD	1.39	1.06
GBP/USD	1.66	1.50
USD/CAD	1.11	1.27
USD/JPY	102.45	121.28

MARCH

M	T	W	T	F	S	S
	1	2	3	4	5	6
7	8	9	10	11	12	13
14	15	16	17	18	19	20
21	22	23	24	25	26	27
28	29	30	31			

APRIL

M	T	W	T	F	S	S
				1	2	3
4	5	6	7	8	9	10
11	12	13	14	15	16	17
18	19	20	21	22	23	24
25	26	27	28	29	30	

MAY

M	T	W	T	F	S	S
						1
2	3	4	5	6	7	8
9	10	11	12	13	14	15
16	17	18	19	20	21	22
23	24	25	26	27	28	29
30	31					

From 1996 to 2014, the best month for Linamar has been May on an average, median and frequency basis. The seasonal period for Linamar finishes on May 12th, but the remainder of the month can still provide solid gains. Care must be taken as June is typically a weak month.

Over the last five years, on average, Linamar has followed its seasonal trend with May being the strongest month and November performing poorly.

In 2014 and 2015, Linamar outperformed the TSX Composite during its seasonal period and in both cases received a boost from strong earnings reported in early May.

BBBY BED BATH & BEYOND
①Feb25-Apr8 ②Aug23-Sep29

Bed Bath & Beyond is a retailer with a focus on selling house merchandise. As the majority of its revenue comes from selling products for the home, the company's seasonal performance is not only affected by retail sales, but also by home sales and starts. According to the company's 2014 annual report, "The Company's sales exhibit seasonality with sales levels generally higher in the calendar months of August, November and December, and generally lower in February".

25% gain & positive 86% of the time

Bed Bath & Beyond has a two periods of seasonal strength. The first period is from February 25th to April 8th and the second from August 23rd to September 29th.

The first period of seasonal strength from late February to early April is the core part of the retail sector's seasonal trend. The tendency is for Bed Bath and Beyond to perform well into the first week in April, leading up to the day the company releases in full-year earnings report.

The second period of seasonal strength is from late August into late September. This period of strength is driven mainly by investors taking a position in the stock ahead of the company's Q2 earnings announcement that typically takes place towards the end of September. This seasonal period tends to perform particularly well if Bed Bath & Beyond has corrected in the summer months relative to the S&P 500.

BBBY* vs. S&P 500 1993 to 2014   Positive ▢

Year	Feb 25 to Apr 8		Aug 23 to Sep 29		Compound Growth	
	S&P 500	BBBY	S&P 500	BBBY	S&P 500	BBBY
1993	0.2	23.1 %	0.9	40.1 %	1.1	72.5 %
1994	-3.7	13.8	0.0	-5.0	-3.7	8.1
1995	3.8	-12.1	4.5	8.9	8.4	-4.3
1996	-2.3	13.9	2.3	32.6	0.0	50.9
1997	-5.5	2.8	3.2	10.6	-2.4	13.7
1998	6.9	22.3	-3.0	25.3	3.7	53.2
1999	7.2	31.0	-5.1	7.7	1.8	41.1
2000	12.0	70.2	-4.1	36.4	7.4	132.2
2001	-9.4	3.9	-10.7	-10.6	-19.1	-7.1
2002	3.3	9.7	-14.1	0.2	-11.3	9.9
2003	5.5	11.2	1.4	-8.9	6.9	1.3
2004	0.0	-2.7	1.5	4.0	1.5	1.2
2005	-1.6	6.4	0.5	-4.1	-1.1	2.1
2006	0.5	13.0	2.9	8.5	3.3	22.6
2007	-0.5	-3.2	4.3	-1.2	3.7	-4.3
2008	0.9	6.8	-14.4	1.8	-13.6	8.7
2009	6.7	47.3	3.4	5.1	10.3	54.8
2010	7.4	11.5	6.8	13.6	14.7	26.6
2011	1.7	13.6	3.3	15.0	5.0	30.6
2012	2.4	19.1	1.9	-5.4	4.3	12.6
2013	3.1	12.9	2.1	3.8	5.3	17.2
2014	0.2	2.7	-0.5	3.4	-0.3	6.2
Avg.	1.8 %	14.4 %	-0.6 %	8.2 %	1.2 %	25 %
Fq>0	73 %	86 %	64 %	73 %	68 %	86 %

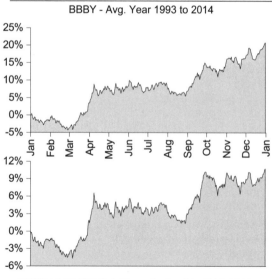

BBBY - Avg. Year 1993 to 2014

BBBY / S&P 500 Rel. Strength- Avg Yr. 1993-2014

Bed Bath & Beyond Performance

BBBY Monthly Performance (1993-2014)

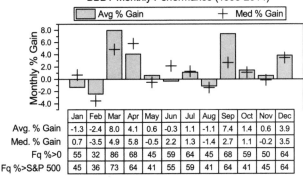

	Jan	Feb	Mar	Apr	May	Jun	Jul	Aug	Sep	Oct	Nov	Dec
Avg. % Gain	-1.3	-2.4	8.0	4.1	0.6	-0.3	1.1	-1.1	7.4	1.4	0.6	3.9
Med. % Gain	0.7	-3.5	4.9	5.8	-0.5	2.2	1.3	-1.4	2.7	1.1	-0.2	3.5
Fq %>0	55	32	86	68	45	59	64	45	68	59	50	64
Fq %>S&P 500	45	36	73	64	41	55	59	41	64	41	45	64

BBBY 5 Year (2010-2014) % Gain

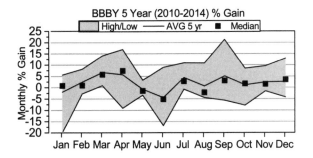

Jan Feb Mar Apr May Jun Jul Aug Sep Oct Nov Dec

BBBY Performance 2014-2015

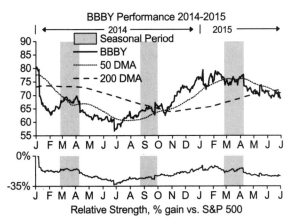

Relative Strength, % gain vs. S&P 500

WEEK 12

**Market Indices & Rates
Weekly Values****

Stock Markets	2014	2015
Dow	16,288	17,998
S&P500	1,866	2,090
Nasdaq	4,303	4,974
TSX	14,327	14,908
FTSE	6,569	6,914
DAX	9,268	12,002
Nikkei	14,344	19,453
Hang Seng	21,449	24,163
Commodities	**2014**	**2015**
Oil	99.51	44.34
Gold	1347.1	1159.6
Bond Yields	**2014**	**2015**
USA 5 Yr Treasury	1.67	1.49
USA 10 Yr T	2.74	2.00
USA 20 Yr T	3.36	2.36
Moody's Aaa	4.42	3.62
Moody's Baa	5.11	4.51
CAN 5 Yr T	1.69	0.77
CAN 10 Yr T	2.46	1.36
Money Market	**2014**	**2015**
USA Fed Funds	0.25	0.25
USA 3 Mo T-B	0.06	0.03
CAN tgt overnight rate	1.00	0.75
CAN 3 Mo T-B	0.84	0.53
Foreign Exchange	**2014**	**2015**
EUR/USD	1.39	1.07
GBP/USD	1.66	1.49
USD/CAD	1.12	1.27
USD/JPY	102.03	120.73

MARCH

M	T	W	T	F	S	S
	1	2	3	4	5	6
7	8	9	10	11	12	13
14	15	16	17	18	19	20
21	22	23	24	25	26	27
28	29	30	31			

APRIL

M	T	W	T	F	S	S
				1	2	3
4	5	6	7	8	9	10
11	12	13	14	15	16	17
18	19	20	21	22	23	24
25	26	27	28	29	30	

MAY

M	T	W	T	F	S	S
						1
2	3	4	5	6	7	8
9	10	11	12	13	14	15
16	17	18	19	20	21	22
23	24	25	26	27	28	29
30	31					

From 1993 to 2014, on average, the best month for Bed Bath & Beyond has been March. April is also a strong month, but the returns have mostly come at the beginning of the month, giving caution to investors as Bed Bath & Beyond weakens into May. September is a also a strong month for Bed Bath & Beyond and is the core part of the second seasonal period from late August to late September. Over the last five years, Bed Bath & Beyond has followed its general seasonal trend with March and April being the strongest months. In 2014 and 2015, Bed Bath & Beyond has been positive in its seasonal periods and it has outperformed the S&P 500.

CANADIANS GIVE 3 CHEERS FOR AMERICAN HOLIDAYS

When I used to work on the retail side of the investment business, I was always amazed at how often the Canadian stock market increased on U.S. holidays, when the U.S. stock market was closed.

The Canadian stock market on U.S. holidays always had light volume, tended not to have large increases or decreases, but nevertheless usually ended the day with a gain.

the U.S stock markets are open. This does not invalidate the *Canadians Give 3 Cheers* trade – it presents more alternatives for the astute investor.

For example, an investor can allocate a portion of money to a standard U.S. holiday trade and another portion to the *Canadian Give 3 Cheers* version. By spreading out the exit days, the overall risk in the trade is reduced.

1% average gain

How the trade works

For the three big holidays in the United States that do not exist in Canada (Memorial, Independence and U.S. Thanksgiving Days), buy at the end of the market day before the holiday (TSX Composite) and sell at the end of the U.S. holiday when the U.S markets are closed.

For U.S. investors to take advantage of this trade, they must have access to the TSX Composite. Unfortunately, SEC regulations do not allow Americans to purchase foreign ETFs.

Generally, markets perform well around most major U.S. holidays, hence the trading strategies for U.S holidays included in this book. The typical U.S. holiday trade is to get into the stock market the day before the holiday and then exit the day after the holiday.

The main reason for the strong performance around these holidays is a lack of institutional involvement in the markets, allowing bullish retail investors to push up the markets.

On the actual American holidays, economic reports are not released in the U.S. and are very seldom released in Canada. During market hours on U.S. holidays, without any strong influences, the TSX Composite tends to float, preferring to wait until the next day before making any significant moves. Despite this laxidasical action during the day, the TSX Composite tends to end the day on a gain. This is true for the three major U.S. holidays that are covered in this book: Memorial Day, Independence Day and U.S. Thanksgiving.

From a theoretical perspective, a lot of the gain that is captured on the U.S. holidays in the Canadian stock market is realized the next day when

S&P/TSX Comp
Gain 1977-2014   Positive ▢

	Memorial	Independence	Thanksgiving	Compound Growth
1977	0.10 %	-0.08 %	0.61 %	0.63 %
1978	-0.05	-0.16	0.57	0.36
1979	1.11	0.23	0.58	1.93
1980	1.64	0.76	0.89	3.32
1981	0.51	-0.15	1.03	1.40
1982	-0.18	-0.01	0.35	0.17
1983	0.29	0.53	0.15	0.97
1984	0.86	-0.11	0.73	1.48
1985	0.61	0.31	0.31	1.24
1986	0.23	-0.02	0.22	0.44
1987	-0.11	1.08	1.57	2.55
1988	0.44	0.08	0.58	1.11
1989	0.10	-0.12	-0.11	-0.13
1990	0.11	0.43	0.02	0.57
1991	0.02	0.18	-0.09	0.11
1992	-0.06	0.35	0.36	0.65
1993	0.42	-0.18	0.14	0.38
1994	-0.19	0.70	0.91	1.43
1995	0.14	0.25	0.29	0.68
1996	0.11	0.25	0.54	0.90
1997	1.08	-0.04	-0.85	0.18
1998	0.56	0.18	0.51	1.25
1999	0.57	1.63	1.14	3.39
2000	0.43	1.04	0.91	2.40
2001	-0.02	-0.23	0.70	0.45
2002	-0.01	0.08	0.38	0.45
2003	0.03	0.03	0.26	0.31
2004	0.84	-0.02	0.55	1.39
2005	0.56	0.39	1.48	2.45
2006	0.70	1.04	0.70	2.46
2007	0.35	-0.03	0.76	1.08
2008	0.24	-0.94	1.28	0.56
2009	0.76	0.36	-1.29	-0.18
2010	0.78	-0.92	0.34	0.19
2011	0.23	0.64	-0.75	0.12
2012	-0.09	0.55	0.44	0.90
2013	0.23	0.17	0.07	0.47
2014	0.05	0.05	-0.77	-0.67
Avg	0.35 %	0.22 %	0.41 %	0.98 %
Fq > 0	79 %	63 %	84 %	92 %

Canadians Give 3 Cheers Performance

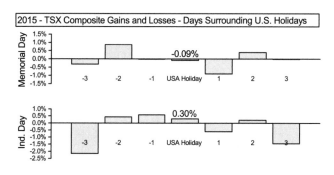

WEEK 13

**Market Indices & Rates
Weekly Values****

Stock Markets	2014	2015
Dow	16,300	17,847
S&P500	1,856	2,075
Nasdaq	4,188	4,927
TSX	14,240	14,930
FTSE	6,587	6,960
DAX	9,403	11,896
Nikkei	14,539	19,594
Hang Seng	21,873	24,481

Commodities	2014	2015
Oil	100.57	48.58
Gold	1303.8	1194.5

Bond Yields	2014	2015
USA 5 Yr Treasury	1.73	1.42
USA 10 Yr T	2.72	1.94
USA 20 Yr T	3.29	2.29
Moody's Aaa	4.33	3.54
Moody's Baa	5.00	4.47
CAN 5 Yr T	1.71	0.78
CAN 10 Yr T	2.45	1.35

Money Market	2014	2015
USA Fed Funds	0.25	0.25
USA 3 Mo T-B	0.05	0.03
CAN tgt overnight rate	1.00	0.75
CAN 3 Mo T-B	0.89	0.55

Foreign Exchange	2014	2015
EUR/USD	1.38	1.09
GBP/USD	1.66	1.49
USD/CAD	1.11	1.25
USD/JPY	102.31	119.46

MARCH

M	T	W	T	F	S	S
	1	2	3	4	5	6
7	8	9	10	11	12	13
14	15	16	17	18	19	20
21	22	23	24	25	26	27
28	29	30	31			

Canadians Give 3 Cheers Performance

In 2014, the TSX Composite was positive for both the Memorial Day and Independence Day. In both cases, the gains were very minor. Unfortunately, the loss on U.S. Thanksgiving Day, more than offset the gains made on the two previous holiday trades.

In 2015, the TSX Composite was slightly negative on Memorial Day. At the time, the S&P 500 was topping out and set its spring time closing high a few days later at 2131 on May 21, 2015.

The S&P 500 corrected sharply at the end of June 2015, setting up well for Independence Day. In the end, the trade was positive and its gains more than offset the loss earlier in the year on Memorial Day.

APRIL

M	T	W	T	F	S	S
				1	2	3
4	5	6	7	8	9	10
11	12	13	14	15	16	17
18	19	20	21	22	23	24
25	26	27	28	29	30	

MAY

M	T	W	T	F	S	S
						1
2	3	4	5	6	7	8
9	10	11	12	13	14	15
16	17	18	19	20	21	22
23	24	25	26	27	28	29
30	31					

APRIL

	MONDAY	TUESDAY	WEDNESDAY
WEEK 14	28	29	30
WEEK 15	4 26	5 25	6 24
WEEK 16	11 19	12 18	13 17
WEEK 17	18 12	19 11	20 10
WEEK 18	25 5	26 4	27 3

THURSDAY		FRIDAY	
31		**1**	29
7	23	**8**	22
14	16	**15**	15
21	9	**22**	8
28	2	**29**	1

MAY

M	T	W	T	F	S	S
						1
2	3	4	5	6	7	8
9	10	11	12	13	14	15
16	17	18	19	20	21	22
23	24	25	26	27	28	29
30	31					

JUNE

M	T	W	T	F	S	S
		1	2	3	4	5
6	7	8	9	10	11	12
13	14	15	16	17	18	19
20	21	22	23	24	25	26
27	28	29	30			

JULY

M	T	W	T	F	S	S
				1	2	3
4	5	6	7	8	9	10
11	12	13	14	15	16	17
18	19	20	21	22	23	24
25	26	27	28	29	30	31

AUGUST

M	T	W	T	F	S	S
1	2	3	4	5	6	7
8	9	10	11	12	13	14
15	16	17	18	19	20	21
22	23	24	25	26	27	28
29	30	31				

APRIL
S U M M A R Y

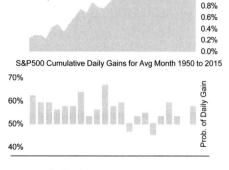

S&P500 Cumulative Daily Gains for Avg Month 1950 to 2015

	Dow Jones	S&P 500	Nasdaq	TSX Comp
Month Rank	1	3	4	7
# Up	43	44	27	17
# Down	22	21	16	13
% Pos	66	68	63	57
% Avg. Gain	2.0	1.5	1.3	0.7

Dow & S&P 1950-2014, Nasdaq 1972-2014, TSX 1985-2014

♦ April, on average, has been the second strongest month for the S&P 500. From 1950 to 2015, April has produced an average gain of 1.5% and been positive 69% of the time. ♦ The first part of April tends to be the strongest (see *18 Day Earnings Month Effect strategy*). ♦ The last part of April tends to be "flat." ♦ Overall, April tends to be a volatile month with the cyclical sectors outperforming. When the defensive sectors outperform in April, it often indicates market weakness ahead.

BEST / WORST APRIL BROAD MKTS. 2006-2015

BEST APRIL MARKETS
♦ Russell 2000 (2009) 15.3%
♦ Nasdaq (2009) 12.3%
♦ Nikkei 225 (2013) 11.8%

WORST APRIL MARKETS
♦ Nikkei 225 (2012) -5.6%
♦ Russell 2000 (2014) -3.9%
♦ Nikkei 225 (2014) -3.5%

Index Values End of Month

	2006	2007	2008	2009	2010	2011	2012	2013	2014	2015
Dow	11,367	13,063	12,820	8,168	11,009	12,811	13,214	14,840	16,581	17,841
S&P 500	1,311	1,482	1,386	873	1,187	1,364	1,398	1,598	1,884	2,086
Nasdaq	2,323	2,525	2,413	1,717	2,461	2,874	3,046	3,329	4,115	4,941
TSX	12,204	13,417	13,937	9,325	12,211	13,945	12,293	12,457	14,652	15,225
Russell 1000	1,373	1,553	1,453	917	1,259	1,458	1,487	1,705	2,019	2,238
Russell 2000	1,900	2,024	1,780	1,212	1,781	2,150	2,030	2,355	2,801	3,032
FTSE 100	6,023	6,449	6,087	4,244	5,553	6,070	5,738	6,430	6,780	6,961
Nikkei 225	16,906	17,400	13,850	8,828	11,057	9,850	9,521	13,861	14,304	19,520

Percent Gain for April

	2006	2007	2008	2009	2010	2011	2012	2013	2014	2015
Dow	2.3	5.7	4.5	7.3	1.4	4.0	0.0	1.8	0.7	0.4
S&P 500	1.2	4.3	4.8	9.4	1.5	2.8	-0.7	1.8	0.6	0.9
Nasdaq	-0.7	4.3	5.9	12.3	2.6	3.3	-1.5	1.9	-2.0	0.8
TSX	0.8	1.9	4.4	6.9	1.4	-1.2	-0.8	-2.3	2.2	2.2
Russell 1000	1.1	4.1	5.0	10.0	1.8	2.9	-0.7	1.7	0.4	0.6
Russell 2000	-0.1	1.7	4.1	15.3	5.6	2.6	-1.6	-0.4	-3.9	-2.6
FTSE 100	1.0	2.2	6.8	8.1	-2.2	2.7	-0.5	0.3	2.8	2.8
Nikkei 225	-0.9	0.7	10.6	8.9	-0.3	1.0	-5.6	11.8	-3.5	1.6

April Market Avg. Performance 2006 to 2015[1]

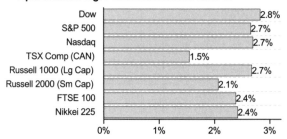

Dow	2.8%
S&P 500	2.7%
Nasdaq	2.7%
TSX Comp (CAN)	1.5%
Russell 1000 (Lg Cap)	2.7%
Russell 2000 (Sm Cap)	2.1%
FTSE 100	2.4%
Nikkei 225	2.4%

Interest Corner Apr[2]

	Fed Funds %[3]	3 Mo. T-Bill %[4]	10 Yr %[5]	20 Yr %[6]
2015	0.25	0.01	2.05	2.49
2014	0.25	0.03	2.67	3.22
2013	0.25	0.05	1.70	2.49
2012	0.25	0.10	1.95	2.73
2011	0.25	0.04	3.32	4.15

(1) Russell Data provided by Russell (2) Federal Reserve Bank of St. Louis- end of month values (3) Target rate set by FOMC (4)(5)(6) Constant yield maturities.

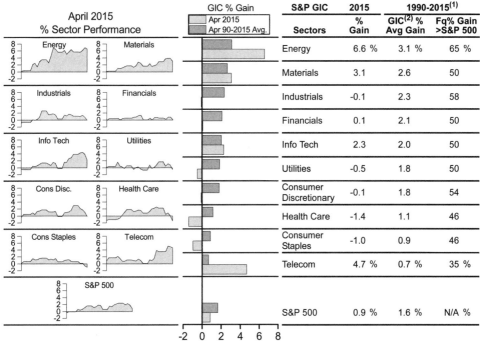

April 2015 % Sector Performance	GIC % Gain	S&P GIC Sectors	2015 % Gain	1990-2015[1] GIC[2] % Avg Gain	Fq% Gain >S&P 500
Energy / Materials		Energy	6.6 %	3.1 %	65 %
Industrials / Financials		Materials	3.1	2.6	50
Info Tech / Utilities		Industrials	-0.1	2.3	58
Cons Disc. / Health Care		Financials	0.1	2.1	50
Cons Staples / Telecom		Info Tech	2.3	2.0	50
S&P 500		Utilities	-0.5	1.8	50
		Consumer Discretionary	-0.1	1.8	54
		Health Care	-1.4	1.1	46
		Consumer Staples	-1.0	0.9	46
		Telecom	4.7 %	0.7 %	35 %
		S&P 500	0.9 %	1.6 %	N/A %

Legend: Apr 2015, Apr 90-2015 Avg.

Sector Commentary

♦ On average, April is one of the strongest months of the year for commodities. In 2015, the energy sector took a reprieve from its multi-month decline. In April, the energy sector produced a gain of 6.6%. ♦ The telecom sector, which on average has been the weakest sector of the market, produced a gain of 4.7%. ♦ The materials sector, followed the overall commodity trend for the month, producing a gain of 3.1%.

Sub-Sector Commentary

♦ After a steep loss in March 2015, the metals and mining sub-sector produced a gain of 12.9% following the uptrending commodity sector in the month of April. ♦ The agriculture sub-sector, typically one of the weaker sub-sectors in the market, also benefited from the general commodity bounce, as the sub-sector produced a gain of 3.1%. ♦ Homebuilders reversed their rapid rise in March, with a steep decline of 11.8% in April. ♦ Both gold and silver tend to be amongst the weaker performing sub-sectors in April. In 2015, both precious metals, lived up to their long-term trend of underperforming the market by producing losses for the month.

SELECTED SUB-SECTORS[3]			
SOX (1995-2015)	-1.3 %	3.7 %	52 %
Railroads	0.3	3.2	58
Chemicals	2.1	3.2	69
Banks	2.1	2.5	54
Transportation	-0.9	2.3	58
Pharma	0.2	1.8	54
Metals & Mining	12.9	1.6	42
Software & Services	3.7	1.6	50
Steel	4.6	1.5	46
Homebuilders	-11.8	1.4	46
Retail	0.0	0.8	42
Gold (London PM)	-0.6	0.2	42
Biotech (1993-2015)	-2.5	0.1	39
Agriculture (1994-2015)	3.1	0.0	55
Silver	-0.5	-0.4	38

(1) Sector data provided by Standard and Poors (2) GIC is short form for Global Industry Classification (3) Sub Sector data provided by Standard and Poors, except where marked by symbol.

18 DAY EARNINGS MONTH EFFECT
Markets Outperform 1st 18 Calendar Days of Earnings Months

Earnings season occurs the first month of every quarter. At this time, public companies report their financials for the previous quarter and often give guidance on future expectations. As a result, investors tend to bid up stocks, anticipating good earnings. Earnings are a major driver of stock market prices as investors generally get in the stock market early, in anticipation of favorable results, which helps to run up stock prices in the first half of the month.

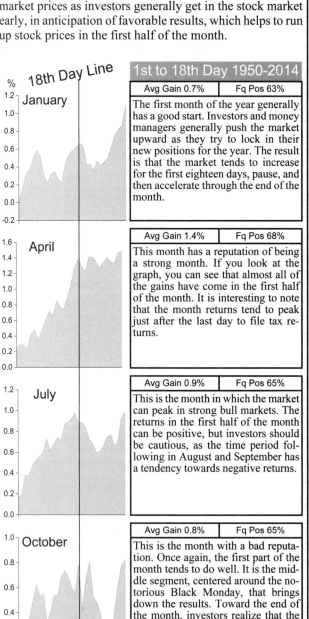

18th Day Line

January

April

July

October

1st to 18th Day 1950-2014

Avg Gain 0.7%	Fq Pos 63%

The first month of the year generally has a good start. Investors and money managers generally push the market upward as they try to lock in their new positions for the year. The result is that the market tends to increase for the first eighteen days, pause, and then accelerate through the end of the month.

Avg Gain 1.4%	Fq Pos 68%

This month has a reputation of being a strong month. If you look at the graph, you can see that almost all of the gains have come in the first half of the month. It is interesting to note that the month returns tend to peak just after the last day to file tax returns.

Avg Gain 0.9%	Fq Pos 65%

This is the month in which the market can peak in strong bull markets. The returns in the first half of the month can be positive, but investors should be cautious, as the time period following in August and September has a tendency towards negative returns.

Avg Gain 0.8%	Fq Pos 65%

This is the month with a bad reputation. Once again, the first part of the month tends to do well. It is the middle segment, centered around the notorious Black Monday, that brings down the results. Toward the end of the month, investors realize that the world has not ended and start to buy stocks again, providing a strong finish to the month.

1st to 18th Day Gain S&P500			
	JAN	APR	JUL	OCT
1950	0.36 %	4.28 %	-3.56 %	2.88 %
1951	4.75	3.41	4.39	1.76
1952	2.02	-3.57	-0.44	-1.39
1953	-2.07	-2.65	0.87	3.38
1954	2.50	3.71	2.91	-1.49
1955	-3.28	4.62	3.24	-4.63
1956	-2.88	-1.53	4.96	2.18
1957	-4.35	2.95	2.45	-4.93
1958	2.78	1.45	1.17	2.80
1959	1.09	4.47	1.23	0.79
1960	-3.34	2.26	-2.14	1.55
1961	2.70	1.75	-0.36	2.22
1962	-4.42	-1.84	2.65	0.12
1963	3.30	3.49	-1.27	2.26
1964	2.05	1.99	2.84	0.77
1965	2.05	2.31	1.87	1.91
1966	1.64	2.63	2.66	2.77
1967	6.80	1.84	3.16	-1.51
1968	-0.94	7.63	1.87	2.09
1969	-1.76	-0.27	-2.82	3.37
1970	-1.24	-4.42	6.83	-0.02
1971	1.37	3.17	0.42	-1.01
1972	1.92	2.40	-1.22	-2.13
1973	0.68	0.02	2.00	1.46
1974	-2.04	0.85	-2.58	13.76
1975	3.50	3.53	-2.09	5.95
1976	7.55	-2.04	0.38	-3.58
1977	-3.85	2.15	0.47	-3.18
1978	-4.77	4.73	1.40	-2.00
1979	3.76	0.11	-1.19	-5.22
1980	2.90	-1.51	6.83	4.83
1981	-0.73	-0.96	-0.34	2.59
1982	-4.35	4.33	1.33	13.54
1983	4.10	4.43	-2.20	1.05
1984	1.59	-0.80	-1.16	1.20
1985	2.44	0.10	1.32	2.72
1986	-1.35	1.46	-5.77	3.25
1987	9.96	-1.64	3.48	-12.16
1988	1.94	0.12	-1.09	2.75
1989	3.17	3.78	4.20	-2.12
1990	-4.30	0.23	1.73	-0.10
1991	0.61	3.53	3.83	1.20
1992	0.42	3.06	1.83	-1.45
1993	0.26	-0.60	-1.06	2.07
1994	1.67	-0.74	2.46	1.07
1995	2.27	0.93	2.52	0.52
1996	-1.25	-0.29	-4.04	3.42
1997	4.78	1.22	3.41	-0.33
1998	-0.92	1.90	4.67	3.88
1999	1.14	2.54	3.36	-2.23
2000	-0.96	-3.80	2.69	-6.57
2001	2.10	6.71	-1.36	2.66
2002	-1.79	-2.00	-10.94	8.48
2003	2.50	5.35	1.93	4.35
2004	2.51	0.75	-3.46	-0.05
2005	-1.32	-2.93	2.50	-4.12
2006	2.55	1.22	0.51	3.15
2007	1.41	4.33	-3.20	1.48
2008	-9.75	5.11	-1.51	-19.36
2009	-5.88	8.99	2.29	2.89
2010	1.88	1.94	3.32	3.81
2011	2.97	-1.56	-1.15	8.30
2012	4.01	-1.66	0.78	1.16
2013	4.2	-1.76	5.17	3.74
2014	-0.52	-0.4	0.92	-4.34
Avg	0.66 %	1.38 %	0.87 %	0.78 %

- 43 -

Earnings Month Effect Performance

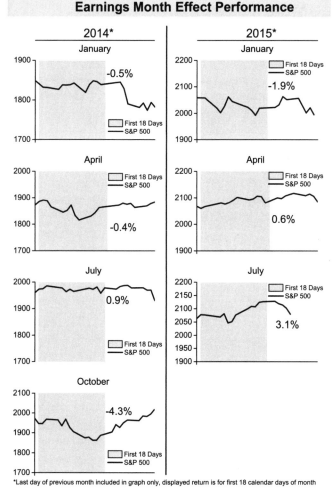

*Last day of previous month included in graph only, displayed return is for first 18 calendar days of month

Market Indices & Rates
Weekly Values**

Stock Markets	2014	2015
Dow	16,510	17,803
S&P500	1,881	2,070
Nasdaq	4,222	4,904
TSX	14,394	14,945
FTSE	6,651	6,827
DAX	9,622	12,005
Nikkei	14,940	19,280
Hang Seng	22,440	25,029

Commodities	2014	2015
Oil	100.47	48.88
Gold	1289.8	1192.0

Bond Yields	2014	2015
USA 5 Yr Treasury	1.75	1.34
USA 10 Yr T	2.77	1.91
USA 20 Yr T	3.35	2.28
Moody's Aaa	4.31	3.49
Moody's Baa	5.02	4.46
CAN 5 Yr T	1.75	0.75
CAN 10 Yr T	2.51	1.33

Money Market	2014	2015
USA Fed Funds	0.25	0.25
USA 3 Mo T-B	0.03	0.03
CAN tgt overnight rate	1.00	0.75
CAN 3 Mo T-B	0.91	0.56

Foreign Exchange	2014	2015
EUR/USD	1.38	1.08
GBP/USD	1.66	1.48
USD/CAD	1.10	1.26
USD/JPY	103.60	119.73

APRIL

M	T	W	T	F	S	S
				1	2	3
4	5	6	7	8	9	10
11	12	13	14	15	16	17
18	19	20	21	22	23	24
25	26	27	28	29	30	

MAY

M	T	W	T	F	S	S
						1
2	3	4	5	6	7	8
9	10	11	12	13	14	15
16	17	18	19	20	21	22
23	24	25	26	27	28	29
30	31					

JUNE

M	T	W	T	F	S	S
		1	2	3	4	5
6	7	8	9	10	11	12
13	14	15	16	17	18	19
20	21	22	23	24	25	26
27	28	29	30			

Earnings Month Effect Performance

In 2014, the first eighteen calendar days of the earnings months were only positive once out of four times (July). The biggest loss occurred in October, as the S&P 500 corrected over global growth concerns. As the *Earnings Month* seasonal trade was finishing in October, the stock market started a strong rally that carried into December.

In 2015, the first eighteen calendar days for earnings months, up until July, were positive two out of the three times. The first eighteen calendar days in January were negative, as the stock market took a reprieve from a strong rally in the second half of December. The opposite cycle happened for second quarter earnings, as the stock market corrected sharply in June and then rebounded in July. The end result was a large 3.1% gain in the first eighteen calendar days of July.

CONSUMER SWITCH
SELL CONSUMER DISCRETIONARY
BUY CONSUMER STAPLES
Consumer Staples Outperform Apr 23 to Oct 27

The *Consumer Switch* strategy has allowed investors to use a set portion of their account to switch between the two related consumer sectors. To use this strategy, investors invest in the consumer discretionary sector from October 28th to April 22nd, and then use the proceeds to invest in the consumer staples sector from April 23rd to October 27th, and then repeat the cycle.

The end result has been outperformance compared with buying and holding both consumer sectors, or buying and holding the broad market.

> *3758% total aggregate gain compared with 538% for the S&P 500*

The basic premise of the strategy is that the consumer discretionary sector tends to outperform during the favorable six months when more money flows into the market, pushing up stock prices. On the other hand, the consumer staples sector tends to outperform when investors are looking for safety and stability of earnings in the six months when the market tends to move into a defensive mode.

Consumer Staples & Discretionary Switch Strategy*			
Investment Period	Buy @ Beginning of Period	% Gain @ End of Period	% Gain Cumulative
90 Apr23 - 90 Oct29	Staples	7.7%	8%
90 Oct29 - 91 Apr23	Discretionary	41.7	53
91 Apr23 - 91 Oct28	Staples	2.1	56
91 Oct28 - 92 Apr23	Discretionary	15.9	81
92 Apr23 - 92 Oct27	Staples	6.3	92
92 Oct27 - 93 Apr23	Discretionary	6.3	104
93 Apr23 - 93 Oct27	Staples	5.8	116
93 Oct27 - 94 Apr25	Discretionary	-3.7	108
94 Apr25 - 94 Oct27	Staples	10.2	129
94 Oct27 - 95 Apr24	Discretionary	4.4	139
95 Apr24 - 95 Oct27	Staples	15.3	176
95 Oct27 - 96 Apr23	Discretionary	17.3	227
96 Apr23 - 96 Oct27	Staples	12.6	265
96 Oct27 - 97 Apr23	Discretionary	5.1	283
97 Apr23 - 97 Oct27	Staples	2.5	293
97 Oct27 - 98 Apr23	Discretionary	35.9	434
98 Apr23 - 98 Oct27	Staples	-0.7	423
98 Oct27 - 99 Apr23	Discretionary	41.8	651
99 Apr23 - 99 Oct27	Staples	-9.7	578
99 Oct27 - 00 Apr24	Discretionary	11.9	659
00 Apr24 - 00 Oct27	Staples	16.5	785
00 Oct27 - 01 Apr23	Discretionary	9.8	872
01 Apr23 - 01 Oct29	Staples	4.0	910
01 Oct29 - 02 Apr23	Discretionary	16.1	1073
02 Apr23 - 02 Oct28	Staples	-13.9	910
02 Oct28 - 03 Apr23	Discretionary	3.0	941
03 Apr23 - 03 Oct27	Staples	8.4	1028
03 Oct27 - 04 Apr23	Discretionary	9.6	1137
04 Apr23 - 04 Oct27	Staples	-7.4	1045
04 Oct27 - 05 Apr25	Discretionary	-2.0	1021
05 Apr25 - 05 Oct27	Staples	-0.5	1016
05 Oct27 - 06 Apr24	Discretionary	9.2	1119
06 Apr24 - 06 Oct27	Staples	10.6	1249
06 Oct27 - 07 Apr23	Discretionary	6.3	1334
07 Apr23 - 07 Oct29	Staples	4.6	1400
07 Oct29 - 08 Apr23	Discretionary	-13.7	1194
08 Apr23 - 08 Oct27	Staples	-21.5	916
08 Oct27 - 09 Apr23	Discretionary	17.7	1096
09 Apr23 - 09 Oct27	Staples	20.6	1342
09 Oct27 - 10 Apr23	Discretionary	29.7	1770
10 Apr23 - 10 Oct27	Staples	2.4	1815
10 Oct27 - 11 Apr25	Discretionary	13.7	2079
11 Apr25 - 11 Oct27	Staples	2.2	2126
11 Oct27 - 12 Apr23	Discretionary	10.9	2368
12 Apr23 - 12 Oct31	Staples	4.7	2485
12 Oct31 - 13 Apr23	Discretionary	17.5	2938
13 Apr23 - 13 Oct28	Staples	2.3	3006
13 Oct28 - 14 Apr23	Discretionary	1.7	3060
14 Apr23 - 14 Oct27	Staples	5.9	3248
14 Oct27 - 15 Apr23	Discretionary	15.2	3758

Total Gains From
Apr 1990 to Apr 2015

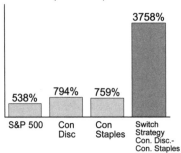

S&P 500 538% | Con Disc 794% | Con Staples 759% | Switch Strategy Con. Disc.- Con. Staples 3758%

* If buy date lands on weekend or holiday, then next day is used

Consumer Discretionary / Consumer Staples Relative Strength Avg. Year 1990 - 2014

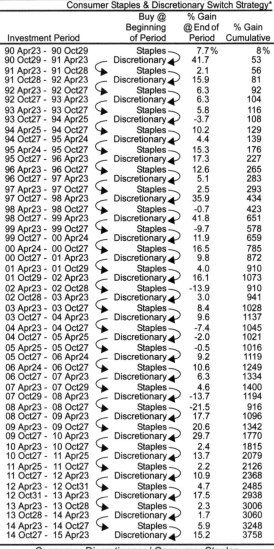

Consumer Switch Performance

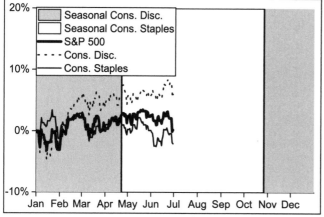

2014

2015

Stock Markets	2014	2015
Dow	16,227	17,935
S&P500	1,844	2,086
Nasdaq	4,086	4,950
TSX	14,329	15,244
FTSE	6,611	7,001
DAX	9,456	12,175
Nikkei	14,395	19,735
Hang Seng	22,802	26,818

Commodities	2014	2015
Oil	102.75	51.79
Gold	1309.8	1205.1

Bond Yields	2014	2015
USA 5 Yr Treasury	1.63	1.36
USA 10 Yr T	2.68	1.93
USA 20 Yr T	3.27	2.31
Moody's Aaa	4.24	3.50
Moody's Baa	4.92	4.47
CAN 5 Yr T	1.70	0.77
CAN 10 Yr T	2.45	1.35

Money Market	2014	2015
USA Fed Funds	0.25	0.25
USA 3 Mo T-B	0.04	0.03
CAN tgt overnight rate	1.00	0.75
CAN 3 Mo T-B	0.91	0.58

Foreign Exchange	2014	2015
EUR/USD	1.38	1.08
GBP/USD	1.67	1.48
USD/CAD	1.09	1.25
USD/JPY	102.01	120.15

APRIL

M	T	W	T	F	S	S
				1	2	3
4	5	6	7	8	9	10
11	12	13	14	15	16	17
18	19	20	21	22	23	24
25	26	27	28	29	30	

MAY

M	T	W	T	F	S	S
						1
2	3	4	5	6	7	8
9	10	11	12	13	14	15
16	17	18	19	20	21	22
23	24	25	26	27	28	29
30	31					

JUNE

M	T	W	T	F	S	S
		1	2	3	4	5
6	7	8	9	10	11	12
13	14	15	16	17	18	19
20	21	22	23	24	25	26
27	28	29	30			

Consumer Switch Strategy Performance

In 2014, the consumer discretionary sector underperformed both the S&P 500 and the consumer staples sector at the beginning of the year when it typically outperforms. In the seasonal period of the year when the consumer staples sector typically outperforms, from April 23rd to October 27th, the consumer staples performed at market and approximately even with the consumer discretionary sector. In the last part of the year, the consumer discretionary sector outperformed the S&P 500 and consumer staples sector, making the overall strategy mildly successful in 2014.

In 2015, in its seasonal period at the beginning of the year, the consumer discretionary sector was the strongest performer, as consumers continued to spend and investors were attracted to the sector for its domestic focus.

NATURAL GAS FIRES UP AND DOWN
①LONG (Mar22-Jun19) ②LONG (Sep5-Dec21)
③SELL SHORT (Dec22-Dec31)

There are two high consumption times for natural gas: winter and summer. The colder it gets in winter, the more natural gas is consumed to keep the furnaces going. The warmer it gets in the summer, the more natural gas is used to produce power for air conditioners.

On the supply side, weather plays a large factor in determining price. During the hurricane season in the Gulf of Mexico, the price of natural gas is affected by the number and severity of hurricanes.

Natural Gas (Cash) Henry Hub LA*
Seasonal Gains 1995 to 2014

Year	Pos. Mar 22 % to Jun 19	Pos. Sep 5 to Dec 21	Neg. (Short) Dec 22 to Dec 31	Pos. Compound Growth
1995	99.4	13.0 %	103.0 %	1.2 %	126.7
1996	-27.4	-6.6	170.4	-46.2	269.2
1997	-9.4	16.8	-13.1	-6.3	7.9
1998	-13.0	-2.6	20.9	-6.7	25.7
1999	18.6	28.9	5.3	-11.2	50.9
2000	356.5	57.1	121.9	0.7	246.3
2001	-74.3	-24.1	21.5	1.5	-9.2
2002	70.0	0.6	61.3	-9.1	77.1
2003	26.4	9.5	47.1	-16.3	87.4
2004	3.6	18.2	54.6	-11.6	103.9
2005	58.4	6.3	14.5	-29.6	57.7
2006	-42.2	-1.8	17.4	-9.5	26.3
2007	30.2	9.2	32.7	2.0	42.1
2008	-21.4	52.2	-21.4	-0.9	20.6
2009	3.6	1.5	208.0	0.7	210.4
2010	-27.4	28.6	10.4	2.4	38.6
2011	-29.6	10.0	-26.1	-1.7	-17.3
2012	15.4	18.7	21.7	0.6	43.7
2013	26.3	-1.4	18.2	-0.2	16.8
2014	-31.1	7.7	-11.8	-12.9	7.2
Avg.	21.6	12.1 %	42.8 %	-7.7 %	71.6

Natural Gas (Henry Hub Spot)- Avg. Year 1995 to 2014

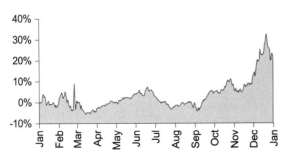

rise between September 5th and December 21st, due to the demands of the heating season. In this period, from 1995 to 2014, natural gas has produced an average gain of 43% and has been positive 82% of the time.

Positive 90% of the time

Natural gas tends to fall in price from December 22nd to December 31st. Although this is a short time period, for the years from 1995 to 2014, natural gas has produced an average loss of 7.7% and has only been positive 35% of the time. Also, in this period, when gains did occur, they were relatively small. The poor performance of natural gas at this time is largely driven by southern U.S. refiners dumping inventory on the market to help mitigate year-end taxes on their inventory.

Applying a strategy of investing in natural gas from March 22nd to June 19th, reinvesting the proceeds from September 5th to December 21st, reinvesting the proceeds again to short natural gas from December 22nd to December 31st, has produced a compounded average return of 72% and has been positive 91% of the time.

Using the natural gas compound strategy has produced returns that are over three times greater than the average annual gain in natural gas. By using the strategy, an investor would have caught most of the large gains and missed most of the large losses.

Natural gas prices tend to rise from mid-March to mid-June ahead of the cooling season demands in the summer. From 1995 to 2014, during the period of March 22nd to June 19th, the spot price of natural gas has on average increased 12% and has been positive 77% of the time. The price of natural gas also tends to

Caution: The cash price for natural gas is extremely volatile and extreme caution should be used. Care must be taken to ensure that investments are within risk tolerances.

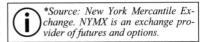

Source: New York Mercantile Exchange. NYMX is an exchange provider of futures and options.

- 47 -

Natural Gas Performance

Natural Gas Monthly Performance (1995-2014)

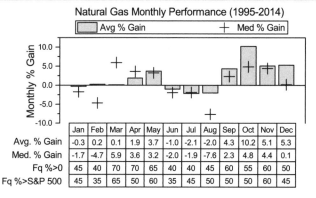

	Jan	Feb	Mar	Apr	May	Jun	Jul	Aug	Sep	Oct	Nov	Dec
Avg. % Gain	-0.3	0.2	0.1	1.9	3.7	-1.0	-2.1	-2.0	4.3	10.2	5.1	5.3
Med. % Gain	-1.7	-4.7	5.9	3.6	3.2	-2.0	-1.9	-7.6	2.3	4.8	4.4	0.1
Fq %>0	45	40	70	70	65	40	40	45	60	55	60	50
Fq %>S&P 500	45	35	65	50	60	35	45	50	50	50	60	45

Natural Gas 5 Year (2010-2014) % Gain

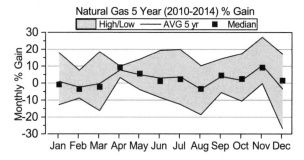

Natural Gas Performance 2014-2015

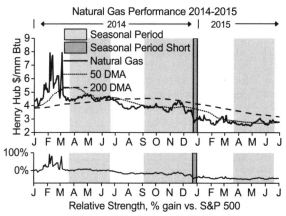

Relative Strength, % gain vs. S&P 500

Market Indices & Rates
Weekly Values**

Stock Markets	2014	2015
Dow	16,317	18,012
S&P500	1,850	2,096
Nasdaq	4,060	4,983
TSX	14,384	15,394
FTSE	6,584	7,058
DAX	9,310	12,097
Nikkei	14,252	19,845
Hang Seng	22,792	27,718

Commodities	2014	2015
Oil	103.97	54.81
Gold	1306.1	1198.9

Bond Yields	2014	2015
USA 5 Yr Treasury	1.67	1.33
USA 10 Yr T	2.67	1.90
USA 20 Yr T	3.23	2.30
Moody's Aaa	4.22	3.47
Moody's Baa	4.86	4.44
CAN 5 Yr T	1.68	0.79
CAN 10 Yr T	2.42	1.36

Money Market	2014	2015
USA Fed Funds	0.25	0.25
USA 3 Mo T-B	0.04	0.02
CAN tgt overnight rate	1.00	0.75
CAN 3 Mo T-B	0.93	0.62

Foreign Exchange	2014	2015
EUR/USD	1.38	1.07
GBP/USD	1.68	1.48
USD/CAD	1.10	1.24
USD/JPY	102.16	119.32

APRIL

M	T	W	T	F	S	S
				1	2	3
4	5	6	7	8	9	10
11	12	13	14	15	16	17
18	19	20	21	22	23	24
25	26	27	28	29	30	

MAY

M	T	W	T	F	S	S
						1
2	3	4	5	6	7	8
9	10	11	12	13	14	15
16	17	18	19	20	21	22
23	24	25	26	27	28	29
30	31					

JUNE

M	T	W	T	F	S	S
		1	2	3	4	5
6	7	8	9	10	11	12
13	14	15	16	17	18	19
20	21	22	23	24	25	26
27	28	29	30			

From 1995 to 2014, on average, September through to November has been the best cluster of positive months for natural gas. Natural gas is a very volatile commodity and as a result there is a large difference between the mean and median performances on a month to month basis.

April and May are also strong months and make up the core of the spring trade. In the last five years, natural gas has generally followed its seasonal trend, with a strong performance in April, a weak summer and a strong autumn. In 2014/2015, the overall return for the combination of natural gas periods was positive.

⬛🍁$ CANADIAN DOLLAR STRONG– TWICE
①April ②Aug20-Sep25

All other things being equal, if oil increases in price, investors favor the Canadian dollar over the U.S. dollar. They do so with good reason, as Canada is a net exporter of oil and benefits from its rising price.

Oil tends to do well in the month of April, which is the core of the main energy seasonal strategy that lasts from February 25th to May 9th.

April has been a strong month for the Canadian dollar relative to the U.S. dollar. The largest losses have had a tendency to occur in years when the Fed Reserve has been aggressively hiking their target rate.

At some point during the years 1987, 2000, 2004 and 2005, the Fed increased their target rate by a total of at least 1% in each year. Since 1971, three of these

CAD vs USD Avg. % Gain 1971 to 2014

years (1987, 2004 and 2005) were three of the biggest losers for the Canadian dollar in the month of April.

The Canadian dollar also has a second period of seasonality, August 20th to September 25th. It is not a coincidence that oil also has a second period of seasonal strength at this time. Although the August 20th to September 25th seasonal period is not as strong as the April seasonal period, it is still a trade worth considering.

CAD vs USD Apr & Aug 20 to Sep 25 % Gain (1971-2015) Source: Bloomberg   Positive ▢

	Apr1-Apr30	Aug20-Sep25		Apr1-Apr30	Aug20-Sep25		Apr1-Apr30	Aug20-Sep25		Apr1-Apr30	Aug20-Sep25		Apr1-Apr30	Aug20-Sep25
			1980	0.29%	-0.15%	1990	0.44%	-0.43%	2000	-1.89%	-0.96%	2010	0.44%	1.32%
1971	-0.10%	0.46%	1981	-0.74	1.08	1991	0.65	0.86	2001	2.76	-1.76	2011	2.44	-4.20
1972	0.53	0.01	1982	0.89	0.78	1992	-0.48	-3.37	2002	-0.48	-0.61	2012	1.05	1.16
1973	-0.41	-0.32	1983	0.64	0.17	1993	-1.02	-0.08	2003	2.50	3.95	2013	1.01	0.39
1974	1.27	-0.40	1984	-0.62	-1.01	1994	0.14	2.22	2004	-4.46	1.57	2014	0.88	-1.58
1975	-1.56	1.33	1985	0.04	-0.32	1995	2.91	0.96	2005	-3.77	3.75	2015	4.67	
1976	0.55	1.41	1986	1.69	0.35	1996	0.15	0.48	2006	4.17	0.64			
1977	0.91	0.31	1987	-2.38	1.41	1997	-0.97	0.79	2007	4.17	6.30			
1978	0.09	-3.22	1988	0.41	0.43	1998	-0.85	1.37	2008	1.81	2.59			
1979	1.61	0.15	1989	0.60	0.55	1999	3.53	1.36	2009	5.59	0.46			
Avg.	0.32%	-0.03%		0.06%	0.38%		0.45%	0.51%		1.62%	1.88%		2.01%	-1.06%

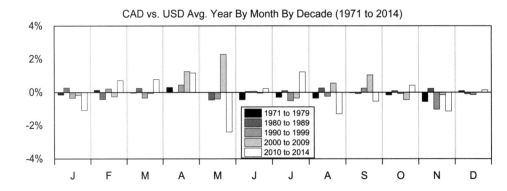

CAD vs. USD Avg. Year By Month By Decade (1971 to 2014)

1971 to 1979
1980 to 1989
1990 to 1999
2000 to 2009
2010 to 2014

CAD/USD Performance

CAD/USD Monthly Performance (1971-2014)

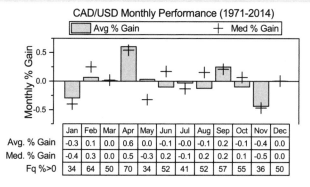

Avg % Gain   + Med % Gain

	Jan	Feb	Mar	Apr	May	Jun	Jul	Aug	Sep	Oct	Nov	Dec
Avg. % Gain	-0.3	0.1	0.0	0.6	0.0	-0.1	-0.0	-0.1	0.2	-0.1	-0.4	0.0
Med. % Gain	-0.4	0.3	0.0	0.5	-0.3	0.2	-0.1	0.2	0.2	0.1	-0.5	0.0
Fq %>0	34	64	50	70	34	52	41	52	57	55	36	50

CAD/USD 5 Year (2010-2014) % Gain

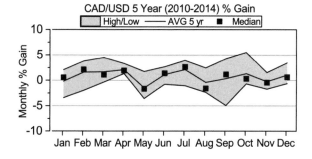

High/Low —— AVG 5 yr ■ Median

CAD/USD Performance 2014-2015

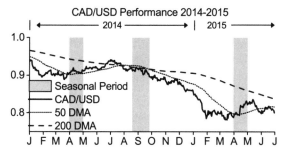

◄——— 2014 ———► | 2015 ———►

Seasonal Period
CAD/USD
50 DMA
200 DMA

Market Indices & Rates
Weekly Values**

Stock Markets	2014	2015
Dow	16,466	18,032
S&P500	1,874	2,107
Nasdaq	4,127	5,038
TSX	14,534	15,373
FTSE	5,349	7,054
DAX	9,524	11,847
Nikkei	14,456	19,977
Hang Seng	22,507	27,754

Commodities	2014	2015
Oil	102.28	55.77
Gold	1291.2	1190.0

Bond Yields	2014	2015
USA 5 Yr Treasury	1.74	1.36
USA 10 Yr T	2.71	1.94
USA 20 Yr T	3.23	2.36
Moody's Aaa	4.22	3.54
Moody's Baa	4.86	4.48
CAN 5 Yr T	1.70	0.90
CAN 10 Yr T	2.43	1.46

Money Market	2014	2015
USA Fed Funds	0.25	0.25
USA 3 Mo T-B	0.03	0.03
CAN tgt overnight rate	1.00	0.75
CAN 3 Mo T-B	0.94	0.66

Foreign Exchange	2014	2015
EUR/USD	1.38	1.08
GBP/USD	1.68	1.50
USD/CAD	1.10	1.22
USD/JPY	102.45	119.47

APRIL

M	T	W	T	F	S	S
				1	2	3
4	5	6	7	8	9	10
11	12	13	14	15	16	17
18	19	20	21	22	23	24
25	26	27	28	29	30	

MAY

M	T	W	T	F	S	S
						1
2	3	4	5	6	7	8
9	10	11	12	13	14	15
16	17	18	19	20	21	22
23	24	25	26	27	28	29
30	31					

JUNE

M	T	W	T	F	S	S
		1	2	3	4	5
6	7	8	9	10	11	12
13	14	15	16	17	18	19
20	21	22	23	24	25	26
27	28	29	30			

Canadian Dollar Performance (CAD/USD)

From 1971 to 2014, April has been the strongest month of the year for CAD/USD on an average, median and frequency basis. September is the second strongest month and makes up the bulk of the second seasonal period of performance for the Canadian dollar. Over the last five years, May and August have been the worst performing months, with July being the best performing month. In 2014, the Canadian dollar started to correct at the beginning of the year, but then stabilized and managed to produce a gain in April. When the energy sector started to correct in the late summer, it put downward pressure on the Canadian dollar during its September seasonal period. The Canadian dollar was once again strong in April 2015, following the rebound in oil prices.

MAY

	MONDAY	TUESDAY	WEDNESDAY
WEEK 19	**2** 29	**3** 28	**4** 27
WEEK 20	**9** 22	**10** 21	**11** 20
WEEK 21	**16** 15	**17** 14	**18** 13
WEEK 22	**23** 8 CAN Market Closed- Victoria Day	**24** 7	**25** 6
WEEK 23	**30** 1 USA Market Closed- Memorial Day	**31**	1

THURSDAY		FRIDAY	
5	26	**6**	25
12	19	**13**	18
19	12	**20**	11
26	5	**27**	4
2		3	

JUNE

M	T	W	T	F	S	S
		1	2	3	4	5
6	7	8	9	10	11	12
13	14	15	16	17	18	19
20	21	22	23	24	25	26
27	28	29	30			

JULY

M	T	W	T	F	S	S
				1	2	3
4	5	6	7	8	9	10
11	12	13	14	15	16	17
18	19	20	21	22	23	24
25	26	27	28	29	30	31

AUGUST

M	T	W	T	F	S	S
1	2	3	4	5	6	7
8	9	10	11	12	13	14
15	16	17	18	19	20	21
22	23	24	25	26	27	28
29	30	31				

SEPTEMBER

M	T	W	T	F	S	S
			1	2	3	4
5	6	7	8	9	10	11
12	13	14	15	16	17	18
19	20	21	22	23	24	25
26	27	28	29	30		

MAY
S U M M A R Y

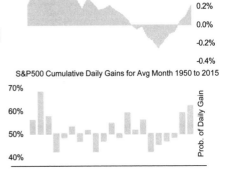

S&P500 Cumulative Daily Gains for Avg Month 1950 to 2015

	Dow Jones	S&P 500	Nasdaq	TSX Comp
Month Rank	9	8	5	2
# Up	33	37	26	19
# Down	32	28	17	11
% Pos	51	57	60	63
% Avg. Gain	0.0	0.2	1.0	1.5

Dow & S&P 1950-2014, Nasdaq 1972-2014, TSX 1985-2014

♦ The S&P 500 often peaks in May and as a result seasonal investors should start to be more cautious with their investments at this time. ♦ After producing a loss for three years in a row from 2010 to 2012, the S&P 500 has produced gains in May for the last three years, including a 1.0% gain in May 2015 ♦ The first few days and the last few days in May tend to be strong and the period in between tends to negative. ♦ A lot of the cyclical sectors finish their seasonal periods at the beginning of May.

BEST / WORST MAY BROAD MKTS. 2006-2015

BEST MAY MARKETS
- ♦ TSX Comp. (2009) 11.2%
- ♦ Nikkei 225 (2009) 7.9%
- ♦ TSX Comp. (2008) 5.6%

WORST MAY MARKETS
- ♦ Nikkei 225 (2010) -11.7%
- ♦ Nikkei 225 (2012) -10.3%
- ♦ Nikkei 225 (2006) -8.5%

Index Values End of Month

	2006	2007	2008	2009	2010	2011	2012	2013	2014	2015
Dow	11,168	13,628	12,638	8,500	10,137	12,570	12,393	15,116	16,717	18,011
S&P 500	1,270	1,531	1,400	919	1,089	1,345	1,310	1,631	1,924	2,107
Nasdaq	2,179	2,605	2,523	1,774	2,257	2,835	2,827	3,456	4,243	5,070
TSX Comp.	11,745	14,057	14,715	10,370	11,763	13,803	11,513	12,650	14,604	15,014
Russell 1000	1,330	1,605	1,477	965	1,157	1,439	1,392	1,739	2,061	2,262
Russell 2000	1,792	2,105	1,860	1,247	1,644	2,108	1,893	2,446	2,820	3,098
FTSE 100	5,724	6,622	6,054	4,418	5,188	5,990	5,321	6,583	6,845	6,984
Nikkei 225	15,467	17,876	14,339	9,523	9,769	9,694	8,543	13,775	14,632	20,563

Percent Gain for May

	2006	2007	2008	2009	2010	2011	2012	2013	2014	2015
Dow	-1.7	4.3	-1.4	4.1	-7.9	-1.9	-6.2	1.9	0.8	1.0
S&P 500	-3.1	3.3	1.1	5.3	-8.2	-1.4	-6.3	2.1	2.1	1.0
Nasdaq	-6.2	3.1	4.6	3.3	-8.3	-1.3	-7.2	3.8	3.1	2.6
TSX Comp.	-3.8	4.8	5.6	11.2	-3.7	-1.0	-6.3	1.6	-0.3	-1.4
Russell 1000	-3.2	3.4	1.6	5.3	-8.1	-1.3	-6.4	2.0	2.1	1.1
Russell 2000	-5.7	4.0	4.5	2.9	-7.7	-2.0	-6.7	3.9	0.7	2.2
FTSE 100	-5.0	2.7	-0.6	4.1	-6.6	-1.3	-7.3	2.4	1.0	0.3
Nikkei 225	-8.5	2.7	3.5	7.9	-11.7	-1.6	-10.3	-0.6	2.3	5.3

May Market Avg. Performance 2006 to 2015[1]

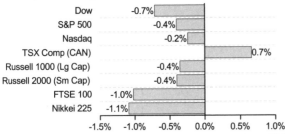

	Dow	-0.7%
S&P 500	-0.4%
Nasdaq	-0.2%
TSX Comp (CAN)	0.7%
Russell 1000 (Lg Cap)	-0.4%
Russell 2000 (Sm Cap)	-0.4%
FTSE 100	-1.0%
Nikkei 225	-1.1%

Interest Corner May[2]

	Fed Funds % [3]	3 Mo. T-Bill % [4]	10 Yr % [5]	20 Yr % [6]
2015	0.25	0.01	2.12	2.63
2014	0.25	0.04	2.48	3.05
2013	0.25	0.04	2.16	2.95
2012	0.25	0.07	1.59	2.27
2011	0.25	0.06	3.05	3.91

(1) Russell Data provided by Russell (2) Federal Reserve Bank of St. Louis- end of month values (3) Target rate set by FOMC (4)(5)(6) Constant yield maturities.

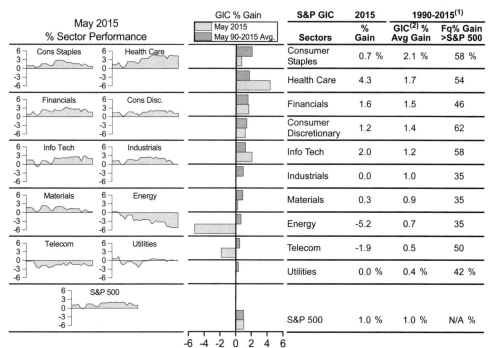

S&P GIC Sectors	2015 % Gain	1990-2015[1] GIC[2] % Avg Gain	1990-2015[1] Fq% Gain >S&P 500
Consumer Staples	0.7 %	2.1 %	58 %
Health Care	4.3	1.7	54
Financials	1.6	1.5	46
Consumer Discretionary	1.2	1.4	62
Info Tech	2.0	1.2	58
Industrials	0.0	1.0	35
Materials	0.3	0.9	35
Energy	-5.2	0.7	35
Telecom	-1.9	0.5	50
Utilities	0.0 %	0.4 %	42 %
S&P 500	1.0 %	1.0 %	N/A %

Sector Commentary

♦ Overall, in May 2015, the sectors that have historically performed well in the month, were the better performing sectors and the sectors that tended to underperform were the weaker sectors. On average, one of the better performing sectors of the market in May has been the health care sector. In May 2015, the sector was boosted by mergers and acquisitions, producing a gain of 4.3%. The energy sector, typically one of the weaker sectors of the market, produced the largest loss of the major sectors, with a loss of 5.2%. After a brief rally in April, the energy sector seemed to get back on its multi-month declining trend.

Sub-Sector Commentary

♦ After a strong April 2015, the metals and mining sector once again put in a poor performance due to concerns of slowing global growth. The sector ended up with a loss of 7.1%. In May, agriculture and biotech have historically been two of the better sub-sectors and have produced average gains of 8.1% and 5.7% respectively. The transportation and railroad sub-sectors both were strong underperformers. The two sub-sectors produced losses of 4.7% and 6.2% respectively.

SELECTED SUB-SECTORS[3]

Agriculture (1994-2015)	8.1 %	2.4 %	55 %
Biotech (1993-2015)	5.7	2.3	70
Banks	2.5	2.1	50
Retail	1.2	1.8	62
Railroads	-6.2	1.5	58
Pharma	3.3	1.3	46
Chemicals	1.2	1.0	50
Metals & Mining	-7.1	0.9	46
Steel	-3.4	0.8	50
Software & Services	0.2	0.7	35
Transportation	-4.7	0.6	50
SOX (1995-2015)	0.2	0.4	52
Gold (London PM)	0.9	0.3	54
Silver	0.9	-0.2	46
Homebuilders	1.5	-1.0	50

1/2 'N' 1/2
First 1/2 of April – Financial Stocks
Second 1/2 of April – Information Technology Stocks

The *1/2 'N' 1/2* strategy is a short-term switch combination that takes advantage of the superior performance of financial stocks in the first half of April and information technology stocks in the second half.

The opportunity exists in mid-April because technology stocks tend to start increasing at the same time financial stocks tend to start decreasing. This creates an ideal switch opportunity between the two sectors.

4.3% gain & 17 times out of 26 better than the S&P 500

Why do financial stocks tend to perform well in the first half of April? It is not a coincidence that the rate on the three month T-Bill tends to bottom in mid-April.

Liquidity is the common denominator that affects both the financial stocks and the money market. Investors sell-off their money market positions in the beginning of April to cover their taxes that are due to the IRS in mid-April. As a result, short-term money market rates tend to decrease.

Decreasing short-term yields are good for financial stocks, particularly banks. Banks tend to make more money with a steeper yield curve. They borrow short-term money (your savings account) and lend out long-term (mortgages). The steeper the curve, the more money banks make.

The end result is that financial stocks benefit from this trend in the first half of April.

On the flip side, investors stop selling their money market positions to cover taxes by mid-month. At this time, short-term yields tend to increase and financial stocks decrease.

Financials & Info Tech* & 1/2 & 1/2
Positive ▢

	April 1st to April 15th		April 16th to April 30		April Compound Growth	
Year	S&P 500	Finan cials	S&P 500	Info Tech	S&P 500	1/2 & 1/2
1990	1.3 %	1.3 %	-3.9 %	-1.9 %	-2.7 %	-0.6 %
1991	1.6	2.3	-1.5	-3.1	0.0	-0.9
1992	3.1	1.0	-0.3	-1.3	2.8	-0.3
1993	-0.7	3.5	-1.8	-2.2	-2.5	1.3
1994	0.1	4.9	1.1	3.5	1.2	8.6
1995	1.7	2.9	1.1	5.8	2.8	8.8
1996	-0.5	-2.3	1.8	8.2	1.3	5.8
1997	-0.3	0.3	6.2	11.3	5.8	11.6
1998	1.6	5.5	-0.7	4.3	0.9	10.0
1999	2.8	5.0	0.9	1.3	3.8	6.4
2000	-9.5	-7.0	7.1	14.8	-3.1	6.8
2001	2.0	0.2	5.6	8.3	7.7	8.5
2002	-3.9	-1.6	-2.3	-3.5	-6.1	-5.1
2003	5.0	9.3	2.9	5.3	8.1	15.1
2004	0.2	-3.0	-1.9	-5.0	-1.7	-7.8
2005	-3.2	-2.6	1.2	2.3	-2.0	-0.4
2006	-0.4	-0.3	1.7	-1.3	1.2	-1.6
2007	2.3	0.5	2.0	2.7	4.3	3.2
2008	0.9	-0.6	3.8	6.8	4.8	6.2
2009	6.8	23.0	2.4	5.8	9.4	30.1
2010	3.6	6.5	-2.1	-2.9	1.5	3.4
2011	-0.5	-1.6	3.3	4.6	2.9	2.9
2012	-2.7	-4.4	2.0	0.0	-0.7	-4.4
2013	-1.1	-0.8	2.9	3.4	1.8	2.6
2014	-1.6	-3.1	2.2	2.4	0.6	-0.8
2015	1.9	1.3	1.0	0.7	2.9	2.0
Avg.	0.4 %	1.5 %	1.3 %	2.7 %	1.7 %	4.3 %

Fortunately, information technology stocks tend to present a good opportunity in mid-April, just when financials stocks are starting to underperform. Very often at this time of the year, technology stocks have corrected after their seasonal period finished in January and have become oversold and are set up for a bounce.

Ⓨ *Alternate Strategy—*
The first few days in May tend to produce gains. An alternate strategy is to hold the information technology position for the first three trading days in May.

ⓘ *The SP GICS Financial Sector # 40 encompasses a wide range financial based companies.*
The SP GICS Information Technology Sector # 45 encompasses a wide range technology based companies. For more information on the information technology sector, see www.standardandpoors.com

1/2 and 1/2 Performance

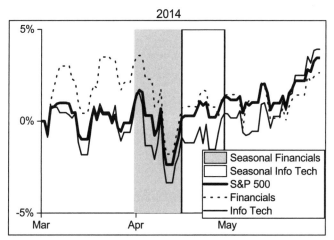

2014

2015

Stock Markets	2014	2015
Dow	16,527	18,010
S&P500	1,879	2,105
Nasdaq	4,109	5,017
TSX	14,639	15,320
FTSE	6,776	7,005
DAX	9,547	11,684
Nikkei	14,384	19,773
Hang Seng	22,245	28,352

Commodities	2014	2015
Oil	100.21	58.28
Gold	1289.0	1194.8

Bond Yields	2014	2015
USA 5 Yr Treasury	1.70	1.42
USA 10 Yr T	2.66	2.03
USA 20 Yr T	3.20	2.47
Moody's Aaa	4.19	3.68
Moody's Baa	4.81	4.61
CAN 5 Yr T	1.67	0.97
CAN 10 Yr T	2.40	1.57

Money Market	2014	2015
USA Fed Funds	0.25	0.25
USA 3 Mo T-B	0.03	0.01
CAN tgt overnight rate	1.00	0.75
CAN 3 Mo T-B	0.95	0.66

Foreign Exchange	2014	2015
EUR/USD	1.39	1.11
GBP/USD	1.69	1.53
USD/CAD	1.10	1.21
USD/JPY	102.38	119.29

MAY

M	T	W	T	F	S	S
						1
2	3	4	5	6	7	8
9	10	11	12	13	14	15
16	17	18	19	20	21	22
23	24	25	26	27	28	29
30	31					

Overall, in 2014 and 2015, the half and half trade underperformed the S&P 500.

In 2014, the financial sector underperformed the S&P 500 in the first half of the April. When the financial sector underperforms, it often means that there is weakness ahead for the S&P 500.

In 2014, this was not the case in the short-term, as the S&P 500 consolidated for most of May and then went on to rally in June and July. The S&P 500 did correct in August and then later in October, taking it back down to April levels.

In 2015, the financial sector underperformed the S&P 500 in the first half of April. Shortly afterwards, the S&P 500 peaked in May and then consolidated in June.

JUNE

M	T	W	T	F	S	S
		1	2	3	4	5
6	7	8	9	10	11	12
13	14	15	16	17	18	19
20	21	22	23	24	25	26
27	28	29	30			

JULY

M	T	W	T	F	S	S
				1	2	3
4	5	6	7	8	9	10
11	12	13	14	15	16	17
18	19	20	21	22	23	24
25	26	27	28	29	30	31

6n6 SIX 'N' SIX
Take a Break for Six Months - May 6th to October 27th

Several times in the last few years, the stock market has corrected sharply in spring, which has prompted many pundits to release reports in the media on "Sell in May and Go Away." But most pundits do not grasp the full value of the favorable six month period for stocks from October 28th to May 5th, compared with the other six months: the unfavorable six month period.

Not only does the favorable period on average have bigger gains more frequently and smaller losses, but the period also on a yearly basis outperforms the unfavorable period 71% of the time (last column in the table with YES values). There is no question which six month period seasonal investors should favor.

$1,474,478 gain on $10,000

The accompanying table uses the S&P 500 to compare the returns made from Oct 28th to May 5th, to the returns made during the remainder of the year.

Starting with $10,000 and investing from October 28th to May 5th every year (October 28th, 1950, to May 5th, 2015) has produced a gain of $1,474,478. On the flip side, being invested from May 6th to October 27th, has actually lost money. An initial investment of $10,000 has lost $2,275 over the same time period.

S&P 500 Unfavorable 6 Month Avg. Gain vs Favorable 6 Month Avg. Gain (1950-2015)

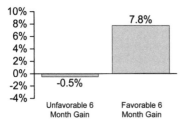

The above growth rates are geometric averages in order to represent the cumulative growth of a dollar investment over time. These figures differ from the arithmetic mean calculations used in the Six 'N' Six Take a Break Strategy, which are used to represent an average year.

	S&P 500 % May 6 to Oct 27	$10,000 Start	S&P 500 % Oct 28 to May 5	$10,000 Start	Oct28-May5 > May6-Oct27
1950/51	8.5%	10,851	15.2%	11,517	YES
1951/52	0.2	10,870	3.7	11,947	YES
1952/53	1.8	11,067	3.9	12,413	YES
1953/54	-3.1	10,727	16.6	14,475	YES
1954/55	13.2	12,141	18.1	17,097	YES
1955/56	11.4	13,528	15.1	19,681	YES
1956/57	-4.6	12,903	0.2	19,711	YES
1957/58	-12.4	11,302	7.9	21,265	YES
1958/59	15.1	13,013	14.5	24,356	
1959/60	-0.6	12,939	-4.5	23,270	
1960/61	-2.3	12,647	24.1	28,869	YES
1961/62	2.7	12,993	-3.1	27,982	
1962/63	-17.7	10,698	28.4	35,929	YES
1963/64	5.7	11,306	9.3	39,264	YES
1964/65	5.1	11,882	5.5	41,440	YES
1965/66	3.1	12,253	-5.0	39,388	
1966/67	-8.8	11,180	17.7	46,364	YES
1967/68	0.6	11,241	3.9	48,171	YES
1968/69	5.6	11,872	0.2	48,249	
1969/70	-6.2	11,141	-19.7	38,722	
1970/71	5.8	11,782	24.9	48,346	YES
1971/72	-9.6	10,647	13.7	54,965	YES
1972/73	3.7	11,046	0.3	55,154	
1973/74	0.3	11,084	-18.0	45,205	
1974/75	-23.2	8,513	28.5	58,073	YES
1975/76	-0.4	8,480	12.4	65,290	YES
1976/77	0.9	8,554	-1.6	64,231	
1977/78	-7.8	7,890	4.5	67,146	YES
1978/79	-2.0	7,732	6.4	71,476	YES
1979/80	-0.1	7,723	5.8	75,605	YES
1980/81	20.2	9,283	1.9	77,047	
1981/82	-8.5	8,498	-1.4	76,001	YES
1982/83	15.0	9,769	21.4	92,293	YES
1983/84	0.3	9,803	-3.5	89,085	
1984/85	3.9	10,183	8.9	97,057	YES
1985/86	4.1	10,604	26.8	123,044	YES
1986/87	0.4	10,651	23.7	152,196	YES
1987/88	-21.0	8,409	11.0	168,904	YES
1988/89	7.1	9,010	10.9	187,380	YES
1989/90	8.9	9,814	1.0	189,242	
1990/91	-10.0	8,837	25.0	236,498	YES
1991/92	0.9	8,916	8.5	256,590	YES
1992/93	0.4	8,952	6.2	272,550	YES
1993/94	4.5	9,356	-2.8	264,789	
1994/95	3.2	9,656	11.6	295,636	YES
1995/96	11.5	10,762	10.7	327,219	
1996/97	9.2	11,757	18.5	387,591	YES
1997/98	5.6	12,419	27.2	493,003	YES
1998/99	-4.5	11,860	26.5	623,489	YES
1999/00	-3.8	11,415	10.5	688,842	YES
2000/01	-3.7	10,992	-8.2	632,435	
2001/02	-12.8	9,586	-2.8	614,583	YES
2002/03	-16.4	8,016	3.2	634,369	YES
2003/04	11.3	8,921	8.8	689,985	
2004/05	0.3	8,952	4.2	718,942	YES
2005/06	0.5	9,000	12.5	808,503	YES
2006/07	3.9	9,350	9.3	883,804	YES
2007/08	2.0	9,534	-8.3	810,240	
2008/09	-39.7	5,750	6.5	862,619	YES
2009/10	17.7	6,766	9.6	934,470	
2010/11	1.4	6,862	12.9	1,067,851	YES
2011/12	-3.8	6,602	6.6	1,138,103	YES
2012/13	3.1	6,809	14.3	1,301,313	YES
2013/14	9.0	7,422	7.1	1,393,667	
2014/15	4.1	7,725	6.5	1,484,478	YES
Total Gain (Loss)	($2,275)			$1,474,478	

6 'n' 6 Strategy Performance

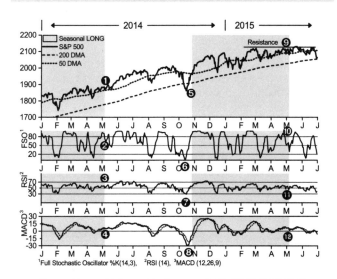

¹Full Stochastic Oscillator %K(14,3), ²RSI (14), ³MACD (12,26,9)

Favorable vs. Unfavorable Seasons 2013-2015 (S&P 500)

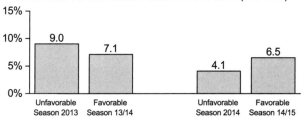

9.0	7.1	4.1	6.5
Unfavorable Season 2013	Favorable Season 13/14	Unfavorable Season 2014	Favorable Season 14/15

Market Indices & Rates
Weekly Values**

Stock Markets	2014	2015
Dow	16,517	17,991
S&P500	1,877	2,098
Nasdaq	4,082	4,965
TSX	14,609	15,165
FTSE	5,450	6,949
DAX	9,541	11,483
Nikkei	14,132	19,336
Hang Seng	21,856	27,678

Commodities	2014	2015
Oil	100.00	59.72
Gold	1295.1	1191.1

Bond Yields	2014	2015
USA 5 Yr Treasury	1.65	1.54
USA 10 Yr T	2.62	2.19
USA 20 Yr T	3.15	2.65
Moody's Aaa	4.17	3.91
Moody's Baa	4.79	4.82
CAN 5 Yr T	1.65	1.08
CAN 10 Yr T	2.37	1.74

Money Market	2014	2015
USA Fed Funds	0.25	0.25
USA 3 Mo T-B	0.03	0.01
CAN tgt overnight rate	1.00	0.75
CAN 3 Mo T-B	0.93	0.67

Foreign Exchange	2014	2015
EUR/USD	1.39	1.12
GBP/USD	1.69	1.52
USD/CAD	1.09	1.21
USD/JPY	101.85	119.79

MAY

M	T	W	T	F	S	S
						1
2	3	4	5	6	7	8
9	10	11	12	13	14	15
16	17	18	19	20	21	22
23	24	25	26	27	28	29
30	31					

JUNE

M	T	W	T	F	S	S
		1	2	3	4	5
6	7	8	9	10	11	12
13	14	15	16	17	18	19
20	21	22	23	24	25	26
27	28	29	30			

JULY

M	T	W	T	F	S	S
				1	2	3
4	5	6	7	8	9	10
11	12	13	14	15	16	17
18	19	20	21	22	23	24
25	26	27	28	29	30	31

Technical Conditions– May 6th to October 27th, 2014

In mid-April, the S&P 500 bounced off its 50 day moving average and continued its ascent into May❶. In early May, the S&P 500 became overbought as the FSO was above 80❷. At the time, the RSI was above 50 and positive❸. The MACD was also heading higher❹.

Technical Conditions– October 28th to May 5th, 2015
Entry Strategy –Buy Position Early–

In early October, the S&P 500 traded below its 50 day moving average and then bounced on its trend line❺. An early buy signal was triggered when the FSO crossed above 20❻. The RSI supported the action by moving above 30❼ and the MACD had a supporting crossover❽.

Exit Strategy –Sell Position Early–

In February 2015, the S&P 500 started to push up against 2100❾ forming a resistance level. As a pattern of higher lows was forming, a bullish ascending triangle developed. Nevertheless, an early sell signal was triggered when the FSO turned down below 80❿ in April. At the time, the RSI was just above 50⓫ and the MACD was positive⓬.

In analysing long-term trends for the broad markets such as the S&P 500 or the TSX Composite, a large data set is preferable because it incorporates various economic cycles. The daily data set for the TSX Composite starts in 1977.

Over this time period, investors have been rewarded for following the six month cycle of investing from October 28th to May 5th, versus the other unfavorable six months, May 6th to October 27th.

Starting with an investment of $10,000 in 1977, investing in the unfavorable six months has produced a loss of $3,205, versus investing in the favorable six months which has produced a gain of $212,404.

$212,404 gain on $10,000 since 1977

The TSX Composite Average Year 1977 to 2014 (graph below) indicates that the market tended to peak in mid-July or the end of August. In our book *Time In Time Out, Outsmart the Stock Market Using Calendar Investment Strategies*, Bruce Lindsay and I analysed a number of market trends and peaks over different decades.

What we found was that the markets tend to peak at the beginning of May or mid-July. The mid-July peak was usually the result of a strong bull market in place that had a lot of momentum.

The main reason that the TSX Composite data shows a peak occurring in July-August is that the data is primarily from the biggest bull market in history, starting in 1982.

TSX Composite % Gain Avg. Year 1977 to 2014

Does a later average peak in the stock market mean that the best six month cycle does not work? No. Dividing the year up into six month

intervals, the period from October to May is far superior compared with the other half of the year.

The table below illustrates the superiority of the best six months over the worst six months. Going down the table year by year, the period from October 28 to May 5th outperforms the period from May 6th to October 27 on a regular basis.

In a strong bull market, investors always have the choice of using a stop loss or technical indicators to help extend the exit point past the May date.

	TSX Comp May 6 to Oct 27	$10,000 Start	TSX Comp Oct 28 to May 5	$10,000 Start
1977/78	-3.9%	9,608	13.1%	11,313
1978/79	12.1	10,775	21.3	13,728
1979/80	2.9	11,084	23.0	16,883
1980/81	22.5	13,579	-2.4	16,479
1981/82	-17.0	11,272	-18.2	13,488
1982/83	16.6	13,138	34.6	18,150
1983/84	-0.9	13,015	-1.9	17,811
1984/85	1.6	13,226	10.7	19,718
1985/86	0.5	13,299	16.5	22,978
1986/87	-1.9	13,045	24.8	28,666
1987/88	-23.4	9,992	15.3	33,050
1988/89	2.7	10,260	5.7	34,939
1989/90	7.9	11,072	-13.3	30,294
1990/91	-8.4	10,148	13.1	34,266
1991/92	-1.6	9,982	-2.0	33,571
1992/93	-2.3	9,750	15.3	38,704
1993/94	10.8	10,801	1.7	39,365
1994/95	-0.1	10,792	0.3	39,483
1995/96	1.3	10,936	18.2	46,671
1996/97	8.3	11,843	10.8	51,725
1997/98	7.3	12,707	17.0	60,510
1998/99	-22.3	9,870	17.1	70,871
1999/00	-0.2	9,853	36.9	97,009
2000/01	-2.9	9,570	-14.4	83,062
2001/02	-12.2	8,399	9.4	90,875
2002/03	-16.4	7,020	4.0	94,476
2003/04	15.1	8,079	10.3	104,252
2004/05	3.9	8,398	7.8	112,379
2005/06	8.1	9,080	19.8	134,587
2006/07	0.0	9,079	12.2	151,053
2007/08	3.8	9,426	-0.2	150,820
2008/09	-40.2	5,638	15.7	174,551
2009/10	11.9	6,307	7.4	187,526
2010/11	5.8	6,674	7.1	200,778
2011/12	-7.4	6,183	-4.8	191,207
2012/13	3.6	6,407	1.1	193,348
2013/14	7.7	6,902	9.7	212,072
2014/15	-1.6	6,795	4.9	222,404
Total Gain (Loss)	**($-3,205)**			**$212,404**

6 'n' 6 Canada Strategy Performance

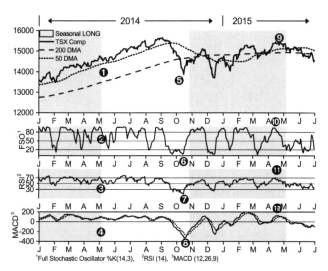

Market Indices & Rates
Weekly Values**

Stock Markets	2014	2015
Dow	16,593	18,152
S&P500	1,886	2,109
Nasdaq	4,107	5,010
TSX	14,622	15,063
FTSE	6,860	6,969
DAX	9,699	11,501
Nikkei	14,275	19,663
Hang Seng	22,528	27,497

Commodities	2014	2015
Oil	101.64	60.01
Gold	1298.2	1207.4

Bond Yields	2014	2015
USA 5 Yr Treasury	1.59	1.54
USA 10 Yr T	2.57	2.24
USA 20 Yr T	3.12	2.74
Moody's Aaa	4.15	4.02
Moody's Baa	4.77	4.94
CAN 5 Yr T	1.58	1.08
CAN 10 Yr T	2.31	1.79

Money Market	2014	2015
USA Fed Funds	0.25	0.25
USA 3 Mo T-B	0.03	0.02
CAN tgt overnight rate	1.00	0.75
CAN 3 Mo T-B	0.92	0.65

Foreign Exchange	2014	2015
EUR/USD	1.37	1.13
GBP/USD	1.68	1.57
USD/CAD	1.09	1.20
USD/JPY	101.87	119.51

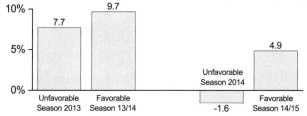

Favorable vs. Unfavorable Seasons 2013-2015 (TSX Composite)

TSX Composite Performance– May 6th to October 27, 2014

At the start of its unfavorable season, the TSX Composite was above its 50 day moving average❶, the FSO had just entered overbought territory above 80❷ and the RSI had just turned down from 70❸. The MACD was positive and rising❹.

October 28th to May 5th, 2015
Entry Strategy –Buy Position Early–

In mid-October, the TSX Composite was trading well below its 50 day moving average❺. An early buy signal was produced when the FSO bounced off 20❻. The RSI supported this move with a strong move above 30❼ and at the same time, the MACD started to trend higher❽.

Exit Strategy –Sell Position Early–

In mid-April, the TSX Composite started to turn down❾ and the FSO registered a sell signal crossing below 80❿. The RSI just turned down from 70⓫ and the MACD was just turning negative ⓬. Overall it was time to exit.

MAY

M	T	W	T	F	S	S
						1
2	3	4	5	6	7	8
9	10	11	12	13	14	15
16	17	18	19	20	21	22
23	24	25	26	27	28	29
30	31					

JUNE

M	T	W	T	F	S	S
		1	2	3	4	5
6	7	8	9	10	11	12
13	14	15	16	17	18	19
20	21	22	23	24	25	26
27	28	29	30			

JULY

M	T	W	T	F	S	S
				1	2	3
4	5	6	7	8	9	10
11	12	13	14	15	16	17
18	19	20	21	22	23	24
25	26	27	28	29	30	31

COSTCO– BUY AT A DISCOUNT
COST ①May26-Jun30 ②Oct4-Dec1

Shoppers are attracted to Costco because of its consistently low prices. They take comfort in the fact that although the prices may not always be the lowest, they are consistently in the lower range.

Costco performs well in the late spring and early summer, and in the autumn and early winter. These two periods are considered to be transition periods where the stock market is moving to and from its unfavorable and favorable seasons. Companies such as Costco that have stable earnings are desirable at these times.

There are two times when Costco is a seasonal bargain: May 26th to June 30th and October 4th to December 1st. From 1990 to 2014, during the period of May 26th to June 30th, Costco has averaged a gain of 5.6% and has been positive 68% of the time. From October 4th to December 1st, Costco has averaged a gain of 9.9% and has been positive 80% of the time.

16.4% gain & positive 92% of the time

Putting both seasonal periods together has produced a 92% positive success rate and an average gain of 16.4%. Although the earlier strong years in the 1990's skews the data to the high-side, Costco has still maintained its strong seasonal performances in both the May to June and the October to December time periods. When investors go shopping for stocks, Costco is one consumer staples company that should be on their list. They should also remember not to bulk up with too much, even if it is selling at a discount.

(i) *COST - stock symbol for Costco which trades on the Nasdaq exchange. Stock data adjusted for stock splits.*

Costco* vs. S&P 500 1990 to 2014   Positive ☐

Year	May 26 to Jun 30 S&P 500	May 26 to Jun 30 COST	Oct 4 to Dec 1 S&P 500	Oct 4 to Dec 1 COST	Compound Growth S&P 500	Compound Growth COST
1990	1.0	16.5%	3.5	26.5%	4.5	47.4%
1991	-1.7	-2.1	-2.4	-3.7	-4.0	-5.7
1992	-1.4	-2.2	5.0	22.7	3.5	20.1
1993	0.4	17.2	0.1	13.4	0.5	32.9
1994	-2.6	10.7	-2.8	-6.3	-5.3	3.7
1995	3.1	19.2	4.2	-2.1	7.4	16.7
1996	-1.2	9.4	9.3	15.5	8.0	26.4
1997	4.5	3.1	1.0	16.6	5.6	20.2
1998	2.1	17.6	17.2	41.1	19.7	65.9
1999	6.9	8.1	9.0	30.7	16.5	41.2
2000	5.3	10.0	-7.8	-3.6	-2.9	6.1
2001	-4.2	9.3	6.3	12.3	1.8	22.6
2002	-8.7	-0.8	14.3	4.6	4.4	3.8
2003	4.4	5.3	3.9	13.5	8.5	19.4
2004	2.5	10.3	5.3	17.3	7.9	29.4
2005	0.1	-1.5	3.1	13.9	3.2	12.2
2006	-0.2	5.0	4.7	6.0	4.5	11.3
2007	-0.8	3.8	-3.8	8.9	-4.6	12.9
2008	-7.0	-1.7	-25.8	-23.5	-30.9	-24.7
2009	3.6	-5.2	8.2	7.5	12.1	1.9
2010	-4.0	-3.0	5.2	5.0	1.0	1.9
2011	0.0	1.2	13.2	6.7	13.2	7.9
2012	3.4	12.5	-2.4	4.3	0.9	17.3
2013	-2.6	-3.3	7.6	9.6	4.7	6.0
2014	3.1	0.2	4.4	11.7	7.6	11.9
Avg.	0.2%	5.6%	3.2%	9.9%	3.5%	16.4%
Fq>0	56%	68%	76%	80%	80%	92%

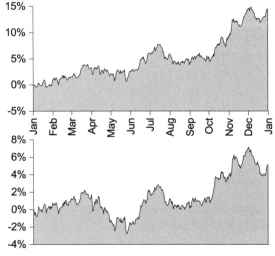

Costco - Avg. Year 1990 to 2014

Costco / S&P 500 Rel. Strength- Avg Yr. 1990-2014

Costco Performance

COST Monthly Performance (1990-2014)

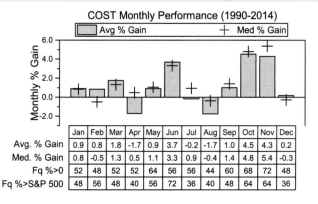

	Jan	Feb	Mar	Apr	May	Jun	Jul	Aug	Sep	Oct	Nov	Dec
Avg. % Gain	0.9	0.8	1.8	-1.7	0.9	3.7	-0.2	-1.7	1.0	4.5	4.3	0.2
Med. % Gain	0.8	-0.5	1.3	0.5	1.1	3.3	0.9	-0.4	1.4	4.8	5.4	-0.3
Fq %>0	52	48	52	52	64	56	56	44	60	68	72	48
Fq %>S&P 500	48	56	48	40	56	72	36	40	48	64	64	36

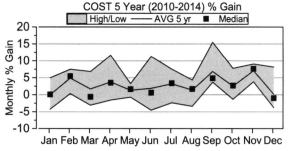

COST 5 Year (2010-2014) % Gain

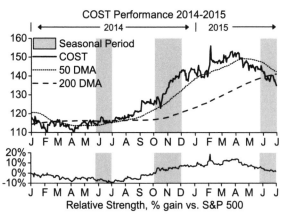

COST Performance 2014-2015

Relative Strength, % gain vs. S&P 500

Market Indices & Rates
Weekly Values**

Stock Markets	2014	2015
Dow	16,514	18,283
S&P500	1,888	2,128
Nasdaq	4,139	5,080
TSX	14,646	15,150
FTSE	6,821	7,003
DAX	9,697	11,795
Nikkei	14,185	20,116
Hang Seng	22,859	27,677

Commodities	2014	2015
Oil	103.73	58.83
Gold	1295.0	1211.5

Bond Yields	2014	2015
USA 5 Yr Treasury	1.55	1.56
USA 10 Yr T	2.54	2.23
USA 20 Yr T	3.12	2.75
Moody's Aaa	4.18	4.07
Moody's Baa	4.78	4.96
CAN 5 Yr T	1.56	1.05
CAN 10 Yr T	2.29	1.77

Money Market	2014	2015
USA Fed Funds	0.25	0.25
USA 3 Mo T-B	0.03	0.02
CAN tgt overnight rate	1.00	0.75
CAN 3 Mo T-B	0.92	0.65

Foreign Exchange	2014	2015
EUR/USD	1.37	1.11
GBP/USD	1.69	1.56
USD/CAD	1.09	1.22
USD/JPY	101.58	120.92

MAY

M	T	W	T	F	S	S
						1
2	3	4	5	6	7	8
9	10	11	12	13	14	15
16	17	18	19	20	21	22
23	24	25	26	27	28	29
30	31					

JUNE

M	T	W	T	F	S	S
		1	2	3	4	5
6	7	8	9	10	11	12
13	14	15	16	17	18	19
20	21	22	23	24	25	26
27	28	29	30			

JULY

M	T	W	T	F	S	S
				1	2	3
4	5	6	7	8	9	10
11	12	13	14	15	16	17
18	19	20	21	22	23	24
25	26	27	28	29	30	31

From 1990 to 2014, October and November have been the best contiguous months for Costco on an average, median and frequency basis. This has been mainly driven by Costco releasing its year-end earnings at the end of September. The other strong month is June, which occurs right after Costco typically announces its Q3 results. Over the last five years, on average, November has been Costco's best month followed by December being its worst month.

In 2014, Costco outperformed the S&P 500 in its Oct. 4th to Dec. 1st seasonal period, but more recently underperformed in its first seasonal period in 2015.

MEMORIAL DAY – BE EARLY & STAY LATE
Positive 2 Market Days Before Memorial Day to 5 Market Days into June

A lot of strategies that focus on investing around holidays concentrate on the market performance the day before and the day after a holiday.

1.0% average gain and positive 62% of the time

Not all holidays were created equal. The typical Memorial Day trade is to invest the day before the holiday and sell the day after. If you invested in the stock market for just these two days, you would be missing out on a lot of gains.

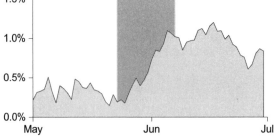

S&P 500% Gain May to June Avg. Year- 1971 to 2015

▨ Memorial Day Trade

Historically, the best strategy has been to invest two market days before Memorial Day and exit five market days into June. Extending the investment into June makes sense. The first few days in June tend to be positive– so why sell early?

The graph shows the average performance of the S&P 500 on a calendar basis for the months of May and June from 1971 to 2015.

The increase from the end of May into June represents the opportunity with the *"Memorial Day - Be Early & Stay Late"* trade.

The graph clearly shows a spike in the market that occurs at the end of the month and carries on into June.

Investors using the typical Memorial Day trade of investing just for the day before and the day after Memorial Day, have missed out on potential gains. The *Memorial Day - Be Early & Stay Late* strategy has produced an average gain of 1.0% and has been positive 62% of the time (S&P 500, 1971 to 2015). Not a bad gain for being invested an average of ten market days.

The *Memorial Day - Be Early & Stay Late* trade can be extended into June primarily because the first market days of the month tend to be positive. These days are part of the end of the month effect. (see *Super Seven* strategy).

2 Market Days Before Memorial Day to
5 Market Days Into June - S&P 500   Positive ☐

			1980	5.1	%	1990	1.1	%	2000	5.2	%	2010	-1.6	%
1971	1.5	%	1981	0.2		1991	0.9		2001	-0.9		2011	-2.7	
1972	-2.4		1982	-2.6		1992	-0.5		2002	-5.4		2012	-0.3	
1973	1.7		1983	-2.1		1993	-1.3		2003	7.0		2013	-0.7	
1974	6.3		1984	1.2		1994	0.4		2004	2.3		2014	3.3	
1975	3.8		1985	4.3		1995	0.9		2005	0.6		2015	-1.6	
1976	-0.7		1986	4.3		1996	0.0		2006	-0.2				
1977	1.0		1987	5.5		1997	2.2		2007	-2.1				
1978	3.1		1988	4.5		1998	-0.5		2008	-2.2				
1979	1.9		1989	2.4		1999	2.3		2009	4.1				
Avg.	1.8	%		2.3	%		0.6	%		0.8	%		-0.6	%

⚅ *History of Memorial Day:*
Originally called Decoration Day in remembrance of those who died in the nation's service. Memorial Day was first observed on May 30th 1868 when flowers were placed on the graves of Union and Confederate soldiers at Arlington National Cemetery. The South acknowledged the day after World War I, when the holiday changed from honoring just those who died fighting in the Civil War to honoring Americans who died fighting in any war. In 1971 Congress passed the National Holiday Act recognizing Memorial Day as the last Monday in May.

Memorial Day Strategy Performance

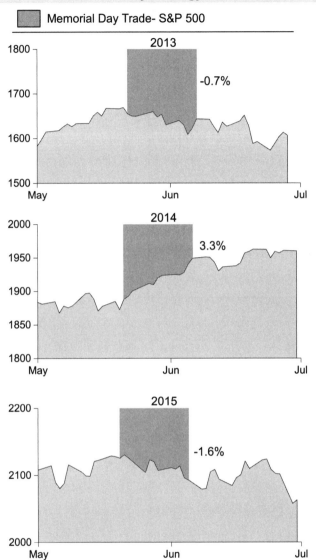

Memorial Day Trade- S&P 500

Market Indices & Rates
Weekly Values**

Stock Markets	2014	2015
Dow	16,681	18,085
S&P500	1,916	2,114
Nasdaq	4,238	5,077
TSX	14,636	15,094
FTSE	5,482	7,002
DAX	9,931	11,622
Nikkei	14,645	20,488
Hang Seng	23,016	27,802

Commodities	2014	2015
Oil	103.28	58.38
Gold	1261.1	1186.9

Bond Yields	2014	2015
USA 5 Yr Treasury	1.53	1.52
USA 10 Yr T	2.47	2.13
USA 20 Yr T	3.05	2.64
Moody's Aaa	4.16	3.95
Moody's Baa	4.70	4.86
CAN 5 Yr T	1.55	0.97
CAN 10 Yr T	2.27	1.69

Money Market	2014	2015
USA Fed Funds	0.25	0.25
USA 3 Mo T-B	0.04	0.01
CAN tgt overnight rate	1.00	0.75
CAN 3 Mo T-B	0.93	0.63

Foreign Exchange	2014	2015
EUR/USD	1.36	1.09
GBP/USD	1.68	1.54
USD/CAD	1.09	1.24
USD/JPY	101.87	123.28

MAY

M	T	W	T	F	S	S
						1
2	3	4	5	6	7	8
9	10	11	12	13	14	15
16	17	18	19	20	21	22
23	24	25	26	27	28	29
30	31					

JUNE

M	T	W	T	F	S	S
		1	2	3	4	5
6	7	8	9	10	11	12
13	14	15	16	17	18	19
20	21	22	23	24	25	26
27	28	29	30			

JULY

M	T	W	T	F	S	S
				1	2	3
4	5	6	7	8	9	10
11	12	13	14	15	16	17
18	19	20	21	22	23	24
25	26	27	28	29	30	31

In 2013, the S&P 500 had a strong run at the beginning of May and then started its pull back just as the *Memorial Day Trade* started. In the end, the *Memorial Day Trade* produced a loss of 0.7%. In 2014, the S&P 500 was flat up until the *Memorial Day Trade*. At the beginning of the trade, the S&P 500 started to rally. In the end, the 2014 *Memorial Day Trade* produced a gain of 3.3%.

In 2015, the S&P 500 was rising up until the *Memorial Day Trade* and started its pull back just as the trade started, producing a loss of 1.6% for the trade. In all three *Memorial Day Trades*, the start of the trade was a pivot point for the S&P 500.

JUNE

	MONDAY	TUESDAY	WEDNESDAY
WEEK 23	30	31	**1** 29
WEEK 24	**6** 24	**7** 23	**8** 22
WEEK 25	**13** 17	**14** 16	**15** 15
WEEK 26	**20** 10	**21** 9	**22** 8
WEEK 27	**27** 3	**28** 2	**29** 1

THURSDAY		FRIDAY	
2	28	**3**	27
9	21	**10**	20
16	14	**17**	13
23	7	**24**	6
30		1	

JULY

M	T	W	T	F	S	S
				1	2	3
4	5	6	7	8	9	10
11	12	13	14	15	16	17
18	19	20	21	22	23	24
25	26	27	28	29	30	31

AUGUST

M	T	W	T	F	S	S
1	2	3	4	5	6	7
8	9	10	11	12	13	14
15	16	17	18	19	20	21
22	23	24	25	26	27	28
29	30	31				

SEPTEMBER

M	T	W	T	F	S	S
			1	2	3	4
5	6	7	8	9	10	11
12	13	14	15	16	17	18
19	20	21	22	23	24	25
26	27	28	29	30		

OCTOBER

M	T	W	T	F	S	S
					1	2
3	4	5	6	7	8	9
10	11	12	13	14	15	16
17	18	19	20	21	22	23
19	20	26	27	28	29	30
31						

JUNE
S U M M A R Y

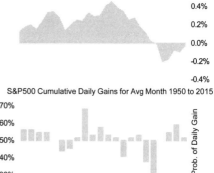

0.6%
0.4%
0.2%
0.0%
-0.2%
-0.4%

S&P500 Cumulative Daily Gains for Avg Month 1950 to 2015

	Dow Jones	S&P 500	Nasdaq	TSX Comp
Month Rank	11	10	6	11
# Up	30	34	25	14
# Down	35	31	18	16
% Pos	46	52	58	47
% Avg. Gain	-0.3	0.0	0.6	-0.3

70%
60%
50%
40%
30%

Prob. of Daily Gain

Dow & S&P 1950-2014, Nasdaq 1972-2014, TSX 1985-2014

♦ On average, June is not a strong month. From 1950 to 2015, it was the third worst month for the S&P 500, producing a flat return of 0.0%. ♦ From year to year, different sectors of the market tend to lead in June and there is not a strong consistent outperforming major sector. ♦ On average, the biotech sector starts its seasonal run in late June. ♦ The last few days of June, the start the successful *Independence Day Trade,* tend to be positive. ♦ In June 2015, the S&P 500 produced a sharp loss of 2.1% after breaking above 2100 in May.

BEST / WORST JUNE BROAD MKTS. 2006-2015

BEST JUNE MARKETS
♦ Nikkei 225 (2012) 5.4%
♦ Russell 2000 (2014) 5.2%
♦ Russell 2000 (2012) 4.8%

WORST JUNE MARKETS
♦ Dow (2008) -10.2%
♦ Nasdaq (2008) -9.1%
♦ S&P 500 (2008) -8.6%

Index Values End of Month

	2006	2007	2008	2009	2010	2011	2012	2013	2014	2015
Dow	11,150	13,409	11,350	8,447	9,774	12,414	12,880	14,910	16,827	17,620
S&P 500	1,270	1,503	1,280	919	1,031	1,321	1,362	1,606	1,960	2,063
Nasdaq	2,172	2,603	2,293	1,835	2,109	2,774	2,935	3,403	4,408	4,987
TSX Comp.	11,613	13,907	14,467	10,375	11,294	13,301	11,597	12,129	15,146	14,553
Russell 1000	1,330	1,573	1,352	966	1,091	1,412	1,443	1,712	2,104	2,216
Russell 2000	1,801	2,072	1,714	1,263	1,515	2,056	1,984	2,429	2,965	3,116
FTSE 100	5,833	6,608	5,626	4,249	4,917	5,946	5,571	6,216	6,744	6,521
Nikkei 225	15,505	18,138	13,481	9,958	9,383	9,816	9,007	13,677	15,162	20,236

Percent Gain for June

	2006	2007	2008	2009	2010	2011	2012	2013	2014	2015
Dow	-0.2	-1.6	-10.2	-0.6	-3.6	-1.2	3.9	-1.4	0.7	-2.2
S&P 500	0.0	-1.8	-8.6	0.0	-5.4	-1.8	4.0	-1.5	1.9	-2.1
Nasdaq	-0.3	0.0	-9.1	3.4	-6.5	-2.2	3.8	-1.5	3.9	-1.6
TSX Comp.	-1.1	-1.1	-1.7	0.0	-4.0	-3.6	0.7	-4.1	3.7	-3.1
Russell 1000	0.0	-2.0	-8.5	0.1	-5.7	-1.9	3.7	-1.5	2.1	-2.0
Russell 2000	0.5	-1.6	-7.8	1.3	-7.9	-2.5	4.8	-0.7	5.2	0.6
FTSE 100	1.9	-0.2	-7.1	-3.8	-5.2	-0.7	4.7	-5.6	-1.5	-6.6
Nikkei 225	0.2	1.5	-6.0	4.6	-4.0	1.3	5.4	-0.7	3.6	-1.6

June Market Avg. Performance 2006 to 2015[1]

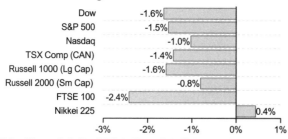

Dow	-1.6%
S&P 500	-1.5%
Nasdaq	-1.0%
TSX Comp (CAN)	-1.4%
Russell 1000 (Lg Cap)	-1.6%
Russell 2000 (Sm Cap)	-0.8%
FTSE 100	-2.4%
Nikkei 225	0.4%

-3%   -2%   -1%   0%   1%

Interest Corner Jun[2]

	Fed Funds % [3]	3 Mo. T-Bill % [4]	10 Yr % [5]	20 Yr % [6]
2015	0.25	0.01	2.35	2.83
2014	0.25	0.04	2.53	3.08
2013	0.25	0.04	2.52	3.22
2012	0.25	0.09	1.67	2.38
2011	0.25	0.03	3.18	4.09

(1) Russell Data provided by Russell (2) Federal Reserve Bank of St. Louis- end of month values (3) Target rate set by FOMC (4)(5)(6) Constant yield maturities.

JUNE SECTOR PERFORMANCE

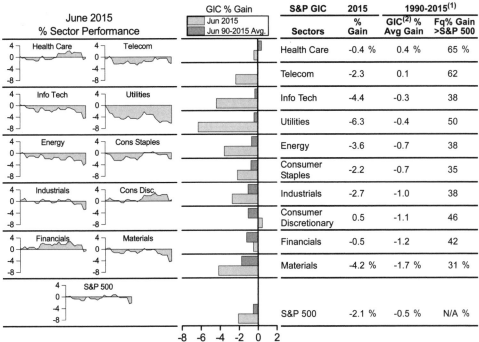

S&P GIC Sectors	2015 % Gain	1990-2015[1] GIC[2] % Avg Gain	1990-2015[1] Fq% Gain >S&P 500
Health Care	-0.4 %	0.4 %	65 %
Telecom	-2.3	0.1	62
Info Tech	-4.4	-0.3	38
Utilities	-6.3	-0.4	50
Energy	-3.6	-0.7	38
Consumer Staples	-2.2	-0.7	35
Industrials	-2.7	-1.0	38
Consumer Discretionary	0.5	-1.1	46
Financials	-0.5	-1.2	42
Materials	-4.2 %	-1.7 %	31 %
S&P 500	-2.1 %	-0.5 %	N/A %

Sector Commentary

♦ In June 2015, the only sector of the market that put in a positive performance was consumer discretionary, producing a small return of 0.5%. At the time, investors were focusing on sectors of the market that produced most of their revenue in the U.S., as the U.S. economy proved stronger than most economies around the world. ♦ Utilities produced a loss of 6.3%, carrying on its negative trend since late January.

Sub-Sector Commentary

♦ After performing well for the first few months of 2015, the agriculture sector produced a large loss of 8.8% as global growth concerns weighed on the sector. ♦ Likewise, the metals and mining, and steel sub-sectors produced losses of 8.7% and 6.9% respectively. ♦ The global growth concerns spilled over into the semiconductor sub-sector as it lost 8.7% in the month. ♦ On a positive note, the biotech sub-sector started its period of seasonal strength with a gain of 1.7%. ♦ The home-builders sub-sector, which is typically one of the weaker sub-sectors in June, produced a strong gain of 6.5% based upon a strong home starts report.

SELECTED SUB-SECTORS[3]

Sub-Sector	% Gain	GIC % Avg Gain	Fq% Gain >S&P 500
Software & Services	-2.4 %	2.1 %	69 %
Pharma	-2.0	0.5	65
Gold (London PM)	-1.7	-0.5	50
Retail	0.4	-0.5	58
Biotech (1993-2015)	1.7	-0.8	48
SOX (1995-2015)	-8.7	-1.0	38
Metals & Mining	-8.7	-1.1	54
Railroads	-4.8	-1.1	38
Steel	-6.9	-1.3	42
Transportation	-4.1	-1.3	31
Home-builders	6.5	-1.4	42
Agriculture (1994-2015)	-8.8	-1.7	32
Chemicals	-3.5	-1.8	31
Banks	2.0	-2.1	31
Silver	-5.8	-2.4	38

(1) Sector data provided by Standard and Poors (2) GIC is short form for Global Industry Classification (3) Sub Sector data provided by Standard and Poors, except where marked by symbol.

BIOTECH SUMMER SOLSTICE
June 23rd to September 13th

The *Biotech Summer Solstice* trade starts on June 23rd and lasts until September 13th. The trade is aptly named as its outperformance starts approximately on the day summer solstice starts– the longest day of the year.

There are two main drivers of the trade: biotech is a good substitute for technology stocks in the summer, and investors want to take a position in the biotech sector before the autumn conferences.

11.6% extra & 87% of the time better than the S&P 500

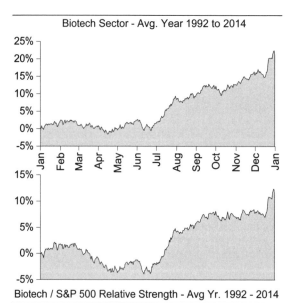

Biotech Sector - Avg. Year 1992 to 2014

Biotech / S&P 500 Relative Strength - Avg Yr. 1992 - 2014

Biotech* vs. S&P 500 1992 to 2014

Jun 23 to Sep 13	S&P 500	Positive		
		Biotech	Diff	
1992	4.0 %	17.9 %	13.8 %	
1993	3.6	3.6	0.0	
1994	3.2	24.2	21.0	
1995	5.0	31.5	26.5	
1996	2.1	7.0	4.9	
1997	2.8	-18.9	-21.7	
1998	-8.5	20.6	29.1	
1999	0.6	64.3	63.7	
2000	2.3	7.6	5.4	
2001	-10.8	-3.6	7.2	
2002	-10.0	8.1	18.2	
2003	2.3	6.4	4.1	
2004	-0.8	8.9	9.6	
2005	1.4	26.0	24.5	
2006	5.8	7.4	1.6	
2007	-1.2	6.0	7.2	
2008	-5.0	11.4	16.5	
2009	16.8	7.7	-9.1	
2010	2.4	2.8	0.4	
2011	-8.9	-3.7	5.2	
2012	9.4	15.6	6.2	
2013	6.0	24.9	18.9	
2014	1.2	14.8	13.6	
Avg	1.0 %	12.6 %	11.6 %	
Fq>0	70 %	87 %	87 %	

As a result, in the summer months when investors tend to be more cautious, they are more willing to commit speculative money into the biotech sector, compared with the technology sector.

The biotech sector is one of the few sectors that starts its outperformance in June. This is in part because of the biotech conferences that occur in autumn and with the possibility of positive announcements, the price of biotech companies on the stock market can increase dramatically. As a result, investors try to lock in positions early.

The biotechnology sector is often considered the cousin of the technology sector, a good place for speculative investments. The sectors are similar as both include concept companies (companies without a product but with good potential).

Despite their similarity, investors view the sectors differently. The technology sector is viewed as being largely dependent on the economy and conversely, the biotech sector as being much less dependent on the economy. The end product of biotechnology companies is mainly medicine, which is not economically sensitive.

(i) *Biotech SP GIC Sector # 352010: Companies primarily engaged in the research, development, manufacturing and/or marketing of products based on genetic analysis and genetic engineering. This includes companies specializing in protein-based therapeutics to treat human diseases.*

Biotech Performance

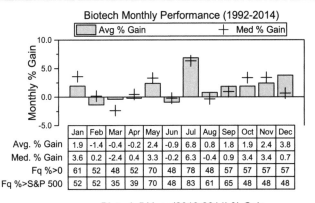

Biotech Monthly Performance (1992-2014)

	Jan	Feb	Mar	Apr	May	Jun	Jul	Aug	Sep	Oct	Nov	Dec
Avg. % Gain	1.9	-1.4	-0.4	-0.2	2.4	-0.9	6.8	0.8	1.8	1.9	2.4	3.8
Med. % Gain	3.6	0.2	-2.4	0.4	3.3	-0.2	6.3	-0.4	0.9	3.4	3.4	0.7
Fq %>0	61	52	48	52	70	48	78	48	57	57	57	57
Fq %>S&P 500	52	52	35	39	70	48	83	61	65	48	48	48

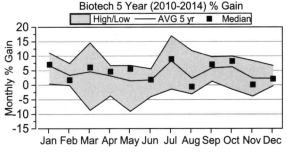

Biotech 5 Year (2010-2014) % Gain

Market Indices & Rates
Weekly Values**

Stock Markets	2014	2015
Dow	16,793	17,977
S&P500	1,933	2,105
Nasdaq	4,268	5,077
TSX	14,770	15,062
FTSE	6,838	6,899
DAX	9,946	11,344
Nikkei	15,039	20,507
Hang Seng	23,126	27,507

Commodities	2014	2015
Oil	102.58	59.65
Gold	1247.1	1184.7

Bond Yields	2014	2015
USA 5 Yr Treasury	1.64	1.65
USA 10 Yr T	2.59	2.31
USA 20 Yr T	3.16	2.80
Moody's Aaa	4.27	4.13
Moody's Baa	4.82	5.04
CAN 5 Yr T	1.59	0.97
CAN 10 Yr T	2.32	1.74

Money Market	2014	2015
USA Fed Funds	0.25	0.25
USA 3 Mo T-B	0.04	0.02
CAN tgt overnight rate	1.00	0.75
CAN 3 Mo T-B	0.93	0.61

Foreign Exchange	2014	2015
EUR/USD	1.36	1.11
GBP/USD	1.68	1.53
USD/CAD	1.09	1.25
USD/JPY	102.51	124.62

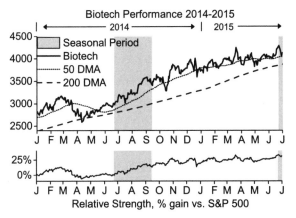

Biotech Performance 2014-2015

Relative Strength, % gain vs. S&P 500

JUNE

M	T	W	T	F	S	S
		1	2	3	4	5
6	7	8	9	10	11	12
13	14	15	16	17	18	19
20	21	22	23	24	25	26
27	28	29	30			

JULY

M	T	W	T	F	S	S
				1	2	3
4	5	6	7	8	9	10
11	12	13	14	15	16	17
18	19	20	21	22	23	24
25	26	27	28	29	30	31

From 1992 to 2014, the best month for the biotech sector has been July on an average, median and frequency basis. The start of the seasonal period for the sector is late June and runs into the middle of September. On the whole, June is actually a negative month, but the tail end of the month often provides a good buying opportunity. Although August has been positive on an average absolute basis, it can be a weaker month and investors should be prepared to exit the sector before the seasonal period finishes. Over the last five years, the sector has demonstrated superior performance in July. In 2014, the sector strongly outperformed the S&P 500 during its seasonal period.

AUGUST

M	T	W	T	F	S	S
1	2	3	4	5	6	7
8	9	10	11	12	13	14
15	16	17	18	19	20	21
22	23	24	25	26	27	28
29	30	31				

SUPER SEVEN DAYS
7 Best Days of the Month

The end of the month tends to be an excellent time to invest: portfolio managers "window dress" (adjust their portfolios to look good for month end reports), investors stop procrastinating and invest their extra cash, and brokers try to increase their commissions by investing their clients' extra cash.

From 1950 to 2014
All 7 days better
than market average

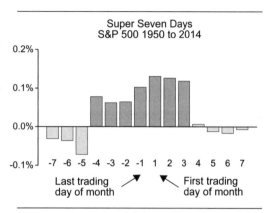

Super Seven Days
S&P 500 1950 to 2014

Last trading day of month ↗   ↖ First trading day of month

All of these factors tend to produce above average returns in the market during the days on either side of month end.

The above graph illustrates the strength of the *Super Seven* days. The *Super Seven* days are the last four trading days of the month and the first three trading days of the next month, represented by the dark columns from day -4 to day 3. All of the *Super Seven* days have daily average gains above the daily market average gain of 0.03% since 1950.

% Gain Super Seven Day Period From 2005 to 2014

	2005	2006	2007	2008	2009	2010	2011	2012	2013	2014	Avg.
Jan	1.8 %	-0.1 %	1.6 %	-4.5 %	-0.5 %	0.0 %	1.2 %	1.4 %	0.6	-1.7 %	-0.2 %
Feb	2.2	-0.4	-5.6	-2.8	4.1	1.0	1.2	0.1	1.6	1.4	-1.0
Mar	0.9	0.8	0.1	1.2	3.5	2.0	1.4	-1.2	-0.2	1.2	0.8
Apr	1.2	0.0	1.5	1.3	4.3	-3.8	0.9	1.4	2.3	0.3	0.9
May	0.2	0.5	1.6	0.1	5.0	2.7	-1.2	-2.7	-2.5	1.4	0.8
Jun	0.3	1.9	1.8	-3.9	-0.2	-4.2	5.6	4.1	2.7	1.8	0.1
Jul	1.3	0.9	-5.6	2.2	2.1	1.1	-5.8	4.0	1.0	-2.9	0.2
Aug	1.7	0.4	0.8	-2.4	-2.4	4.7	0.5	1.5	-0.1	0.0	-0.1
Sep	-1.6	1.8	1.4	-7.3	-1.0	1.1	-1.6	-0.4	-1.1	-1.5	-0.6
Oct	2.0	-1.3	-0.8	12.2	-1.9	1.0	2.6	0.3	0.2	3.2	1.1
Nov	-0.3	1.0	5.5	8.8	-0.6	3.7	8.2	0.2	-0.7	0.5	1.6
Dec	0.4	-0.1	-5.7	7.7	0.9	1.5	1.2	2.8	-0.4	-3.8	0.4
Avg.	0.8 %	0.0 %	0.0 %	1.1 %	0.4 %	1.1 %	1.2 %	1.0 %	0.3	0.0 %	0.3 %

From 2005 to 2014, the super seven strategy has worked very well and has produced an average gain of 0.3% per month. On an annualized basis, this return is greater than 4.2% per year. Given that the average month has twenty-two trading days, the *Super Seven* strategy has investors in the market for less than one third of the time. On a time-adjusted basis, adjusting returns for the amount of time in the market, the strategy has produced much greater gains than a buy and hold discipline.

If there is one time of the month that investors should be concentrating on investing, it is the last four trading days of the current month and the first three of the next month.

Super Seven Strategy Performance

2014 - S&P 500 - % Gains Last 4 Days of Month & First 3 Days of Next Month

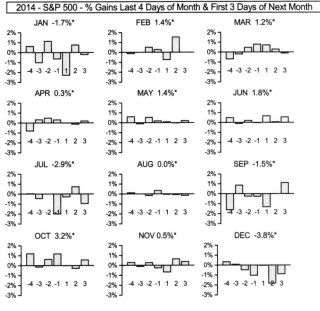

Market Indices & Rates
Weekly Values**

Stock Markets	2014	2015
Dow	16,849	17,894
S&P500	1,942	2,094
Nasdaq	4,323	5,049
TSX	14,916	14,804
FTSE	6,842	6,801
DAX	9,968	11,172
Nikkei	15,052	20,278
Hang Seng	23,237	27,036

Commodities	2014	2015
Oil	105.32	60.09
Gold	1262.8	1180.0

Bond Yields	2014	2015
USA 5 Yr Treasury	1.69	1.75
USA 10 Yr T	2.62	2.42
USA 20 Yr T	3.17	2.88
Moody's Aaa	4.28	4.20
Moody's Baa	4.82	5.13
CAN 5 Yr T	1.59	1.04
CAN 10 Yr T	2.33	1.84

Money Market	2014	2015
USA Fed Funds	0.25	0.25
USA 3 Mo T-B	0.04	0.02
CAN tgt overnight rate	1.00	0.75
CAN 3 Mo T-B	0.93	0.62

Foreign Exchange	2014	2015
EUR/USD	1.36	1.13
GBP/USD	1.68	1.55
USD/CAD	1.09	1.23
USD/JPY	102.14	123.66

2015 - S&P 500 - % Gains Last 4 Days of Month & First 3 Days of Next Month

*% Cumulative Gain Return over full 7 days, **Scale changed due to magnitude of gains

JUNE

M	T	W	T	F	S	S
		1	2	3	4	5
6	7	8	9	10	11	12
13	14	15	16	17	18	19
20	21	22	23	24	25	26
27	28	29	30			

JULY

M	T	W	T	F	S	S
				1	2	3
4	5	6	7	8	9	10
11	12	13	14	15	16	17
18	19	20	21	22	23	24
25	26	27	28	29	30	31

AUGUST

M	T	W	T	F	S	S
1	2	3	4	5	6	7
8	9	10	11	12	13	14
15	16	17	18	19	20	21
22	23	24	25	26	27	28
29	30	31				

Super Seven Performance

The *Super Seven* strategy has faltered over the last two years. In some cases the returns have been strong, but generally the negative returns have more than offset the positive returns.

In 2014, the S&P 500 was successful seven out of twelve *Super Seven* trades, but on average the negative results were larger than the positive results, leading to an overall loss.

In 2015, so far the *Super Seven* strategy has been negative five out of the six times. The S&P 500 in early 2015 traded in a very tight range looking for direction. The end result was generally weaker performance in the last few days of the month and then a positive start to the next month. Overall, the last few days of the month have had the greatest impact on the Super Seven.

INDEPENDENCE DAY – THE FULL TRADE PROFIT BEFORE & AFTER FIREWORKS

Two Market Days Before June Month End To 5 Market Days After Independence Day

The beginning of July is a time for celebration and the markets tend to agree.

Based on previous market data, the best way to take advantage of this trend is to be invested for the two market days prior to June month end and hold until five market days after Independence Day. This time period has produced above average returns on a fairly consistent basis.

Since 1950, 0.9% avg. gain & 71% of the time positive

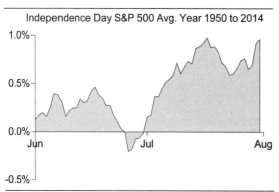

Independence Day S&P 500 Avg. Year 1950 to 2014

The typical *Independence Day Trade* put forward by quite a few pundits has been to invest one or two days before the holiday and take profits one or two days after the holiday.

Although this strategy has produced profits, it has left a lot of money on the table. This strategy misses out on the positive days at the end of June and on the full slate of positive days after Independence Day.

The beginning part of the *Independence Day Trade* positive trend is driven by two combining factors.

First, portfolio managers "window dress" (buying stocks that have a favorable perception in the market); thereby pushing stock prices up at the end of the month.

Second, investors have become "wise" to the *Independence Day Trade* and try to jump in before other investors.

Depending on market conditions at the time, investors should consider extending the exit date until eighteen calendar days in July. With July being an earnings month, the market can continue to rally until mid-month (see *18 Day Earnings Month Strategy*).

> **(i)** *History of Independence Day:*
> *Independence Day is celebrated on July 4th because that is the day when the Continental Congress adopted the final draft of the Declaration of Independence in 1776. Independence Day was made an official holiday at the end of the War of Independence in 1783. In 1941 Congress declared the 4th of July a federal holiday.*

S&P 500, 2 Market Days Before June Month End To 5 Market Days after Independence Day % Gain 1950 to 2015   Positive [ ]

Year	%	Year	%	Year	%	Year	%	Year	%	Year	%	Year	%
1950	-4.4	1960	-0.1	1970	1.5	1980	1.4	1990	1.7	2000	1.8	2010	0.4
1951	1.5	1961	1.7	1971	3.2	1981	-2.4	1991	1.4	2001	-2.6	2011	1.8
1952	0.9	1962	9.8	1972	0.3	1982	-0.6	1992	2.8	2002	-4.7	2012	0.7
1953	0.8	1963	0.5	1973	2.1	1983	1.5	1993	-0.6	2003	1.2	2013	4.5
1954	2.9	1964	2.3	1974	-8.8	1984	-0.7	1994	0.4	2004	-1.7	2014	0.5
1955	4.9	1965	5.0	1975	-0.2	1985	1.5	1995	1.8	2005	1.5	2015	-1.2
1956	3.4	1966	2.1	1976	2.4	1986	-2.6	1996	-2.8	2006	2.1		
1957	3.8	1967	1.3	1977	-0.6	1987	0.4	1997	3.7	2007	0.8		
1958	2.0	1968	2.3	1978	0.6	1988	-0.6	1998	2.7	2008	-3.4		
1959	3.3	1969	-1.5	1979	1.3	1989	0.9	1999	5.1	2009	-4.3		
Avg.	**1.9%**		2.3%		0.2%		-0.1%		1.8%		-0.9%		1.1%

Independence Day Strategy Performance

☐ Independence Day Trade

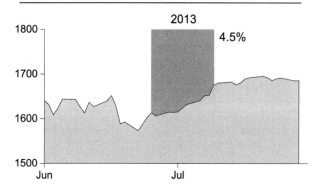

2013 — 4.5%

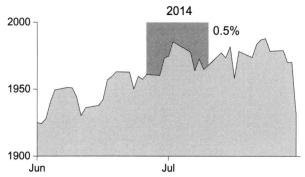

2014 — 0.5%

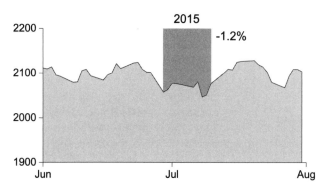

2015 — -1.2%

Market Indices & Rates
Weekly Values**

Stock Markets	2014	2015
Dow	16,873	17,953
S&P500	1,952	2,102
Nasdaq	4,350	5,080
TSX	15,085	14,733
FTSE	6,787	6,704
DAX	9,945	11,029
Nikkei	15,147	20,206
Hang Seng	23,210	26,727

Commodities	2014	2015
Oil	106.58	59.89
Gold	1283.8	1188.5

Bond Yields	2014	2015
USA 5 Yr Treasury	1.72	1.65
USA 10 Yr T	2.63	2.32
USA 20 Yr T	3.17	2.81
Moody's Aaa	4.27	4.17
Moody's Baa	4.81	5.10
CAN 5 Yr T	1.57	0.95
CAN 10 Yr T	2.28	1.75

Money Market	2014	2015
USA Fed Funds	0.25	0.25
USA 3 Mo T-B	0.03	0.01
CAN tgt overnight rate	1.00	0.75
CAN 3 Mo T-B	0.94	0.62

Foreign Exchange	2014	2015
EUR/USD	1.36	1.13
GBP/USD	1.70	1.58
USD/CAD	1.08	1.23
USD/JPY	101.98	123.18

JUNE

M	T	W	T	F	S	S
		1	2	3	4	5
6	7	8	9	10	11	12
13	14	15	16	17	18	19
20	21	22	23	24	25	26
27	28	29	30			

JULY

M	T	W	T	F	S	S
				1	2	3
4	5	6	7	8	9	10
11	12	13	14	15	16	17
18	19	20	21	22	23	24
25	26	27	28	29	30	31

AUGUST

M	T	W	T	F	S	S
1	2	3	4	5	6	7
8	9	10	11	12	13	14
15	16	17	18	19	20	21
22	23	24	25	26	27	28
29	30	31				

In 2013, the *Independence Day Trade* worked very well as investors pushed up stock prices in the anticipation of strong earnings. The S&P 500 tailed off after the *Independence Day Trade* ended.

In 2014, the S&P 500 rallied in June and continued its momentum into July for a successful *Independence Day Trade*.

In 2015, the S&P 500 declined in June and continued its decline into the *Independence Day Trade* to produce a loss of 1.2%.

Nikkei 225- Avoid for Six Months
May 6th to November 13th

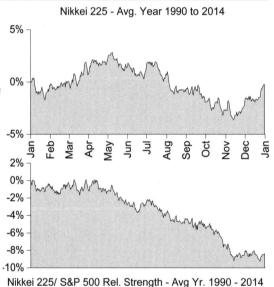

In the second half of the 1980's, the Nikkei 225 was climbing rapidly as Japanese businesses were increasing their exports around the world. Over-confidence and speculation developed bubbles in the stock market and real estate market. In 1990, in an attempt to control the overheated economy and speculation, the Bank of Japan tightened the money supply repeatedly and by the beginning of October, the Nikkei 225 had lost almost half its value.

7.9% loss & positive 16% of the time

Nikkei 225* vs. S&P 500
1990 to 2014

May 6 to Nov 13	S&P 500	Nikkei 225	Diff
		Negative	
1990	-6.1%	-20.6%	-14.4%
1991	4.4	-7.8	-12.2
1992	1.3	-5.6	-7.0
1993	4.7	-11.6	-16.3
1994	2.4	-1.5	-3.9
1995	13.9	4.1	-9.8
1996	14.0	-3.2	-17.1
1997	10.4	-21.0	-31.4
1998	0.9	-8.5	-9.5
1999	3.6	9.3	5.7
2000	-5.7	-20.5	-14.8
2001	-10.1	-30.5	-20.4
2002	-17.8	-27.0	-9.2
2003	14.2	30.7	16.5
2004	5.6	-6.3	-11.9
2005	5.3	28.7	23.4
2006	4.4	-6.6	-11.0
2007	-1.6	-13.0	-11.4
2008	-35.3	-41.4	-6.1
2009	21.0	8.8	-12.2
2010	2.9	-12.1	-14.9
2011	-5.3	-14.9	-9.6
2012	0.4	-7.7	-8.1
2013	10.4	6.4	-4.0
2014	8.2	20.3	12.1
Avg	1.8%	-6.0%	-7.9%
Fq > 0	72%	28%	16%

Nikkei 225 - Avg. Year 1990 to 2014

Nikkei 225/ S&P 500 Rel. Strength - Avg Yr. 1990 - 2014

Although it is possible that the Nikkei 225's secular decline has skewed its seasonal average trend, historically avoiding most stock markets around the world from May to October has generally been beneficial on a risk-reward basis and the Nikkei 225 is no exception. From 1990 to 2014, during the period of May 6th to November 13th, the Nikkei 225 has produced an average loss of 7.9% and has only been positive 16% of the time. The Nikkei 225's secular decline starting in the 1990's may have artificially boosted the magnitude of its underperformance during its unfavorable period from May 6th to November 13th. However, since its low in 2009, during its unfavorable period, the Nikkei 225 has underperformed the S&P 500 every year except 2014.

After Shinza Abe was elected for a second term as Prime Minister of Japan in December 2012, he introduced expansionary policies to stimulate the economy. His "three arrows" policy of fiscal stimulus, monetary easing and structural reforms was well received by the investors. Japan has continued on its expansionary monetary policy, helping to boost the Nikkei 225. Nevertheless, investors would still be wise to pay heed to the Nikkei's unfavorable period.

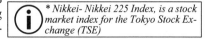
Nikkei- Nikkei 225 Index, is a stock market index for the Tokyo Stock Exchange (TSE)

Nikkei 225 Performance

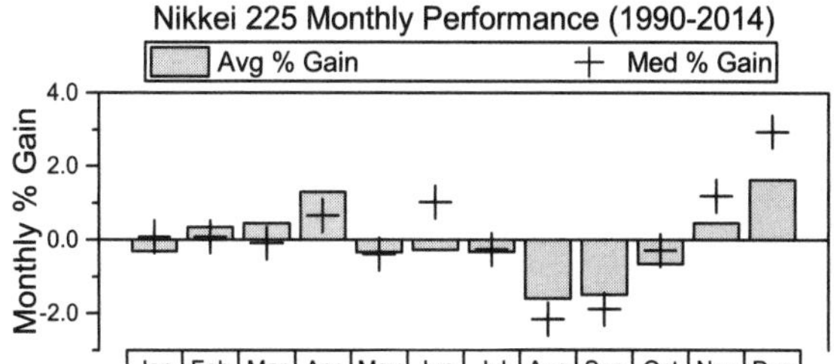
Nikkei 225 Monthly Performance (1990-2014)
Avg % Gain
Med % Gain
Monthly % Gain
4.0
2.0
0.0
-2.0

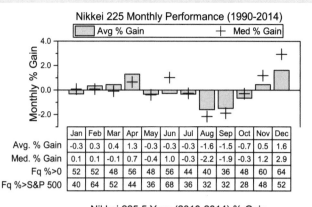

	Jan	Feb	Mar	Apr	May	Jun	Jul	Aug	Sep	Oct	Nov	Dec
Avg. % Gain	-0.3	0.3	0.4	1.3	-0.3	-0.3	-0.3	-1.6	-1.5	-0.7	0.5	1.6
Med. % Gain	0.1	0.1	-0.1	0.7	-0.4	1.0	-0.3	-2.2	-1.9	-0.3	1.2	2.9
Fq %>0	52	52	48	56	48	56	44	40	36	48	60	64
Fq %>S&P 500	40	64	52	44	36	68	36	32	32	28	48	52

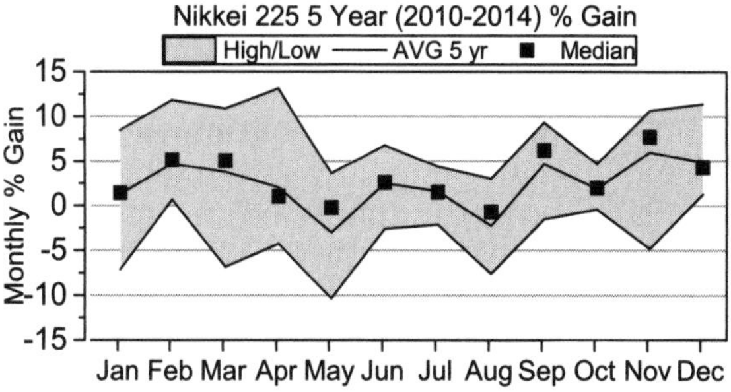
Nikkei 225 5 Year (2010-2014) % Gain
High/Low
AVG 5 yr
Median
Monthly % Gain
15
10
5
0
-5
-10
-15
Jan Feb Mar Apr May Jun Jul Aug Sep Oct Nov Dec

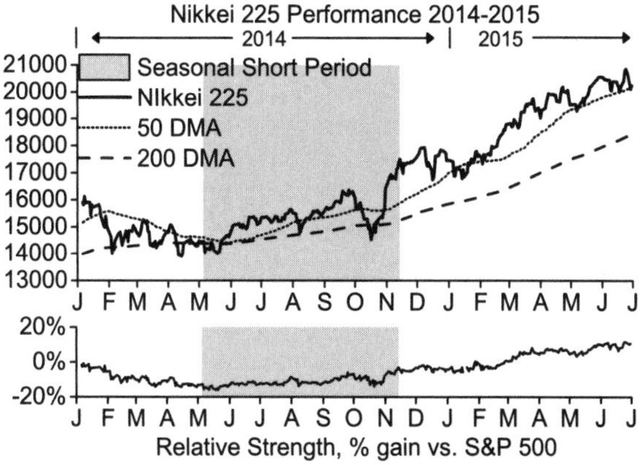
Nikkei 225 Performance 2014-2015
2014
2015
21000
20000
19000
18000
17000
16000
15000
14000
13000
Seasonal Short Period
NIkkei 225
50 DMA
200 DMA
J F M A M J J A S O N D J F M A M J J
20%
0%
-20%
J F M A M J J A S O N D J F M A M J J
Relative Strength, % gain vs. S&P 500

From 1990 to 2014, the Nikkei 225 on average has had negative performance during the six month unfavorable period for stocks from May to October. Over the last five years, the Nikkei 225 has on average generally followed its seasonal trend of weaker performance in the summer months, but September on an average and median basis has performed better than its long-term average from 1990 to 2014.

In 2014, the Nikkei 225 started the year underperforming the S&P 500, but with the advent of quantitative easing by the Bank of Japan, the Nikkei 225 outperformed the S&P 500 with strong absolute performance.

WEEK 26

Market Indices & Rates
Weekly Values**

Stock Markets	**2014**	**2015**
Dow	16,864	18,013
S&P500	1,958	2,112
Nasdaq	4,375	5,126
TSX	15,034	14,870
FTSE	6,763	6,813
DAX	9,869	11,488
Nikkei	15,283	20,717
Hang Seng	22,994	27,126
Commodities	**2014**	**2015**
Oil	106.46	59.95
Gold	1315.6	1176.1
Bond Yields	**2014**	**2015**
USA 5 Yr Treasury	1.68	1.71
USA 10 Yr T	2.57	2.41
USA 20 Yr T	3.12	2.90
Moody's Aaa	4.20	4.26
Moody's Baa	4.76	5.22
CAN 5 Yr T	1.58	0.99
CAN 10 Yr T	2.28	1.82
Money Market	**2014**	**2015**
USA Fed Funds	0.25	0.25
USA 3 Mo T-B	0.03	0.01
CAN tgt overnight rate	1.00	0.75
CAN 3 Mo T-B	0.95	0.58
Foreign Exchange	**2014**	**2015**
EUR/USD	1.36	1.12
GBP/USD	1.70	1.58
USD/CAD	1.07	1.23
USD/JPY	101.78	123.73

JUNE

M	T	W	T	F	S	S
		1	2	3	4	5
6	7	8	9	10	11	12
13	14	15	16	17	18	19
20	21	22	23	24	25	26
27	28	29	30			

JULY

M	T	W	T	F	S	S
				1	2	3
4	5	6	7	8	9	10
11	12	13	14	15	16	17
18	19	20	21	22	23	24
25	26	27	28	29	30	31

AUGUST

M	T	W	T	F	S	S
1	2	3	4	5	6	7
8	9	10	11	12	13	14
15	16	17	18	19	20	21
22	23	24	25	26	27	28
29	30	31				

JULY

	MONDAY	TUESDAY	WEDNESDAY
WEEK 27	27	28	29
WEEK 28	**4** 27 USA Market Closed - Independence Day	**5** 26	**6** 25
WEEK 29	**11** 20	**12** 19	**13** 18
WEEK 30	**18** 13	**19** 12	**20** 11
WEEK 31	**25** 6	**26** 5	**27** 4

THURSDAY	FRIDAY
30	**1** 30
	CAN Market Closed- Canada Day
7 24	**8** 23
14 17	**15** 16
21 10	**22** 9
28 3	**29** 2

AUGUST

M	T	W	T	F	S	S
1	2	3	4	5	6	7
8	9	10	11	12	13	14
15	16	17	18	19	20	21
22	23	24	25	26	27	28
29	30	31				

SEPTEMBER

M	T	W	T	F	S	S
			1	2	3	4
5	6	7	8	9	10	11
12	13	14	15	16	17	18
19	20	21	22	23	24	25
26	27	28	29	30		

OCTOBER

M	T	W	T	F	S	S
					1	2
3	4	5	6	7	8	9
10	11	12	13	14	15	16
17	18	19	20	21	22	23
19	20	26	27	28	29	30
31						

NOVEMBER

M	T	W	T	F	S	S
	1	2	3	4	5	6
7	8	9	10	11	12	13
14	15	16	17	18	19	20
21	22	23	24	25	26	27
28	29	30				

JULY
S U M M A R Y

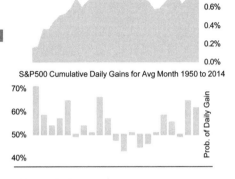

S&P500 Cumulative Daily Gains for Avg Month 1950 to 2014

	Dow Jones	S&P 500	Nasdaq	TSX Comp
Month Rank	4	6	10	6
# Up	40	35	22	20
# Down	25	30	21	10
% Pos	62	54	51	67
% Avg. Gain	1.1	1.0	0.2	0.9

Dow & S&P 1950-2014, Nasdaq 1972-2014, TSX 1985-2014

♦ When a summer rally occurs, the gains are usually made in July. ♦ Typically, it is the first part of July that produces the gains as the market rallies for Independence Day and into the first eighteen calendar days (see the *18 Days Earnings Month Effect*). In 2014, July produced a strong gain of 0.9% during its first eighteen calendar days. ♦ On average, volatility starts to increase in July and continues this trend into October. ♦ Two major sector opportunities in July are gold and energy.

BEST / WORST JULY BROAD MKTS. 2005-2014

BEST JULY MARKETS
♦ Russell 2000 (2009) 9.5%
♦ Dow (2009) 8.6%
♦ FTSE 100 (2009) 8.5%

WORST JULY MARKETS
♦ Russell 2000 (2007) -6.9%
♦ Russell 2000 (2014) -6.1%
♦ TSX Comp (2008) -6.0%

Index Values End of Month

	2005	2006	2007	2008	2009	2010	2011	2012	2013	2014
Dow	10,641	11,186	13,212	11,378	9,172	10,466	12,143	13,009	15,500	16,563
S&P 500	1,234	1,277	1,455	1,267	987	1,102	1,292	1,379	1,686	1,931
Nasdaq	2,185	2,091	2,546	2,326	1,979	2,255	2,756	2,940	3,626	4,370
TSX Comp.	10,423	11,831	13,869	13,593	10,787	11,713	12,946	11,665	12,487	15,331
Russell 1000	1,288	1,331	1,523	1,334	1,038	1,165	1,380	1,458	1,802	2,068
Russell 2000	1,689	1,741	1,929	1,776	1,384	1,618	1,981	1,956	2,598	2,784
FTSE 100	5,282	5,928	6,360	5,412	4,608	5,258	5,815	5,635	6,621	6,730
Nikkei 225	11,900	15,457	17,249	13,377	10,357	9,537	9,833	8,695	13,668	15,621

Percent Gain for July

	2005	2006	2007	2008	2009	2010	2011	2012	2013	2014
Dow	3.6	0.3	-1.5	0.2	8.6	7.1	-2.2	1.0	4.0	-1.6
S&P 500	3.6	0.5	-3.2	-1.0	7.4	6.9	-2.1	1.3	4.9	-1.5
Nasdaq	6.2	-3.7	-2.2	1.4	7.8	6.9	-0.6	0.2	6.6	-0.9
TSX Comp.	5.3	1.9	-0.3	-6.0	4.0	3.7	-2.7	0.6	2.9	1.2
Russell 1000	3.8	0.1	-3.2	-1.3	7.5	6.8	-2.3	1.1	5.2	-1.7
Russell 2000	6.3	-3.3	-6.9	3.6	9.5	6.8	-3.7	-1.4	6.9	-6.1
FTSE 100	3.3	1.6	-3.7	-3.8	8.5	6.9	-2.2	1.2	6.5	-0.2
Nikkei 225	2.7	-0.3	-4.9	-0.8	4.0	1.6	0.2	-3.5	-0.1	3.0

July Market Avg. Performance 2005 to 2014[1]

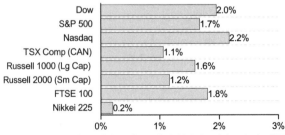

	Dow	2.0%
	S&P 500	1.7%
	Nasdaq	2.2%
	TSX Comp (CAN)	1.1%
	Russell 1000 (Lg Cap)	1.6%
	Russell 2000 (Sm Cap)	1.2%
	FTSE 100	1.8%
	Nikkei 225	0.2%

Interest Corner Jul[2]

	Fed Funds % [3]	3 Mo. T-Bill % [4]	10 Yr % [5]	20 Yr % [6]
2014	0.25	0.03	2.58	3.07
2013	0.25	0.04	2.60	3.34
2012	0.25	0.11	1.51	2.21
2011	0.25	0.10	2.82	3.77
2010	0.25	0.15	2.94	3.74

(1) Russell Data provided by Russell (2) Federal Reserve Bank of St. Louis- end of month values (3) Target rate set by FOMC (4)(5)(6) Constant yield maturities.

July 2014 % Sector Performance	GIC % Gain	S&P GIC	2014	1990-2014[1]	
	Jul 2014 / Jul 90-2014 Avg.	Sectors	% Gain	GIC[2] % Avg Gain	Fq% Gain >S&P 500
Financials / Energy		Financials	-1.6 %	1.3 %	48 %
		Energy	-3.4	1.1	64
Materials / Info Tech		Materials	-2.0	1.1	60
		Info Tech	1.4	1.0	48
Health Care / Cons Staples		Health Care	0.0	0.7	44
		Consumer Staples	-3.4	0.7	56
Industrials / Cons Disc.		Industrials	-4.1	0.5	48
		Consumer Discretionary	-1.4	0.1	52
Utilities / Telecom		Utilities	-6.9	-0.2	44
		Telecom	2.6 %	-0.2 %	48 %
S&P 500		S&P 500	-1.5 %	0.7 %	N/A %

-8 -6 -4 -2 0 2 4 6

Sector Commentary

♦ July is an earnings month and the stock market performed positively into the start of the earnings season in July 2014 as part of the *18 Calendar Days Earning Month Effect*. ♦ The rest of July was not so positive and only two of the major sectors performed positively: information technology and telecom. ♦ The worst performing major sector was the utilities sector which produced a loss of 6.9% after peaking in June. ♦ Industrials kept up its poor performance as concerns remained over a global growth slowdown.

Sub-Sector Commentary

♦ In July 2014, the biotech sector put in a strong performance of 6.3%. ♦ Agriculture produced a strong gain of 5.2%. This was more of a bounce from the large decline of 8.8% in June. ♦ The homebuilders sub-sector produced a very large loss of 14.0% as concerns over the economy took its toll, particularly after the large gain of 6.5 % in June. ♦ The semiconductor sub-sector produced a loss of 4.5%, despite a gain for the overall technology sector in July.

SELECTED SUB-SECTORS[3]			
Biotech (1993-2014)	6.3 %	6.8 %	82 %
Railroads	-1.5	2.4	64
Silver	-0.9	1.6	64
Banks	-1.4	1.4	64
Chemicals	-2.3	1.4	56
Transportation	-2.1	1.1	44
Retail	-0.7	0.7	56
Homebuilders	-14.0	0.5	44
Gold (London PM)	-2.3	0.5	52
Metals & Mining	2.0	0.4	48
SOX (1995-2014)	-4.5	0.2	40
Pharma	-2.7	0.1	48
Steel	-2.4	-0.5	48
Agriculture (1994-2014)	5.2	-1.1	48
Software & Services	1.7	-1.7	28

(1) Sector data provided by Standard and Poors (2) GIC is short form for Global Industry Classification (3) Sub Sector data provided by Standard and Poors, except where marked by symbol.

VIX | Volatility Index
July 3rd to October 9th

The Chicago Board Options Exchange Market Volatility Index (VIX) is often referred to as a fear index as it measures investors' expectations of market volatility over the next thirty day period. The higher the VIX value, the greater the expectation of volatility and vice versa.

From 1990 to June 2015, the long-term average of the VIX is 19.9. In this time period, the VIX has bottomed at approximately 10 in the mid-90's, and the mid-00's. In both cases, the VIX dropped below 10 for a few days.

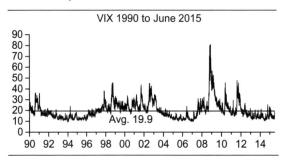

VIX 1990 to June 2015

Avg. 19.9

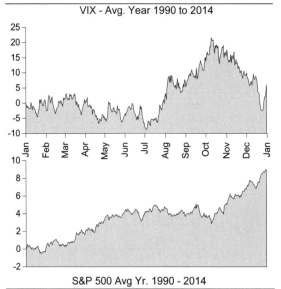

VIX - Avg. Year 1990 to 2014

S&P 500 Avg Yr. 1990 - 2014

VIX* vs. S&P 500 1990 to 2014		
		Positive
July 3 to Oct 9	S&P 500	VIX %Gain
1990	-15.1%	88.9%
1991	-0.2	5.2
1992	-2.2	47.8
1993	3.3	6.3
1994	2.0	3.9
1995	6.2	30.5
1996	3.4	13.4
1997	7.4	13.3
1998	-14.1	138.8
1999	-4.0	9.8
2000	-3.6	22.9
2001	-14.6	85.7
2002	-18.1	45.5
2003	4.5	-1.1
2004	-0.3	-0.2
2005	0.1	28.0
2006	6.3	-10.7
2007	3.0	4.7
2008	-27.9	146.6
2009	19.5	-17.3
2010	13.9	-31.2
2011	-13.8	128.1
2012	5.6	-2.6
2013	2.6	19.2
2014	-2.4	73.4
Avg	-1.5%	34.0%
Fq > 0	52%	76%

tunity for seasonal investors to adjust their portfolios in order to manage risk.

From 1990 to 2014, during the period of July 3rd to October 9th, the VIX has increased 76% of the time. On average, the VIX tends to start increasing in July, particularly after the earnings season gets underway. After mid-July, without the expectation of strong earnings ahead, investors tend to focus on the economic forecasts that often become more dire in the second half of the year. In addition, stock market analysts tend to reduce their earnings forecasts at this time. Both of these effects tend to add volatility in the markets, increasing the VIX. The VIX tends to peak in October as the stock market often starts to establishing a rising trend at this time.

Levels below 15 are often associated with investor complacency, as investors are expecting very little volatility. Very often when a stock market correction occurs in this state, it can be sharp and severe.

Knowing the trends of the VIX can be useful in adjusting the amount of risk in a portfolio. Knowing the seasonal trends of the VIX provides an annual oppor-

ⓘ * VIX - ticker symbol for the Chicago Board Options Exchange Market Volatility Index, measure implied volatility of S&P 500 index options

VIX Performance

2014

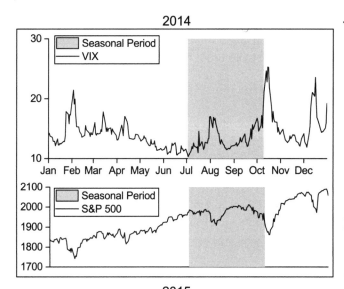

2015

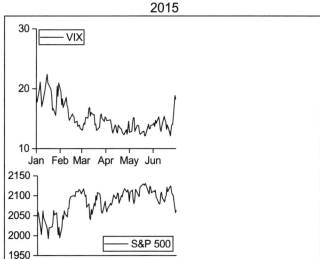

**Market Indices & Rates
Weekly Values***

Stock Markets	2013	2014
Dow	15,008	16,957
S&P500	1,619	1,973
Nasdaq	3,448	4,453
TSX	12,156	15,194
FTSE	6,328	6,819
DAX	7,905	9,937
Nikkei	14,067	15,329
Hang Seng	20,532	23,455

Commodities	2013	2014
Oil	100.51	104.81
Gold	1242.0	1321.2

Bond Yields	2013	2014
USA 5 Yr Treasury	1.45	1.68
USA 10 Yr T	2.56	2.60
USA 20 Yr T	3.25	3.16
Moody's Aaa	4.33	4.23
Moody's Baa	5.36	4.80
CAN 5 Yr T	1.80	1.58
CAN 10 Yr T	2.45	2.29

Money Market	2013	2014
USA Fed Funds	0.25	0.25
USA 3 Mo T-B	0.04	0.02
CAN tgt overnight rate	1.00	1.00
CAN 3 Mo T-B	1.03	0.94

Foreign Exchange	2013	2014
EUR/USD	1.30	1.36
GBP/USD	1.51	1.71
USD/CAD	1.05	1.07
USD/JPY	100.29	101.78

JULY

M	T	W	T	F	S	S
				1	2	3
4	5	6	7	8	9	10
11	12	13	14	15	16	17
18	19	20	21	22	23	24
25	26	27	28	29	30	31

AUGUST

M	T	W	T	F	S	S
1	2	3	4	5	6	7
8	9	10	11	12	13	14
15	16	17	18	19	20	21
22	23	24	25	26	27	28
29	30	31				

SEPTEMBER

M	T	W	T	F	S	S
			1	2	3	4
5	6	7	8	9	10	11
12	13	14	15	16	17	18
19	20	21	22	23	24	25
26	27	28	29	30		

An increase in volatility typically occurs at the beginning of July, just ahead of earnings season. Despite the pickup in volatility ahead of earnings, the S&P 500 tends to perform well for the first half of the month.

In 2014, volatility was consistently trending down from March, right up until the end of June. A rise in volatility occurred right on seasonal cue in July and then continued to increase during its seasonal period and spiked at the end.

In 2015, volatility followed a similar pattern, decreasing from the beginning of the year. The difference compared to the previous year, is that volatility spiked at the end of June, just ahead of its seasonal period when it typically increases.

GOLD SHINES

(Metal)   Gold (Metal) Outperforms – July 12th to October 9th

For many years, gold was thought to be a dead investment. It was only the "gold bugs" that espoused the virtues of investing in the precious metal. Investors were mesmerized with technology stocks, and central bankers confident of their currencies, were selling gold, "left, right and center."

3.8% gain & positive 68% of the time

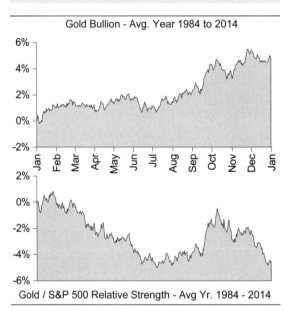

Gold Bullion - Avg. Year 1984 to 2014

Gold / S&P 500 Relative Strength - Avg Yr. 1984 - 2014

Gold (Metal) London PM* vs S&P 500
1984 to 2014

| Jul 12 to | | Positive | |
Oct 9th	S&P 500	Gold	Diff
1984	7.4 %	0.5 %	-6.9 %
1985	-5.4	4.1	9.5
1986	-2.6	25.2	27.8
1987	0.9	3.9	3.0
1988	2.8	-7.5	-10.3
1989	9.4	-4.2	-13.6
1990	-15.5	12.1	27.6
1991	0.0	-2.9	-2.8
1992	-2.9	0.4	3.3
1993	2.7	-8.8	-11.5
1994	1.6	1.6	0.0
1995	4.3	-0.1	-4.3
1996	7.9	-0.4	-8.3
1997	5.9	4.4	-1.5
1998	-15.5	2.8	18.2
1999	-4.8	25.6	30.4
2000	-5.3	-4.5	0.8
2001	-10.5	8.4	18.8
2002	-16.2	1.7	17.9
2003	4.1	7.8	3.8
2004	0.8	3.8	2.9
2005	-1.9	11.4	13.4
2006	6.1	-8.8	-14.9
2007	3.1	11.0	8.0
2008	-26.6	-8.2	18.4
2009	21.9	15.2	- 6.7
2010	8.1	11.0	2.9
2011	-12.4	6.2	18.6
2012	7.5	12.5	5.0
2013	-1.1	1.5	2.6
2014	-2.0	-8.1	-6.1
Avg.	-0.9 %	3.8 %	4.7 %
Fq > 0	52 %	68 %	65 %

In the early 2000's, investors started to take a shine to gold, boosting its returns. On a seasonal basis, on average from 1984 to 2014, gold has performed well relative to the stock market from July 12th to October 9th. The reasons for gold's seasonal changes in price are largely related to jewellery production and European Central banks selling cycles (see *Golden Times* strategy page).

The movement of gold stock prices, represented by the index (XAU) on the Philadelphia Exchange, coincides closely with the price of gold. Although there is a strong correlation between gold and gold stocks, there are other factors, such as company operations and hedging policies, which determine each company's price in the market. Gold has typically started its seasonal strong period a few weeks earlier than gold stocks and finished just after gold stocks have turned down.

Investors should know that gold can have a run in the month of November. Although this is a positive time for gold, producing an average gain of 1.7% and being positive 68% of the time (1984 to 2014), the trouble is in the following month. December has a history of being negative for gold, producing an average loss of 0.4% and only being positive 45% of the time. This compares with the S&P 500, which over the same time period has produced a 2% average gain and has been positive 81% of the time.

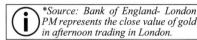

Source: Bank of England- London PM represents the close value of gold in afternoon trading in London.

Gold Bullion Performance

Gold Monthly Performance (1984-2014)

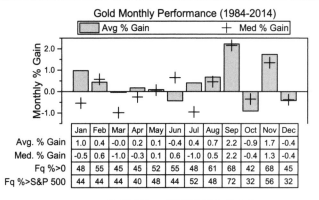

	Jan	Feb	Mar	Apr	May	Jun	Jul	Aug	Sep	Oct	Nov	Dec
Avg. % Gain	1.0	0.4	-0.0	0.2	0.1	-0.4	0.4	0.7	2.2	-0.9	1.7	-0.4
Med. % Gain	-0.5	0.6	-1.0	-0.3	0.1	0.6	-1.0	0.5	2.2	-0.4	1.3	-0.4
Fq %>0	48	55	45	45	52	55	48	61	68	42	68	45
Fq %>S&P 500	44	44	44	40	48	44	52	48	72	32	56	32

Gold 5 Year (2010-2014) % Gain

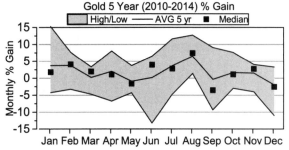

Gold Performance 2014-2015

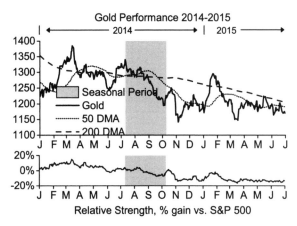

Relative Strength, % gain vs. S&P 500

Market Indices & Rates
Weekly Values**

Stock Markets	2013	2014
Dow	15,348	16,955
S&P500	1,660	1,969
Nasdaq	3,538	4,415
TSX	12,354	15,153
FTSE	6,511	6,729
DAX	8,093	9,762
Nikkei	14,396	15,275
Hang Seng	20,977	23,346

Commodities	2013	2014
Oil	104.81	102.60
Gold	1262.3	1326.8

Bond Yields	2013	2014
USA 5 Yr Treasury	1.48	1.69
USA 10 Yr T	2.64	2.57
USA 20 Yr T	3.36	3.11
Moody's Aaa	4.37	4.19
Moody's Baa	5.41	4.76
CAN 5 Yr T	1.78	1.56
CAN 10 Yr T	2.46	2.25

Money Market	2013	2014
USA Fed Funds	0.25	0.25
USA 3 Mo T-B	0.04	0.03
CAN tgt overnight rate	1.00	1.00
CAN 3 Mo T-B	1.02	0.94

Foreign Exchange	2013	2014
EUR/USD	1.30	1.36
GBP/USD	1.50	1.71
USD/CAD	1.05	1.07
USD/JPY	100.00	101.54

JULY

M	T	W	T	F	S	S
				1	2	3
4	5	6	7	8	9	10
11	12	13	14	15	16	17
18	19	20	21	22	23	24
25	26	27	28	29	30	31

AUGUST

M	T	W	T	F	S	S
1	2	3	4	5	6	7
8	9	10	11	12	13	14
15	16	17	18	19	20	21
22	23	24	25	26	27	28
29	30	31				

SEPTEMBER

M	T	W	T	F	S	S
			1	2	3	4
5	6	7	8	9	10	11
12	13	14	15	16	17	18
19	20	21	22	23	24	25
26	27	28	29	30		

From 1984 to 2014, the best month for gold bullion on an average, median and frequency basis has been September. The worst month in the same yearly period is September's contiguous month October. This juxtaposition, presents interesting challenges on an exit strategy, as it is sometimes best that investors leave the seasonal trade early. Over the last five years, August has been the best month and September one of the worst months, making an early exit the best strategy.

In 2014, gold underperformed during its seasonal period, particularly in September.

GOLDEN TIMES

(Stocks) Gold Stocks Outperform – July 27th to September 25th

Gold stocks were shunned for many years. It is only recently that interest in the sector has increased again. What few investors know is that even during the twenty year bear market in gold that started in 1981, it was possible to make money in gold stocks.

5.8% gain when the S&P 500 has been negative

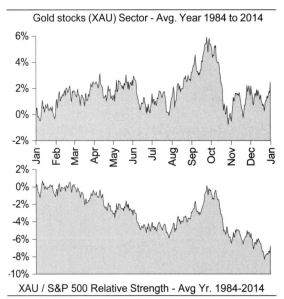

Gold stocks (XAU) Sector - Avg. Year 1984 to 2014

XAU / S&P 500 Relative Strength - Avg Yr. 1984-2014

On average from 1984 (start of the XAU index) to 2014, gold stocks as represented by the XAU index, have outperformed the S&P 500 from July 27th to September 25th. One factor that has led to a rise in the price of gold stocks in August and September is the Indian festival and wedding season that starts in October and finishes in November during Diwali. The Indian culture places a great emphasis on gold as a store of value and a lot of it is "consumed" as jewellery during the festival and wedding season. The price of gold tends to increase in the months preceding this season as the jewellery fabricators purchase gold to make their final product.

The August-September increase in gold stocks coincides with the time that a lot of investors are pulling their money out of the broad market and are looking for a place to invest. This makes gold a very attractive investment at this time of the year.

Be careful. Just as the gold stocks tend to go up in August-September, they also tend to go down in Octo-

XAU (Gold Stocks)* vs S&P 500 and Gold (1984 to 2014)

| | XAU>S&P 500 | | |
| | XAU>Gold | | |
Jul 27 to Sep 25	S&P 500	Gold	XAU
1984	10.4 %	0.3 %	20.8 %
1985	-6.1	3.6	-5.5
1986	-3.5	23.0	36.9
1987	3.5	1.9	23.0
1988	1.7	-7.2	-11.9
1989	1.8	-1.3	10.5
1990	-13.4	9.5	3.8
1991	1.6	-3.1	-11.9
1992	0.7	-2.2	-3.8
1993	1.9	-8.7	-7.3
1994	1.4	2.5	18.2
1995	3.6	-0.8	-1.0
1996	7.9	-0.7	-1.0
1997	-0.1	0.2	8.7
1998	-8.4	1.2	12.0
1999	-5.2	6.5	16.9
2000	-0.9	-2.3	-2.8
2001	-15.8	7.7	3.2
2002	-1.5	6.6	29.8
2003	0.5	7.6	11.0
2004	2.4	4.4	16.5
2005	-1.3	9.3	20.5
2006	4.6	-4.8	-11.9
2007	2.3	8.7	14.0
2008	-3.9	-3.5	-18.5
2009	6.7	4.2	6.0
2010	3.0	9.6	14.7
2011	-14.7	4.7	-13.7
2012	6.0	9.5	23.4
2013	0.1	-0.6	-5.5
2014	-0.6	-6.3	-16.4
Avg.	-0.5 %	2.6 %	5.8 %
Fq > 0	58 %	61 %	58 %

ber. Historically, this negative trend has been caused by European Central banks selling some of their gold holdings in autumn when their annual allotment of possible sales is renewed yearly. In recent years, European Central banks have reduced gold sales and have even become net buyers. This has muted gold's negative trend in October. Nevertheless, gold stocks have still underperformed. From October 1st to October 27th, for the period 1984 to 2014, XAU has produced an average loss of 5.3% and has only been positive 35% of the time.

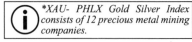

*XAU- PHLX Gold Silver Index consists of 12 precious metal mining companies.

Gold Stocks Performance

XAU Monthly Performance (1984-2014)

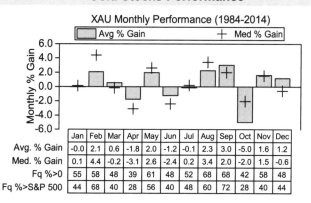

| | Avg % Gain | | | | | | | | | + | Med % Gain | |

	Jan	Feb	Mar	Apr	May	Jun	Jul	Aug	Sep	Oct	Nov	Dec
Avg. % Gain	-0.0	2.1	0.6	-1.8	2.0	-1.2	-0.1	2.3	3.0	-5.0	1.6	1.2
Med. % Gain	0.1	4.4	-0.2	-3.1	2.6	-2.4	0.2	3.4	2.0	-2.0	1.5	-0.6
Fq %>0	55	58	48	39	61	48	52	68	68	42	58	48
Fq %>S&P 500	44	68	40	28	56	40	48	60	72	28	40	44

XAU 5 Year (2010-2014) % Gain

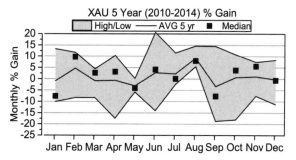

| | High/Low | —— AVG 5 yr | ■ Median |

Jan Feb Mar Apr May Jun Jul Aug Sep Oct Nov Dec

XAU Performance 2014-2015

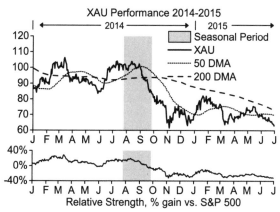

| ← 2014 → | 2015 → |

Seasonal Period
—— XAU
········· 50 DMA
— — 200 DMA

Relative Strength, % gain vs. S&P 500

Market Indices & Rates
Weekly Values**

Stock Markets	2013	2014
Dow	15,500	17,066
S&P500	1,684	1,974
Nasdaq	3,603	4,416
TSX	12,586	15,190
FTSE	6,596	6,746
DAX	8,272	9,767
Nikkei	14,653	15,331
Hang Seng	21,339	23,461

Commodities	2013	2014
Oil	106.98	101.68
Gold	1290.5	1305.4

Bond Yields	2013	2014
USA 5 Yr Treasury	1.35	1.69
USA 10 Yr T	2.54	2.53
USA 20 Yr T	3.28	3.06
Moody's Aaa	4.31	4.16
Moody's Baa	5.29	4.73
CAN 5 Yr T	1.69	1.50
CAN 10 Yr T	2.39	2.19

Money Market	2013	2014
USA Fed Funds	0.25	0.25
USA 3 Mo T-B	0.03	0.02
CAN tgt overnight rate	1.00	1.00
CAN 3 Mo T-B	1.01	0.94

Foreign Exchange	2013	2014
EUR/USD	1.31	1.36
GBP/USD	1.52	1.71
USD/CAD	1.04	1.07
USD/JPY	99.93	101.48

JULY

M	T	W	T	F	S	S
				1	2	3
4	5	6	7	8	9	10
11	12	13	14	15	16	17
18	19	20	21	22	23	24
25	26	27	28	29	30	31

AUGUST

M	T	W	T	F	S	S
1	2	3	4	5	6	7
8	9	10	11	12	13	14
15	16	17	18	19	20	21
22	23	24	25	26	27	28
29	30	31				

SEPTEMBER

M	T	W	T	F	S	S
			1	2	3	4
5	6	7	8	9	10	11
12	13	14	15	16	17	18
19	20	21	22	23	24	25
26	27	28	29	30		

From 1984 to 2014, gold stocks have outperformed in September on an average and frequency basis, but not on a median basis. February has been the best month on a median basis. Part of the reason for September's lower median return is that gold stocks tend to correct sharply before the end of September.

Over the last five years, August has been one of the strongest months and September one of the weakest, making an early exit from the seasonal strategy the best course of action.

In 2014, gold stocks corrected sharply before the end of August and then went on to perform poorly in September.

Oil stocks tend to outperform the market from July 24th to October 3rd. Earlier in the year, there is another seasonal period of outperformance from late February to early May. Although the first seasonal period has had an incredible record of outperformance, the second seasonal period in July is still noteworthy.

While the seasonal period has more to do with inventories during the switch from producing heating oil to gasoline, the second seasonal period is more related to the conversion of production from gasoline to heating oil and the effects of the hurricane season.

1.6% extra

XOI* vs. S&P 500 1984 to 2014			
	Jul 24 to Oct 3 S&P 500	Positive XOI	Diff
1984	9.1 %	9.0 %	-0.1 %
1985	-4.3	6.7	11.0
1986	-2.1	15.7	17.7
1987	6.6	-1.2	-7.8
1988	3.0	-3.6	-6.6
1989	5.6	5.7	0.1
1990	-12.4	-0.5	11.8
1991	1.3	0.7	-0.7
1992	-0.4	2.9	3.3
1993	3.2	7.8	4.6
1994	1.9	-3.6	-5.5
1995	5.2	-2.2	-7.4
1996	10.5	7.7	-2.8
1997	3.0	8.9	5.9
1998	-12.0	1.4	13.5
1999	-5.5	-2.1	3.3
2000	-3.6	12.2	15.8
2001	-10.0	-5.1	4.8
2002	2.7	7.3	4.6
2003	4.2	5.5	1.4
2004	4.2	10.9	6.7
2005	-0.6	14.3	14.9
2006	7.6	-8.5	-16.9
2007	-0.1	-4.2	-4.1
2008	-14.3	-18.1	-3.8
2009	5.0	3.0	-2.0
2010	4.0	8.5	4.5
2011	-18.3	-26.0	-7.7
2012	7.4	6.1	-1.3
2013	-0.8	-0.8	0.0
2014	-1.0	-10.8	-9.8
Avg	-0.3 %	1.5 %	1.6 %
Fq > 0	55 %	58 %	55 %

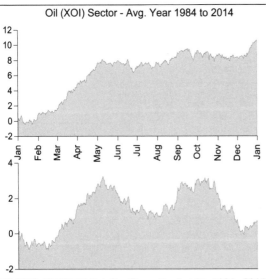

Oil (XOI) Sector - Avg. Year 1984 to 2014

Oil (XOI) / S&P 500 Relative Strength - Avg Yr. 1984 - 2014

First, there is a large difference between how heating oil and gasoline are stored and consumed. For individuals and businesses, gasoline is consumed in an immediate fashion. It is stored by the local distributor and the supplies are drawn upon as needed. Heating oil, on the other hand, is largely inventoried by individuals, farms and business operations in rural areas.

The inventory process starts before the cold weather arrives. The production facilities have to start switching from gasoline to heating oil, dropping their inventory levels and boosting prices. Second, the hurricane season can play havoc with the production of oil and drive up prices substantially. The official duration of the hurricane season in the Gulf of Mexico is from June 1st to November 30th, but most major hurricanes occur in September and early October.

The threat of a strong hurricane can shut down the oil platforms temporarily, interrupting production. If a strong hurricane strikes the platforms, it can do significant damage and put the them out of commission for an extended period of time.

(i) *NYSE Arca Oil Index (XOI): An index designed to represent a cross section of widely held oil corporations involved in various phases of the oil industry.*

For more information on the XOI index, see www.cboe.com

NYSE Arca Oil Index (XOI) Performance

XOI Monthly Performance (1984-2014)

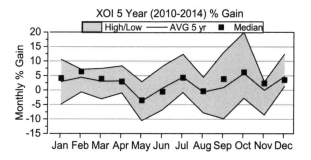

	Jan	Feb	Mar	Apr	May	Jun	Jul	Aug	Sep	Oct	Nov	Dec
Avg. % Gain	0.5	0.8	3.1	2.9	0.9	-0.9	0.7	1.0	-0.1	-0.1	-0.6	2.1
Med. % Gain	0.1	1.6	2.7	2.3	0.8	-1.8	2.2	0.5	0.0	-0.0	0.8	1.0
Fq %>0	52	55	74	81	65	39	58	58	52	48	55	65
Fq %>S&P 500	35	55	68	61	42	35	52	61	58	48	35	55

XOI 5 Year (2010-2014) % Gain

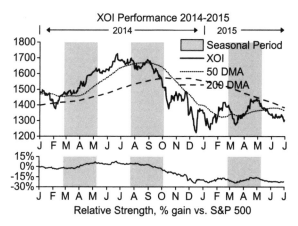

XOI Performance 2014-2015

Relative Strength, % gain vs. S&P 500

Market Indices & Rates
Weekly Values**

Stock Markets	2013	2014
Dow	15,554	17,059
S&P500	1,691	1,982
Nasdaq	3,596	4,455
TSX	12,699	15,362
FTSE	6,597	6,787
DAX	8,314	9,708
Nikkei	14,572	15,354
Hang Seng	21,834	23,900

Commodities	2013	2014
Oil	105.93	105.66
Gold	1330.5	1303.5

Bond Yields	2013	2014
USA 5 Yr Treasury	1.36	1.69
USA 10 Yr T	2.57	2.49
USA 20 Yr T	3.30	3.01
Moody's Aaa	4.34	4.12
Moody's Baa	5.25	4.68
CAN 5 Yr T	1.71	1.48
CAN 10 Yr T	2.43	2.13

Money Market	2013	2014
USA Fed Funds	0.25	0.25
USA 3 Mo T-B	0.03	0.03
CAN tgt overnight rate	1.00	1.00
CAN 3 Mo T-B	1.00	0.94

Foreign Exchange	2013	2014
EUR/USD	1.32	1.35
GBP/USD	1.54	1.70
USD/CAD	1.03	1.08
USD/JPY	99.37	101.60

JULY

M	T	W	T	F	S	S
				1	2	3
4	5	6	7	8	9	10
11	12	13	14	15	16	17
18	19	20	21	22	23	24
25	26	27	28	29	30	31

AUGUST

M	T	W	T	F	S	S
1	2	3	4	5	6	7
8	9	10	11	12	13	14
15	16	17	18	19	20	21
22	23	24	25	26	27	28
29	30	31				

SEPTEMBER

M	T	W	T	F	S	S
			1	2	3	4
5	6	7	8	9	10	11
12	13	14	15	16	17	18
19	20	21	22	23	24	25
26	27	28	29	30		

From 1984 to 2014, oil stocks have had a secondary seasonal period from late July to early October. The returns in this secondary seasonal period have largely been focused in August.

Over the last five years, the returns in the secondary seasonal period have been positive, but August has been a weaker month.

In 2014, oil stocks declined during the secondary seasonal period, with September being the weakest month in the period. At the end of the seasonal period, oil stocks continued to decline until mid-December.

Seasonal Investment Timeline[1]

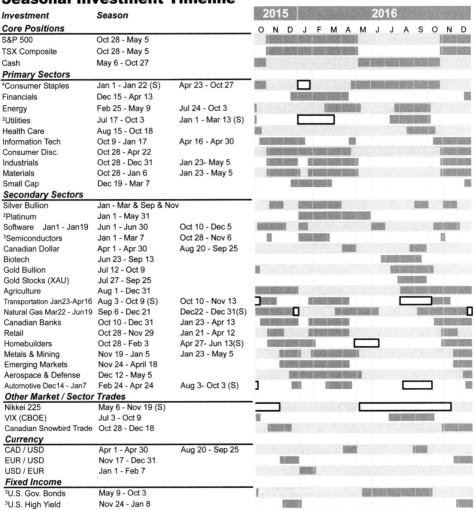

Investment	Season		2015 → 2016 (O N D J F M A M J J A S O N D)
Core Positions			
S&P 500	Oct 28 - May 5		
TSX Composite	Oct 28 - May 5		
Cash	May 6 - Oct 27		
Primary Sectors			
[4]Consumer Staples	Jan 1 - Jan 22 (S)	Apr 23 - Oct 27	
Financials	Dec 15 - Apr 13		
Energy	Feb 25 - May 9	Jul 24 - Oct 3	
[2]Utilities	Jul 17 - Oct 3	Jan 1 - Mar 13 (S)	
Health Care	Aug 15 - Oct 18		
Information Tech	Oct 9 - Jan 17	Apr 16 - Apr 30	
Consumer Disc.	Oct 28 - Apr 22		
Industrials	Oct 28 - Dec 31	Jan 23- May 5	
Materials	Oct 28 - Jan 6	Jan 23 - May 5	
Small Cap	Dec 19 - Mar 7		
Secondary Sectors			
Silver Bullion	Jan - Mar & Sep & Nov		
[2]Platinum	Jan 1 - May 31		
Software Jan1 - Jan19	Jun 1 - Jun 30	Oct 10 - Dec 5	
[3]Semiconductors	Jan 1 - Mar 7	Oct 28 - Nov 6	
Canadian Dollar	Apr 1 - Apr 30	Aug 20 - Sep 25	
Biotech	Jun 23 - Sep 13		
Gold Bullion	Jul 12 - Oct 9		
Gold Stocks (XAU)	Jul 27 - Sep 25		
Agriculture	Aug 1 - Dec 31		
Transportation Jan23-Apr16	Aug 3 - Oct 9 (S)	Oct 10 - Nov 13	
Natural Gas Mar22 - Jun19	Sep 6 - Dec 21	Dec22 - Dec 31(S)	
Canadian Banks	Oct 10 - Dec 31	Jan 23 - Apr 13	
Retail	Oct 28 - Nov 29	Jan 21 - Apr 12	
Homebuilders	Oct 28 - Feb 3	Apr 27- Jun 13(S)	
Metals & Mining	Nov 19 - Jan 5	Jan 23 - May 5	
Emerging Markets	Nov 24 - April 18		
Aerospace & Defense	Dec 12 - May 5		
Automotive Dec14 - Jan7	Feb 24 - Apr 24	Aug 3- Oct 3 (S)	
Other Market / Sector Trades			
Nikkei 225	May 6 - Nov 19 (S)		
VIX (CBOE)	Jul 3 - Oct 9		
Canadian Snowbird Trade	Oct 28 - Dec 18		
Currency			
CAD / USD	Apr 1 - Apr 30	Aug 20 - Sep 25	
EUR / USD	Nov 17 - Dec 31		
USD / EUR	Jan 1 - Feb 7		
Fixed Income			
[3]U.S. Gov. Bonds	May 9 - Oct 3		
[3]U.S. High Yield	Nov 24 - Jan 8		

Long Investment ▓▓▓▓   Short Investment (S) ▭   [1] Holiday, End of Month, Witches' Hangover, - et al not included.
[2]Thackray's 2012 Investor's Guide [3]Thackray's 2013 Investor's Guide [4]Thackray's 2014 Investor's Guide [5]Thackray's 2015 Investor's Guide

Seasonal Investment Timeline[1]

Investment Stocks	Season		2015	2016
			O N D J F M A M J J A S O N D	

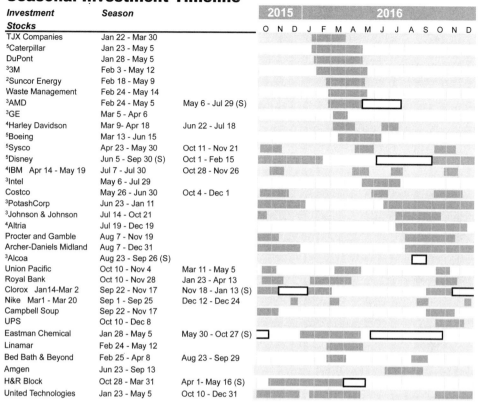

Investment Stocks	Season	
TJX Companies	Jan 22 - Mar 30	
[5]Caterpillar	Jan 23 - May 5	
DuPont	Jan 28 - May 5	
[3]3M	Feb 3 - May 12	
[2]Suncor Energy	Feb 18 - May 9	
Waste Management	Feb 24 - May 14	
[3]AMD	Feb 24 - May 5	May 6 - Jul 29 (S)
[3]GE	Mar 5 - Apr 6	
[4]Harley Davidson	Mar 9- Apr 18	Jun 22 - Jul 18
[5]Boeing	Mar 13 - Jun 15	
[5]Sysco	Apr 23 - May 30	Oct 11 - Nov 21
[5]Disney	Jun 5 - Sep 30 (S)	Oct 1 - Feb 15
[4]IBM Apr 14 - May 19	Jul 7 - Jul 30	Oct 28 - Nov 26
[3]Intel	May 6 - Jul 29	
Costco	May 26 - Jun 30	Oct 4 - Dec 1
[3]PotashCorp	Jun 23 - Jan 11	
[3]Johnson & Johnson	Jul 14 - Oct 21	
[4]Altria	Jul 19 - Dec 19	
Procter and Gamble	Aug 7 - Nov 19	
Archer-Daniels Midland	Aug 7 - Dec 31	
[3]Alcoa	Aug 23 - Sep 26 (S)	
Union Pacific	Oct 10 - Nov 4	Mar 11 - May 5
Royal Bank	Oct 10 - Nov 28	Jan 23 - Apr 13
Clorox Jan14-Mar 2	Sep 22 - Nov 17	Nov 18 - Jan 13 (S)
Nike Mar1 - Mar 20	Sep 1 - Sep 25	Dec 12 - Dec 24
Campbell Soup	Sep 22 - Nov 17	
UPS	Oct 10 - Dec 8	
Eastman Chemical	Jan 28 - May 5	May 30 - Oct 27 (S)
Linamar	Feb 24 - May 12	
Bed Bath & Beyond	Feb 25 - Apr 8	Aug 23 - Sep 29
Amgen	Jun 23 - Sep 13	
H&R Block	Oct 28 - Mar 31	Apr 1- May 16 (S)
United Technologies	Jan 23 - May 5	Oct 10 - Dec 31

Long Investment ▨▨▨▨   Short Investment (S) ☐☐☐☐   [1] Holiday, End of Month, Witches' Hangover, - et al not included.

[2]Thackray's 2012 Investor's Guide [3]Thackray's 2013 Investor's Guide [4]Thackray's 2014 Investor's Guide [5]Thackray's 2015 Investor's Guide

AUGUST

	MONDAY	TUESDAY	WEDNESDAY
WEEK 32	**1** 30 CAN Market Closed- Civic Day	**2** 29	**3** 28
WEEK 33	**8** 23	**9** 22	**10** 21
WEEK 34	**15** 16	**16** 15	**17** 14
WEEK 35	**22** 9	**23** 8	**24** 7
WEEK 36	**29** 2	**30** 1	**31**

THURSDAY	FRIDAY
4 27	**5** 26
11 20	**12** 19
18 13	**19** 12
25 6	**26** 5
1	2

SEPTEMBER

M	T	W	T	F	S	S
			1	2	3	4
5	6	7	8	9	10	11
12	13	14	15	16	17	18
19	20	21	22	23	24	25
26	27	28	29	30		

OCTOBER

M	T	W	T	F	S	S
					1	2
3	4	5	6	7	8	9
10	11	12	13	14	15	16
17	18	19	20	21	22	23
19	20	26	27	28	29	30
31						

NOVEMBER

M	T	W	T	F	S	S
	1	2	3	4	5	6
7	8	9	10	11	12	13
14	15	16	17	18	19	20
21	22	23	24	25	26	27
28	29	30				

DECEMBER

M	T	W	T	F	S	S
			1	2	3	4
5	6	7	8	9	10	11
12	13	14	15	16	17	18
19	20	21	22	23	24	25
26	27	28	29	30	31	

AUGUST
S U M M A R Y

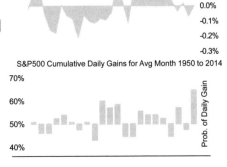

S&P500 Cumulative Daily Gains for Avg Month 1950 to 2014

	Dow Jones	S&P 500	Nasdaq	TSX Comp
Month Rank	10	9	11	10
# Up	37	36	23	17
# Down	28	29	20	13
% Pos	57	55	52	57
% Avg. Gain	-0.1	0.0	0.2	-0.1

Dow & S&P 1950-2014, Nasdaq 1972-2014 TSX 1985-2014

♦ August is typically a marginal month and has been the fourth worst month for the S&P 500 from 1950 to 2014, producing a flat return of 0.0%. ♦ If there is a summer rally in July, it is often in jeopardy in August. ♦ In July 2014, the S&P 500's rally faded at the beginning of August, but came back to life in the second week. In August, the S&P 500 ended producing a gain of 3.8% ♦ The TSX Composite is usually one of the better performing markets in August, but the strength of the market is largely dependent on oil and gold stocks.

BEST / WORST AUGUST BROAD MKTS. 2005-2014

BEST AUGUST MARKETS
- ♦ FTSE 100 (2009) 6.5%
- ♦ Russell 2000 (2014) 4.8%
- ♦ Nasdaq (2014) 4.8%

WORST AUGUST MARKETS
- ♦ Nikkei 225 (2011) -8.9%
- ♦ Russell 2000 (2011) -8.8%
- ♦ Russell 2000 (2010) -7.5%

Index Values End of Month

	2005	2006	2007	2008	2009	2010	2011	2012	2013	2014
Dow	10,482	11,381	13,358	11,544	9,496	10,015	11,614	13,091	14,810	17,098
S&P 500	1,220	1,304	1,474	1,283	1,021	1,049	1,219	1,407	1,633	2,003
Nasdaq	2,152	2,184	2,596	2,368	2,009	2,114	2,579	3,067	3,590	4,580
TSX Comp.	10,669	12,074	13,660	13,771	10,868	11,914	12,769	11,949	12,654	15,626
Russell 1000	1,275	1,360	1,540	1,350	1,073	1,110	1,297	1,490	1,748	2,149
Russell 2000	1,656	1,791	1,970	1,838	1,422	1,496	1,806	2,018	2,512	2,919
FTSE 100	5,297	5,906	6,303	5,637	4,909	5,225	5,395	5,712	6,413	6,820
Nikkei 225	12,414	16,141	16,569	13,073	10,493	8,824	8,955	8,840	13,389	15,425

Percent Gain for August

	2005	2006	2007	2008	2009	2010	2011	2012	2013	2014
Dow	-1.5	1.7	1.1	1.5	3.5	-4.3	-4.4	0.6	-4.4	3.2
S&P 500	-1.1	2.1	1.3	1.2	3.4	-4.7	-5.7	2.0	-3.1	3.8
Nasdaq	-1.5	4.4	2.0	1.8	1.5	-6.2	-6.4	4.3	-1.0	4.8
TSX Comp.	2.4	2.1	-1.5	1.3	0.8	1.7	-1.4	2.4	1.3	1.9
Russell 1000	-1.1	2.2	1.1	1.2	3.4	-4.7	-6.0	2.2	-3.0	3.9
Russell 2000	-1.9	2.8	2.2	3.5	2.8	-7.5	-8.8	3.2	-3.3	4.8
FTSE 100	0.3	-0.4	-0.9	4.2	6.5	-0.6	-7.2	1.4	-3.1	1.3
Nikkei 225	4.3	4.4	-3.9	-2.3	1.3	-7.5	-8.9	1.7	-2.0	-1.3

August Market Avg. Performance 2005 to 2014[1]

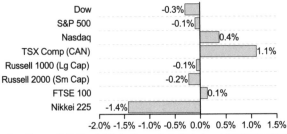

Dow	-0.3%
S&P 500	-0.1%
Nasdaq	0.4%
TSX Comp (CAN)	1.1%
Russell 1000 (Lg Cap)	-0.1%
Russell 2000 (Sm Cap)	-0.2%
FTSE 100	0.1%
Nikkei 225	-1.4%

Interest Corner Aug[2]

	Fed Funds %[3]	3 Mo. T-Bill %[4]	10 Yr %[5]	20 Yr %[6]
2014	0.25	0.03	2.35	2.83
2013	0.25	0.03	2.78	3.46
2012	0.25	0.09	1.57	2.29
2011	0.25	0.02	2.23	3.19
2010	0.25	0.14	2.47	3.23

(1) Russell Data provided by Russell (2) Federal Reserve Bank of St. Louis- end of month values (3) Target rate set by FOMC (4)(5)(6) Constant yield maturities.

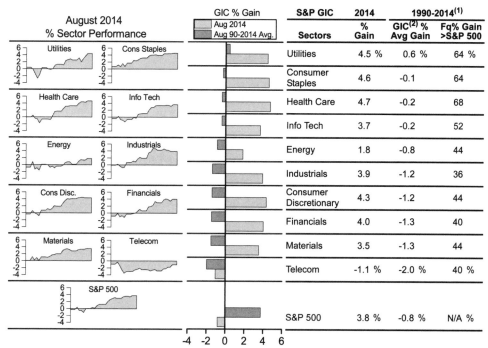

S&P GIC Sectors	2014 % Gain	1990-2014[1] GIC[2] % Avg Gain	1990-2014[1] Fq% Gain >S&P 500
Utilities	4.5 %	0.6 %	64 %
Consumer Staples	4.6	-0.1	64
Health Care	4.7	-0.2	68
Info Tech	3.7	-0.2	52
Energy	1.8	-0.8	44
Industrials	3.9	-1.2	36
Consumer Discretionary	4.3	-1.2	44
Financials	4.0	-1.3	40
Materials	3.5	-1.3	44
Telecom	-1.1 %	-2.0 %	40 %
S&P 500	3.8 %	-0.8 %	N/A %

Sector Commentary

♦ In August 2014, all of the major sectors gained ground except the telecom sector which produced a loss of 1.1%. ♦ The biggest gaining sector was the health care sector, which was supported by mergers and acquisitions. ♦ The consumer staples and discretionary sectors were also big winners in August, based upon strong retail numbers. ♦ The utilities sector also performed well, producing a gain of 4.5%. Although the utilities sector typically performs well in August, the sector was surprisingly strong given the strong performance of the S&P 500. Typically, when the S&P 500 produces a strong gain, the utilities sector does not outperform it.

Sub-Sector Commentary

♦ Biotech produced a very strong gain of 10.3% in August as it continued its strong run from July. ♦ The homebuilders sector snapped back after a large loss in July, to produce a gain of 7.2%. ♦ Agriculture started its seasonal run on a positive note with a gain of 7.5%. ♦ Gold was flat for the month and silver produced a loss of 5.9%.

SELECTED SUB-SECTORS[3]

Biotech (1993-2014)	10.3 %	1.0 %	64 %
Gold (London PM)	0.0	0.6	48
Agriculture (1994-2014)	7.5	0.6	52
Home-builders	7.2	0.1	56
SOX (1995-2014)	6.2	-0.3	50
Pharma	3.5	-0.3	60
Silver	-5.9	-0.4	48
Retail	8.3	-0.4	60
Software & Services	2.5	-0.6	56
Metals & Mining	2.5	-1.1	48
Banks	2.8	-1.2	36
Chemicals	3.8	-1.5	44
Railroads	5.9	-2.2	44
Transportation	4.2	-2.7	32
Steel	8.9	-3.4	48

(1) Sector data provided by Standard and Poors (2) GIC is short form for Global Industry Classification (3) Sub Sector data provided by Standard and Poors, except where marked by symbol.

ARCHER-DANIELS-MIDLAND
PLANT YOUR SEEDS FOR GROWTH
August 7th to December 31st

The agriculture sector generally performs well in the last five months of the year and ADM is no exception. If you had to choose just one part of the year in which to invest in ADM, it would have to be the last five months. From August 7th to December 31st, for the years 1990 to 2014, ADM produced an average gain of 13.7% and was positive 84% of the time.

13.7% gain & positive 84% of the time positive

The business of "growing" really takes place in the last part of the year. This is the harvest season for the northern hemisphere and the time when cash flows in the agriculture business. As a result, investors are much more interested in committing money to the agriculture sector.

Aug 7 to Dec 31	S&P 500	ADM	Diff
1990	-1.3%	0.1%	1.3%
1991	6.8	41.1	34.3
1992	3.6	3.1	-0.5
1993	4.0	1.7	-2.3
1994	0.5	31.9	31.4
1995	10.2	17.2	7.0
1996	11.8	27.5	15.6
1997	1.1	1.2	0.2
1998	12.8	9.4	-3.4
1999	13.0	-9.8	-22.8
2000	-9.8	58.5	68.2
2001	-4.4	14.6	19.0
2002	2.4	13.6	11.2
2003	15.0	16.7	1.7
2004	13.9	42.9	29.0
2005	1.8	18.7	16.9
2006	10.9	-21.9	-32.7
2007	0.1	34.5	34.5
2008	-29.9	5.4	35.3
2009	11.8	9.3	-2.6
2010	12.1	-0.3	-12.5
2011	4.9	-0.1	-5.0
2012	2.3	8.3	6.0
2013	8.9	14.5	5.7
2014	7.2	6.9	-0.3
Avg	4.4%	13.7%	9.4%
Fq > 0	84%	84%	64%

ADM* vs. S&P 500 1990 to 2014 — Positive

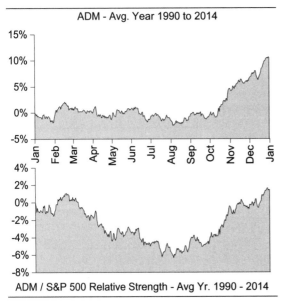

ADM - Avg. Year 1990 to 2014

ADM / S&P 500 Relative Strength - Avg Yr. 1990 - 2014

On the other hand, the first seven months leading up to the favorable season (January 1st to August 6th) has produced an average loss of 2.4% and has only been positive 44% of the time.

Investors should avoid investing in ADM for the first seven months of the year. In fact, shorting ADM during the first seven months of the year and then switching to a long position for the last five months has proven to be a profitable strategy.

Seasonal investors can take advantage of the growing interest in the agriculture sector in the second half of the year by investing at the beginning of August. The idea is to get in before everyone else and get out when interest in the sector is at a maximum, towards the end of the year.

Investing in ADM for the last five months of the year has produced very strong results over the long-term.

(i) *ADM - stock symbol for Archer-Daniels-Midland which trades on the NYSE. Archer-Daniels-Midland Company engages in the manufacture and sale of protein meal, vegetable oil, corn sweeteners, flour, biodiesel, ethanol, and other value-added food and feed ingredients. Data adjusted for stock splits.*

ADM Performance

ADM Monthly Performance (1990-2014)

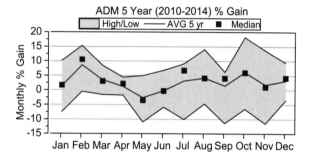

	Jan	Feb	Mar	Apr	May	Jun	Jul	Aug	Sep	Oct	Nov	Dec
Avg. % Gain	-0.8	1.4	-0.7	-1.4	2.4	-1.6	-0.6	0.7	0.0	5.3	2.9	3.3
Med. % Gain	-2.8	0.8	-1.6	0.6	3.3	-1.8	0.8	1.0	1.4	4.9	1.1	2.6
Fq %>0	36	56	40	52	60	40	52	56	56	72	56	60
Fq %>S&P 500	36	56	28	36	60	24	48	56	56	76	48	52

ADM 5 Year (2010-2014) % Gain

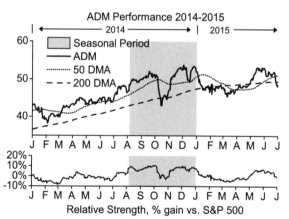

ADM Performance 2014-2015

Relative Strength, % gain vs. S&P 500

WEEK 31

Market Indices & Rates
Weekly Values**

Stock Markets	2013	2014
Dow	15,566	16,766
S&P500	1,695	1,955
Nasdaq	3,641	4,415
TSX	12,587	15,393
FTSE	6,616	6,756
DAX	8,325	9,493
Nikkei	13,934	15,588
Hang Seng	21,994	24,618

Commodities	2013	2014
Oil	105.50	99.79
Gold	1318.5	1295.0

Bond Yields	2013	2014
USA 5 Yr Treasury	1.40	1.73
USA 10 Yr T	2.64	2.53
USA 20 Yr T	3.38	3.03
Moody's Aaa	4.42	4.13
Moody's Baa	5.32	4.72
CAN 5 Yr T	1.78	1.49
CAN 10 Yr T	2.50	2.13

Money Market	2013	2014
USA Fed Funds	0.25	0.25
USA 3 Mo T-B	0.04	0.03
CAN tgt overnight rate	1.00	1.00
CAN 3 Mo T-B	1.00	0.95

Foreign Exchange	2013	2014
EUR/USD	1.33	1.34
GBP/USD	1.52	1.69
USD/CAD	1.03	1.09
USD/JPY	98.47	102.44

AUGUST

M	T	W	T	F	S	S
1	2	3	4	5	6	7
8	9	10	11	12	13	14
15	16	17	18	19	20	21
22	23	24	25	26	27	28
29	30	31				

SEPTEMBER

M	T	W	T	F	S	S
			1	2	3	4
5	6	7	8	9	10	11
12	13	14	15	16	17	18
19	20	21	22	23	24	25
26	27	28	29	30		

Although ADM's period of seasonal strength starts in August, the real sweet spot of the trade starts in October, which is its strongest month of the year on an average, median and frequency basis. On an average and median basis, November and December are also strong months.

Over the last five years, the dispersion between the maximum and minimum monthly returns has been large, but the overall seasonal strategy has been positive.

In 2014, the seasonal strategy for ADM was positive, despite a dip in October when the S&P 500 also corrected sharply.

OCTOBER

M	T	W	T	F	S	S
					1	2
3	4	5	6	7	8	9
10	11	12	13	14	15	16
17	18	19	20	21	22	23
24	25	26	27	28	29	30
31						

TRANSPORTATION— ON A ROLL

①LONG (Jan23-Apr16) ②SELL SHORT (Aug1-Oct9) ③LONG (Oct10-Nov13)

The transportation sector can provide a "hilly" ride as the seasonal trends rise and fall throughout the year.

Activity in the transportation sub-sectors in rails, airlines and freight, tends to bottom in February.

16.9% gain & positive 92% of the time

Increased transportation activity in the spring, coupled with a typically positive economic outlook in the first part of the year, creates a positive seasonal trend, starting January 23rd and lasting until April 16th.

The next seasonal period is a weak period, giving investors an opportunity to sell short the sector and profit from its decline. This negative seasonal period lasts from August 1st to October 9th and is largely the result of investors questioning economic growth at this time of the year.

The third seasonal period is positive and occurs from October 10th to November 13th. This trend is the result of a generally improved economic outlook at this time of the year and investors wanting to get into the sector ahead of earnings announcements.

The SP GICS Transportation Sector encompasses a wide range transportation based companies. For more information, see www.standardandpoors.com

Transportation Sector* vs. S&P 500 1990 to 2014

Negative Short ☐ Positive Long ▒

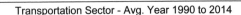

Year	Jan 23 to Apr 16 S&P 500	Jan 23 to Apr 16 Trans port	Aug 1 to Oct 9 S&P 500	Aug 1 to Oct 9 Trans port	Oct 10 to Nov 13 S&P 500	Oct 10 to Nov 13 Trans port	Compound Growth S&P 500	Compound Growth Trans port
1990	4.4 %	4.1 %	-14.3 %	-19.2 %	4.1	3.3 %	-6.9 %	28.1 %
1991	18.1	11.4	-2.8	0.5	5.5	9.6	21.0	21.5
1992	-0.5	3.7	-5.1	-9.1	4.9	14.1	-0.9	29.1
1993	2.9	9.1	2.7	-0.3	1.1	6.4	6.9	16.5
1994	-6.0	-10.7	-0.7	-9.3	1.6	0.8	-5.2	-1.6
1995	9.6	10.5	2.9	-1.3	2.4	5.0	15.5	17.6
1996	5.2	9.4	8.9	4.9	4.9	6.1	20.1	10.4
1997	-2.9	-2.0	1.7	0.9	-5.6	-5.4	-6.7	-8.2
1998	15.1	12.2	-12.2	-16.5	14.4	12.5	15.6	47.0
1999	7.7	17.7	0.6	-11.0	4.5	4.0	13.1	35.8
2000	-5.9	-2.7	-2.0	-6.0	-3.6	13.0	-11.1	16.6
2001	12.2	0.1	-12.8	-20.0	7.8	14.1	-17.4	37.0
2002	0.8	6.9	-14.8	-11.2	13.6	8.2	-2.4	28.6
2003	0.2	0.6	4.9	4.9	1.9	8.0	7.1	3.3
2004	-0.8	-2.9	1.9	6.6	5.5	11.1	6.6	0.7
2005	-2.2	-5.1	-3.1	-0.5	3.3	9.0	-2.1	3.9
2006	2.2	13.2	5.8	6.4	2.5	3.8	10.8	9.9
2007	3.2	4.8	7.6	-0.2	-5.4	-2.9	5.0	1.9
2008	4.1	19.1	-28.2	-23.5	0.2	4.0	-25.1	52.9
2009	4.6	7.2	8.5	6.7	2.1	5.9	15.8	5.9
2010	9.2	17.4	5.8	7.9	2.9	2.5	18.9	10.9
2011	2.8	2.2	-10.6	-11.8	9.4	11.4	0.6	26.9
2012	4.1	-2.0	4.5	-3.5	-4.6	-1.1	3.8	0.3
2013	5.5	3.5	-1.7	1.8	7.6	10.9	11.5	12.7
2014	1.0	1.7	-0.1	2.6	5.8	14.9	6.6	13.8
Avg.	2.8 %	5.2 %	-2.1 %	-4.0 %	3.5 %	6.7 %	4.0 %	16.9 %
Fq>0	72 %	76 %	48	40 %	84 %	88 %	64 %	92 %

Transportation Sector - Avg. Year 1990 to 2014

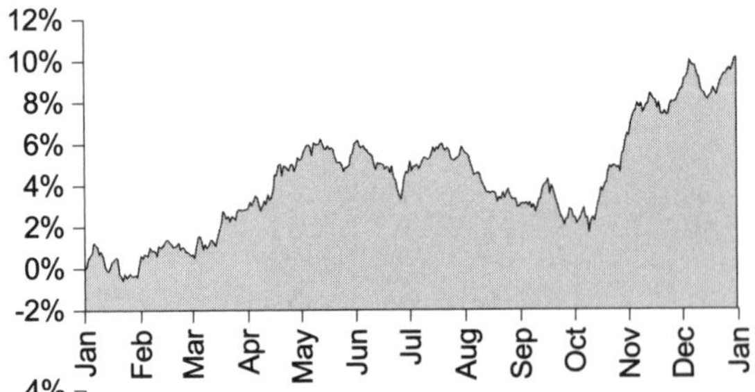

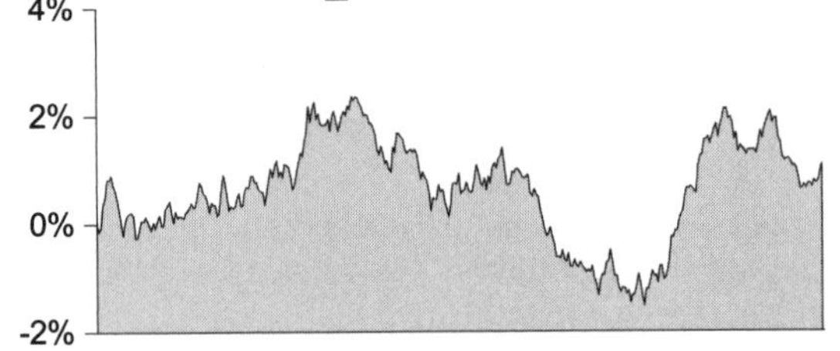

Transportation / S&P 500 Rel. Strength- Avg Yr. 1990-2014

Transportation Performance

Transportation Monthly Performance (1990-2014)

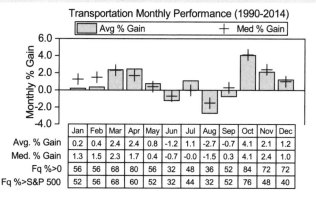

	Jan	Feb	Mar	Apr	May	Jun	Jul	Aug	Sep	Oct	Nov	Dec
Avg. % Gain	0.2	0.4	2.4	2.4	0.8	-1.2	1.1	-2.7	-0.7	4.1	2.1	1.2
Med. % Gain	1.3	1.5	2.3	1.7	0.4	-0.7	-0.0	-1.5	0.3	4.1	2.4	1.0
Fq %>0	56	56	68	80	56	32	48	36	52	84	72	72
Fq %>S&P 500	52	56	68	60	52	32	44	32	52	76	48	40

Transportation 5 Year (2010-2014) % Gain

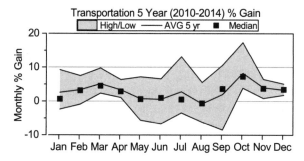

Transportation Performance 2014-2015

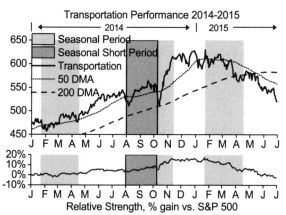

Relative Strength, % gain vs. S&P 500

WEEK 32

Market Indices & Rates
Weekly Values**

Stock Markets	2013	2014
Dow	15,505	16,473
S&P500	1,697	1,924
Nasdaq	3,668	4,360
TSX	12,494	15,176
FTSE	6,570	6,632
DAX	8,323	9,104
Nikkei	13,941	15,193
Hang Seng	21,840	24,510

Commodities	2013	2014
Oil	105.12	97.50
Gold	1295.0	1299.4

Bond Yields	2013	2014
USA 5 Yr Treasury	1.38	1.64
USA 10 Yr T	2.62	2.47
USA 20 Yr T	3.39	3.00
Moody's Aaa	4.44	4.14
Moody's Baa	5.34	4.73
CAN 5 Yr T	1.77	1.48
CAN 10 Yr T	2.50	2.09

Money Market	2013	2014
USA Fed Funds	0.25	0.25
USA 3 Mo T-B	0.05	0.03
CAN tgt overnight rate	1.00	1.00
CAN 3 Mo T-B	0.99	0.96

Foreign Exchange	2013	2014
EUR/USD	1.33	1.34
GBP/USD	1.54	1.68
USD/CAD	1.04	1.09
USD/JPY	97.05	102.28

AUGUST

M	T	W	T	F	S	S
1	2	3	4	5	6	7
8	9	10	11	12	13	14
15	16	17	18	19	20	21
22	23	24	25	26	27	28
29	30	31				

SEPTEMBER

M	T	W	T	F	S	S
			1	2	3	4
5	6	7	8	9	10	11
12	13	14	15	16	17	18
19	20	21	22	23	24	25
26	27	28	29	30		

OCTOBER

M	T	W	T	F	S	S
					1	2
3	4	5	6	7	8	9
10	11	12	13	14	15	16
17	18	19	20	21	22	23
24	25	26	27	28	29	30
31						

The transportation sector has a roller coaster seasonal trend. In the early part of the year it typically outperforms, and then underperforms in the summer, and then outperforms at the end of the year. From 1990 to 2014, October has been the best month for the transportation sector on an average, median and frequency basis.

Over the last five years, on average, generally the transportation sector has followed its seasonal pattern throughout the year.

In 2014, through the combination of ups and downs, the transportation sector outperformed the S&P 500 and in its first seasonal leg of 2015, it has underperformed.

AGRICULTURE MOOOVES
LAST 5 MONTHS OF THE YEAR – Aug to Dec

The agriculture sector has typically performed well during the last five months of the year (August to December).

This is the result of the major summer growing season in the northern hemisphere producing cash for the growers and subsequently, increasing sales for the farming suppliers.

71% of the time
better than the S&P 500

Although this sector can represent a good opportunity, investors should be wary of the wide performance swings. Out of the twenty-one cycles from 1994 to 2014, during August to December, there have been six years with absolute returns greater than +25% or less than -25%, and eleven years of returns greater than +10% or less than -10%. In other words, this sector is very volatile.

Agriculture* vs. S&P 500 1994 to 2014

Aug 1 to Dec 31	S&P 500	Positive		
		Agri	Diff	
1994	0.2 %	8.0 %	7.8 %	
1995	9.6	31.7	22.1	
1996	15.8	30.2	14.5	
1997	1.7	14.7	13.0	
1998	9.7	-3.4	-13.1	
1999	10.6	-2.6	-13.2	
2000	-7.7	68.0	75.7	
2001	-5.2	12.5	17.7	
2002	-3.5	6.0	9.5	
2003	12.3	15.8	3.6	
2004	10.0	44.6	34.6	
2005	1.1	7.5	6.4	
2006	11.1	-27.4	-38.5	
2007	0.9	38.2	37.3	
2008	-28.7	0.7	29.4	
2009	12.9	4.0	-9.0	
2010	14.2	9.9	-4.2	
2011	-2.7	-5.9	-3.2	
2012	3.4	5.0	1.6	
2013	9.7	19.0	9.4	
2014	6.6	12.1	5.4	
Avg.	3.9 %	13.7 %	9.8 %	
Fq > 0	76 %	81 %	71 %	

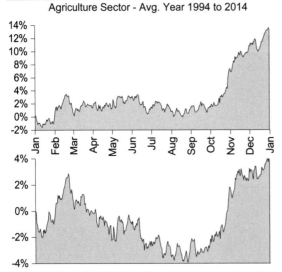

Agriculture Sector - Avg. Year 1994 to 2014

Agriculture / S&P 500 Relative Strength - Avg Yr. 1994-2014

On a year by year basis, the agriculture sector produced its biggest gain during its seasonally strong period in 2000, producing a gain of 68%. It is interesting to note that this is the same year that the technology sector's bubble burst.

After realizing that technology stocks were not going to grow to the sky, investors started to have an epiphany– that the world might be running out of food and

as a result, interest in the agriculture sector started to pick up.

In the second half of 2006, the agriculture sector corrected after a strong run in the first half of the year. In 2007 and the first half of 2008, the agriculture sector once again rocketed upwards due to the increase in prices of agricultural products.

Although food prices have had some reprieve with the global slowdown, the world population is still increasing and imbalances in food supply and demand will continue to exist in the future.

Investors should consider "moooving" into the agriculture sector for the last five months of the year.

*The SP GICS Agriculture Sector # 30202010
For more information on the agriculture sector, see www.standardandpoors.com

Agriculture Performance

Agriculture Monthly Performance (1994-2014)

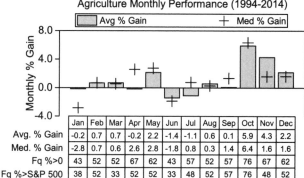

	Jan	Feb	Mar	Apr	May	Jun	Jul	Aug	Sep	Oct	Nov	Dec
Avg. % Gain	-0.2	0.7	0.7	-0.2	2.2	-1.4	-1.1	0.6	0.1	5.9	4.3	2.2
Med. % Gain	-2.8	0.7	0.6	2.6	2.8	-1.8	0.8	0.3	1.4	6.4	1.6	1.6
Fq %>0	43	52	52	67	62	43	57	52	57	76	67	62
Fq %>S&P 500	38	52	33	52	52	33	48	52	57	76	48	52

Agriculture 5 Year (2010-2014) % Gain

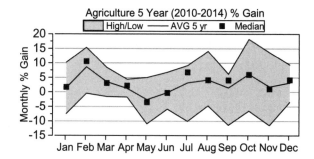

Agriculture Performance 2014-2015

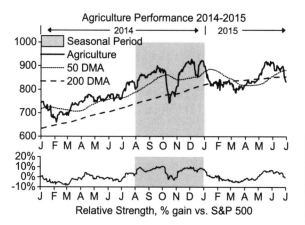

Relative Strength, % gain vs. S&P 500

Market Indices & Rates
Weekly Values**

Stock Markets	2013	2014
Dow	15,280	16,632
S&P500	1,677	1,946
Nasdaq	3,647	4,429
TSX	12,663	15,279
FTSE	6,551	6,659
DAX	8,396	9,153
Nikkei	13,768	15,228
Hang Seng	22,467	24,796

Commodities	2013	2014
Oil	106.92	97.19
Gold	1339.0	1308.9

Bond Yields	2013	2014
USA 5 Yr Treasury	1.50	1.59
USA 10 Yr T	2.73	2.41
USA 20 Yr T	3.50	2.95
Moody's Aaa	4.56	4.08
Moody's Baa	5.44	4.71
CAN 5 Yr T	1.89	1.52
CAN 10 Yr T	2.63	2.07

Money Market	2013	2014
USA Fed Funds	0.25	0.25
USA 3 Mo T-B	0.05	0.04
CAN tgt overnight rate	1.00	1.00
CAN 3 Mo T-B	0.99	0.96

Foreign Exchange	2013	2014
EUR/USD	1.33	1.34
GBP/USD	1.55	1.67
USD/CAD	1.03	1.09
USD/JPY	97.63	102.34

AUGUST

M	T	W	T	F	S	S
1	2	3	4	5	6	7
8	9	10	11	12	13	14
15	16	17	18	19	20	21
22	23	24	25	26	27	28
29	30	31				

SEPTEMBER

M	T	W	T	F	S	S
			1	2	3	4
5	6	7	8	9	10	11
12	13	14	15	16	17	18
19	20	21	22	23	24	25
26	27	28	29	30		

OCTOBER

M	T	W	T	F	S	S
					1	2
3	4	5	6	7	8	9
10	11	12	13	14	15	16
17	18	19	20	21	22	23
24	25	26	27	28	29	30
31						

From 1994 to 2014, October has been the sweet spot for the agriculture seasonal trade. On an average, median and frequency basis, October has also been the best month of the year over the same yearly period.

Over the last five years, on average, the general trend provided nominal seasonal benefits. The big anomaly was the sector's strong performance in May on an average and median basis.

In 2014, the agriculture sector produced a positive performance and outperformed the S&P 500. At the end of its seasonal period, the agriculture sector started to underperform.

AMGEN
June 23rd to September 13th

Biotech has a period of seasonal strength from June 23rd to September 13th (see *Biotech Summer Solstice* strategy). Amgen is considered one of the major biotech companies and has a similar seasonal trend. Amgen has an additional benefit during the biotech seasonal period, as it typically releases its second quarter earnings towards the end of July. This gives Amgen a seasonal boost as investors buy Amgen ahead of their earnings in anticipation of any possible good news.

Strong earnings are particularly welcome in the second quarter, as the first quarter tends to be the weakest quarter of the year for Amgen. The first quarter of the year tends to be weak due to slower sales and the effects of wholesale inventory over-stocking at the end of the previous year.

15.7% gain & positive 84% of the time

From 1990 to 2014, in its seasonal period, Amgen has produced an average gain of 15.7% and has been positive 84% of the time. During this same time period, it has beaten the S&P 500 by an average 15.1% and has outperformed it 84% of the time. This is a strong track record of outperformance, especially the percentage of times that Amgen has beaten the S&P 500.

AMGN* vs. S&P 500 - 1990 to 2014		Positive	
Jun 23 to Sep 13	S&P 500	AGMN	Diff
1990	-10.4%	29.5%	39.8%
1991	1.6	42.4	40.9
1992	4.0	17.9	13.9
1993	3.6	3.4	-0.2
1994	3.2	24.3	21.1
1995	5.0	31.4	26.4
1996	2.1	7.0	4.9
1997	2.8	-19.0	-21.8
1998	-8.5	20.6	29.1
1999	0.6	64.3	63.7
2000	2.3	7.9	5.6
2001	-10.8	-1.6	9.3
2002	-10.0	12.9	23.0
2003	2.3	5.5	3.2
2004	-0.8	9.1	9.8
2005	1.4	36.0	34.5
2006	5.8	6.4	0.6
2007	-1.2	2.1	3.3
2008	-5.0	39.2	44.2
2009	16.8	14.8	-2.0
2010	2.4	-3.1	-5.5
2011	-8.9	-5.6	3.3
2012	9.4	15.0	5.6
2013	6.0	17.1	11.1
2014	1.2	14.0	12.8
Avg	0.6%	15.7%	15.1%
Fq > 0	68%	84%	84%

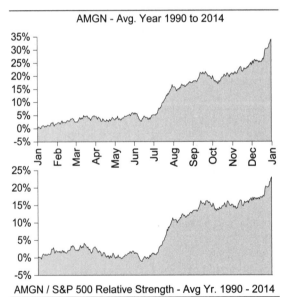

AMGN - Avg. Year 1990 to 2014

AMGN / S&P 500 Relative Strength - Avg Yr. 1990 - 2014

place in the summer months when the stock market typically does not have strong results and the selection of seasonal long trades are limited.

The seasonal trade for Amgen focuses on the sweet spot of its best performance, but like the biotech sector, on average the second half of the year for Amgen is much stronger than the first half of the year. From July 1st to December 31st, for the yearly period 1990 to 2014, Amgen has produced an average gain of 23.3% and has been positive 80% of the time. This compares to the weaker first half of the year, where the average gain over the same yearly period is 5.3% and the frequency of positive performance is 52%.

The Amgen seasonal trade is a valued trade not just because of its strong results, but also because of the time of year when the trade occurs. The trade takes

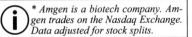

(i) *Amgen is a biotech company. Amgen trades on the Nasdaq Exchange. Data adjusted for stock splits.*

Amgen Performance

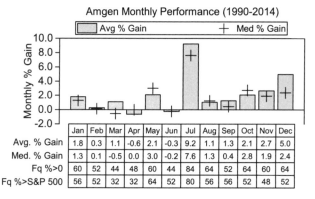

Amgen Monthly Performance (1990-2014)

	Jan	Feb	Mar	Apr	May	Jun	Jul	Aug	Sep	Oct	Nov	Dec
Avg. % Gain	1.8	0.3	1.1	-0.6	2.1	-0.3	9.2	1.1	1.3	2.1	2.7	5.0
Med. % Gain	1.3	0.1	-0.5	0.0	3.0	-0.2	7.6	1.3	0.4	2.8	1.9	2.4
Fq %>0	60	52	44	48	60	44	84	64	52	64	60	64
Fq %>S&P 500	56	52	32	32	64	52	80	56	56	52	48	52

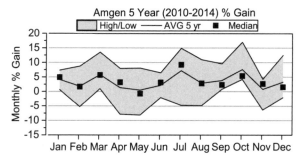

Amgen 5 Year (2010-2014) % Gain

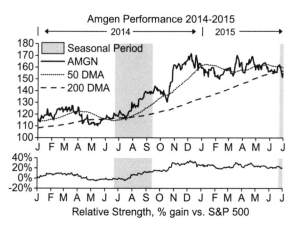

Amgen Performance 2014-2015

Relative Strength, % gain vs. S&P 500

WEEK 34

Market Indices & Rates
Weekly Values**

Stock Markets	2013	2014
Dow	14,977	16,956
S&P500	1,652	1,984
Nasdaq	3,620	4,527
TSX	12,654	15,494
FTSE	6,450	6,766
DAX	8,353	9,327
Nikkei	13,521	15,470
Hang Seng	22,002	25,069

Commodities	2013	2014
Oil	105.51	95.86
Gold	1370.7	1288.2

Bond Yields	2013	2014
USA 5 Yr Treasury	1.64	1.63
USA 10 Yr T	2.86	2.41
USA 20 Yr T	3.61	2.93
Moody's Aaa	4.67	4.08
Moody's Baa	5.55	4.70
CAN 5 Yr T	1.96	1.54
CAN 10 Yr T	2.72	2.08

Money Market	2013	2014
USA Fed Funds	0.25	0.25
USA 3 Mo T-B	0.04	0.03
CAN tgt overnight rate	1.00	1.00
CAN 3 Mo T-B	0.99	0.94

Foreign Exchange	2013	2014
EUR/USD	1.34	1.33
GBP/USD	1.56	1.66
USD/CAD	1.04	1.09
USD/JPY	97.99	103.41

AUGUST

M	T	W	T	F	S	S
1	2	3	4	5	6	7
8	9	10	11	12	13	14
15	16	17	18	19	20	21
22	23	24	25	26	27	28
29	30	31				

SEPTEMBER

M	T	W	T	F	S	S
			1	2	3	4
5	6	7	8	9	10	11
12	13	14	15	16	17	18
19	20	21	22	23	24	25
26	27	28	29	30		

From 1990 to 2014, the best month of the year for Amgen was July on an average, median and frequency basis. The gains in July were substantially above the other months of the year.

Over the last five years, the seasonal trade has worked well, mainly with the strong support from July's results.

In 2014, Amgen was performing at market coming into its seasonal period. Shortly after its seasonal period started, Amgen started to perform well, once again outperforming the S&P 500.

OCTOBER

M	T	W	T	F	S	S
					1	2
3	4	5	6	7	8	9
10	11	12	13	14	15	16
17	18	19	20	21	22	23
24	25	26	27	28	29	30
31						

HEALTH CARE
AUGUST PRESCRIPTION RENEWAL
August 15th to October 18th

Health care stocks have traditionally been classified as defensive stocks because of their stable earnings. Pharmaceutical and other health care companies typically still perform relatively well in an economic downturn.

Even in tough times, people still need to take their medication. As a result, investors have typically found comfort in this sector starting in the late summer and riding the momentum into mid-October.

> **2.6% extra & 17 out of 25 times better than the S&P 500**

Health Care* vs. S&P 500 Performance 1990 to 2014			
Aug 15 to Oct 18	S&P 500	Positive Health Care	Diff
1990	-9.9 %	-1.3 %	8.6 %
1991	0.7	1.3	0.6
1992	-1.9	-9.0	-7.1
1993	4.1	13.5	9.5
1994	1.2	7.2	6.0
1995	4.9	11.7	6.7
1996	7.4	9.4	2.1
1997	2.1	5.8	3.7
1998	-0.6	3.0	3.6
1999	-5.5	-0.5	5.0
2000	-10.0	6.9	16.9
2001	-10.0	-0.4	9.6
2002	-3.8	2.4	6.2
2003	4.9	-0.5	-5.4
2004	4.6	-0.8	-5.4
2005	-4.2	-3.1	1.2
2006	7.7	6.4	-1.3
2007	8.0	6.0	-2.0
2008	-27.3	-20.4	6.8
2009	8.3	5.1	-3.3
2010	9.8	8.2	-1.6
2011	4.0	3.2	-0.8
2012	3.8	6.9	3.1
2013	3.5	4.3	0.8
2014	-3.5	-1.1	2.5
Avg	-0.1 %	2.6 %	2.6 %
Fq > 0	60 %	64 %	68 %

Health Care Sector - Avg. Year 1990 to 2014

Health Care / S&P 500 - Avg Yr. 1990 - 2014

From August 15th to October 18th (1990 to 2014), health care stocks have had a tendency to outperform the S&P 500 on a yearly basis.

During this time period, the broad market (S&P 500) produced an average loss of 0.1%, compared with the health care stocks that produced a gain of 2.6%.

Despite competing with a runaway market in 2003 and legal problems which required drugs to be withdrawn from the market in 2004, the sector has beaten the S&P 500 seventeen out of twenty-five times from 1990 to 2014 in its seasonal period.

The real benefit of investing in the health care sector has been the positive returns that have been generated when the market has typically been negative.

Since 1950, August and September have been the worst two-month combination for gains in the broad stock market.

Having an alternative sector to invest in during the summer and early autumn is a valuable asset.

> *Alternate Strategy—As the health care sector has had a tendency to perform at par with the broad market from late October to early December, an alternative strategy is to continue holding the health care sector during this time period if the fundamentals or technicals are favorable.*

> **Health Care SP GIC Sector# 35: An index designed to represent a cross section of health care companies. For more information on the health care sector, see www.standardand-poors.com.*

Health Care Performance

Health Care Monthly Performance (1990-2014)

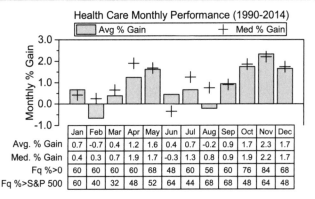

	Jan	Feb	Mar	Apr	May	Jun	Jul	Aug	Sep	Oct	Nov	Dec
Avg. % Gain	0.7	-0.7	0.4	1.2	1.6	0.4	0.7	-0.2	0.9	1.7	2.3	1.7
Med. % Gain	0.4	0.3	0.7	1.9	1.7	-0.3	1.3	0.8	0.9	1.9	2.2	1.7
Fq %>0	60	60	60	60	68	48	60	56	60	76	84	68
Fq %>S&P 500	60	40	32	48	52	64	44	68	68	48	64	48

Health Care 5 Year (2010-2014) % Gain

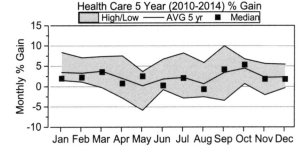

Health Care Performance 2014-2015

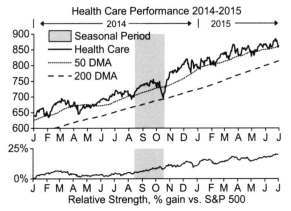

Market Indices & Rates
Weekly Values**

Stock Markets	2013	2014
Dow	14,840	17,097
S&P500	1,639	2,000
Nasdaq	3,608	4,567
TSX	12,663	15,601
FTSE	5,153	6,820
DAX	8,227	9,520
Nikkei	13,473	15,511
Hang Seng	21,768	24,929

Commodities	2013	2014
Oil	108.30	94.67
Gold	1410.3	1286.6

Bond Yields	2013	2014
USA 5 Yr Treasury	1.60	1.66
USA 10 Yr T	2.76	2.37
USA 20 Yr T	3.48	2.85
Moody's Aaa	4.54	3.98
Moody's Baa	5.40	4.61
CAN 5 Yr T	1.92	1.53
CAN 10 Yr T	2.61	2.02

Money Market	2013	2014
USA Fed Funds	0.25	0.25
USA 3 Mo T-B	0.03	0.03
CAN tgt overnight rate	1.00	1.00
CAN 3 Mo T-B	0.99	0.94

Foreign Exchange	2013	2014
EUR/USD	1.33	1.32
GBP/USD	1.55	1.66
USD/CAD	1.05	1.09
USD/JPY	97.94	103.96

AUGUST

M	T	W	T	F	S	S
1	2	3	4	5	6	7
8	9	10	11	12	13	14
15	16	17	18	19	20	21
22	23	24	25	26	27	28
29	30	31				

SEPTEMBER

M	T	W	T	F	S	S
				1	2	3	4
5	6	7	8	9	10	11
12	13	14	15	16	17	18
19	20	21	22	23	24	25
26	27	28	29	30		

OCTOBER

M	T	W	T	F	S	S
					1	2
3	4	5	6	7	8	9
10	11	12	13	14	15	16
17	18	19	20	21	22	23
24	25	26	27	28	29	30
31						

Over the long-term, on average, August is one of the worst performing months for the health care sector and yet the middle of the month starts off the sector's seasonal period. In this case, averages can be deceiving. Since 1990, not only is the median positive in August, but also the frequency of outperformance relative to the S&P 500 is high, at 68%. Nevertheless, the second half of August is the better performing half. Over the last five years, the health care sector's average performance throughout the year has placed August as the weakest month of the year and the best two performing months as September and October. In 2014, the health care sector produced a loss in its seasonal period, but outperformed the S&P 500.

SEPTEMBER

	MONDAY	TUESDAY	WEDNESDAY
WEEK 36	29	30	31
WEEK 37	**5** 25 USA Market Closed- Labor Day CAN Market Closed- Labor Day	**6** 24	**7** 23
WEEK 38	**12** 18	**13** 17	**14** 16
WEEK 39	**19** 11	**20** 10	**21** 9
WEEK 40	**26** 4	**27** 3	**28** 2

THURSDAY		FRIDAY	
1	29	**2**	28
8	22	**9**	21
15	15	**16**	14
22	8	**23**	7
29	1	**30**	

OCTOBER

M	T	W	T	F	S	S
					1	2
3	4	5	6	7	8	9
10	11	12	13	14	15	16
17	18	19	20	21	22	23
19	20	26	27	28	29	30
31						

NOVEMBER

M	T	W	T	F	S	S
	1	2	3	4	5	6
7	8	9	10	11	12	13
14	15	16	17	18	19	20
21	22	23	24	25	26	27
28	29	30				

DECEMBER

M	T	W	T	F	S	S
			1	2	3	4
5	6	7	8	9	10	11
12	13	14	15	16	17	18
19	20	21	22	23	24	25
26	27	28	29	30	31	

JANUARY

M	T	W	T	F	S	S
						1
2	3	4	5	6	7	8
9	10	11	12	13	14	15
16	17	18	19	20	21	22
23	24	25	26	27	28	29
30	31					

SEPTEMBER
S U M M A R Y

	Dow Jones	S&P 500	Nasdaq	TSX Comp
Month Rank	12	12	12	12
# Up	26	29	23	12
# Down	39	36	20	18
% Pos	40	45	53	40
% Avg. Gain	-0.8	-0.5	-0.5	-1.6

Dow & S&P 1950-2014, Nasdaq 1972-2014, TSX 1985-2014

S&P500 Cumulative Daily Gains for Avg Month 1950 to 2014

♦ September has the reputation of being the worst month of the year. From 1950 to 2014, September produced an average loss of 0.5% and was only positive 45% of the time. ♦ The last part of September tends to be negative. ♦ When a rally occurs in September, it is usually the result of a large external event, such as an increase in monetary stimulus. ♦ In September 2014, the stock market started to correct early in the month based upon concerns of slowing global growth.

BEST / WORST SEPTEMBER BROAD MKTS. 2005-2014

BEST SEPTEMBER MARKETS
♦ Russell 2000 (2010) 12.3%
♦ Nasdaq (2010) 12.0%
♦ Nikkei 225 (2005) 9.4%

WORST SEPTEMBER MARKETS
♦ TSX Comp. (2008) -14.7%
♦ Nikkei 225 (2008) -13.9%
♦ FTSE 100 (2008) -13.0%

Index Values End of Month

	2005	2006	2007	2008	2009	2010	2011	2012	2013	2014
Dow	10,569	11,679	13,896	10,851	9,712	10,788	10,913	13,437	15,130	17,043
S&P 500	1,229	1,336	1,527	1,166	1,057	1,141	1,131	1,441	1,682	1,972
Nasdaq	2,152	2,258	2,702	2,092	2,122	2,369	2,415	3,116	3,771	4,493
TSX Comp.	11,012	11,761	14,099	11,753	11,395	12,369	11,624	12,317	12,787	14,961
Russell 1000	1,285	1,391	1,597	1,219	1,115	1,211	1,198	1,526	1,806	2,108
Russell 2000	1,660	1,803	2,002	1,689	1,502	1,680	1,601	2,081	2,669	2,738
FTSE 100	5,478	5,961	6,467	4,903	5,134	5,549	5,129	5,742	6,462	6,623
Nikkei 225	13,574	16,128	16,786	11,260	10,133	9,369	8,700	8,870	14,456	16,174

Percent Gain for September

	2005	2006	2007	2008	2009	2010	2011	2012	2013	2014
Dow	0.8	2.6	4.0	-6.0	2.3	7.7	-6.0	2.6	2.2	-0.3
S&P 500	0.7	2.5	3.6	-9.1	3.6	8.8	-7.2	2.4	3.0	-1.6
Nasdaq	0.0	3.4	4.0	-11.6	5.6	12.0	-6.4	1.6	5.1	-1.9
TSX Comp.	3.2	-2.6	3.2	-14.7	4.8	3.8	-9.0	3.1	1.1	-4.3
Russell 1000	0.8	2.3	3.7	-9.7	3.9	9.0	-7.6	2.4	3.3	-1.9
Russell 2000	0.2	0.7	1.6	-8.1	5.6	12.3	-11.4	3.1	6.2	-6.2
FTSE 100	3.4	0.9	2.6	-13.0	4.6	6.2	-4.9	0.5	0.8	-2.9
Nikkei 225	9.4	-0.1	1.3	-13.9	-3.4	6.2	-2.8	0.3	8.0	4.9

September Market Avg. Performance 2005 to 2014[1]

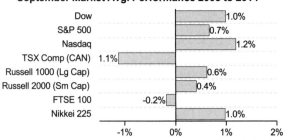

Dow	1.0%
S&P 500	0.7%
Nasdaq	1.2%
TSX Comp (CAN)	1.1%
Russell 1000 (Lg Cap)	0.6%
Russell 2000 (Sm Cap)	0.4%
FTSE 100	-0.2%
Nikkei 225	1.0%

Interest Corner Sep[2]

	Fed Funds % [3]	3 Mo. T-Bill % [4]	10 Yr % [5]	20 Yr % [6]
2014	0.25	0.02	2.52	2.98
2013	0.25	0.02	2.64	3.41
2012	0.25	0.10	1.65	2.42
2011	0.25	0.02	1.92	2.66
2010	0.25	0.16	2.53	3.38

(1) Russell Data provided by Russell (2) Federal Reserve Bank of St. Louis- end of month values (3) Target rate set by FOMC (4)(5)(6) Constant yield maturities.

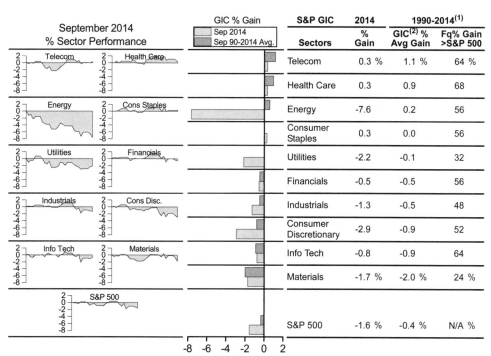

S&P GIC Sectors	2014 % Gain	1990-2014[1] GIC[2] % Avg Gain	1990-2014[1] Fq% Gain >S&P 500
Telecom	0.3 %	1.1 %	64 %
Health Care	0.3	0.9	68
Energy	-7.6	0.2	56
Consumer Staples	0.3	0.0	56
Utilities	-2.2	-0.1	32
Financials	-0.5	-0.5	56
Industrials	-1.3	-0.5	48
Consumer Discretionary	-2.9	-0.9	52
Info Tech	-0.8	-0.9	64
Materials	-1.7 %	-2.0 %	24 %
S&P 500	-1.6 %	-0.4 %	N/A %

GIC % Gain — Sep 2014 / Sep 90-2014 Avg.

September 2014 % Sector Performance

Sector Commentary

♦ In September 2014, the energy sector, typically a stronger sector in the month, produced a large loss of 7.6% as a glut of oil started to enter the market. ♦ The consumer discretionary sector also lost a lot of ground, producing a loss of 2.9%. ♦ The materials sector was impacted by slowing global growth. ♦ The defensive sectors, consumer staples, health care and telecom lived up to their seasonal track record of better performing sectors, with all three sectors performing positively in September.

Sub-Sector Commentary

♦ September is typically the month when precious metals tend to perform well. In September 2014, both gold and silver underperformed as investors were concerned about the possibility of the U.S. Federal Reserve raising interest rates. ♦ The metals and mining sector continued its slide with a 7.6% loss. ♦ The railroads, usually a weak performing sub-sector, produced a large gain of 3.5%, as the sub-sector was still on an overall uptrend. Investors were pushing up the sub-sector based upon U.S. growth running ahead of expectations.

SELECTED SUB-SECTORS[3]

Gold (London PM)	-5.4 %	2.7 %	64 %
Biotech (1993-2014)	0.1	2.0	68
Silver	-12.1	1.7	68
Pharma	2.0	1.1	64
Software & Services	0.0	0.8	72
Agriculture (1994-2014)	2.5	0.1	57
Retail	-2.6	-0.6	44
Home-builders	-4.7	-0.6	60
Transporta-tion	2.3	-0.7	52
Banks	1.3	-0.8	56
Railroads	3.5	-0.8	36
Chemicals	-0.2	-1.7	32
Metals & Mining	-7.6	-1.8	44
SOX (1995-2014)	-1.1	-3.0	40
Steel	-2.6	-3.5	44

(1) Sector data provided by Standard and Poors (2) GIC is short form for Global Industry Classification (3) Sub Sector data provided by Standard and Poors, except where marked by symbol.

PROCTER AND GAMBLE
SOMETHING FOR EVERYONE – Aug 7 to Nov 19

In the investors' eyes, Procter and Gamble is a relatively defensive investment, as the company is in the consumer packaged goods business and its revenues are generated in over 180 countries. Defensive stocks have a reputation of producing sub-par performance compared with the broad market. This is not the case with PG, as on average, it has outperformed the S&P 500 over the last twenty-five years during its seasonally strong period.

10.0% gain & positive 88% of the time

Interestingly, on average, the gains have been produced largely in the second half of the year. In the first half of the year, PG has been relatively flat and has underperformed the S&P 500.

PG* vs. S&P 500 - 1990 to 2014

Aug 7 to Nov 19	S&P 500	PG	Diff
1990	-4.5%	8.3%	12.8%
1991	-2.9	-2.2	0.7
1992	0.7	10.1	9.4
1993	3.1	17.7	14.6
1994	1.0	19.3	18.3
1995	7.4	27.8	20.4
1996	12.0	18.6	6.5
1997	-1.6	0.2	1.9
1998	5.8	14.0	8.2
1999	9.4	18.7	9.3
2000	-6.5	31.8	38.3
2001	-4.1	11.2	15.3
2002	4.3	-0.7	-5.0
2003	7.8	8.2	0.4
2004	10.0	2.5	-7.5
2005	1.8	6.2	4.4
2006	9.5	7.4	-2.1
2007	-2.3	12.0	14.4
2008	-37.4	-8.1	29.3
2009	9.8	20.8	11.0
2010	7.0	6.7	-0.3
2011	1.4	4.4	3.0
2012	-0.5	3.2	3.7
2013	5.3	3.2	-2.2
2014	6.7	9.4	2.7
Avg	1.7%	10.0%	8.3%
Fq > 0	68%	88%	80%

PG - Avg. Year 1990 to 2014

PG / S&P 500 Relative Strength - Avg Yr. 1990 - 2014

From a seasonal perspective, the best time to invest in PG has been from August 7th to November 19th. During this period, from 1990 to 2014, PG on average produced a gain of 10.0% and was positive 88% of the time. In addition, it substantially outperformed the S&P 500, generating an extra profit of 8.3% and beating its performance 80% of the time.

Investors will often seek sanctuary in defensive stocks in late summer and early autumn. Although August is not typically the worst month of the year, it does have a weak risk-reward profile. With the dreaded month of September falling right after August, investors become "gun shy" and start to become more conservative in August.

This trend benefits PG as more investors switch over to defensive companies. PG's outperformance, on average, starts to occur just after it releases its fourth quarter earnings at the beginning of August.

PG continues to outperform the S&P 500 through September and October. For the S&P 500, September on average is the worst month of the year and October is the most volatile month. The outperformance of PG continues into mid-November.

PG's seasonally strong period extends past the seasonal period for the consumer staples sector. It is possible that investors wait until after PG's first quarter results are released in the beginning of November before adjusting their portfolios.

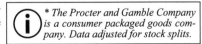
The Procter and Gamble Company is a consumer packaged goods company. Data adjusted for stock splits.

Procter & Gamble Performance

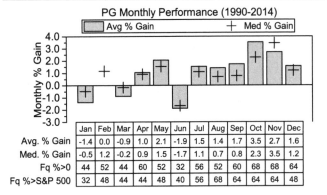

PG Monthly Performance (1990-2014)

Avg % Gain   + Med % Gain

	Jan	Feb	Mar	Apr	May	Jun	Jul	Aug	Sep	Oct	Nov	Dec
Avg. % Gain	-1.4	0.0	-0.9	1.0	2.1	-1.9	1.5	1.4	1.7	3.5	2.7	1.6
Med. % Gain	-0.5	1.2	-0.2	0.9	1.5	-1.7	1.1	0.7	0.8	2.3	3.5	1.2
Fq %>0	44	52	44	60	52	32	56	52	60	68	68	64
Fq %>S&P 500	32	48	44	44	48	40	56	68	64	64	64	48

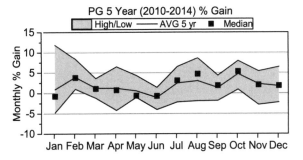

PG 5 Year (2010-2014) % Gain

High/Low —— AVG 5 yr ■ Median

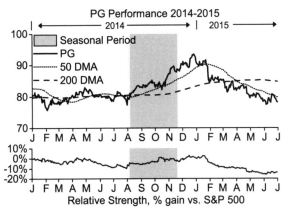

PG Performance 2014-2015

Seasonal Period
PG
50 DMA
200 DMA

Relative Strength, % gain vs. S&P 500

Market Indices & Rates
Weekly Values**

Stock Markets	2013	2014
Dow	14,906	17,088
S&P500	1,651	2,002
Nasdaq	3,645	4,579
TSX	12,791	15,606
FTSE	6,506	6,852
DAX	8,226	9,617
Nikkei	13,906	15,644
Hang Seng	22,423	25,071

Commodities	2013	2014
Oil	108.67	94.04
Gold	1390.8	1271.3

Bond Yields	2013	2014
USA 5 Yr Treasury	1.76	1.70
USA 10 Yr T	2.92	2.44
USA 20 Yr T	3.59	2.93
Moody's Aaa	4.67	4.03
Moody's Baa	5.49	4.69
CAN 5 Yr T	2.06	1.57
CAN 10 Yr T	2.72	2.08

Money Market	2013	2014
USA Fed Funds	0.25	0.25
USA 3 Mo T-B	0.02	0.03
CAN tgt overnight rate	1.00	1.00
CAN 3 Mo T-B	1.00	0.93

Foreign Exchange	2013	2014
EUR/USD	1.32	1.31
GBP/USD	1.56	1.64
USD/CAD	1.05	1.09
USD/JPY	99.57	104.92

SEPTEMBER

M	T	W	T	F	S	S
			1	2	3	4
5	6	7	8	9	10	11
12	13	14	15	16	17	18
19	20	21	22	23	24	25
26	27	28	29	30		

OCTOBER

M	T	W	T	F	S	S
					1	2
3	4	5	6	7	8	9
10	11	12	13	14	15	16
17	18	19	20	21	22	23
24	25	26	27	28	29	30
31						

NOVEMBER

M	T	W	T	F	S	S
	1	2	3	4	5	6
7	8	9	10	11	12	13
14	15	16	17	18	19	20
21	22	23	24	25	26	27
28	29	30				

From 1990 to 2014, October was the strongest month for Procter & Gamble on an average and frequency basis. Over the same time period, June was the weakest month, although generally the first few months of the year tend to be weaker.

Over the last five years, Procter & Gamble has generally followed its average seasonal trend. The exception is February's relatively strong performance.

In 2014, Procter & Gamble started its outperformance a few days before its seasonal period and managed to outperform the S&P 500 during its seasonal period.

H&R BLOCK

(NEW) HRB

①LONG (Oct28-Mar31)
②SELL SHORT (Apr1-May16)

H&R Block has a seasonal business based upon its clients' need to file taxes. Although most corporate clients file their taxes at quarter end, a large part of H&R Block's revenue is produced from personal tax returns that are filed by mid-April in the U.S.

The April personal tax deadline provides an opportunity for seasonal investors. H&R Block's stock price tends to get pushed up ahead of tax season as average investors get into the stock ahead of the company's busy time.

The positive seasonal period for H&R Block is from October 28th to March 31st. In this time period, from 1989 to 2015, H&R Block produced an average gain of 12.5% and was positive 73% of the time.

16.5% gain

At the beginning of April, investors' enthusiasm wanes as they anticipate H&R Block's decreasing revenues in the near future as tax season winds down. The result is H&R Block's stock price starts to underperform the S&P 500.

The best time to short sell H&R Block is from April 1st to May 16th. In this period, from 1989 to 2015, H&R Block has produced an average loss of 3.7% and has only been positive 27% of the time.

Given that the short sell seasonal period follows right after the seasonally strong period for H&R Block, it is best to use technical analysis to help determine the best time to switch from a long position to a short sell position.

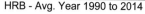

HRB* vs. S&P 500 1989/90 to 2014/15

Positive Long ☐ Negative Short ☐

Year	Oct 28 to Mar 31 S&P 500	HRB	Apr 1 to May 16 S&P 500	HRB	Compound Growth S&P 500	HRB
1989/90	1.5 %	12.4 %	4.1 %	2.0 %	5.7 %	10.2 %
1990/91	23.1	35.4	-0.8	-1.5	22.1	37.4
1991/92	5.1	-4.0	1.6	-2.7	6.7	-1.4
1992/93	7.9	0.7	-2.7	-12.5	5.0	13.3
1993/94	-4.1	8.2	-0.3	-7.5	-4.3	16.3
1994/95	7.5	0.6	5.5	-6.4	13.4	7.0
1995/96	11.4	-12.4	3.0	-3.4	14.7	-9.4
1996/97	8.0	17.4	9.6	8.2	18.4	7.8
1997/98	25.6	36.8	0.6	-9.8	26.4	50.2
1998/99	20.8	1.5	4.0	-1.5	25.6	3.1
1999/00	15.6	15.0	-2.2	-26.7	13.1	45.7
2000/01	-15.9	44.9	10.7	15.7	-6.9	22.1
2001/02	3.9	30.9	-4.3	4.1	-0.6	25.6
2002/03	-5.5	-2.7	11.3	-9.8	5.2	6.8
2003/04	9.2	7.6	-2.7	-10.7	6.3	19.1
2004/05	4.9	8.9	-1.3	-1.9	3.6	11.0
2005/06	9.8	-9.9	-0.2	1.7	9.6	-11.4
2006/07	3.2	-1.8	6.6	8.9	9.9	-10.5
2007/08	-13.9	-5.1	7.8	14.1	-7.2	-18.5
2008/09	-6.0	17.7	10.7	-23.4	4.0	45.1
2009/10	10.0	-5.3	-2.9	-4.7	6.8	-0.9
2010/11	12.1	45.8	0.3	-5.2	12.4	53.4
2011/12	9.6	7.3	-5.9	-10.8	3.1	18.9
2012/13	11.1	65.8	5.2	-2.0	16.9	69.1
2013/14	6.4	6.0	0.3	-6.7	6.7	13.1
2014/15	5.4	3.6	2.7	-2.3	8.2	5.9
Avg	6.4 %	12.5 %	2.3 %	-3.7 %	8.7 %	16.5 %
Fq>0	81 %	73 %	62 %	27 %	85 %	77 %

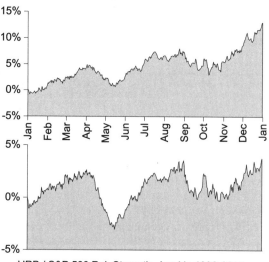

HRB - Avg. Year 1990 to 2014

HRB / S&P 500 Rel. Strength- Avg Yr. 1990-2014

H&R Block Performance

HRB Monthly Performance (1990-2014)

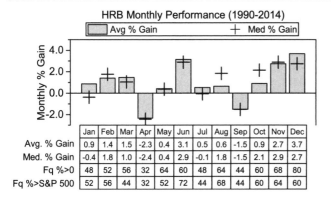

	Jan	Feb	Mar	Apr	May	Jun	Jul	Aug	Sep	Oct	Nov	Dec
Avg. % Gain	0.9	1.4	1.5	-2.3	0.4	3.1	0.5	0.6	-1.5	0.9	2.7	3.7
Med. % Gain	-0.4	1.8	1.0	-2.4	0.4	2.9	-0.1	1.8	-1.5	2.1	2.9	2.7
Fq %>0	48	52	56	32	64	60	48	64	44	60	68	80
Fq %>S&P 500	52	56	44	32	52	72	44	68	44	60	64	60

HRB 5 Year (2010-2014) % Gain

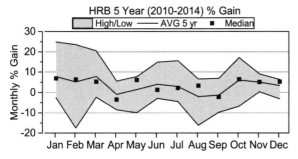

HRB Performance 2014-2015

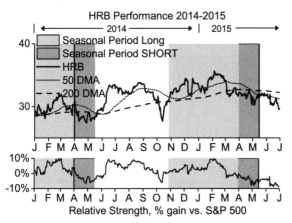

Relative Strength, % gain vs. S&P 500

Market Indices & Rates
Weekly Values**

Stock Markets	2013	2014
Dow	15,251	17,046
S&P500	1,683	1,994
Nasdaq	3,720	4,578
TSX	12,786	15,517
FTSE	6,575	6,820
DAX	8,444	9,702
Nikkei	14,369	15,820
Hang Seng	22,907	24,788

Commodities	2013	2014
Oil	108.26	92.44
Gold	1351.7	1247.7

Bond Yields	2013	2014
USA 5 Yr Treasury	1.73	1.78
USA 10 Yr T	2.92	2.54
USA 20 Yr T	3.61	3.01
Moody's Aaa	4.70	4.13
Moody's Baa	5.54	4.79
CAN 5 Yr T	2.13	1.66
CAN 10 Yr T	2.78	2.19

Money Market	2013	2014
USA Fed Funds	0.25	0.25
USA 3 Mo T-B	0.02	0.02
CAN tgt overnight rate	1.00	1.00
CAN 3 Mo T-B	0.99	0.93

Foreign Exchange	2013	2014
EUR/USD	1.33	1.29
GBP/USD	1.58	1.62
USD/CAD	1.03	1.10
USD/JPY	99.76	106.71

SEPTEMBER

M	T	W	T	F	S	S
			1	2	3	4
5	6	7	8	9	10	11
12	13	14	15	16	17	18
19	20	21	22	23	24	25
26	27	28	29	30		

OCTOBER

M	T	W	T	F	S	S
					1	2
3	4	5	6	7	8	9
10	11	12	13	14	15	16
17	18	19	20	21	22	23
24	25	26	27	28	29	30
31						

NOVEMBER

M	T	W	T	F	S	S
	1	2	3	4	5	6
7	8	9	10	11	12	13
14	15	16	17	18	19	20
21	22	23	24	25	26	27
28	29	30				

From 1990 to 2014, H&R Block performed well in the last two months of the year to the end of March. April tends to be the worst performing month on an average, median and frequency basis. Given the juxtaposition of the strong seasonal period and the weak seasonal period, sometimes H&R Block will start to weaken before the end of its strong seasonal period.

Over the last five years, H&R Block has followed its average seasonal trend, with a positive finish to the year and into the New Year, and a negative April. In 2014 and 2015, the overall combination of long and short positions have been successful.

INFORMATION TECHNOLOGY
USE IT OR LOSE IT
October 9th to January 17th

Information technology– the sector that investors love to love and love to hate. In recent years, most investors have made and lost money in this sector. When the sector is performing well, it can perform really well. When it is performing poorly, it can perform really poorly. From 1989 to 2015, during its seasonal period of October 9th to January 17th, the information technology sector has produced an average gain of 10.5% and has been positive 76% of the time.

4.8% extra compared with the S&P 500

Technology stocks get bid up at the end of the year for three reasons.

First, a lot of companies operate with year end budgets and if they do not spend the money in their budget, they lose it.

In the last few months of the year, whatever money they have, they spend. Hence, the saying "use it or lose it."

The number one purchase item for this budget flush is technology equipment. An upgrade in technology equipment is something which a large number of employees in the company can benefit from and is easy to justify.

Second, consumers indirectly help push up technology stocks by purchasing electronic items during the holiday season.

Retail sales ramp up significantly on Black Friday, the Friday after Thanksgiving. Investors anticipate the upswing in sales and buy technology stocks.

Third, the "Conference Effect" helps maintain the momentum in January. This phenomenon is the result of investors increasing positions ahead of major conferences in order to benefit from positive announcements.

In the case of the information technology sector, investors increase their holdings ahead of the Las Vegas Consumer Electronics Conference that typically occurs in the second week of January.

Info Tech* & Nasdaq vs S&P 500
Oct 9 to Jan 17, 1989/90 to 2014/15

	S&P 500	Info Tech	Nas daq	Diff IT- S&P500	Diff Nas- S&P500
1989/90	-6.0 %	-6.9 %	-9.3 %	-1.0 %	-3.3 %
1990/91	4.6	13.4	8.0	8.8	3.3
1991/92	10.0	16.4	21.2	6.4	11.2
1992/93	7.2	11.2	21.5	4.0	14.3
1993/94	2.8	12.5	3.7	9.7	0.8
1994/95	3.3	16.0	3.0	12.7	-0.3
1995/96	4.1	-8.9	-1.4	-13.0	-5.5
1996/97	10.8	21.2	8.8	10.4	-2.0
1997/98	-1.3	-14.2	-10.3	-12.9	-9.0
1998/99	29.6	71.8	65.5	42.2	35.9
1999/00	9.7	29.2	40.8	19.5	31.1
2001/01	-5.6	-21.7	-20.2	-16.1	-14.5
2001/02	7.2	26.8	23.7	19.6	16.5
2002/03	12.9	30.0	21.9	17.0	8.9
2003/04	10.3	14.2	13.0	4.0	2.8
2004/05	5.6	6.8	8.7	1.2	3.2
2005/06	7.3	9.7	10.2	2.4	2.9
2006/07	6.0	7.1	7.8	1.1	1.8
2007/08	-14.1	-14.9	-15.8	-0.7	-1.7
2008/09	-13.7	-12.0	-12.1	1.6	1.6
2009/10	6.6	9.9	7.7	3.3	1.1
2010/11	11.0	13.6	14.7	2.6	3.7
2011/12	12.0	8.4	10.0	-3.6	-1.9
2012/13	1.7	-2.9	0.8	-4.7	-1.0
2013/14	11.1	15.1	13.6	4.0	2.5
2014/15	2.6	2.5	3.7	-0.1	1.1
Avg	5.7 %	10.5 %	9.9 %	4.8 %	4.3 %
Fq > 0	84 %	76 %	80 %	72 %	68 %

Positive

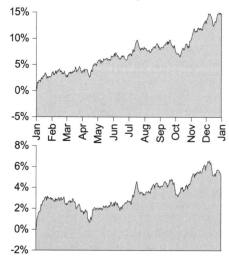

InfoTech Sector % Gain Avg. Year 1990 to 2014

Info Tech / S&P 500 - Avg Yr. 1990 - 2014

Information Technology SP GIC Sector 45: An index designed to represent a cross section of information technology companies.

Information Technology Performance

Info Tech Monthly Performance (1990-2014)

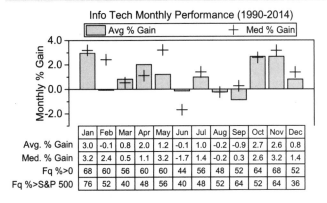

	Jan	Feb	Mar	Apr	May	Jun	Jul	Aug	Sep	Oct	Nov	Dec
Avg. % Gain	3.0	-0.1	0.8	2.0	1.2	-0.1	1.0	-0.2	-0.9	2.7	2.6	0.8
Med. % Gain	3.2	2.4	0.5	1.1	3.2	-1.7	1.4	-0.2	0.3	2.6	3.2	1.4
Fq %>0	68	60	56	60	60	44	56	48	52	64	68	52
Fq %>S&P 500	76	52	40	48	56	40	48	52	64	52	64	36

Info Tech 5 Year (2010-2014) % Gain

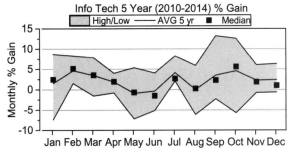

Info Tech Performance 2014-2015

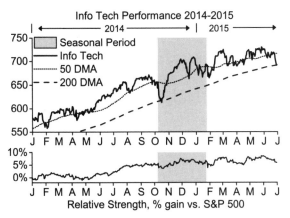

Relative Strength, % gain vs. S&P 500

**Market Indices & Rates
Weekly Values****

Stock Markets	2013	2014
Dow	15,558	17,173
S&P500	1,712	2,001
Nasdaq	3,762	4,561
TSX	12,863	15,437
FTSE	6,595	6,807
DAX	8,643	9,710
Nikkei	14,581	16,047
Hang Seng	23,263	24,269

Commodities	2013	2014
Oil	106.23	93.54
Gold	1330.4	1228.6

Bond Yields	2013	2014
USA 5 Yr Treasury	1.54	1.82
USA 10 Yr T	2.79	2.61
USA 20 Yr T	3.53	3.10
Moody's Aaa	4.67	4.21
Moody's Baa	5.49	4.89
CAN 5 Yr T	2.05	1.71
CAN 10 Yr T	2.73	2.26

Money Market	2013	2014
USA Fed Funds	0.25	0.25
USA 3 Mo T-B	0.01	0.02
CAN tgt overnight rate	1.00	1.00
CAN 3 Mo T-B	0.99	0.92

Foreign Exchange	2013	2014
EUR/USD	1.35	1.29
GBP/USD	1.60	1.63
USD/CAD	1.03	1.10
USD/JPY	98.99	108.08

SEPTEMBER

M	T	W	T	F	S	S
			1	2	3	4
5	6	7	8	9	10	11
12	13	14	15	16	17	18
19	20	21	22	23	24	25
26	27	28	29	30		

OCTOBER

M	T	W	T	F	S	S
					1	2
3	4	5	6	7	8	9
10	11	12	13	14	15	16
17	18	19	20	21	22	23
24	25	26	27	28	29	30
31						

NOVEMBER

M	T	W	T	F	S	S
	1	2	3	4	5	6
7	8	9	10	11	12	13
14	15	16	17	18	19	20
21	22	23	24	25	26	27
28	29	30				

From 1990 to 2014, on average, the technology sector performed well from October to January. The seasonal period for the technology sector lies within these four contiguous months, starting on October 9th and ending on January 17th.

Over the last five years, the technology sector has on average followed its seasonal trend. The largest anomaly has been the strong performance in February. October was the strongest month and also had the widest dispersion in returns.

In 2014, the technology sector was positive and outperformed the S&P 500 in its seasonal period.

🇨🇦 CANADIAN BANKS — IN-OUT-IN AGAIN
①Oct10-Dec 31   ②Jan23-Apr13

Canadian banks have their year-end on October 31st. Why does this matter? Typically, banks clean up their "books" at their year-end, by announcing any bad news. In addition, this is often the time period when the banks announce their positive news, including increases in dividends.

11.2% gain & positive 81% of the time

The Canadian bank sector, from October 10th to December 31st for the years 1989/1990 to 2014/2015, has been positive 81% of the time and has produced an average gain of 5.4%. From January 23rd to April 13th, the sector has been positive 73% of the time and has produced an average gain of 5.6%. On a compound basis, the strategy has been positive 81% of the time and produced an average gain of 11.2%.

In the table above, Canadian bank returns in December have been separated out to show the impact of bank earnings on returns. In December, Canadian banks on average have provided gains 77% of the time, but they have underperformed the TSX Composite. If Canadian banks have performed well leading into their earnings, they often pause in December.

ⓘ *Banks SP GIC Canadian Sector Level 2 An index designed to represent a cross section of Canadian banking companies.*

Canadian Banks* vs. S&P 500 1990 to 2014

Positive ☐   1989 to 2014

Year	Oct 10 to Dec 31 TSX-Comp	Oct 10 to Dec 31 Cdn. Banks	Jan 23 to Apr 13 TSX-Comp	Jan 23 to Apr 13 Cdn. Banks	Compound Growth TSX-Comp	Compound Growth Cdn. Banks	Dec 1 Dec 31 TSX-Comp	Dec 1 Dec 31 Cdn. Banks
89/90	-1.7 %	-1.8 %	-6.3 %	-9.1 %	-7.9	-10.8 %	0.7 %	-1.4 %
90/91	3.7	8.9	9.8	14.6	13.9	24.8	3.4	5.5
91/92	5.2	10.2	-6.8	-11.6	-2.0	-2.6	1.9	4.6
92/93	4.1	2.5	10.7	14.4	15.2	17.3	2.1	1.8
93/94	6.3	6.8	-5.6	-13.3	0.3	-7.4	3.4	5.1
94/95	-1.8	3.4	5.0	10.0	3.1	13.8	2.9	0.9
95/96	4.9	3.5	3.6	-3.2	8.6	0.1	1.1	1.5
96/97	9.0	15.1	-6.2	0.7	2.3	15.9	-1.5	-1.9
97/98	-6.1	7.6	19.9	38.8	12.6	49.4	2.9	4.2
98/99	18.3	28.0	4.8	13.0	24.0	44.6	2.2	3.0
99/00	18.2	5.1	3.8	22.1	22.8	28.3	11.8	0.7
00/01	-14.4	1.7	-14.1	-6.7	-26.4	-5.1	1.3	9.6
01/02	11.9	6.5	2.3	8.2	14.5	15.1	3.5	3.4
02/03	16.1	21.3	-4.3	2.6	11.1	24.4	0.7	2.6
03/04	8.1	5.1	2.0	2.1	10.3	7.4	4.6	2.0
04/05	4.9	6.2	4.5	6.9	9.6	13.5	2.4	4.7
05/06	6.2	8.4	5.5	2.7	12.1	11.3	4.1	2.1
06/07	10.4	8.4	6.9	3.2	18.0	11.8	1.2	3.7
07/08	-3.0	-10.4	8.2	-3.5	5.0	-13.5	1.1	-7.7
08/09	-6.4	-14.8	9.4	24.4	2.4	6.1	-3.1	-11.2
09/10	2.7	2.4	6.7	15.2	9.6	18.0	2.6	0.1
10/11	7.2	-0.2	4.3	9.1	11.9	8.9	3.8	-0.5
11/12	3.2	3.1	-2.9	1.1	0.2	4.2	-2.0	2.7
12/13	1.3	4.4	-3.8	-2.0	-2.5	2.3	1.6	1.5
13/14	7.0	9.0	1.9	1.6	9.1	10.7	1.7	0.9
14/15	1.2	-0.9	4.2	4.4	5.4	3.5	-0.8	-4.3
Avg.	4.5 %	5.4 %	2.4 %	5.6 %	7.0 %	11.2 %	2.1 %	1.3 %
Fq>0	77 %	81 %	69	73 %	85 %	81 %	85 %	77 %

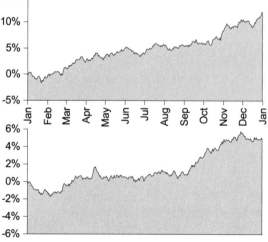

Canadian Banking Sector - Avg. Year 1990 to 2014

Cdn. Banking / TSX Comp Rel. Strength- Avg Yr. 1990-2014

Canadian Banks Performance

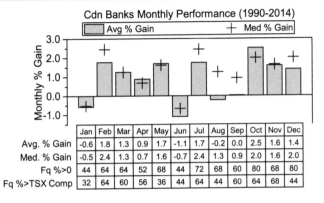

Cdn Banks Monthly Performance (1990-2014)

	Jan	Feb	Mar	Apr	May	Jun	Jul	Aug	Sep	Oct	Nov	Dec
Avg. % Gain	-0.6	1.8	1.3	0.9	1.7	-1.1	1.7	-0.2	0.0	2.5	1.6	1.4
Med. % Gain	-0.5	2.4	1.3	0.7	1.6	-0.7	2.4	1.3	0.9	2.0	1.6	2.0
Fq %>0	44	64	64	52	68	44	72	68	60	80	68	80
Fq %>TSX Comp	32	64	60	56	36	44	64	44	60	64	68	44

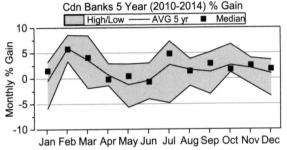

Cdn Banks 5 Year (2010-2014) % Gain

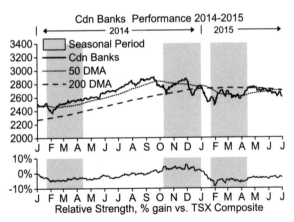

Cdn Banks Performance 2014-2015

Relative Strength, % gain vs. TSX Composite

Market Indices & Rates
Weekly Values**

Stock Markets	2013	2014
Dow	15,319	17,100
S&P500	1,696	1,985
Nasdaq	3,773	4,514
TSX	12,836	15,059
FTSE	6,552	6,689
DAX	8,658	9,601
Nikkei	14,728	16,244
Hang Seng	23,218	23,832

Commodities	2013	2014
Oil	103.10	93.19
Gold	1326.8	1216.1

Bond Yields	2013	2014
USA 5 Yr Treasury	1.43	1.79
USA 10 Yr T	2.66	2.55
USA 20 Yr T	3.41	3.01
Moody's Aaa	4.54	4.10
Moody's Baa	5.37	4.82
CAN 5 Yr T	1.92	1.65
CAN 10 Yr T	2.59	2.18

Money Market	2013	2014
USA Fed Funds	0.25	0.25
USA 3 Mo T-B	0.02	0.01
CAN tgt overnight rate	1.00	1.00
CAN 3 Mo T-B	0.98	0.92

Foreign Exchange	2013	2014
EUR/USD	1.35	1.28
GBP/USD	1.61	1.63
USD/CAD	1.03	1.11
USD/JPY	98.65	108.96

SEPTEMBER

M	T	W	T	F	S	S
			1	2	3	4
5	6	7	8	9	10	11
12	13	14	15	16	17	18
19	20	21	22	23	24	25
26	27	28	29	30		

OCTOBER

M	T	W	T	F	S	S
					1	2
3	4	5	6	7	8	9
10	11	12	13	14	15	16
17	18	19	20	21	22	23
24	25	26	27	28	29	30
31						

NOVEMBER

M	T	W	T	F	S	S
	1	2	3	4	5	6
7	8	9	10	11	12	13
14	15	16	17	18	19	20
21	22	23	24	25	26	27
28	29	30				

From 1990 to 2014, October has been the best month for Canadian banks on an average and frequency basis. One of the weaker months of the year is September. This juxtaposition makes the timing of the transition into the seasonal period that starts in October important. The second seasonal leg starts in late January. On average, January is a weak month making the timing of the transition critical.

Over the last five years, February has been the best month of the year for Canadian banks. In the late 2014 seasonal leg, Canadian banks underperformed the TSX Composite, but later managed to outperform in the 2015 seasonal leg.

OCTOBER

	MONDAY	TUESDAY	WEDNESDAY
WEEK 41	**3** 28	**4** 27	**5** 26
WEEK 42	**10** 21 USA Bond Market Closed- Columbus Day CAN Market Closed- Thanksgiving Day	**11** 20	**12** 19
WEEK 43	**17** 14	**18** 13	**19** 12
WEEK 44	**24** 7	**25** 6	**26** 5
WEEK 45	**31**	1	2

OCTOBER

THURSDAY		FRIDAY	
6	25	**7**	24
13	18	**14**	17
20	11	**21**	10
27	4	**28**	3
3		4	

NOVEMBER

M	T	W	T	F	S	S
	1	2	3	4	5	6
7	8	9	10	11	12	13
14	15	16	17	18	19	20
21	22	23	24	25	26	27
28	29	30				

DECEMBER

M	T	W	T	F	S	S
		1	2	3	4	
5	6	7	8	9	10	11
12	13	14	15	16	17	18
19	20	21	22	23	24	25
26	27	28	29	30	31	

JANUARY

M	T	W	T	F	S	S
						1
2	3	4	5	6	7	8
9	10	11	12	13	14	15
16	17	18	19	20	21	22
23	24	25	26	27	28	29
30	31					

FEBRUARY

M	T	W	T	F	S	S
		1	2	3	4	5
6	7	8	9	10	11	12
13	14	15	16	17	18	19
20	21	22	23	24	25	26
27	28					

OCTOBER
S U M M A R Y

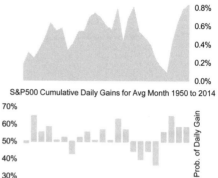

S&P500 Cumulative Daily Gains for Avg Month 1950 to 2014

	Dow Jones	S&P 500	Nasdaq	TSX Comp
Month Rank	7	7	8	9
# Up	39	39	24	19
# Down	26	26	19	11
% Pos	60	60	56	63
% Avg. Gain	0.5	0.8	0.7	0.1

Dow & S&P 1950-2014, Nasdaq 1972-2014, TSX 1985-2014

♦ October, on average, is the most volatile month of the year and often provides opportunities for short-term traders. The first half of October tends to be positive. ♦ The second half of the month, leading up to the last four days, tends to be negative, and prone to large drops. ♦ Seasonal opportunities in mid-October include Canadian banks, technology and transportation. ♦ In late October, a lot of sectors start their seasonal period, including the materials, industrials, consumer discretionary and retail sectors.

BEST / WORST OCTOBER BROAD MKTS. 2005-2014

BEST OCTOBER MARKETS
- ♦ Russell 2000 (2011) 15.0%
- ♦ Nasdaq (2011) 11.1%
- ♦ Russell 1000 (2011) 11.1%

WORST OCTOBER MARKETS
- ♦ Nikkei 225 (2008) -23.8%
- ♦ Russell 2000 (2008) -20.9%
- ♦ Nasdaq (2008) -17.7%

Index Values End of Month

	2005	2006	2007	2008	2009	2010	2011	2012	2013	2014
Dow	10,440	12,081	13,930	9,325	9,713	11,118	11,955	13,096	15,546	17,391
S&P 500	1,207	1,378	1,549	969	1,036	1,183	1,253	1,412	1,757	2,018
Nasdaq	2,120	2,367	2,859	1,721	2,045	2,507	2,684	2,977	3,920	4,631
TSX Comp.	10,383	12,345	14,625	9,763	10,911	12,676	12,252	12,423	13,361	14,613
Russell 1000	1,261	1,437	1,623	1,004	1,089	1,256	1,331	1,498	1,883	2,157
Russell 2000	1,607	1,906	2,058	1,336	1,399	1,748	1,842	2,035	2,734	2,916
FTSE 100	5,317	6,129	6,722	4,377	5,045	5,675	5,544	5,783	6,731	6,547
Nikkei 225	13,607	16,399	16,738	8,577	10,035	9,202	8,988	8,928	14,328	16,414

Percent Gain for October

	2005	2006	2007	2008	2009	2010	2011	2012	2013	2014
Dow	-1.2	3.4	0.2	-14.1	0.0	3.1	9.5	-2.5	2.8	2.0
S&P 500	-1.8	3.2	1.5	-16.9	-2.0	3.7	10.8	-2.0	4.5	2.3
Nasdaq	-1.5	4.8	5.8	-17.7	-3.6	5.9	11.1	-4.5	3.9	3.1
TSX Comp.	-5.7	5.0	3.7	-16.9	-4.2	2.5	5.4	0.9	4.5	-2.3
Russell 1000	-1.9	3.3	1.6	-17.6	-2.3	3.8	11.1	-1.8	4.3	2.3
Russell 2000	-3.2	5.7	2.8	-20.9	-6.9	4.0	15.0	-2.2	2.5	6.5
FTSE 100	-2.9	2.8	3.9	-10.7	-1.7	2.3	8.1	0.7	4.2	-1.2
Nikkei 225	0.2	1.7	-0.3	-23.8	-1.0	-1.8	3.3	0.7	-0.9	1.5

October Market Avg. Performance 2005 to 2014[1]

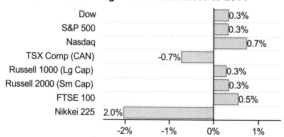

Dow	0.3%
S&P 500	0.3%
Nasdaq	0.7%
TSX Comp (CAN)	-0.7%
Russell 1000 (Lg Cap)	0.3%
Russell 2000 (Sm Cap)	0.3%
FTSE 100	0.5%
Nikkei 225	2.0%

Interest Corner Oct[2]

	Fed Funds %[3]	3 Mo. T-Bill %[4]	10 Yr %[5]	20 Yr %[6]
2014	0.25	0.01	2.35	2.81
2013	0.25	0.04	2.57	3.33
2012	0.25	0.11	1.72	2.46
2011	0.25	0.01	2.17	2.89
2010	0.25	0.12	2.63	3.64

(1) Russell Data provided by Russell (2) Federal Reserve Bank of St. Louis- end of month values (3) Target rate set by FOMC (4)(5)(6) Constant yield maturities.

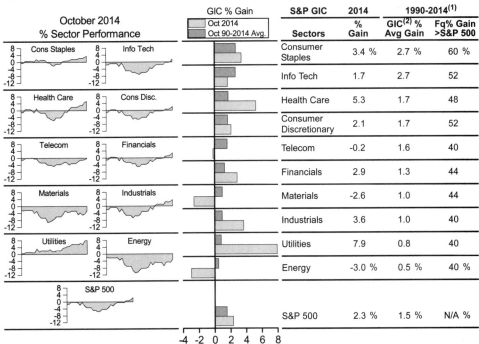

October 2014 % Sector Performance

S&P GIC Sectors	2014 % Gain	1990-2014[1] GIC[2] % Avg Gain	Fq% Gain >S&P 500
Consumer Staples	3.4 %	2.7 %	60 %
Info Tech	1.7	2.7	52
Health Care	5.3	1.7	48
Consumer Discretionary	2.1	1.7	52
Telecom	-0.2	1.6	40
Financials	2.9	1.3	44
Materials	-2.6	1.0	44
Industrials	3.6	1.0	40
Utilities	7.9	0.8	40
Energy	-3.0 %	0.5 %	40 %
S&P 500	2.3 %	1.5 %	N/A %

GIC % Gain — Oct 2014 / Oct 90-2014 Avg.

Sector Commentary

♦ The defensive sectors are on average the top performing sectors of the market in October. In 2014, the first half of October was sharply negative and once earnings started to roll in, the stock market rebounded. Through the up and down markets, the defensive sectors were the top performers. The utilities sector produced a gain of 7.9%, the health care sector a gain of 5.3% and the consumer staples sector a gain of 3.4%. ♦ The energy sector continued on its downward spiral, producing a loss of 3.0%. The materials sector also produced a loss of 2.6%.

Sub-Sector Commentary

♦ With the U.S. economy still one of the strongest economies in the world and with a strong surge in home sales, the homebuilders sub-sector produced a gain of 10.3%. ♦ Railroads continued their solid performance with a gain of 6.0%. ♦ The biotech sub-sector's strong seasonal period ended in mid-September. In 2014, the momentum of the sub-sector carried into October. ♦ Gold and silver often perform poorly in October and 2014 was no exception. ♦ The metals and mining sub-sector followed its seasonal trend of underperformance, with a loss of 7.2%.

SELECTED SUB-SECTORS[3]			
Agriculture (1994-2014)	-8.0 %	5.9 %	76 %
Railroads	6.0	4.4	72
Software & Services	0.4	4.1	60
Transportation	5.9	4.1	76
Pharma	3.0	2.2	60
Steel	-2.5	2.1	40
SOX (1995-2014)	0.4	1.8	40
Chemicals	-2.6	1.8	52
Retail	2.5	1.8	56
Biotech (1993-2014)	7.9	1.7	45
Homebuilders	10.3	1.1	40
Banks	1.4	0.8	36
Metals & Mining	-7.2	0.0	36
Gold (London PM)	-4.3	-1.1	24
Silver	-5.3	-1.5	32

CANADIAN SNOWBIRD TRADE
October 28th to December 18th

Canadians that flock to the U.S. in their retirement years in order to avoid the Canadian cold winters have been bestowed the title of snowbirds.

As snowbirds make their annual pilgrimage to the U.S., all Canadians should consider reallocating some of their Canadian investments to the U.S., as the U.S. stock market tends to outperform the Canadian stock market from October 28th to December 18th. In this period, during the years 1985 to 2014, the S&P 500 has produced an average gain of 3.7% and has been positive 77% of the time.

3.7% gain &
positive 77% of the time

Over the same time period, the TSX Composite is also positive, but historically, it has not performed as well as the S&P 500. There is a cluster of years from 1999 to 2006 where the TSX Composite outperformed the S&P 500 frequently. This anomaly in the data set is mainly the result of the commodity super bull that was taking place at the time and largely favored the Canadian stock market.

TSX Comp vs. S&P 500 1985 to 2014			
			Positive
Oct 28 to Dec 18	TSX Comp	S&P 500	Diff
1985	9.1%	11.9%	2.8%
1986	0.6	3.4	2.8
1987	9.8	6.9	-2.9
1988	-3.2	-0.4	2.9
1989	1.9	2.6	0.7
1990	4.9	8.3	3.4
1991	-3.0	-0.2	2.8
1992	1.0	5.5	4.4
1993	0.6	0.4	-0.2
1994	-3.5	-1.5	1.9
1995	6.4	4.7	-1.7
1996	3.2	4.4	1.2
1997	-0.1	8.9	9.0
1998	6.0	11.5	5.6
1999	15.5	9.6	-5.9
2000	-3.4	-4.1	-0.8
2001	8.3	3.5	-4.8
2002	2.4	-0.7	-3.2
2003	6.0	5.6	-0.4
2004	3.8	6.1	2.3
2005	8.7	7.5	-1.2
2006	4.2	3.3	-0.9
2007	-6.6	-5.2	1.3
2008	-1.3	4.3	5.6
2009	3.7	3.7	0.0
2010	5.1	5.2	0.2
2011	-6.7	-5.1	1.6
2012	0.3	2.5	2.2
2013	-0.5	2.9	3.4
2014	-0.8	5.1	5.9
Avg	2.4%	3.7%	1.3%
Fq > 0	67%	77%	63%

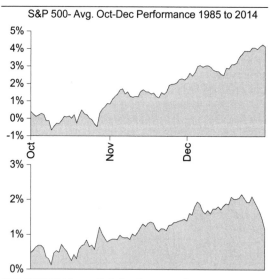

S&P 500- Avg. Oct-Dec Performance 1985 to 2014

S&P 500/TSX Comp Relative Strength- Oct-Dec1985-2014

nate of the TSX Composite's under-performance at this time.

Investors should note that the last part of December, on average starting December 19th, the TSX Composite has outperformed the S&P 500 mainly as a result of gold and oil stocks having a small bounce into year-end.

Investors should monitor the relative performance of gold and oil stocks in order to determine if the *Canadian Snowbird Trade* should be exited early.

Two major commodities that affect the TSX Composite much more than the S&P 500 are gold and oil. Both commodities tend to have weak performance from October to December and are a major determi-

Canadian Snowbird Strategy Performance

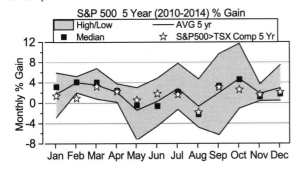

S&P 500 Monthly Performance (1985-2014)

Legend: ☐ Avg % Gain   + Med % Gain

	Jan	Feb	Mar	Apr	May	Jun	Jul	Aug	Sep	Oct	Nov	Dec
Avg. % Gain	1.2	0.5	1.4	1.5	1.4	-0.0	0.8	-0.4	-0.7	0.9	1.2	1.9
Med. % Gain	2.0	0.9	1.5	1.2	1.7	0.0	-0.5	0.9	-0.8	1.9	2.0	1.4
Fq %>0	67	67	67	67	73	57	47	57	47	67	67	80
Fq %> TSX Comp	50	47	57	67	47	53	43	43	60	53	57	47

S&P 500 5 Year (2010-2014) % Gain

Legend: ☐ High/Low ■ Median — AVG 5 yr ☆ S&P500>TSX Comp 5 Yr

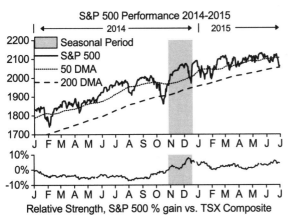

S&P 500 Performance 2014-2015

Legend: ☐ Seasonal Period, — S&P 500, ···· 50 DMA, – – 200 DMA

Relative Strength, S&P 500 % gain vs. TSX Composite

Market Indices & Rates
Weekly Values**

Stock Markets	2013	2014
Dow	15,105	16,946
S&P500	1,688	1,962
Nasdaq	3,797	4,465
TSX	12,793	14,859
FTSE	6,453	6,560
DAX	8,627	9,369
Nikkei	14,259	15,987
Hang Seng	23,049	23,076

Commodities	2013	2014
Oil	103.12	91.44
Gold	1309.9	1211.9

Bond Yields	2013	2014
USA 5 Yr Treasury	1.39	1.73
USA 10 Yr T	2.64	2.47
USA 20 Yr T	3.42	2.92
Moody's Aaa	4.58	4.00
Moody's Baa	5.41	4.76
CAN 5 Yr T	1.87	1.60
CAN 10 Yr T	2.55	2.11

Money Market	2013	2014
USA Fed Funds	0.25	0.25
USA 3 Mo T-B	0.02	0.02
CAN tgt overnight rate	1.00	1.00
CAN 3 Mo T-B	0.97	0.92

Foreign Exchange	2013	2014
EUR/USD	1.36	1.26
GBP/USD	1.62	1.62
USD/CAD	1.03	1.12
USD/JPY	97.68	109.24

OCTOBER

M	T	W	T	F	S	S
					1	2
3	4	5	6	7	8	9
10	11	12	13	14	15	16
17	18	19	20	21	22	23
24	25	26	27	28	29	30
31						

NOVEMBER

M	T	W	T	F	S	S
	1	2	3	4	5	6
7	8	9	10	11	12	13
14	15	16	17	18	19	20
21	22	23	24	25	26	27
28	29	30				

DECEMBER

M	T	W	T	F	S	S
			1	2	3	4
5	6	7	8	9	10	11
12	13	14	15	16	17	18
19	20	21	22	23	24	25
26	27	28	29	30	31	

The core of the *Canadian Snowbird* trade is November, which on average has been one of the strongest months for the S&P 500, since 1985. Although the core months of the *Canadian Snowbird* trade, October, November and December, all have success rates of the S&P 500 outperforming the TSX Composite less than 60% of the time, the total *Canadian Snowbird* trade has a success rate of 63%. On average, over the last five years the S&P 500 has outperformed the TSX Composite in every month except May and August. In 2014, the S&P 500 started to strongly outperform the TSX Composite in the summer and the trend continued into the *Canadian Snowbird* trade period.

HOMEBUILDERS—
TIME TO BREAK & TIME TO BUILD
①SELL SHORT (Apr27-Jun13) ②LONG (Oct28-Feb3)

The homebuilders sector has been in the spotlight for the last few years: first when the mortgage meltdown occurred in 2007 and 2008, and more recently, as the housing market has bounced back giving the homebuilders sector a boost.

18% extra & positive 20 times out of 25

Historically, the best time to be in the homebuilders sector has been from October 28th to February 3rd. In this time period, during the years 1990/91 to 2014/15, the homebuilders sector has produced an average gain of 18.0% and have been positive 92% of the time.

In the two years where losses occurred, the drawdowns were relatively small, at least compared to the large gains that the homebuilders sector has produced during its strong seasonal time period.

Generally the rest of the year, other than the strong seasonal period, is a time that seasonal investors should avoid the homebuilders sector, as not only has the average performance relative to the S&P 500 been negative, but the sector has produced both large gains and losses. In other words, the risk is substantially higher that a large drawdown will occur.

This is particularly true for the time period from April 27th to June 13th. In this time period from 1990 to 2015, the homebuilders sector produced an average loss of 3.6% and was only positive 32% of the time.

(i) *Homebuilders: SP GIC Sector: An index designed to represent a cross section of homebuilding companies.* For more information, see www.standardandpoors.com.

Homebuilders (HB)* vs. S&P 500 1990/91 to 2014/15
Negative Short [ ]   Positive Long [ ]

	SHORT Apr 27 to Jun 13		LONG Oct 28 to Feb 3		Compound Growth	
Year	S&P 500	HB	S&P 500	HB	S&P 500	HB
1990/91	9.6 %	7.9 %	12.6 %	58.0 %	1.8 %	45.5 %
1991/92	-0.4	-4.8	6.6	41.2	7.0	48.0
1992/93	0.2	-11.5	6.9	26.7	6.7	41.2
1993/94	3.2	12.6	3.5	8.6	0.2	-5.1
1994/95	1.6	-4.0	2.8	-4.0	1.1	-0.2
1995/96	4.6	11.1	9.7	16.7	4.7	3.7
1996/97	2.2	10.6	12.2	6.3	9.8	-4.9
1997/98	16.7	22.6	14.7	24.8	-4.5	-3.4
1998/99	-0.8	-10.6	19.4	12.4	20.4	24.2
1999/00	-4.9	-7.1	9.9	-3.9	15.3	2.9
2000/01	0.6	-3.8	-2.2	18.6	-2.7	23.1
2001/02	0.6	-17.5	1.6	43.1	1.0	68.1
2002/03	-6.2	-5.3	-4.2	6.7	1.8	12.3
2003/04	10.0	31.5	10.2	7.6	-0.8	-26.3
2004/05	0.1	-2.6	5.7	23.7	5.6	26.9
2005/06	4.3	11.9	7.2	14.8	2.7	1.1
2006/07	-6.3	-27.1	5.2	16.8	11.7	48.4
2007/08	1.4	-7.9	-9.1	8.8	-10.4	17.4
2008/09	-2.7	-25.3	-1.2	27.7	1.4	60.0
2009/10	9.2	-25.1	3.2	15.5	-6.3	44.4
2010/11	-9.9	-22.9	10.5	12.9	21.5	38.7
2011/12	-5.6	-11.2	4.7	35.0	10.6	50.1
2012/13	-6.1	-9.3	7.2	13.7	13.7	24.3
2013/14	3.4	-7.2	-1.0	10.1	-4.4	18.1
2014/15	3.9	4.5	4.5	7.8	0.4	3.0
Avg.	1.1 %	-3.6 %	5.6 %	18.0 %	4.3 %	22.5 %
Fq>0	64 %	32 %	80 %	92 %	76 %	80 %

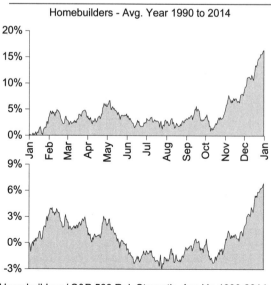

Homebuilders - Avg. Year 1990 to 2014

Homebuilders / S&P 500 Rel. Strength- Avg Yr. 1990-2014

Homebuilders Performance

Homebuilders Monthly Performance (1990-2014)

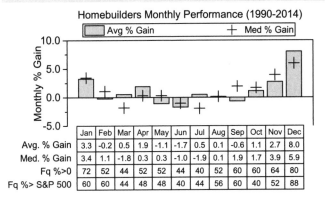

	Jan	Feb	Mar	Apr	May	Jun	Jul	Aug	Sep	Oct	Nov	Dec
Avg. % Gain	3.3	-0.2	0.5	1.9	-1.1	-1.7	0.5	0.1	-0.6	1.1	2.7	8.0
Med. % Gain	3.4	1.1	-1.8	0.3	0.3	-1.0	-1.9	0.1	1.9	1.7	3.9	5.9
Fq %>0	72	52	44	52	52	44	40	52	60	60	64	80
Fq %> S&P 500	60	60	44	48	48	40	44	56	60	40	52	88

Homebuilders 5 Year (2010-2014) % Gain

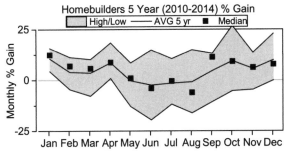

Homebuilders Performance 2014-2015

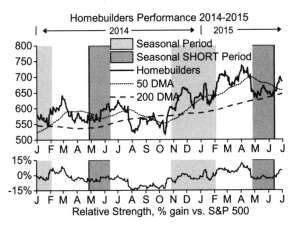

Relative Strength, % gain vs. S&P 500

Market Indices & Rates
Weekly Values**

Stock Markets	2013	2014
Dow	14,976	16,782
S&P500	1,677	1,941
Nasdaq	3,739	4,393
TSX	12,800	14,535
FTSE	6,412	6,463
DAX	8,615	9,017
Nikkei	14,077	15,610
Hang Seng	23,071	23,325

Commodities	2013	2014
Oil	102.63	87.62
Gold	1304.2	1213.8

Bond Yields	2013	2014
USA 5 Yr Treasury	1.43	1.61
USA 10 Yr T	2.68	2.36
USA 20 Yr T	3.43	2.82
Moody's Aaa	4.58	3.92
Moody's Baa	5.38	4.68
CAN 5 Yr T	1.89	1.52
CAN 10 Yr T	2.58	2.04

Money Market	2013	2014
USA Fed Funds	0.25	0.25
USA 3 Mo T-B	0.05	0.01
CAN tgt overnight rate	1.00	1.00
CAN 3 Mo T-B	0.93	0.90

Foreign Exchange	2013	2014
EUR/USD	1.35	1.27
GBP/USD	1.60	1.61
USD/CAD	1.04	1.12
USD/JPY	97.53	108.08

OCTOBER

M	T	W	T	F	S	S
					1	2
3	4	5	6	7	8	9
10	11	12	13	14	15	16
17	18	19	20	21	22	23
24	25	26	27	28	29	30
31						

NOVEMBER

M	T	W	T	F	S	S
	1	2	3	4	5	6
7	8	9	10	11	12	13
14	15	16	17	18	19	20
21	22	23	24	25	26	27
28	29	30				

DECEMBER

M	T	W	T	F	S	S
			1	2	3	4
5	6	7	8	9	10	11
12	13	14	15	16	17	18
19	20	21	22	23	24	25
26	27	28	29	30	31	

From 1990 to 2014, the best month of the year for the home-builders sector has been December on an average, median and frequency basis. On average, it has been best to enter the sector in late October and exit in early February. The following months do not perform particularly well for the sector and in particular, May and June are weak performing months.

Over the last five years, on average, the homebuilders sector has followed its general seasonal trend. The anomaly has been the strength of September, as the homebuilders sector started its seasonal run early. In 2014, the combination of seasonal long and short positions outperformed the S&P 500.

 **UNITED TECHNOLOGIES**
①Jan23-May5　②Oct10-Dec31

United Technologies is a conglomerate industrial company and as such has similar seasonal periods to the industrial sector. The difference is that United Technologies starts one of its seasonal periods earlier in October. The industrial sector starts its seasonal period on October 28th, whereas United Technologies starts its seasonal period on October 10th.

During the time period from October 10th to October 27th, in the years 1990 to 2014, United Technologies has produced an average gain of 3.0% and has been positive 68% of the time. As a result, it is worthwhile to consider entering a position in United Technologies before the start of the industrial sector's seasonal period. When United Technologies outperforms in early October, it is often a precursor of what to expect for the broad market.

The combined trade of January 23rd to May 5th and October 10th to December 31st has produced a 20.2% gain and has been successful 100% of the time since 1990.

Investors should note that being positive 100% of the time in the past does not guarantee the success of the trade in the future. Nevertheless, it does indicate the strength of the seasonal trade.

9.5% extra & positive 25 times out of 25

Given that United Technologies produces 6% of its revenues from China (Reuters), investors should be looking to the strength of the Chinese economy in order to help determine the possible strength of the United Technologies seasonal trade.

(i) *United Technologies Corporation is a multinational conglomerate in the industrial sector. For more information, see UTC.com*

UTX* vs. S&P 500 - 1990 to 2014 Positive ▢

Year	Jan 23 to May 5 S&P 500	UTX	Oct 10 to Dec 31 S&P 500	UTX	Compound Growth S&P 500	UTX
1990	2.4 %	10.2 %	8.2 %	5.2 %	10.8 %	15.9 %
1991	16.0	4.0	10.7	27.3	28.4	32.4
1992	-0.3	-0.9	8.2	4.1	7.9	3.1
1993	1.9	4.7	1.3	8.5	3.3	13.7
1994	-4.9	-0.4	0.9	1.2	-4.0	0.8
1995	11.9	15.0	6.5	12.0	19.2	28.8
1996	4.6	14.1	6.3	7.8	11.2	23.0
1997	5.6	15.9	0.0	-7.5	5.6	7.3
1998	15.8	31.5	24.9	41.7	44.6	86.3
1999	10.0	27.2	10.0	9.7	20.9	39.6
2000	-0.6	7.7	-5.8	12.2	-6.4	20.9
2001	-5.7	9.9	8.6	26.7	2.5	39.2
2002	-4.1	7.6	13.3	25.9	8.6	35.5
2003	5.5	-2.6	7.1	14.7	12.9	11.8
2004	-2.0	-9.6	8.0	11.8	5.9	1.1
2005	0.4	2.3	4.4	11.5	4.8	14.1
2006	5.1	18.0	5.0	-4.1	10.4	13.2
2007	5.8	6.1	-6.2	-5.7	-0.7	0.0
2008	7.4	11.0	-0.7	15.7	6.6	28.4
2009	9.2	5.9	4.1	11.7	13.7	18.2
2010	6.8	6.5	7.9	8.0	15.3	15.0
2011	4.0	10.4	8.8	2.3	13.2	12.9
2012	4.1	3.6	-1.1	6.1	3.0	9.9
2013	8.2	6.5	11.6	10.7	20.7	17.8
2014	2.2	0.6	6.8	15.1	9.1	15.8
Avg.	4.4 %	8.2 %	6.0 %	10.9 %	10.7 %	20.2 %
Fq>0	76 %	84 %	80 %	88 %	88 %	100 %

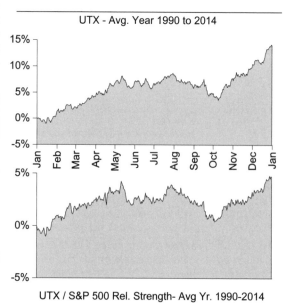

UTX - Avg. Year 1990 to 2014

UTX / S&P 500 Rel. Strength- Avg Yr. 1990-2014

- 125 -

UTX Performance

UTX Monthly Performance (1990-2014)

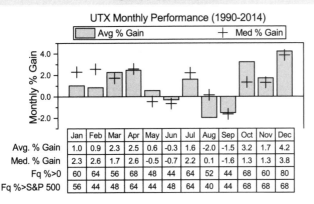

	Jan	Feb	Mar	Apr	May	Jun	Jul	Aug	Sep	Oct	Nov	Dec
Avg. % Gain	1.0	0.9	2.3	2.5	0.6	-0.3	1.6	-2.0	-1.5	3.2	1.7	4.2
Med. % Gain	2.3	2.6	1.7	2.6	-0.5	-0.7	2.2	0.1	-1.6	1.3	1.3	3.8
Fq %>0	60	64	56	68	48	44	64	52	44	68	60	80
Fq %>S&P 500	56	44	48	64	44	48	64	40	44	68	68	68

UTX 5 Year (2010-2014) % Gain

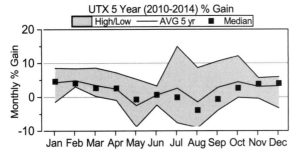

UTX Performance 2014-2015

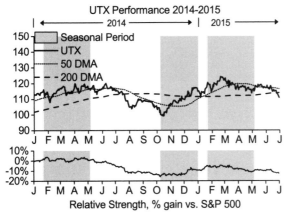

Relative Strength, % gain vs. S&P 500

WEEK 42

Market Indices & Rates
Weekly Values**

Stock Markets	2013	2014
Dow	15,323	16,255
S&P500	1,721	1,873
Nasdaq	3,845	4,226
TSX	13,015	14,047
FTSE	6,565	6,295
DAX	8,810	8,729
Nikkei	14,514	14,820
Hang Seng	23,250	23,051

Commodities	2013	2014
Oil	101.48	82.96
Gold	1293.1	1234.7

Bond Yields	2013	2014
USA 5 Yr Treasury	1.39	1.41
USA 10 Yr T	2.66	2.19
USA 20 Yr T	3.41	2.67
Moody's Aaa	4.55	3.83
Moody's Baa	5.32	4.62
CAN 5 Yr T	1.88	1.43
CAN 10 Yr T	2.59	1.95

Money Market	2013	2014
USA Fed Funds	0.25	0.25
USA 3 Mo T-B	0.08	0.02
CAN tgt overnight rate	1.00	1.00
CAN 3 Mo T-B	0.92	0.88

Foreign Exchange	2013	2014
EUR/USD	1.36	1.28
GBP/USD	1.61	1.60
USD/CAD	1.03	1.13
USD/JPY	98.23	106.61

OCTOBER

M	T	W	T	F	S	S
					1	2
3	4	5	6	7	8	9
10	11	12	13	14	15	16
17	18	19	20	21	22	23
24	25	26	27	28	29	30
31						

NOVEMBER

M	T	W	T	F	S	S
	1	2	3	4	5	6
7	8	9	10	11	12	13
14	15	16	17	18	19	20
21	22	23	24	25	26	27
28	29	30				

DECEMBER

M	T	W	T	F	S	S
			1	2	3	4
5	6	7	8	9	10	11
12	13	14	15	16	17	18
19	20	21	22	23	24	25
26	27	28	29	30	31	

From 1990 to 2014, the best month for United Technologies is December on an average, median and frequency basis. December is the last month of the autumn seasonal period and as such, investors should give the stock some leeway to demonstrate its strength at this time. Over the last five years, United Technologies has generally followed its seasonal trend with weaker summer months. The dispersion of returns in the summer months was much larger than at other times, despite the average poor performance at this time. In the 2014/15 seasonal trade, United Technologies started off strong and faded in the springtime, but still ended up positive and outperforming the S&P 500.

The *Retail – Shop Early* strategy is the second retail sector strategy of the year and it occurs before the biggest shopping season of the year – the Christmas holiday season.

3.0% extra & 80% of the time better than S&P 500

The time to go shopping for retail stocks is at the end of October, which is about one month before Thanksgiving. It is the time when two favorable influences happen at the same time.

Retail Sector - Avg. Year 1990 to 2014

Retail / S&P 500 Relative Strength - Avg Yr. 1990 - 2014

First, historically, the three best months in a row for the stock market have been November, December and January. The end of October usually represents an excellent buying opportunity, not only for the next three months, but the next six months.

Second, investors tend to buy retail stocks in anticipation of a strong holiday sales season. At the same time that the market tends to increase, investors are attracted back into the retail sector.

Retail sales tend to be lower in the summer and a lot of investors view investing in retail stocks at this time as dead money. During the summertime, investors prefer not to invest in this sector until it comes back

into favor towards the end of October.

The trick to investing is not to be too early, but early. If an investor gets into a sector too early, they can suffer from the frustration of having dead money– having an investment that goes nowhere, while the rest of the market increases.

If an investor moves into a sector too late, there is very little upside potential. In fact, this can be a dangerous strategy because if the sales or earnings numbers disappoint the analysts, the sector can severely correct.

For the *Retail – Shop Early* strategy, the time to enter is approximately one month before Black Friday.

The end of October is also typically a good time to enter the broad market.

| Oct 28 | Positive | | |
to Nov 29	S&P 500	Retail	Diff
1990	3.8 %	9.9 %	6.0 %
1991	-2.3	2.7	5.0
1992	2.8	5.5	2.8
1993	-0.6	6.3	6.9
1994	-2.3	0.4	2.7
1995	4.8	9.5	4.7
1996	8.0	0.4	-7.6
1997	8.9	16.9	7.9
1998	11.9	20.4	8.4
1999	8.6	14.1	5.5
2000	-2.7	9.9	12.6
2001	3.2	7.9	4.7
2002	4.3	-1.7	-6.0
2003	2.6	2.5	-0.1
2004	4.7	7.0	2.3
2005	6.7	9.9	3.2
2006	1.6	0.2	-1.4
2007	-4.3	-7.5	-3.2
2008	5.6	7.5	1.9
2009	2.6	3.6	1.0
2010	0.5	5.2	4.7
2011	-7.0	-4.5	2.5
2012	0.3	5.1	4.8
2013	2.6	5.0	2.4
2014	5.4	8.9	3.5
Avg.	2.8 %	5.8 %	3.0 %
Fq > 0	76 %	88 %	80 %

Retail Sector vs. S&P 500 1990 to 2014

Retail Performance

Retail Monthly Performance (1990-2014)

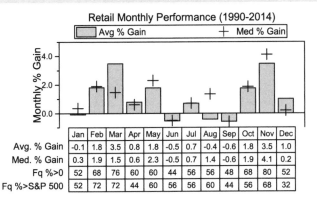

	Jan	Feb	Mar	Apr	May	Jun	Jul	Aug	Sep	Oct	Nov	Dec
Avg. % Gain	-0.1	1.8	3.5	0.8	1.8	-0.5	0.7	-0.4	-0.6	1.8	3.5	1.0
Med. % Gain	0.3	1.9	1.5	0.6	2.3	-0.5	0.7	1.4	-0.6	1.9	4.1	0.2
Fq %>0	52	68	76	60	60	44	56	56	48	68	80	52
Fq %>S&P 500	52	72	72	44	60	56	56	60	44	56	68	32

Retail 5 Year (2010-2014) % Gain

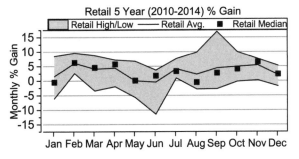

Retail Performance 2014-2015

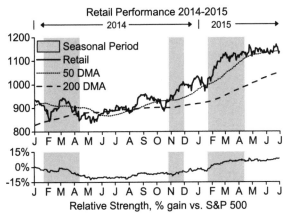

Relative Strength, % gain vs. S&P 500

Market Indices & Rates Weekly Values**

Stock Markets	2013	2014
Dow	15,471	16,592
S&P500	1,752	1,938
Nasdaq	3,926	4,411
TSX	13,280	14,446
FTSE	6,692	6,369
DAX	8,940	8,916
Nikkei	14,481	15,108
Hang Seng	23,058	23,240

Commodities	2013	2014
Oil	97.53	82.11
Gold	1334.9	1240.8

Bond Yields	2013	2014
USA 5 Yr Treasury	1.32	1.47
USA 10 Yr T	2.55	2.25
USA 20 Yr T	3.32	2.73
Moody's Aaa	4.46	3.93
Moody's Baa	5.21	4.68
CAN 5 Yr T	1.76	1.45
CAN 10 Yr T	2.46	1.98

Money Market	2013	2014
USA Fed Funds	0.25	0.25
USA 3 Mo T-B	0.04	0.02
CAN tgt overnight rate	1.00	1.00
CAN 3 Mo T-B	0.91	0.89

Foreign Exchange	2013	2014
EUR/USD	1.38	1.27
GBP/USD	1.62	1.61
USD/CAD	1.04	1.12
USD/JPY	97.68	107.50

OCTOBER

M	T	W	T	F	S	S
					1	2
3	4	5	6	7	8	9
10	11	12	13	14	15	16
17	18	19	20	21	22	23
24	25	26	27	28	29	30
31						

NOVEMBER

M	T	W	T	F	S	S
	1	2	3	4	5	6
7	8	9	10	11	12	13
14	15	16	17	18	19	20
21	22	23	24	25	26	27
28	29	30				

DECEMBER

M	T	W	T	F	S	S
			1	2	3	4
5	6	7	8	9	10	11
12	13	14	15	16	17	18
19	20	21	22	23	24	25
26	27	28	29	30	31	

From 1990 to 2014, the two best months for the retail sector were March and November, on an average basis. November is the core part of the autumn retail seasonal trade and has the highest median performance. Over the last five years, on average the retail sector has followed its general seasonal pattern, with the strongest months being February, April and November. These months are part of either the spring seasonal trade or the autumn seasonal trade. In 2014, the retail sector outperformed the S&P 500 in its autumn seasonal period and in 2015, it outperformed in its spring seasonal period.

INDUSTRIAL STRENGTH
① Oct28-Dec31 ② Jan23-May5

The industrial sector's seasonal trends are largely the same as the broad market, such as the S&P 500. Although the trends are similar, there still exists an opportunity to take advantage of the time period when the industrial sector tends to outperform.

11.9% gain & positive 92% of the time

Industrials tend to outperform in the favorable six months, but there is an opportunity to temporarily get out of the sector to avoid a time period when the sector has, on average, decreased before turning positive again.

The overall strategy is to be invested in the industrial sector from October 28th to December 31st, sell at the end of the day on the 31st, and re-enter the sector to be invested from January 23rd to May 5th.

Using the complete *Industrial Strength* strategy from 1989/90 to 2014/15, the industrial sector has produced a total compounded average annual gain of 11.9%.

In addition, it has been positive 92% of the time and has outperformed the S&P 500, 73% of the time.

During the time period from January 1st to January 22nd, the industrial sector has on average lost 0.7% and has only been positive 50% of the time.

It should be noted that longer term investors may decide to be invested during the whole time period from October 28th to May 5th.

Shorter term investors may decide to use technical analysis to determine, if and when, they should temporarily sell the industrials sector during its weak period from January 1st to January 22nd.

Industrials* vs. S&P 500 1989/90 to 2014/15   Positive ☐

Year	Oct 28 to Dec 31 S&P 500	Oct 28 to Dec 31 Ind.	Jan 23 to May 5 S&P 500	Jan 23 to May 5 Ind.	Compound Growth S&P 500	Compound Growth Ind.
1989/90	5.5 %	6.9 %	2.4 %	5.5 %	8.0 %	12.7 %
1990/91	8.4	10.7	16.0	15.2	25.7	27.5
1991/92	8.6	7.2	-0.3	-1.0	8.2	6.1
1992/93	4.1	6.3	1.9	5.4	6.1	12.0
1993/94	0.4	5.1	-4.9	-6.7	-4.5	-2.0
1994/95	-1.4	-0.5	11.9	12.4	10.3	11.8
1995/96	6.3	10.7	4.6	7.6	11.1	19.1
1996/97	5.7	4.5	5.6	5.2	11.6	9.9
1997/98	10.7	10.5	15.8	11.5	28.2	23.2
1998/99	15.4	10.5	10.0	19.5	26.9	32.1
1999/00	13.3	10.8	-0.6	4.5	12.6	15.8
2000/01	-4.3	1.8	-5.7	4.7	-9.7	6.6
2001/02	3.9	8.1	-4.1	-5.3	-0.3	2.4
2002/03	-2.0	-1.3	5.5	8.6	3.4	7.1
2003/04	7.8	11.6	-2.0	-3.3	5.7	7.9
2004/05	7.7	8.7	0.4	0.2	8.1	8.9
2005/06	5.9	7.6	5.1	14.3	11.3	23.0
2006/07	3.0	3.1	5.8	6.8	9.0	10.1
2007/08	-4.4	-3.4	7.4	9.7	2.7	6.0
2008/09	6.4	7.1	9.2	6.1	16.2	13.7
2009/10	4.9	6.4	6.8	13.4	12.0	20.6
2010/11	6.4	8.1	4.0	4.9	10.6	13.5
2011/12	-2.1	-1.0	4.1	0.3	1.9	-0.7
2012/13	1.0	4.1	8.2	4.9	9.3	9.2
2013/14	5.0	7.3	2.2	1.6	7.3	9.0
2014/15	5.0	5.2	1.3	-1.0	6.3	4.1
Avg.	4.7 %	6.0 %	4.3 %	5.6 %	9.2 %	11.9 %
Fq > 0	81 %	85 %	77 %	81 %	88 %	92 %

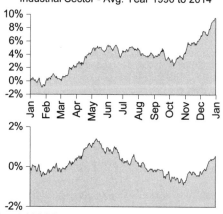

Industrial Sector - Avg. Year 1990 to 2014

Industrial / S&P 500 Rel. Strength - Avg Yr. 1990 - 2014

> *Alternate Strategy—*
> *Investors can bridge the gap between the two positive seasonal trends for the industrials sector by holding from October 28th to May 5th. Longer term investors may prefer this strategy, shorter term investors can use technical tools to determine the appropriate strategy.*

> ⓘ *The SP GICS Industrial Sector. For more information on the industrials sector, see www.standardandpoors.com*

- 129 -

Industrials Performance

Industrials Monthly Performance (1990-2014)

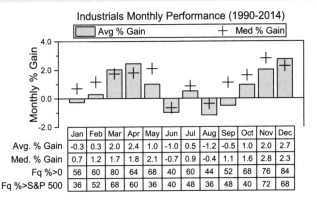

	Jan	Feb	Mar	Apr	May	Jun	Jul	Aug	Sep	Oct	Nov	Dec
Avg. % Gain	-0.3	0.3	2.0	2.4	1.0	-1.0	0.5	-1.2	-0.5	1.0	2.0	2.7
Med. % Gain	0.7	1.2	1.7	1.8	2.1	-0.7	0.9	-0.4	1.1	1.6	2.8	2.3
Fq %>0	56	60	80	64	68	40	60	44	52	68	76	84
Fq %>S&P 500	36	52	68	60	36	40	48	36	48	40	72	68

Industrials 5 Year (2010-2014) % Gain

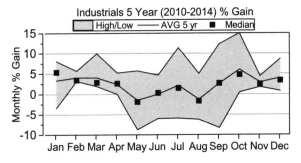

Industrials Performance 2014-2015

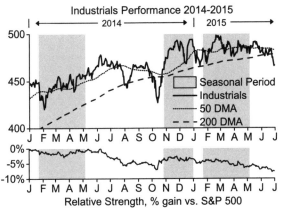

Relative Strength, % gain vs. S&P 500

WEEK 44

Market Indices & Rates
Weekly Values**

Stock Markets	2013	2014
Dow	15,606	17,077
S&P500	1,763	1,988
Nasdaq	3,933	4,559
TSX	13,393	14,539
FTSE	6,749	6,446
DAX	9,011	9,099
Nikkei	14,351	15,669
Hang Seng	23,083	23,637

Commodities	2013	2014
Oil	96.93	81.26
Gold	1339.2	1209.6

Bond Yields	2013	2014
USA 5 Yr Treasury	1.32	1.57
USA 10 Yr T	2.57	2.32
USA 20 Yr T	3.34	2.78
Moody's Aaa	4.48	3.92
Moody's Baa	5.23	4.72
CAN 5 Yr T	1.73	1.53
CAN 10 Yr T	2.44	2.04

Money Market	2013	2014
USA Fed Funds	0.25	0.25
USA 3 Mo T-B	0.04	0.02
CAN tgt overnight rate	1.00	1.00
CAN 3 Mo T-B	0.90	0.89

Foreign Exchange	2013	2014
EUR/USD	1.37	1.26
GBP/USD	1.60	1.61
USD/CAD	1.04	1.12
USD/JPY	98.28	109.28

OCTOBER

M	T	W	T	F	S	S
					1	2
3	4	5	6	7	8	9
10	11	12	13	14	15	16
17	18	19	20	21	22	23
24	25	26	27	28	29	30
31						

NOVEMBER

M	T	W	T	F	S	S
	1	2	3	4	5	6
7	8	9	10	11	12	13
14	15	16	17	18	19	20
21	22	23	24	25	26	27
28	29	30				

DECEMBER

M	T	W	T	F	S	S
			1	2	3	4
5	6	7	8	9	10	11
12	13	14	15	16	17	18
19	20	21	22	23	24	25
26	27	28	29	30	31	

From 1990 to 2014, the real sweet spot for the industrial sector trade, on average, has been November and December. The worst two months have been June and August.

Over the last five years, on average, the industrial sector has somewhat followed its seasonal trend, with its poorest performance in the summer months and its better performance in the autumn months.

In 2014, the industrial sector performed approximately at market for its autumn seasonal leg and then outperformed for its 2015 spring seasonal leg.

NOVEMBER

	MONDAY	TUESDAY	WEDNESDAY
WEEK 45	31	**1** 29	**2** 28
WEEK 46	**7** 23	**8** 22	**9** 21
WEEK 47	**14** 16	**15** 15	**16** 14
WEEK 48	**21** 9	**22** 8	**23** 7
WEEK 49	**28** 2	**29** 1	**30**

THURSDAY	FRIDAY
3 27	**4** 26
10 20	**11** 19
	USA Bond Market Closed- Veterans Day
	CAD Bond Market Closed- Remembrance Day
17 13	**18** 12
24 6	**25** 5
USA Market Closed- Thanksgiving Day	USA Early Market Close Thanksgiving
1	2

DECEMBER

M	T	W	T	F	S	S
			1	2	3	4
5	6	7	8	9	10	11
12	13	14	15	16	17	18
19	20	21	22	23	24	25
26	27	28	29	30	31	

JANUARY

M	T	W	T	F	S	S
						1
2	3	4	5	6	7	8
9	10	11	12	13	14	15
16	17	18	19	20	21	22
23	24	25	26	27	28	29
30	31					

FEBRUARY

M	T	W	T	F	S	S
		1	2	3	4	5
6	7	8	9	10	11	12
13	14	15	16	17	18	19
20	21	22	23	24	25	26
27	28					

MARCH

M	T	W	T	F	S	S
		1	2	3	4	5
6	7	8	9	10	11	12
13	14	15	16	17	18	19
20	21	22	23	24	25	26
27	28	29	30	31		

NOVEMBER
S U M M A R Y

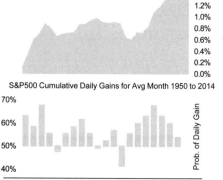

S&P500 Cumulative Daily Gains for Avg Month 1950 to 2014

	Dow Jones	S&P 500	Nasdaq	TSX Comp
Month Rank	3	2	3	8
# Up	44	43	29	18
# Down	21	22	14	12
% Pos	68	66	67	60
% Avg. Gain	1.5	1.5	1.7	0.6

Dow & S&P 1950-2014, Nasdaq 1972-2014, TSX 1985-2014

♦ November, on average, is one of the better months of the year and from 1950 to 2014, the S&P 500 produced an average gain of 1.5% and has been positive 66% of the time. ♦ In November, the cyclical sectors start to increase their relative performance to the S&P 500, with the metals and mining sector starting its period of seasonal strength on November 16th. ♦ For investors looking for a short-term investment, the day before and the day after Thanksgiving are on average the two strongest days of the year.

BEST / WORST NOVEMBER BROAD MKTS. 2005-2014

BEST NOVEMBER MARKETS
♦ Nikkei 225 (2013) 9.3%
♦ Nikkei 225 (2005) 9.3%
♦ Nikkei 225 (2010) 8.0%

WORST NOVEMBER MARKETS
♦ Russell 2000 (2008) -12.0%
♦ Nasdaq (2008) -10.8%
♦ Russell 1000 (2008) -7.9%

Index Values End of Month

	2005	2006	2007	2008	2009	2010	2011	2012	2013	2014
Dow	10,806	12,222	13,372	8,829	10,345	11,006	12,046	13,026	16,086	17,828
S&P 500	1,249	1,401	1,481	896	1,096	1,181	1,247	1,416	1,806	2,068
Nasdaq	2,233	2,432	2,661	1,536	2,145	2,498	2,620	3,010	4,060	4,792
TSX Comp.	10,824	12,752	13,689	9,271	11,447	12,953	12,204	12,239	13,395	14,745
Russell 1000	1,306	1,464	1,550	925	1,150	1,258	1,324	1,506	1,932	2,209
Russell 2000	1,683	1,954	1,908	1,176	1,441	1,807	1,833	2,043	2,840	2,916
FTSE 100	5,423	6,049	6,433	4,288	5,191	5,528	5,505	5,867	6,651	6,723
Nikkei 225	14,872	16,274	15,681	8,512	9,346	9,937	8,435	9,446	15,662	17,460

Percent Gain for November

	2005	2006	2007	2008	2009	2010	2011	2012	2013	2014
Dow	3.5	1.2	-4.0	-5.3	6.5	-1.0	0.8	-0.5	3.5	2.5
S&P 500	3.5	1.6	-4.4	-7.5	5.7	-0.2	-0.5	0.3	2.8	2.5
Nasdaq	5.3	2.7	-6.9	-10.8	4.9	-0.4	-2.4	1.1	3.6	3.5
TSX Comp.	4.2	3.3	-6.4	-5.0	4.9	2.2	-0.4	-1.5	0.3	0.9
Russell 1000	3.5	1.9	-4.5	-7.9	5.6	0.1	-0.5	0.5	2.6	2.4
Russell 2000	4.7	2.5	-7.3	-12.0	3.0	3.4	-0.5	0.4	3.9	0.0
FTSE 100	2.0	-1.3	-4.3	-2.0	2.9	-2.6	-0.7	1.5	-1.2	2.7
Nikkei 225	9.3	-0.8	-6.3	-0.8	-6.9	8.0	-6.2	5.8	9.3	6.4

November Market Avg. Performance 2005 to 2014[1]

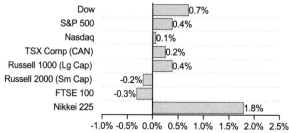

Dow 0.7%
S&P 500 0.4%
Nasdaq 0.1%
TSX Comp (CAN) 0.2%
Russell 1000 (Lg Cap) 0.4%
Russell 2000 (Sm Cap) -0.2%
FTSE 100 -0.3%
Nikkei 225 1.8%

-1.0% -0.5% 0.0% 0.5% 1.0% 1.5% 2.0% 2.5%

Interest Corner Nov[2]

	Fed Funds %[3]	3 Mo. T-Bill %[4]	10 Yr %[5]	20 Yr %[6]
2014	0.25	0.02	2.18	2.62
2013	0.25	0.06	2.75	3.54
2012	0.25	0.08	1.62	2.37
2011	0.25	0.01	2.08	2.77
2010	0.25	0.17	2.81	3.80

(1) Russell Data provided by Russell (2) Federal Reserve Bank of St. Louis- end of month values (3) Target rate set by FOMC (4)(5)(6) Constant yield maturities.

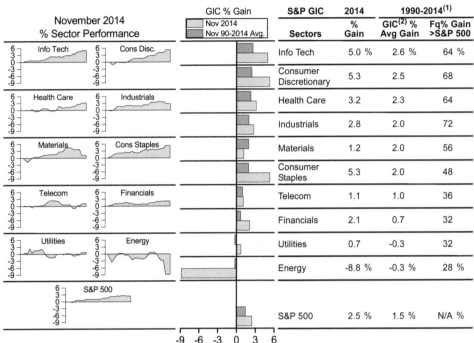

| S&P GIC | 2014 | 1990-2014[1] | |
Sectors	% Gain	GIC[2] % Avg Gain	Fq% Gain >S&P 500
Info Tech	5.0 %	2.6 %	64 %
Consumer Discretionary	5.3	2.5	68
Health Care	3.2	2.3	64
Industrials	2.8	2.0	72
Materials	1.2	2.0	56
Consumer Staples	5.3	2.0	48
Telecom	1.1	1.0	36
Financials	2.1	0.7	32
Utilities	0.7	-0.3	32
Energy	-8.8 %	-0.3 %	28 %
S&P 500	2.5 %	1.5 %	N/A %

GIC % Gain: Nov 2014 / Nov 90-2014 Avg.

November 2014 % Sector Performance

Sector Commentary

♦ In November 2014, the S&P 500 started off on a strong note and ended up producing a gain of 2.5%. ♦ November proved to be a very well behaved seasonal month, with the sectors that typically outperform, performing well and the sectors that tend to be weaker, underperforming the S&P 500. ♦ The top performing sectors were the consumer staples and consumer discretionary sectors, both with gains of 5.3%. ♦ Information technology also performed extremely well with a 5.0% gain for the month. Since 1990, information technology has on average been the best performing sector. ♦ On average, the worst performing sector in November has been the energy sector. In 2014, it lived up to its reputation and produced a large loss of 8.8%.

Sub-Sector Commentary

♦ The agriculture sub-sector has only outperformed the S&P 500 48% of the time since 1994, but on average has strongly outperformed on a percentage gain basis. ♦ In November 2014, the agriculture sub-sector produced a gain of 12.1%. ♦ The home-builders sub-sector continued on its strong October upward trajectory and produced an 11.3% gain in November.

SELECTED SUB-SECTORS[3]

Agriculture (1994-2014)	12.1 %	4.3 %	48 %
Retail	6.0	3.5	68
SOX (1995-2014)	7.0	3.3	55
Steel	-0.2	2.9	52
Home-builders	11.3	2.7	52
Software & Services	2.7	2.3	68
Pharma	4.4	2.2	60
Transportation	5.1	2.1	48
Biotech (1993-2014)	-1.7	1.8	45
Chemicals	1.1	1.8	48
Gold (London PM)	1.6	1.7	56
Metals & Mining	-1.7	1.5	52
Silver	-1.4	1.4	52
Railroads	0.5	1.0	52
Banks	0.9	0.7	44

(1) Sector data provided by Standard and Poors (2) GIC is short form for Global Industry Classification (3) Sub Sector data provided by Standard and Poors, except where marked by symbol.

MATERIAL STOCKS — MATERIAL GAINS
①Oct28-Jan6 ②Jan23-May5

Materials Composition – CAUTION

The U.S. materials sector is substantially different from the Canadian materials sector. The U.S. sector has over a 60% weight in chemical companies, versus the Canadian sector which has over a 60% weight in gold companies.

The materials sector (U.S.) generally does well during the favorable six months of the year, from the end of October to the beginning of May. The sector is economically sensitive and is leveraged to economic forecasts. Generally, if the economy is expected to slow, the materials sector tends to decline and vice versa.

Positive 96% of the time

The materials sector has two seasonal periods. The first period is from October 28th to January 6th and second period is from January 23rd to May 5th.

In the first seasonal period, the materials sector has produced an average gain of 7.0% in the years from 1990 to 2014 and has been positive 85% of the time.

The second seasonal period from January 23rd to May 5th, has produced an average gain of 7.3% (almost double the S&P 500) and has been positive 77% of the time.

The time period in between the two seasonal periods, from January 7th to January 22nd, has had an average loss of 2.4% and only been positive 38% of the time (1989/90 to 2014/15). Investors may decide to bridge the gap between the two seasonal periods if the materials sector has strong momentum at the beginning of January.

The complete materials strategy is to be invested from October 28th to January 6th, out of the sector from January 7th to the 22nd, and back in from January 23rd to May 5th. This strategy has produced an average gain of 14.8% and has been positive 96% of the time.

Materials* vs. S&P 500 1989/90 to 2014/15 Positive ☐

Year	Oct 28 to Jan6 S&P 500	Mat.	Jan 23 to May 5 S&P 500	Mat.	Compound Growth S&P 500	Mat.
1989/90	5.1 %	9.1 %	2.4 %	-3.1 %	7.7 %	5.7 %
1990/91	5.4	9.2	16.0	15.3	22.2	26.0
1991/92	8.8	1.5	-0.3	5.5	8.5	7.1
1992/93	3.8	5.6	1.9	4.3	5.8	10.2
1993/94	0.5	9.4	-4.9	-5.3	-4.4	3.6
1994/95	-1.1	-3.5	11.9	6.1	10.7	2.4
1995/96	6.4	7.6	4.6	11.1	11.3	19.5
1996/97	6.7	2.3	5.6	2.3	12.6	4.6
1997/98	10.2	1.4	15.8	20.9	27.7	22.6
1998/99	19.4	6.1	10.0	31.5	31.3	39.6
1999/00	8.2	15.7	-0.6	-7.1	7.6	7.5
2000/01	-5.9	19.2	-5.7	15.1	-11.2	37.2
2001/02	6.2	8.5	-4.1	14.9	1.8	24.7
2002/03	3.5	9.2	5.5	2.7	9.2	12.1
2003/04	9.0	16.6	-2.0	-3.0	6.8	13.1
2004/05	5.6	5.4	0.4	0.3	6.0	5.8
2005/06	9.0	16.3	5.1	14.7	14.6	33.5
2006/07	2.4	3.2	5.8	10.7	8.3	14.2
2007/08	-8.1	-5.1	7.4	16.7	-1.2	10.8
2008/09	10.1	12.0	9.2	23.3	20.3	38.1
2009/10	6.9	13.8	6.8	3.0	14.2	17.2
2010/11	7.7	11.7	4.0	4.2	12.1	16.4
2011/12	-0.5	-2.3	4.1	-2.7	3.5	-4.9
2012/13	3.9	7.2	8.2	0.0	12.3	7.2
2013/14	3.8	3.1	2.2	4.3	6.1	7.5
2014/15	2.1	-0.7	1.3	2.9	3.4	2.2
Avg.	5.0 %	7.0 %	4.3 %	7.3 %	9.5 %	14.8 %
Fq > 0	85 %	85 %	77 %	77 %	88 %	96 %

Materials Sector - Avg. Year 1990 to 2014

Materials / S&P 500 Rel. Strength - Avg Yr. 1990 - 2014

> **Ⓨ** *Alternate Strategy—*
> *Investors can bridge the gap between the two positive seasonal trends for the materials sector by holding from October 28th to May 5th. Longer term investors may prefer this strategy. Shorter term investors can use technical tools to determine the appropriate strategy.*

> **ⓘ** **The SP GICS Materials Sector encompasses a wide range of materials based companies.*
> *For more information on the materials sector, see www.standardandpoors.com*

Materials Performance

Materials Monthly Performance (1990-2014)

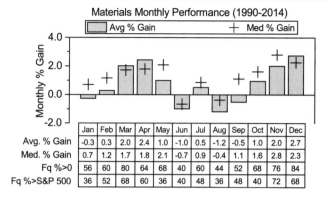

	Jan	Feb	Mar	Apr	May	Jun	Jul	Aug	Sep	Oct	Nov	Dec
Avg. % Gain	-0.3	0.3	2.0	2.4	1.0	-1.0	0.5	-1.2	-0.5	1.0	2.0	2.7
Med. % Gain	0.7	1.2	1.7	1.8	2.1	-0.7	0.9	-0.4	1.1	1.6	2.8	2.3
Fq %>0	56	60	80	64	68	40	60	44	52	68	76	84
Fq %>S&P 500	36	52	68	60	36	40	48	36	48	40	72	68

Materials 5 Year (2010-2014) % Gain

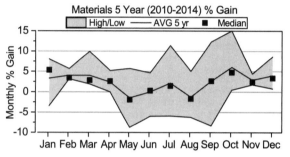

Materials Performance 2014-2015

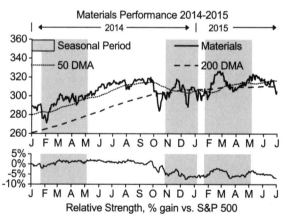

Relative Strength, % gain vs. S&P 500

Market Indices & Rates
Weekly Values**

Stock Markets	2013	2014
Dow	15,672	17,473
S&P500	1,764	2,023
Nasdaq	3,917	4,631
TSX	13,355	14,546
FTSE	6,732	6,520
DAX	9,049	9,281
Nikkei	14,219	16,868
Hang Seng	22,978	23,731

Commodities	2013	2014
Oil	94.32	78.24
Gold	1307.9	1155.2

Bond Yields	2013	2014
USA 5 Yr Treasury	1.36	1.63
USA 10 Yr T	2.68	2.36
USA 20 Yr T	3.46	2.79
Moody's Aaa	4.60	3.90
Moody's Baa	5.36	4.76
CAN 5 Yr T	1.79	1.53
CAN 10 Yr T	2.54	2.05

Money Market	2013	2014
USA Fed Funds	0.25	0.25
USA 3 Mo T-B	0.05	0.03
CAN tgt overnight rate	1.00	1.00
CAN 3 Mo T-B	0.90	0.90

Foreign Exchange	2013	2014
EUR/USD	1.35	1.25
GBP/USD	1.60	1.59
USD/CAD	1.04	1.14
USD/JPY	98.58	114.42

NOVEMBER

M	T	W	T	F	S	S
	1	2	3	4	5	6
7	8	9	10	11	12	13
14	15	16	17	18	19	20
21	22	23	24	25	26	27
28	29	30				

DECEMBER

M	T	W	T	F	S	S
			1	2	3	4
5	6	7	8	9	10	11
12	13	14	15	16	17	18
19	20	21	22	23	24	25
26	27	28	29	30	31	

JANUARY

M	T	W	T	F	S	S
						1
2	3	4	5	6	7	8
9	10	11	12	13	14	15
16	17	18	19	20	21	22
23	24	25	26	27	28	29
30	31					

From 1990 to 2014, on average, the four best months for the materials sector were March, April, November and December. March and April make up the core part of the spring leg of the seasonal trade and November and December make up the core part of the winter leg. Over the last five years, the materials sector has on average, generally followed its seasonal trend with weaker performance in the summer months. In 2014, the materials sector outperformed the S&P 500 in its first seasonal leg, but then underperformed in its second seasonal leg as concerns of slowing global growth weighed on the sector. In its 2015 seasonal leg, it once again outperformed the S&P 500

SOX (SEMICONDUCTOR)
TIME TO PUT ON YOUR SOX TRADE
① Oct28-Nov6   ② Jan1-Feb15

Many investors think of the semiconductor sector as the technology sector on steroids, but there are some differences.

The seasonal trends in the semiconductor sector are largely driven by the ordering cycle of semiconductors and economic expectations.

14.7% gain &
positive 86% of the time

Demand for semiconductors tends to reach a low in the second quarter and the beginning of the third quarter. It tends to reach a peak towards the end of the third quarter and into the fourth quarter. Most of the major semiconductor companies report their third quarter earnings in mid-October. Although this quarter realizes some of the seasonal earnings peak, the market tends to be volatile in this month and investors defer their entry into the sector until the market shows consistent strength, typically towards the end of October.

The first quarter of the year tends to be positive for semiconductor companies as the sector tends to perform well into mid-February.

As a result of the cyclical demand for semiconductors, the semiconductor sector has two periods of seasonal strength, with a short period of market performance in between.

The first period of seasonal strength is very short, starting on October 28th and finishing on November 6th. In this time period, from 1994 to 2014 the semiconductor sector has produced an average gain of 6.0% and has been positive 90% of the time. The second period of seasonal strength is from January 1st to February 15th. In this time period, from 1995 to 2015, the semiconductor sector has produced an average gain of 7.8% and has been positive 81% of the time.

SOX Semiconductor* vs. S&P 500   Positive ☐
1994/95 to 2014/15

Year	Oct 28 to Nov 6 S&P 500	SOX	Jan 1 to Feb 15 S&P 500	SOX	Compound Growth S&P 500	SOX
1994/95	-0.8 %	1.4 %	5.5 %	13.9 %	4.7 %	15.5 %
1995/96	1.5	1.5	5.8	-4.5	7.3	-3.1
1996/97	3.4	7.6	9.1	19.5	12.8	28.6
1997/98	7.0	9.9	5.1	16.4	12.4	27.9
1998/99	7.1	11.1	0.1	11.8	7.2	24.2
1999/00	5.7	25.9	-4.6	35.4	0.8	70.5
2000/01	3.8	8.8	0.5	23.4	4.3	34.2
2001/02	1.3	8.2	-3.8	6.2	-2.6	14.9
2002/03	2.9	12.8	-5.1	-3.1	-2.3	9.2
2003/04	2.6	13.8	3.1	0.5	5.7	14.3
2004/05	3.6	1.7	-0.2	1.4	3.5	3.1
2005/06	3.5	5.7	2.5	12.3	6.1	18.6
2006/07	0.2	1.1	2.7	1.3	2.9	2.4
2007/08	-1.0	0.8	-8.1	-14.8	-9.0	-14.2
2008/09	6.6	3.2	-8.5	4.0	-2.4	7.3
2009/10	0.6	-2.5	-3.6	-7.5	-3.0	-9.8
2010/11	3.7	5.8	5.6	12.0	9.5	18.6
2011/12	-2.4	-1.1	6.8	16.8	4.2	15.5
2012/13	1.2	4.5	6.6	11.6	7.8	16.5
2013/14	0.6	1.7	-0.5	4.5	0.1	6.3
2014/15	3.6	4.7	1.9	2.7	5.5	7.5
Avg.	2.6 %	6.0 %	1.0 %	7.8 %	3.6 %	14.7 %
Fq > 0	86 %	90 %	62 %	81 %	76 %	86 %

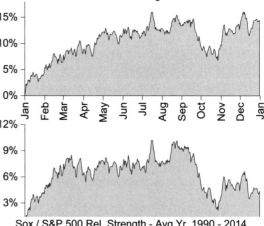

SOX PHLX Semiconductor - Avg. Year 1995 to 2014

Sox / S&P 500 Rel. Strength - Avg Yr. 1990 - 2014

Ⓨ *Alternate Strategy—*
Investors can bridge the gap between the two positive seasonal trends for the semiconductor sector by holding from October 28th to March 1st. Longer term investors may prefer this strategy, shorter term investors can use technical tools to determine the appropriate strategy.

ⓘ *PHLX Semiconductor Index (SOX):*
For more information on the PHLX Semiconductor Index (SOX), see www.nasdaq.com.

SOX Performance

SOX Monthly Performance (1995-2014)

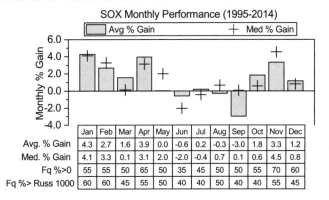

	Jan	Feb	Mar	Apr	May	Jun	Jul	Aug	Sep	Oct	Nov	Dec
Avg. % Gain	4.3	2.7	1.6	3.9	0.0	-0.6	0.2	-0.3	-3.0	1.8	3.3	1.2
Med. % Gain	4.1	3.3	0.1	3.1	2.0	-2.0	-0.4	0.7	0.1	0.6	4.5	0.8
Fq %>0	55	55	50	65	50	35	45	50	50	55	70	60
Fq %> Russ 1000	60	60	45	55	50	40	40	50	40	40	55	45

SOX 5 Year (2010-2014) % Gain

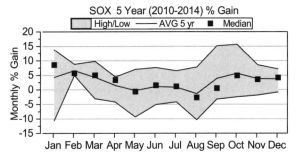

SOX Performance 2014-2015

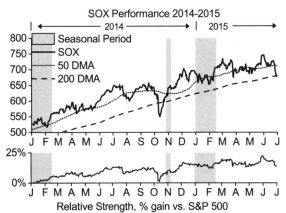

Relative Strength, % gain vs. S&P 500

Market Indices & Rates
Weekly Values**

Stock Markets	2013	2014
Dow	15,839	17,626
S&P500	1,782	2,039
Nasdaq	3,953	4,671
TSX	13,394	14,790
FTSE	6,689	6,628
DAX	9,112	9,287
Nikkei	14,694	17,197
Hang Seng	22,823	23,920

Commodities	2013	2014
Oil	93.93	76.51
Gold	1281.9	1162.8

Bond Yields	2013	2014
USA 5 Yr Treasury	1.40	1.64
USA 10 Yr T	2.74	2.36
USA 20 Yr T	3.53	2.80
Moody's Aaa	4.67	3.94
Moody's Baa	5.43	4.80
CAN 5 Yr T	1.81	1.54
CAN 10 Yr T	2.59	2.05

Money Market	2013	2014
USA Fed Funds	0.25	0.25
USA 3 Mo T-B	0.08	0.02
CAN tgt overnight rate	1.00	1.00
CAN 3 Mo T-B	0.93	0.90

Foreign Exchange	2013	2014
EUR/USD	1.35	1.25
GBP/USD	1.60	1.58
USD/CAD	1.05	1.13
USD/JPY	99.65	115.64

NOVEMBER

M	T	W	T	F	S	S
	1	2	3	4	5	6
7	8	9	10	11	12	13
14	15	16	17	18	19	20
21	22	23	24	25	26	27
28	29	30				

DECEMBER

M	T	W	T	F	S	S
			1	2	3	4
5	6	7	8	9	10	11
12	13	14	15	16	17	18
19	20	21	22	23	24	25
26	27	28	29	30	31	

JANUARY

M	T	W	T	F	S	S
						1
2	3	4	5	6	7	8
9	10	11	12	13	14	15
16	17	18	19	20	21	22
23	24	25	26	27	28	29
30	31					

From 1995 to 2014, on average, the semiconductor sector produced gains in the months from October to April. The end of October and the beginning of November make up most of the gains for both months in the autumn seasonal trade. January and the first part of February tend to be strong and make up the second, longer winter seasonal leg for the semiconductor sector. Over the last five years, the semiconductor sector has on average followed its general seasonal trend by performing well in January, poorly in the summer months and then performing well in October and November. In 2014 and 2015, the seasonal trades were positive and outperformed the S&P 500.

At the macro level, the metals and mining (M&M) sector is driven by future economic growth expectations. When worldwide growth expectations are increasing, there is a greater need for raw materials– when growth expectations are decreasing, the need is less.

Within the macro trend, the M&M sector has traditionally followed the overall market cycle of performing well from autumn until spring. This is the time of year that investors have a positive outlook on the economy and as a result, the cyclical sectors tend to outperform, including the metals and mining sector.

12.3% gain and positive 69% of the time

The metals and mining sector has two seasonal "sweet spots" – the first from November 19th to January 5th and the second from January 23rd to May 5th.

Investors have the option to hold and "bridge the gap" across the two sweet spots, but over the long-term, nimble traders have been able to capture extra value by being out of the sector from January 6th to the 22nd. During this period, from 1990 to 2015, the metals and mining sector has produced an average loss of 2.6% and has only been positive 50% of the time.

From a portfolio perspective, it is important to consider reducing exposure at the beginning of May. The danger of holding on too long is that the sector tends not to perform well in the late summer, particularly in September.

For more information on the metals and mining sector, see www.standardandpoors.com

Metals & Mining* vs. S&P 500 1989/90 to 2014/15				Positive	
	Nov 19 to Jan 5		Jan 23 to May 5		Compound Growth
Year	S&P 500	M&M	S&P 500	M&M	S&P 500	M&M
1989/90	3.1 %	6.3 %	2.4 %	-4.6 %	5.6 %	1.4 %
1990/91	1.2	6.4	16.0	7.1	17.4	13.9
1991/92	8.9	1.0	-0.3	-1.7	8.5	-0.7
1992/93	2.7	12.5	1.9	3.2	4.7	16.1
1993/94	0.9	9.0	-4.9	-11.1	-4.1	-3.1
1994/95	-0.2	-1.2	11.9	-3.0	11.6	-4.1
1995/96	2.8	8.3	4.6	5.8	7.5	14.6
1996/97	1.5	-1.9	5.6	-1.2	7.2	-3.0
1997/98	4.1	-4.5	15.8	19.3	20.6	13.9
1998/99	8.8	-7.9	10.0	31.0	19.6	20.6
1999/00	-1.6	21.7	-0.6	-10.4	-2.2	9.1
2000/01	-5.1	17.0	-5.7	19.6	-10.5	40.0
2001/02	3.0	5.5	-4.1	12.8	-1.3	19.0
2002/03	0.9	9.3	5.5	3.2	6.4	12.8
2003/04	8.5	18.2	-2.0	-12.1	6.4	3.9
2004/05	0.0	-8.4	0.4	-4.0	0.4	-12.0
2005/06	2.0	17.3	5.1	27.3	7.2	49.4
2006/07	0.6	3.0	5.8	17.2	6.5	20.8
2007/08	-3.2	0.9	7.4	27.4	3.9	28.5
2008/09	8.0	43.8	9.2	30.6	17.9	87.8
2009/10	2.4	6.3	6.8	4.8	9.4	11.3
2010/11	6.7	15.0	4.0	-1.6	11.0	13.1
2011/12	5.4	1.2	4.1	-16.0	9.7	-15.0
2012/13	7.8	3.9	8.2	-16.8	16.6	-13.6
2013/14	2.2	1.2	2.2	2.6	4.4	3.8
2014/15	-1.5	-14.2	1.3	5.3	-0.3	-9.7
Avg.	2.7 %	6.5 %	4.3 %	5.2 %	7.1 %	12.3 %
Fq > 0	81 %	77 %	77 %	58 %	81 %	69 %

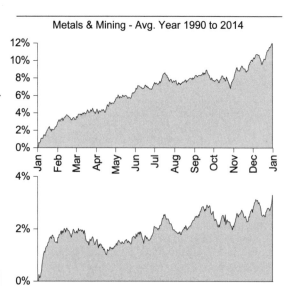

Metals & Mining - Avg. Year 1990 to 2014

Metals & Mining / S&P 500 Rel. Strength- Avg Yr. 1990-2014

Metals & Mining Performance

Metals & Mining Monthly Performance (1990-2014)

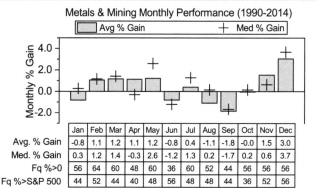

	Jan	Feb	Mar	Apr	May	Jun	Jul	Aug	Sep	Oct	Nov	Dec
Avg. % Gain	-0.8	1.1	1.2	1.1	1.2	-0.8	0.4	-1.1	-1.8	-0.0	1.5	3.0
Med. % Gain	0.3	1.2	1.4	-0.3	2.6	-1.2	1.3	0.2	-1.7	0.2	0.6	3.7
Fq %>0	56	64	60	48	60	36	60	52	44	56	56	56
Fq %>S&P 500	44	52	44	40	48	56	48	48	44	36	52	56

Metals & Mining 5 Year (2010-2014) % Gain

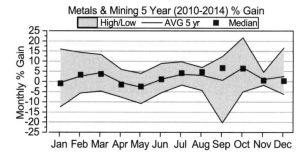

Metals & Mining Performance 2014-2015

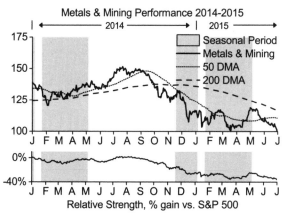

Relative Strength, % gain vs. S&P 500

Market Indices & Rates Weekly Values**

Stock Markets	2013	2014
Dow	15,984	17,710
S&P500	1,792	2,052
Nasdaq	3,953	4,693
TSX	13,457	15,004
FTSE	6,692	6,701
DAX	9,207	9,490
Nikkei	15,223	17,253
Hang Seng	23,659	23,497

Commodities	2013	2014
Oil	93.86	75.36
Gold	1260.5	1193.0

Bond Yields	2013	2014
USA 5 Yr Treasury	1.37	1.64
USA 10 Yr T	2.74	2.33
USA 20 Yr T	3.54	2.78
Moody's Aaa	4.65	3.96
Moody's Baa	5.40	4.84
CAN 5 Yr T	1.77	1.52
CAN 10 Yr T	2.58	2.02

Money Market	2013	2014
USA Fed Funds	0.25	0.25
USA 3 Mo T-B	0.08	0.02
CAN tgt overnight rate	1.00	1.00
CAN 3 Mo T-B	0.94	0.90

Foreign Exchange	2013	2014
EUR/USD	1.35	1.25
GBP/USD	1.62	1.57
USD/CAD	1.05	1.13
USD/JPY	100.52	117.50

NOVEMBER

M	T	W	T	F	S	S
	1	2	3	4	5	6
7	8	9	10	11	12	13
14	15	16	17	18	19	20
21	22	23	24	25	26	27
28	29	30				

DECEMBER

M	T	W	T	F	S	S
			1	2	3	4
5	6	7	8	9	10	11
12	13	14	15	16	17	18
19	20	21	22	23	24	25
26	27	28	29	30	31	

JANUARY

M	T	W	T	F	S	S
						1
2	3	4	5	6	7	8
9	10	11	12	13	14	15
16	17	18	19	20	21	22
23	24	25	26	27	28	29
30	31					

From 1990 to 2014, the strongest month for the metals and mining sector was December, on an average and median basis. Overall, the metals and mining sector does not have a strong track record of positive performance and outperforming the S&P 500, in any month. Nevertheless, the seasonal trend provides value, particularly in a stronger commodity cycle.

Over the last five years, on average the metals and mining sector's monthly performance has not followed its seasonal trend. The seasonal period from the end of November 2014, until the beginning of January did not perform well, like many other commodity sectors.

THANKSGIVING
GIVE THANKS & TAKE RETURNS
Day Before and After – Two of the Best Days

We have a lot to be thankful for on Thanksgiving Day. As a bonus, the market day before and the market day after Thanksgiving, on average, have been two of the best days of the year in the stock market.

Each day, by itself, has produced spectacular results. From 1950 to 2014, the S&P 500 has had an average gain of 0.4% on the day before Thanksgiving and 0.3% on the day after Thanksgiving.

> *The day before Thanksgiving and the day after have had an average cumulative return of 0.7% and together have been positive 85% of the time*

To put the performance of these two days in perspective, the average daily return of the S&P 500 over the same time period is 0.03%.

The gains the day before Thanksgiving and the day after are almost ten times better than the average market and have a much greater frequency of being positive.

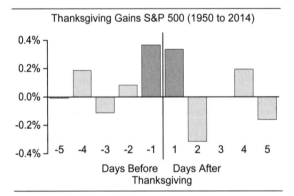

Thanksgiving Gains S&P 500 (1950 to 2014)

Days Before   Days After
Thanksgiving

Ⓨ *Alternate Strategy — Although the focus has been on the performance of two specific days, the day before and the day after Thanksgiving, the holiday occurs at the end of November which tends to be a strong month. December, the next month is also strong. Investors have an option of expanding their trade to include the "Santa Arrives Early & Stays Late" Strategy.*

ⓘ *History of Thanksgiving:*
It was originally a "thanksgiving feast" by the pilgrims for surviving their first winter. Initially it was celebrated sporadically and the holiday, when it was granted, had its date changed several times. It was not until 1941 that it was proclaimed to be the 4th Thursday in November.

S&P500	Day Before	Day After
1950	1.4	0.8
1951	-0.2	-1.1
1952	0.6	0.5
1953	0.1	0.6
1954	0.6	1.0
1955	0.1	-0.1
1956	-0.5	1.1
1957	2.9	1.1
1958	1.7	1.1
1959	0.2	0.5
1960	0.1	0.6
1961	-0.1	0.2
1962	0.6	1.2
1963	-0.2	1.4
1964	-0.3	-0.3
1965	0.2	0.1
1966	0.7	0.8
1967	0.6	0.3
1968	0.5	0.6
1969	0.4	0.6
1970	0.4	1.0
1971	0.2	1.8
1972	0.6	0.3
1973	1.1	-0.3
1974	0.7	0.0
1975	0.3	0.3
1976	0.4	0.7
1977	0.4	0.2
1978	0.5	0.3
1979	0.2	0.8
1980	0.6	0.2
1981	0.4	0.8
1982	0.7	0.7
1983	0.1	0.1
1984	0.2	1.5
1985	0.9	-0.2
1986	0.2	0.2
1987	-0.9	-1.5
1988	0.7	-0.7
1989	0.7	0.6
1990	0.2	-0.3
1991	-0.4	-0.4
1992	0.4	0.2
1993	0.3	0.2
1994	0.0	0.5
1995	-0.3	0.3
1996	-0.1	0.3
1997	0.1	0.4
1998	0.3	0.5
1999	0.9	0.0
2000	-1.9	1.5
2001	-0.5	1.2
2002	2.8	-0.3
2003	0.4	0.0
2004	0.4	0.1
2005	0.3	0.2
2006	0.2	-0.4
2007	-1.6	1.7
2008	3.5	1.0
2009	0.5	-1.7
2010	1.5	-0.7
2011	-2.2	-0.3
2012	0.2	1.3
2013	0.2	-0.1
2014	0.3	-0.3
Total Avg %	0.4%	0.3%
Fq > 0	78%	72%

(Legend: □ Positive; vertical text reads "THANKSGIVING DAY")

- 141 -

Thanksgiving Strategy Performance

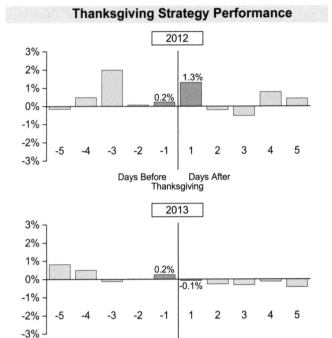

2012

Days Before | Days After
Thanksgiving

2013

Days Before | Days After
Thanksgiving

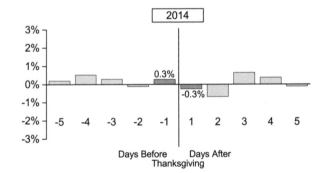

2014

Days Before | Days After
Thanksgiving

In 2012, the day before Thanksgiving produced a small gain and the day after, a large gain. Overall, the trade was a solid success.

In 2013, the net returns from the day before and the day after Thanksgiving were small. In fact, the days surrounding Thanksgiving were unusually quiet, producing either small gains or losses.

In 2014, the S&P 500 had a solid run starting in mid-October. The S&P 500 paused slightly around Thanksgiving, and did not produce a gain.

WEEK 48

Market Indices & Rates
Weekly Values**

Stock Markets	2013	2014
Dow	16,082	17,822
S&P500	1,805	2,069
Nasdaq	4,029	4,773
TSX	13,390	14,959
FTSE	6,657	6,727
DAX	9,347	9,904
Nikkei	15,595	17,375
Hang Seng	23,768	23,968

Commodities	2013	2014
Oil	93.16	72.44
Gold	1246.8	1194.3

Bond Yields	2013	2014
USA 5 Yr Treasury	1.36	1.56
USA 10 Yr T	2.74	2.25
USA 20 Yr T	3.52	2.68
Moody's Aaa	4.62	3.88
Moody's Baa	5.37	4.74
CAN 5 Yr T	1.73	1.45
CAN 10 Yr T	2.54	1.92

Money Market	2013	2014
USA Fed Funds	0.25	0.25
USA 3 Mo T-B	0.07	0.02
CAN tgt overnight rate	1.00	1.00
CAN 3 Mo T-B	0.94	0.91

Foreign Exchange	2013	2014
EUR/USD	1.36	1.25
GBP/USD	1.63	1.57
USD/CAD	1.06	1.13
USD/JPY	101.98	118.06

NOVEMBER

M	T	W	T	F	S	S
	1	2	3	4	5	6
7	8	9	10	11	12	13
14	15	16	17	18	19	20
21	22	23	24	25	26	27
28	29	30				

DECEMBER

M	T	W	T	F	S	S
			1	2	3	4
5	6	7	8	9	10	11
12	13	14	15	16	17	18
19	20	21	22	23	24	25
26	27	28	29	30	31	

JANUARY

M	T	W	T	F	S	S
						1
2	3	4	5	6	7	8
9	10	11	12	13	14	15
16	17	18	19	20	21	22
23	24	25	26	27	28	29
30	31					

DECEMBER

	MONDAY	TUESDAY	WEDNESDAY
WEEK 49	28	29	30
WEEK 50	**5** 26	**6** 25	**7** 24
WEEK 51	**12** 19	**13** 18	**14** 17
WEEK 52	**19** 12	**20** 11	**21** 10
WEEK 01	**26** 5 CAN Market Closed- Christmas Day USA Market Closed- Christmas Day	**27** 4 CAN Market Closed- Boxing Day	**28** 3

THURSDAY		FRIDAY	
1	30	**2**	29
8	23	**9**	22
15	16	**16**	15
22	9	**23**	8
29	2	**30**	1

JANUARY

M	T	W	T	F	S	S
						1
2	3	4	5	6	7	8
9	10	11	12	13	14	15
16	17	18	19	20	21	22
23	24	25	26	27	28	29
30	31					

FEBRUARY

M	T	W	T	F	S	S
		1	2	3	4	5
6	7	8	9	10	11	12
13	14	15	16	17	18	19
20	21	22	23	24	25	26
27	28					

MARCH

M	T	W	T	F	S	S
		1	2	3	4	5
6	7	8	9	10	11	12
13	14	15	16	17	18	19
20	21	22	23	24	25	26
27	28	29	30	31		

APRIL

M	T	W	T	F	S	S
					1	2
3	4	5	6	7	8	9
10	11	12	13	14	15	16
17	18	19	20	21	22	23
24	25	26	27	28	29	30

DECEMBER
S U M M A R Y

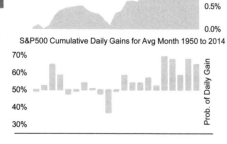

	Dow Jones	S&P 500	Nasdaq	TSX Comp
Month Rank	2	1	2	1
# Up	46	49	25	26
# Down	19	16	18	4
% Pos	71	75	58	87
% Avg. Gain	1.7	1.7	1.8	2.2

Dow & S&P 1950-2014, Nasdaq 1972-2014, TSX 1985-2014

♦ December is typically one of the strongest months of the year for the S&P 500. From 1950 to 2014, the S&P 500 produced an average gain of 1.7% and was positive 75% of the time. ♦ Most of the gains for the S&P 500 are in the second half of the month. ♦ The Nasdaq tends to outperform the S&P 500 starting mid-December. ♦ The small cap sector also starts to outperform mid-month. The small cap sector trade has been positive for the last six years in a row.

BEST / WORST DECEMBER BROAD MKTS. 2005-2014

BEST DECEMBER MARKETS
- ♦ Nikkei 225 (2009) 12.8%
- ♦ Nikkei 225 (2012) 10.0%
- ♦ Nikkei 225 (2005) 8.3%

WORST DECEMBER MARKETS
- ♦ TSX Comp. (2008) -3.1%
- ♦ Nikkei 225 (2007) -2.4%
- ♦ FTSE 100 (2014) -2.3%

Index Values End of Month

	2005	2006	2007	2008	2009	2010	2011	2012	2013	2014
Dow	10,718	12,463	13,265	8,776	10,428	11,578	12,218	13,104	16,577	17,823
S&P 500	1,248	1,418	1,468	903	1,115	1,258	1,258	1,426	1,848	2,059
Nasdaq	2,205	2,415	2,652	1,577	2,269	2,653	2,605	3,020	4,177	4,736
TSX Comp.	11,272	12,908	13,833	8,988	11,746	13,443	11,955	12,434	13,622	14,632
Russell 1000	1,306	1,480	1,538	938	1,176	1,340	1,333	1,518	1,981	2,200
Russell 2000	1,673	1,958	1,904	1,241	1,554	1,948	1,841	2,111	2,892	2,994
FTSE 100	5,619	6,221	6,457	4,434	5,413	5,900	5,572	5,898	6,749	6,566
Nikkei 225	16,111	17,226	15,308	8,860	10,546	10,229	8,455	10,395	16,291	17,451

Percent Gain for December

	2005	2006	2007	2008	2009	2010	2011	2012	2013	2014
Dow	-0.8	2.0	-0.8	-0.6	0.8	5.2	1.4	0.6	3.0	0.0
S&P 500	-0.1	1.3	-0.9	0.8	1.8	6.5	0.9	0.7	2.4	-0.4
Nasdaq	-1.2	-0.7	-0.3	2.7	5.8	6.2	-0.6	0.3	2.9	-1.2
TSX Comp.	4.1	1.2	1.1	-3.1	2.6	3.8	-2.0	1.6	1.7	-0.8
Russell 1000	0.0	1.1	-0.8	1.3	2.3	6.5	0.7	0.8	2.5	-0.4
Russell 2000	-0.6	0.2	-0.2	5.6	7.9	7.8	0.5	3.3	1.8	2.7
FTSE 100	3.6	2.8	0.4	3.4	4.3	6.7	1.2	0.5	1.5	-2.3
Nikkei 225	8.3	5.8	-2.4	4.1	12.8	2.9	0.2	10.0	4.0	-0.1

December Market Avg. Performance 2005 to 2014[1]

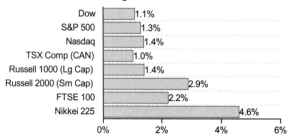

	Interest Corner Dec[2]			
	Fed Funds %[3]	3 Mo. T-Bill %[4]	10 Yr %[5]	20 Yr %[6]
2014	0.25	0.04	2.17	2.47
2013	0.25	0.07	3.04	3.72
2012	0.25	0.05	1.78	2.54
2011	0.25	0.02	1.89	2.57
2010	0.25	0.12	3.30	4.13

(1) Russell Data provided by Russell (2) Federal Reserve Bank of St. Louis- end of month values (3) Target rate set by FOMC (4)(5)(6) Constant yield maturities.

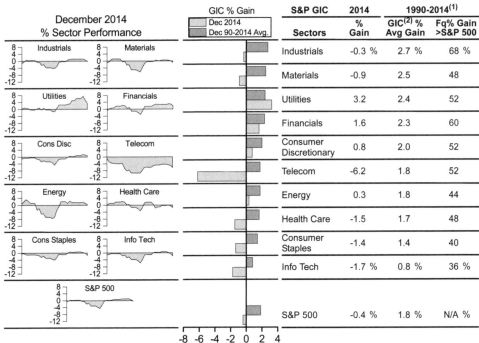

S&P GIC Sectors	2014 % Gain	1990-2014[1] GIC[2] % Avg Gain	Fq% Gain >S&P 500
Industrials	-0.3 %	2.7 %	68 %
Materials	-0.9	2.5	48
Utilities	3.2	2.4	52
Financials	1.6	2.3	60
Consumer Discretionary	0.8	2.0	52
Telecom	-6.2	1.8	52
Energy	0.3	1.8	44
Health Care	-1.5	1.7	48
Consumer Staples	-1.4	1.4	40
Info Tech	-1.7 %	0.8 %	36 %
S&P 500	-0.4 %	1.8 %	N/A %

Sector Commentary

♦ In December 2014, the S&P 500 produced a small loss of 0.4%. ♦ Despite the weak stock market, the defensive telecom sector produced a loss of 6.2%. ♦ On the other hand, the utilities sector, finished the month with a strong 3.2% gain. ♦ The information technology sector, which tends to take a pause and underperform the S&P 500 in its seasonal period that runs from October into January, produced a loss of 1.7%. ♦ The consumer staples and health care sectors, both defensive sectors, produced losses of 1.4% and 1.5% respectively.

Sub-Sector Commentary

♦ The homebuilders sub-sector typically performs well in December, but after a strong rally in previous months, the sector suffered a loss of 2.3%. ♦ Both the metals and mining and the steel sub-sectors, which tend to be strong in December, lost 8.3% and 6.5% respectively. ♦ Banks put in a solid performance of 2.5%. ♦ Based upon strong retail numbers from the holiday season, the retail sub-sector produced a gain of 2.1%. It is typically one of the weaker sub-sectors in December.

SELECTED SUB-SECTORS[3]			
Homebuilders	-2.3 %	8.0 %	88 %
Steel	-6.5	5.2	68
Biotech (1993-2014)	-1.8	4.3	50
Metals & Mining	-8.3	3.0	56
Agriculture (1994-2014)	-1.3	2.2	52
Banks	2.5	2.1	60
Chemicals	0.2	2.1	60
Railroads	0.8	1.8	52
Software & Services	-0.7	1.7	44
Silver	0.0	1.2	48
Transportation	0.8	1.2	40
Pharma	-2.5	1.2	40
SOX (1995-2014)	0.2	1.2	45
Retail	2.1	1.0	32
Gold (London PM)	2.0	-0.1	32

EMERGING MARKETS(USD)– TRUNCATED SIX MONTH SEASONAL
November 24th to April 18th

Emerging markets become popular periodically, mainly after they have had a strong run, or if they have suffered a major correction and investors perceive them to have a lot of value.

Markets around the world tend to have the same broad seasonal trends, including the emerging markets. Typically, emerging markets will outperform when the U.S. market is increasing and underperform when it is decreasing.

The exceptions to this usually occurs if there is a global economic contraction underway, or economic growth is in question, and investors seek the "safety" of the U.S. market. In this case, the emerging markets can underperform the U.S. market.

10.7% gain & positive 84% of the time positive

Seasonal investors have benefited from concentrating their emerging market exposure in a truncated, or shorter version, of the favorable six month seasonal period.

Emerging Markets (USD)* vs. S&P 500
1990/91 to 2014/15

Nov 24 to Apr 18	S&P 500	Positive Em. Mkts.	Diff
1990/91	23.8%	33.8%	10.5%
1991/92	10.6	37.5	26.8
1992/93	5.6	11.8	6.2
1993/94	-4.0	3.7	7.8
1994/95	12.3	-16.4	-28.7
1995/96	7.6	14.7	7.1
1996/97	2.4	7.1	4.7
1997/98	16.6	6.7	-9.9
1998/99	11.0	18.1	7.1
1999/00	2.6	3.5	0.8
2000/01	-6.4	-4.6	1.8
2001/02	-2.3	22.3	24.5
2002/03	-4.0	0.0	4.0
2003/04	9.6	19.5	9.9
2004/05	-2.6	4.3	7.0
2005/06	3.3	24.7	21.4
2006/07	4.7	13.2	8.5
2007/08	-3.5	-0.9	2.6
2008/09	8.7	37.6	28.9
2009/10	7.8	5.6	-2.2
2010/11	10.5	6.6	-3.9
2011/12	19.2	15.6	-3.6
2012/13	9.4	0.1	-9.3
2013/14	3.3	0.3	-3.1
2014/15	0.9	3.8	3.0
Avg	5.9%	10.7%	4.9%
Fq > 0	76%	84%	72%

Emerging Mkts. (USD)- Avg. Year 1990 to 2014

Emerg. Mkts. (USD)/S&P 500 Rel. Str. - Avg Yr. 1990-2014

ing markets sector (USD) produced an average rate of return of 10.7% and has been positive 84% of the time.

As the world has grappled with the sub-prime crisis and then the EU crisis in the last few years, investors have sought the safety of the U.S. markets and as a result, emerging markets have underperformed.

As worldwide economic growth gains traction in the future, seasonal investors should consider adding emerging markets to their portfolio from November 24th to April 18th.

The seasonally strong period for the emerging markets sector is from November 24th to April 18th. In this time period, from 1990/91 to 2014/15, the emerg-

(i) *Emerging Markets (USD)- For more information on the emerging markets, see www.standardand-poors.com*

Emerging Markets Performance

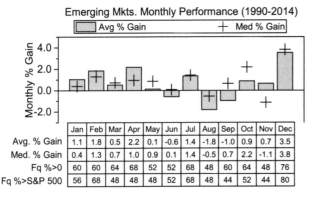

Emerging Mkts. Monthly Performance (1990-2014)

	Jan	Feb	Mar	Apr	May	Jun	Jul	Aug	Sep	Oct	Nov	Dec
Avg. % Gain	1.1	1.8	0.5	2.2	0.1	-0.6	1.4	-1.8	-1.0	0.9	0.7	3.5
Med. % Gain	0.4	1.3	0.7	1.0	0.9	0.1	1.4	-0.5	0.7	2.2	-1.1	3.8
Fq %>0	60	60	64	68	52	52	68	48	60	64	48	76
Fq %>S&P 500	56	68	48	48	48	52	68	48	44	52	44	80

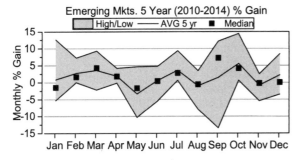

Emerging Mkts. 5 Year (2010-2014) % Gain

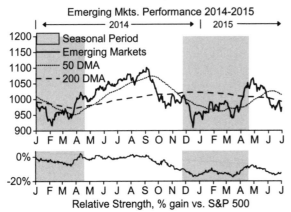

Emerging Mkts. Performance 2014-2015

Relative Strength, % gain vs. S&P 500

Stock Markets	2013	2014
Dow	15,931	17,886
S&P500	1,796	2,068
Nasdaq	4,043	4,762
TSX	13,305	14,589
FTSE	6,538	6,707
DAX	9,205	9,962
Nikkei	15,458	17,756
Hang Seng	23,827	23,657

Commodities	2013	2014
Oil	96.42	67.18
Gold	1226.0	1199.4

Bond Yields	2013	2014
USA 5 Yr Treasury	1.46	1.60
USA 10 Yr T	2.84	2.27
USA 20 Yr T	3.61	2.69
Moody's Aaa	4.69	3.90
Moody's Baa	5.44	4.79
CAN 5 Yr T	1.79	1.44
CAN 10 Yr T	2.64	1.93

Money Market	2013	2014
USA Fed Funds	0.25	0.25
USA 3 Mo T-B	0.06	0.02
CAN tgt overnight rate	1.00	1.00
CAN 3 Mo T-B	0.93	0.90

Foreign Exchange	2013	2014
EUR/USD	1.36	1.24
GBP/USD	1.64	1.57
USD/CAD	1.07	1.14
USD/JPY	102.50	119.73

DECEMBER

M	T	W	T	F	S	S
			1	2	3	4
5	6	7	8	9	10	11
12	13	14	15	16	17	18
19	20	21	22	23	24	25
26	27	28	29	30	31	

JANUARY

M	T	W	T	F	S	S
						1
2	3	4	5	6	7	8
9	10	11	12	13	14	15
16	17	18	19	20	21	22
23	24	25	26	27	28	29
30	31					

FEBRUARY

M	T	W	T	F	S	S
		1	2	3	4	5
6	7	8	9	10	11	12
13	14	15	16	17	18	19
20	21	22	23	24	25	26
27	28					

From 1990 to 2014, December has been the strongest month of the year for emerging markets on an average, median and frequency basis. Although November tends to be a negative month, the last part of the month tends to be a good launching point into the seasonal period for emerging markets.

Over the last five years, September has been the strongest month, but has also had the largest dispersion between the biggest and smallest gains.

In its 2014/2015 seasonal period, the emerging markets sector was positive and outperformed the S&P 500.

Aerospace & Defense Sector Flying High
December 12th to May 5th

The aerospace and defense sector is highly dependent on government purchases and as a result is subject not only to economic cycles, but also the political environment. Despite the fact that outside variables have a large impact on aerospace and defense orders, the sector has a seasonal trend.

The aerospace and defense sector has a seasonal trend that is similar to the overall broad market's seasonal trend. The big difference is that aerospace and defense has a track record of strongly outperforming the S&P 500 up until the beginning of May.

5.2% gain & positive 77% of the time

The difference in the sector's seasonal trend compared with the S&P 500's trend is largely the result of the U.S. governments procurement cycle, which has a year-end of September 30th. The first quarter of the government's fiscal year (October, November and December) tends to be the weakest for orders, as typically major purchases are made towards the end of the last fiscal quarter and the new fiscal quarter is slow to get off the ground. Government procurement tends to pick up at the start of the new calendar year, helping to boost aerospace and defense stocks up until the beginning of May.

Aerospace & Defense* vs. S&P 500
1989/90 to 2014/15

Dec 12 to May 5	S&P 500	Aero & Def.	Diff (Positive)
1989/90	-2.9%	6.1%	9.0%
1990/91	16.7	11.6	-5.1
1991/92	10.4	10.1	-0.3
1992/93	2.5	14.3	11.9
1993/94	-2.7	2.7	5.4
1994/95	16.4	26.0	9.7
1995/96	3.6	11.6	8.0
1996/97	12.1	8.0	-4.1
1997/98	16.8	11.5	-5.3
1998/99	15.5	29.1	13.6
1999/00	1.1	3.6	2.5
2000/01	-8.2	-0.9	7.4
2001/02	-5.6	23.3	28.9
2002/03	2.4	-7.4	-9.8
2003/04	4.7	5.6	0.9
2004/05	-1.3	4.1	5.4
2005/06	5.3	21.0	15.8
2006/07	6.6	9.0	2.5
2007/08	-4.8	-2.5	2.3
2008/09	3.5	8.5	5.1
2009/10	5.4	12.8	7.4
2010/11	7.6	13.0	5.4
2011/12	9.1	7.4	-1.7
2012/13	13.1	14.7	1.7
2013/14	5.8	8.9	3.1
2014/15	2.7	3.0	0.3
Avg	5.2%	9.8%	4.6%
Fq > 0	77%	88%	77%

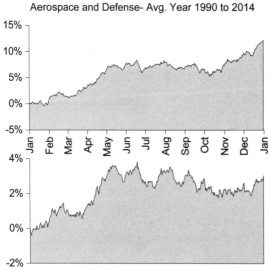

Aerospace and Defense- Avg. Year 1990 to 2014

Aerospace & Def./ S&P 500 Rel. Str. - Avg Yr. 1990 - 2014

been positive 88% of the time. Compared to the S&P 500, it has produced an extra 4.6% and outperformed it 77% of the time.

In the other seven months of the year, from May 6th to December 11th, the aerospace and defense sector has only had a gain of 2.2% and has underperformed the S&P 500, 40% of the time. In this time period, there have been eight years of gains greater than 10% and five years of losses greater than 10%. In other words, the results in the unfavorable period for the sector tend to be volatile.

From 1989/90 to 2014/15, during its seasonal period, December 12th to May 5th, the aerospace and defense sector has produced an average gain of 9.8% and has

 *For more information on the aerospace and defense sector, see www.standardandpoors.com

Aerospace & Defense Performance

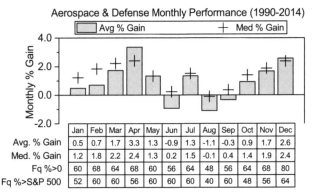

Aerospace & Defense Monthly Performance (1990-2014)

	Jan	Feb	Mar	Apr	May	Jun	Jul	Aug	Sep	Oct	Nov	Dec
Avg. % Gain	0.5	0.7	1.7	3.3	1.3	-0.9	1.3	-1.1	-0.3	0.9	1.7	2.6
Med. % Gain	1.2	1.8	2.2	2.4	1.3	0.2	1.5	-0.1	0.4	1.4	1.9	2.4
Fq %>0	60	68	64	68	60	56	64	48	56	64	68	80
Fq %>S&P 500	52	60	60	56	60	60	60	40	60	48	56	64

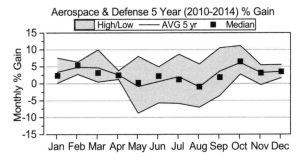

Aerospace & Defense 5 Year (2010-2014) % Gain

Stock Markets	2013	2014
Dow	15,867	17,613
S&P500	1,789	2,037
Nasdaq	4,026	4,711
TSX	13,202	13,966
FTSE	6,495	6,493
DAX	9,082	9,813
Nikkei	15,504	17,558
Hang Seng	23,472	23,524

Commodities	2013	2014
Oil	97.48	61.11
Gold	1244.3	1216.5

Bond Yields	2013	2014
USA 5 Yr Treasury	1.51	1.61
USA 10 Yr T	2.86	2.19
USA 20 Yr T	3.60	2.55
Moody's Aaa	4.66	3.75
Moody's Baa	5.40	4.72
CAN 5 Yr T	1.81	1.39
CAN 10 Yr T	2.65	1.84

Money Market	2013	2014
USA Fed Funds	0.25	0.25
USA 3 Mo T-B	0.07	0.03
CAN tgt overnight rate	1.00	1.00
CAN 3 Mo T-B	0.93	0.89

Foreign Exchange	2013	2014
EUR/USD	1.38	1.24
GBP/USD	1.64	1.57
USD/CAD	1.06	1.15
USD/JPY	103.03	119.12

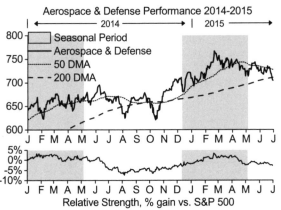

Aerospace & Defense Performance 2014-2015

Relative Strength, % gain vs. S&P 500

DECEMBER

M	T	W	T	F	S	S
			1	2	3	4
5	6	7	8	9	10	11
12	13	14	15	16	17	18
19	20	21	22	23	24	25
26	27	28	29	30	31	

JANUARY

M	T	W	T	F	S	S
						1
2	3	4	5	6	7	8
9	10	11	12	13	14	15
16	17	18	19	20	21	22
23	24	25	26	27	28	29
30	31					

FEBRUARY

M	T	W	T	F	S	S
		1	2	3	4	5
6	7	8	9	10	11	12
13	14	15	16	17	18	19
20	21	22	23	24	25	26
27	28					

From 1990 to 2014, on a monthly average basis, the aerospace and defense sector has increased its gains from January to May, with April being the best month. The summer months have tended to be the weaker months, with August being the weakest.

Over the last five years, on average, the first few months of the year have been stronger than the average month for the rest of the year. The outlier has been October, with an average gain of over 5%. In the December 2014 to May 2015 seasonal period, the aerospace and defense sector was positive and outperformed the S&P 500.

DO THE "NAZ" WITH SANTA
Nasdaq Gives More at Christmas – Dec 15th to Jan 23rd

One of the best times to invest in the major stock markets is the period around Christmas. The markets are generally positive at this time of the year as investors reposition their portfolios for the start of the new year. A lot of investors are familiar with the *Small Cap Effect* opportunity that starts approximately at this time of the year, where small caps tend to outperform from mid-December to the beginning of March (*see Small Cap Effect*), but few investors know that the last half of December and the first half of January is also a seasonally strong period for the Nasdaq.

82% of time better than S&P 500

The Nasdaq tends to perform well in the last two weeks of December, as investors typically increase their investment allocation to higher beta investments, including the Nasdaq, to finish the year.

In addition, the major sector drivers of the Nasdaq (biotech and technology), tend to perform well in the second half of December and the first half of January. Biotech tends to perform well in the last half of December and technology tends to perform well in the first half of January. The end result is a Nasdaq Christmas trade that lasts from December 15th to January 23rd. In this time period, for the years 1971/72 to 2014/15, the Nasdaq has outperformed the S&P 500 by an average 2.2% per year. This rate of return is considered to be very high given that the length of the favorable period is just over one month. Even more impressive is the 82% frequency that the Nasdaq outperforms the S&P 500.

Nasdaq vs. S&P 500 Dec 15th to Jan 23rd 1971/72 To 2014/15

Dec 15 to Jan 23	S&P 500	Positive		
		Nasdaq	Diff	
1971/72	6.1 %	7.5 %	1.3 %	
1972/73	0.0	-0.7	-0.7	
1973/74	4.1	6.8	2.8	
1974/75	7.5	8.9	1.4	
1975/76	13.0	13.8	0.9	
1976/77	-1.7	2.8	4.5	
1977/78	-5.1	-3.5	1.6	
1978/79	4.7	6.2	1.4	
1979/80	4.1	5.6	1.5	
1980/81	0.8	3.3	2.5	
1981/82	-6.0	-5.0	1.0	
1982/83	4.7	5.5	0.8	
1983/84	0.9	1.4	0.4	
1984/85	9.0	13.3	4.3	
1985/86	-2.7	0.8	3.5	
1986/87	9.2	10.2	1.0	
1987/88	1.8	9.1	7.3	
1988/89	3.3	4.6	1.3	
1989/90	-5.5	-3.8	1.7	
1990/91	1.0	4.1	3.1	
1991/92	7.9	15.2	7.2	
1992/93	0.8	7.2	6.4	
1993/94	2.5	5.7	3.2	
1994/95	2.4	4.7	2.3	
1995/96	-0.7	-1.0	-0.3	
1996/97	6.7	7.3	0.6	
1997/98	0.4	2.6	2.1	
1998/99	7.4	18.9	11.6	
1999/00	2.7	18.6	15.9	
2000/01	1.5	4.1	2.6	
2001/02	0.5	-1.6	-2.0	
2002/03	-0.2	1.9	2.1	
2003/04	6.3	9.0	2.7	
2004/05	-3.0	-5.8	-2.9	
2005/06	-0.7	-0.6	0.1	
2006/07	0.2	-0.9	-1.1	
2007/08	-8.8	-12.1	-3.3	
2008/09	-5.4	-4.1	1.3	
2009/10	-2.0	-0.3	1.7	
2010/11	3.4	2.4	-1.0	
2011/12	8.6	9.6	1.1	
2012/13	5.8	6.1	0.4	
2013/14	3.0	5.5	2.5	
2014/15	2.5	2.2	-0.2	
Avg	2.1 %	4.2 %	2.2 %	
Fq > 0	70 %	73 %	82 %	

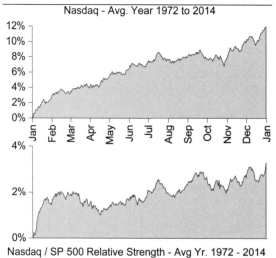

Nasdaq - Avg. Year 1972 to 2014

Nasdaq / SP 500 Relative Strength - Avg Yr. 1972 - 2014

Y *Alternate Strategy — For those investors who favor the Nasdaq, an alternative strategy is to invest in the Nasdaq at an earlier date: October 28th. Historically, on average the Nasdaq has started its outperformance at this time. The "Do the Naz with Santa" strategy focuses on the sweet spot of the Nasdaq's outperformance.*

i *Nasdaq is a market that has a focused on biotech and technology and is typically more volatile than the S&P 500.*

Nasdaq Performance

Nasdaq Monthly Performance (1972-2014)

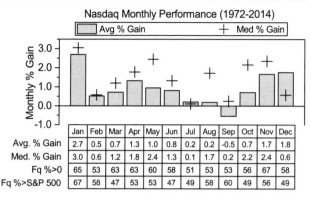

	Jan	Feb	Mar	Apr	May	Jun	Jul	Aug	Sep	Oct	Nov	Dec
Avg. % Gain	2.7	0.5	0.7	1.3	1.0	0.8	0.2	0.2	-0.5	0.7	1.7	1.8
Med. % Gain	3.0	0.6	1.2	1.8	2.4	1.3	0.1	1.7	0.2	2.2	2.4	0.6
Fq %>0	65	53	63	63	60	58	51	53	53	56	67	58
Fq %>S&P 500	67	58	47	53	53	47	49	58	60	49	56	49

Nasdaq 5 Year (2010-2014) % Gain

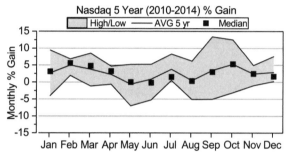

Nasdaq Performance 2014-2015

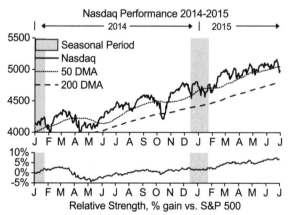

Relative Strength, % gain vs. S&P 500

Market Indices & Rates
Weekly Values**

Stock Markets	2013	2014
Dow	16,066	17,438
S&P500	1,801	2,021
Nasdaq	4,057	4,662
TSX	13,298	14,119
FTSE	6,538	6,372
DAX	9,233	9,608
Nikkei	15,550	17,101
Hang Seng	23,006	22,847

Commodities	2013	2014
Oil	98.04	55.79
Gold	1217.7	1200.4

Bond Yields	2013	2014
USA 5 Yr Treasury	1.58	1.61
USA 10 Yr T	2.89	2.14
USA 20 Yr T	3.61	2.47
Moody's Aaa	4.59	3.74
Moody's Baa	5.35	4.72
CAN 5 Yr T	1.83	1.35
CAN 10 Yr T	2.68	1.80

Money Market	2013	2014
USA Fed Funds	0.25	0.25
USA 3 Mo T-B	0.07	0.04
CAN tgt overnight rate	1.00	1.00
CAN 3 Mo T-B	0.91	0.90

Foreign Exchange	2013	2014
EUR/USD	1.37	1.24
GBP/USD	1.63	1.57
USD/CAD	1.06	1.16
USD/JPY	103.67	118.24

DECEMBER

M	T	W	T	F	S	S
			1	2	3	4
5	6	7	8	9	10	11
12	13	14	15	16	17	18
19	20	21	22	23	24	25
26	27	28	29	30	31	

JANUARY

M	T	W	T	F	S	S
						1
2	3	4	5	6	7	8
9	10	11	12	13	14	15
16	17	18	19	20	21	22
23	24	25	26	27	28	29
30	31					

FEBRUARY

M	T	W	T	F	S	S
		1	2	3	4	5
6	7	8	9	10	11	12
13	14	15	16	17	18	19
20	21	22	23	24	25	26
27	28					

From 1972 to 2014, the best month of the year for the Nasdaq has been January on an average and median basis. January is the core of the Nasdaq trade. December is also a positive month, but on a median and frequency basis, it is weaker than most other months. It is the first part of December that tends to be weaker for the Nasdaq, leading to a mid-month entry into the Nasdaq trade. Over the last five years, the strongest months of the year for the Nasdaq have been February, March, April and October. January was positive in the same time frame, but just not as strong. The 2014/15 Nasdaq trade was positive but fell slightly behind the performance of the S&P 500.

SMALL CAP (SMALL COMPANY) EFFECT
Small Companies Outperform - Dec 19th to Mar 7th

At different stages of the business cycle, small capitalization companies (small caps represented by Russell 2000), perform better than large capitalization companies (large caps represented by Russell 1000).

Evidence shows that the small caps relative outperformance also has a seasonal component as they typically outperform large caps from December 19th to March 7th.

26 times out of 36 better than the Russell 1000

Russell 2000 - Avg. Year 1979 to 2014

Russell 2000 / Russell 1000 - Avg Yr. 1979 - 2014

The core part of the small cap seasonal strategy occurs in January and includes what has been described as the January Effect (Wachtel 1942, 184).

This well documented anomaly of superior performance of stocks in the month of January is based upon the tenet that investors sell stocks in December for tax loss reasons, artificially driving down prices, and creating a great opportunity for astute investors.

In recent times, the January Effect start date has shifted to mid-December and is more pronounced for small caps as their prices are more volatile than large caps. At the beginning of the year, small cap stocks benefit from a phenomenon that I have coined, "beta out of the gate, and coast." If small cap stocks are outperforming at the beginning of the year, money managers will gravitate to the sector in order to produce

Wachtel, S.B. 1942. Certain observations on seasonal movements in stock prices. The Journal of Business and Economics (Winter): 184.

**Russell 2000 vs. Russell 1000* % Gains
Dec 19th to Mar 7th 1979/80 to 2014/15**

Positive ▢

Dec 19 - Mar7	Russell 1000	Russell 2000	Diff
1979/80	-1.3 %	-0.4 %	0.9 %
1980/81	-2.8	4.0	6.8
1981/82	-12.4	-12.1	0.3
1982/83	11.8	19.8	8.0
1983/84	-6.4	-7.5	-1.1
1984/85	7.7	17.1	9.4
1985/86	8.2	11.7	3.5
1986/87	17.2	21.3	4.1
1987/88	8.3	16.4	8.0
1988/89	6.9	9.1	2.5
1989/90	-2.0	-1.9	0.2
1990/91	14.6	29.0	14.4
1991/92	6.0	16.8	10.8
1992/93	1.4	5.0	3.5
1993/94	0.5	5.7	5.3
1994/95	5.3	5.5	0.2
1995/96	8.3	7.8	-0.5
1996/97	9.5	3.5	-6.0
1997/98	10.2	10.3	0.1
1998/99	7.3	0.2	-7.2
1999/00	-1.7	27.7	29.4
2000/01	-5.2	4.7	9.8
2001/02	1.6	1.9	0.4
2002/03	-6.7	-7.8	-1.0
2003/04	6.4	9.6	3.3
2004/05	2.8	0.3	-2.5
2005/06	0.8	5.6	4.7
2006/07	-1.6	-0.8	0.9
2007/08	-10.9	-12.5	-1.5
2008/09	-22.2	-26.7	-4.5
2009/10	3.6	9.1	5.5
2010/11	5.5	4.2	-1.3
2011/12	11.3	10.2	-1.1
2012/13	7.1	10.3	3.1
2013/14	4.2	6.1	2.0
2014/15	1.0	2.1	1.1
Avg.	2.6 %	5.7 %	3.1 %
Fq > 0	69 %	78 %	69 %

returns that are above their index benchmark. Once above average returns have been "locked in," the managers then rotate from their small cap overweight positions back to index large cap positions and coast for the rest of the year with above average returns. The overall process boosts small cap stocks at the beginning of the year.

(i) *Russell 2000 (small cap index): The 2000 smallest companies in the Russell 3000 stock index (a broad market index). Russell 1000 (large cap index): The 1000 largest companies in the Russell 3000 stock index*

For more information on the Russell indexes, see www.Russell.com

Small Cap Performance

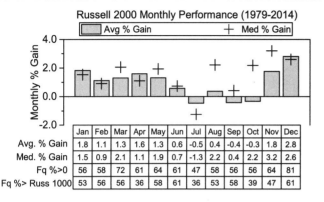

Russell 2000 Monthly Performance (1979-2014)

	Jan	Feb	Mar	Apr	May	Jun	Jul	Aug	Sep	Oct	Nov	Dec
Avg. % Gain	1.8	1.1	1.3	1.6	1.3	0.6	-0.5	0.4	-0.4	-0.3	1.8	2.8
Med. % Gain	1.5	0.9	2.1	1.1	1.9	0.7	-1.3	2.2	0.4	2.2	3.2	2.6
Fq %>0	56	58	72	61	64	61	47	58	56	56	64	81
Fq %> Russ 1000	53	56	56	36	58	61	36	53	58	39	47	61

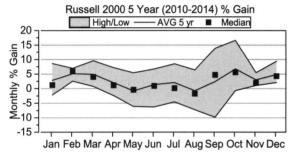

Russell 2000 5 Year (2010-2014) % Gain

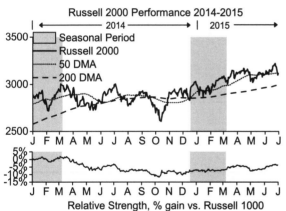

Russell 2000 Performance 2014-2015

Relative Strength, % gain vs. Russell 1000

Market Indices & Rates
Weekly Values**

Stock Markets	2013	2014
Dow	16,403	18,017
S&P500	1,836	2,083
Nasdaq	4,157	4,782
TSX	13,518	14,545
FTSE	6,708	6,595
DAX	9,539	9,894
Nikkei	16,063	17,779
Hang Seng	23,115	23,364

Commodities	2013	2014
Oil	99.38	55.56
Gold	1206.8	1185.5

Bond Yields	2013	2014
USA 5 Yr Treasury	1.72	1.74
USA 10 Yr T	2.99	2.24
USA 20 Yr T	3.66	2.54
Moody's Aaa	4.56	3.79
Moody's Baa	5.35	4.75
CAN 5 Yr T	1.91	1.43
CAN 10 Yr T	2.72	1.89

Money Market	2013	2014
USA Fed Funds	0.25	0.25
USA 3 Mo T-B	0.07	0.03
CAN tgt overnight rate	1.00	0.80
CAN 3 Mo T-B	0.90	0.90

Foreign Exchange	2013	2014
EUR/USD	1.37	1.22
GBP/USD	1.64	1.56
USD/CAD	1.06	1.16
USD/JPY	104.54	120.33

DECEMBER

M	T	W	T	F	S	S
			1	2	3	4
5	6	7	8	9	10	11
12	13	14	15	16	17	18
19	20	21	22	23	24	25
26	27	28	29	30	31	

JANUARY

M	T	W	T	F	S	S
						1
2	3	4	5	6	7	8
9	10	11	12	13	14	15
16	17	18	19	20	21	22
23	24	25	26	27	28	29
30	31					

FEBRUARY

M	T	W	T	F	S	S
		1	2	3	4	5
6	7	8	9	10	11	12
13	14	15	16	17	18	19
20	21	22	23	24	25	26
27	28					

From 1979 to 2014, the best month for the Russell 2000 has been December on an average and frequency basis. On average, the Russell 2000 continued its strong performance into March. Although April is also a positive month, the Russell 2000 only outperformed the Russell 1000 (large cap stocks), thirty-six percent of the time. Over the last five years, on average, the Russell 2000 has been positive in December through to March, but performance has waned into the summer months. After being flat since March 2014 and underperforming the Russell 1000, the Russell 2000 was positive and outperformed the Russell 1000 in its 2014/2015 seasonal period.

FINANCIALS (U.S.) YEAR END CLEAN UP
December 15th to April 13th

The U.S. financial sector often starts its strong performance in October, steps up its performance in mid-December and then strongly outperforms the S&P 500 starting in mid-January.

Extra 2.2% & 65% of the time better than the S&P 500

In the 1990s and early 2000s, financial stocks benefited from the tailwind of falling interest rates. During this period, with a few exceptions, this sector has participated in both the rallies and the declines.

Financials* vs. S&P 500
1989/90 to 2014/15

Dec 15 to Apr 13	S&P 500	Positive Financials	Diff
1989/90	-1.9 %	-9.9 %	-8.0 %
1990/91	16.4	29.2	12.8
1991/92	5.6	9.2	3.5
1992/93	3.8	17.9	14.1
1993/94	-3.6	-0.4	3.2
1994/95	11.9	14.0	2.1
1995/96	3.2	5.5	2.3
1996/97	1.2	4.7	3.4
19/9798	16.4	19.7	3.3
1998/99	18.3	24.9	6.6
1999/00	2.7	4.0	1.3
2000/01	-11.7	-4.8	6.9
2001/02	-1.1	6.5	7.6
2002/03	-2.4	-1.8	0.6
2003/04	5.2	6.7	1.5
2004/05	-2.5	-6.2	-3.7
2005/06	1.3	1.1	-0.2
2006/07	1.9	-2.2	-4.1
2007/08	-9.2	-14.1	-4.9
2008/09	-2.4	-7.0	-4.6
2009/10	7.5	15.2	7.8
2010/11	5.9	4.6	-1.3
2011/12	13.1	20.7	7.7
2012/13	12.4	16.0	3.6
2013/14	2.3	1.0	-1.3
2014/15	4.5	1.1	-3.4
Avg.	3.8 %	6.0 %	2.2 %
Fq > 0	69 %	69 %	65 %

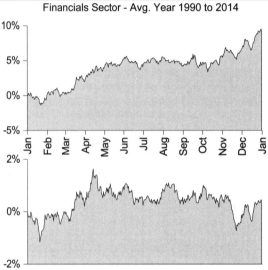

Financials Sector - Avg. Year 1990 to 2014

Financials / S&P 500 Relative Strength - Avg Yr. 1990-2014

On the other hand, a tighter monetary policy will slow the economy and reduce bank profits. Given this volatile situation, investors should concentrate their financial investments during the sector's strong seasonal period.

It should be noted that Canadian banks have their year-ends at the end of October (reporting in November) and as such, their seasonally strong period starts in October.

The main driver for the strong seasonal performance of the financial sector has been the year-end earnings of the banks that start to report in mid-January. A strong performance from mid-December has been the result of investors getting into the market early to take advantage of positive year-end earnings.

Interest rates are at historic lows and the U.S. Federal Reserve is poised to raise its target interest rate. If and when the Federal Reserve starts to increase its target interest rate, banks should benefit in the short-term as their net interest margin will increase. A large portion of their loans are tied to the Federal Reserve's target rate and with an increase in the target rate, the banks will earn more money. Although the interest that they will have to pay out will also increase, the rate of increase will be much slower.

*Financial SP GIC Sector # 40:
For more information on the financial sector, see www.standardandpoors.com

Financials Performance

Financials Monthly Performance (1990-2014)

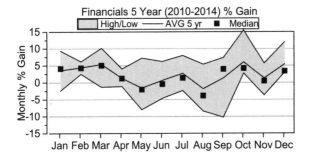

	Jan	Feb	Mar	Apr	May	Jun	Jul	Aug	Sep	Oct	Nov	Dec
Avg. % Gain	0.0	-0.1	2.1	2.2	1.5	-1.2	1.3	-1.3	-0.5	1.3	0.7	2.3
Med. % Gain	0.7	1.8	0.1	1.3	1.9	-0.1	1.8	0.8	1.7	1.4	2.1	1.9
Fq %>0	52	64	56	60	64	48	60	52	60	64	56	76
Fq %>S&P 500	64	64	60	52	44	40	48	40	56	44	32	60

Financials 5 Year (2010-2014) % Gain

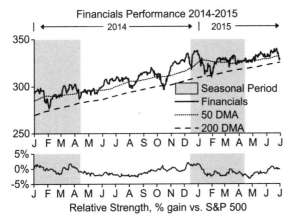

Financials Performance 2014-2015

From 1990 to 2014, December through to March, the core of the seasonal time period for the financial sector, have been the only months (other than September) that have outperformed the S&P 500 more than half of the time. Over the same yearly time period, there is a large dispersion between the monthly averages and the medians, indicating the performance inconsistency of the financial sector. These results have been largely skewed by the 2008-2009 financial crisis. Over the last five years, the summer months have been the weaker months for the financial sector, consistent with the seasonal trend. In its 2014/15 seasonal period, the financial sector underperformed the S&P 500.

JANUARY

M	T	W	T	F	S	S
						1
2	3	4	5	6	7	8
9	10	11	12	13	14	15
16	17	18	19	20	21	22
23	24	25	26	27	28	29
30	31					

FEBRUARY

M	T	W	T	F	S	S
		1	2	3	4	5
6	7	8	9	10	11	12
13	14	15	16	17	18	19
20	21	22	23	24	25	26
27	28					

MARCH

M	T	W	T	F	S	S
		1	2	3	4	5
6	7	8	9	10	11	12
13	14	15	16	17	18	19
20	21	22	23	24	25	26
27	28	29	30	31		

APRIL

M	T	W	T	F	S	S
					1	2
3	4	5	6	7	8	9
10	11	12	13	14	15	16
17	18	19	20	21	22	23
24	25	26	27	28	29	30

MAY

M	T	W	T	F	S	S
1	2	3	4	5	6	7
8	9	10	11	12	13	14
15	16	17	18	19	20	21
22	23	24	25	26	27	28
29	30	31				

JUNE

M	T	W	T	F	S	S
		1	2	3	4	
5	6	7	8	9	10	11
12	13	14	15	16	17	18
19	20	21	22	23	24	25
26	27	28	29	30		

APPENDIX

STOCK MARKET RETURNS

S&P 500 PERCENT CHANGES

	JAN	FEB	MAR	APR	MAY	JUN
1950	1.5 %	1.0 %	0.4 %	4.5 %	3.9 %	− 5.8 %
1951	6.1	0.6	− 1.8	4.8	− 4.1	− 2.6
1952	1.6	− 3.6	4.8	− 4.3	2.3	4.6
1953	− 0.7	− 1.8	− 2.4	− 2.6	− 0.3	− 1.6
1954	5.1	0.3	3.0	4.9	3.3	0.1
1955	1.8	0.4	− 0.5	3.8	− 0.1	8.2
1956	− 3.6	3.5	6.9	− 0.2	− 6.6	3.9
1957	− 4.2	− 3.3	2.0	3.7	3.7	− 0.1
1958	4.3	2.1	3.1	3.2	1.5	2.6
1959	0.4	− 0.1	0.1	3.9	1.9	− 0.4
1960	− 7.1	0.9	− 1.4	− 1.8	2.7	2.0
1961	6.3	2.7	2.6	0.4	1.9	− 2.9
1962	− 3.8	1.6	− 0.6	− 6.2	− 8.6	− 8.2
1963	4.9	− 2.9	3.5	4.9	1.4	− 2.0
1964	2.7	1.0	1.5	0.6	1.1	1.6
1965	3.3	− 0.1	− 1.5	3.4	− 0.8	− 4.9
1966	0.5	− 1.8	− 2.2	2.1	− 5.4	− 1.6
1967	7.8	0.2	3.9	4.2	− 5.2	1.8
1968	− 4.4	− 3.1	0.9	8.0	1.3	0.9
1969	− 0.8	− 4.7	3.4	2.1	− 0.2	− 5.6
1970	− 7.6	5.3	0.1	− 9.0	− 6.1	− 5.0
1971	4.0	0.9	3.7	3.6	− 4.2	− 0.9
1972	1.8	2.5	0.6	0.4	1.7	− 2.2
1973	− 1.7	− 3.7	− 0.1	− 4.1	− 1.9	− 0.7
1974	− 1.0	− 0.4	− 2.3	− 3.9	− 3.4	− 1.5
1975	12.3	6.0	2.2	4.7	4.4	4.4
1976	11.8	− 1.1	3.1	− 1.1	− 1.4	4.1
1977	− 5.1	− 2.2	− 1.4	0.0	− 2.4	4.5
1978	− 6.2	− 2.5	2.5	8.5	0.4	− 1.8
1979	4.0	− 3.7	5.5	0.2	− 2.6	3.9
1980	5.8	− 0.4	− 10.2	4.1	4.7	2.7
1981	− 4.6	1.3	3.6	− 2.3	− 0.2	− 1.0
1982	− 1.8	− 6.1	− 1.0	4.0	− 3.9	− 2.0
1983	3.3	1.9	3.3	7.5	− 1.2	3.2
1984	− 0.9	− 3.9	1.3	0.5	− 5.9	1.7
1985	7.4	0.9	− 0.3	− 0.5	5.4	1.2
1986	0.2	7.1	5.3	− 1.4	5.0	1.4
1987	13.2	3.7	2.6	− 1.1	0.6	4.8
1988	4.0	4.2	− 3.3	0.9	0.3	4.3
1989	7.1	− 2.9	2.1	5.0	3.5	− 0.8
1990	− 6.9	0.9	2.4	− 2.7	9.2	− 0.9
1991	4.2	6.7	2.2	0.0	3.9	− 4.8
1992	− 2.0	1.0	− 2.2	2.8	0.1	− 1.7
1993	0.7	1.0	1.9	− 2.5	2.3	0.1
1994	3.3	− 3.0	− 4.6	1.2	1.2	− 2.7
1995	2.4	3.6	2.7	2.8	3.6	2.1
1996	3.3	0.7	0.8	1.3	2.3	0.2
1997	6.1	0.6	− 4.3	5.8	5.9	4.3
1998	1.0	7.0	5.0	0.9	− 1.9	3.9
1999	4.1	− 3.2	3.9	3.8	− 2.5	5.4
2000	− 5.1	− 2.0	9.7	− 3.1	− 2.2	2.4
2001	3.5	− 9.2	− 6.4	7.7	0.5	− 2.5
2002	− 1.6	− 2.1	3.7	− 6.1	− 0.9	− 7.2
2003	− 2.7	− 1.7	0.8	8.1	5.1	1.1
2004	1.7	1.2	− 1.6	− 1.7	1.2	1.8
2005	− 2.5	1.9	− 1.9	− 2.0	3.0	0.0
2006	2.5	0.0	1.1	1.2	− 3.1	0.0
2007	1.4	− 2.2	1.0	4.3	3.3	− 1.8
2008	− 6.1	− 3.5	− 0.6	4.8	1.1	− 8.6
2009	− 8.6	− 11.0	8.5	9.4	5.3	0.0
2010	− 3.7	2.9	5.9	1.5	− 8.2	− 5.4
2011	2.3	3.2	− 0.1	2.8	− 1.4	− 1.8
2012	4.4	4.1	3.1	− 0.7	− 6.3	4.0
2013	5.0	1.1	3.6	1.8	2.1	− 1.5
2014	− 3.6	4.3	0.7	0.6	2.1	1.9
FQ POS*	40/ 65	36 / 65	43 / 65	44 / 65	37 / 65	34 / 65
% FQ POS*	62 %	55 %	66 %	68 %	57 %	52 %
AVG GAIN*	1.1 %	0.0 %	1.2 %	1.5 %	0.2 %	0.0 %
RANK GAIN*	5	11	4	3	8	10

S&P 500 PERCENT CHANGES — STOCK MKT

JUL	AUG	SEP	OCT	NOV	DEC		YEAR
0.8 %	3.3 %	5.6 %	0.4 %	— 0.1 %	4.6 %	**1950**	21.7 %
6.9	3.9	— 0.1	— 1.4	— 0.3	3.9	**1951**	16.5
1.8	— 1.5	— 2.0	— 0.1	4.6	3.5	**1952**	11.8
2.5	— 5.8	0.1	5.1	0.9	0.2	**1953**	— 6.6
5.7	— 3.4	8.3	— 1.9	8.1	5.1	**1954**	45.0
6.1	— 0.8	1.1	— 3.0	7.5	— 0.1	**1955**	26.4
5.2	— 3.8	— 4.5	0.5	— 1.1	3.5	**1956**	2.6
1.1	— 5.6	— 6.2	— 3.2	1.6	— 4.1	**1957**	— 14.3
4.3	1.2	4.8	2.5	2.2	5.2	**1958**	38.1
3.5	— 1.5	— 4.6	1.1	1.3	2.8	**1959**	8.5
— 2.5	2.6	— 6.0	— 0.2	4.0	4.6	**1960**	— 3.0
3.3	2.0	— 2.0	2.8	3.9	0.3	**1961**	23.1
6.4	1.5	— 4.8	0.4	10.2	1.3	**1962**	— 11.8
— 0.3	4.9	— 1.1	3.2	— 1.1	2.4	**1963**	18.9
1.8	— 1.6	2.9	0.8	— 0.5	0.4	**1964**	13.0
1.3	2.3	3.2	2.7	— 0.9	0.9	**1965**	9.1
— 1.3	— 7.8	— 0.7	4.8	0.3	— 0.1	**1966**	— 13.1
4.5	— 1.2	3.3	— 3.5	0.8	2.6	**1967**	20.1
— 1.8	1.1	3.9	0.7	4.8	— 4.2	**1968**	7.7
— 6.0	4.0	— 2.5	4.3	— 3.4	— 1.9	**1969**	— 11.4
7.3	4.4	3.4	— 1.2	4.7	5.7	**1970**	0.1
— 3.2	3.6	— 0.7	— 4.2	— 0.3	8.6	**1971**	10.8
0.2	3.4	— 0.5	0.9	4.6	1.2	**1972**	15.6
3.8	— 3.7	4.0	— 0.1	— 11.4	1.7	**1973**	— 17.4
— 7.8	— 9.0	— 11.9	16.3	— 5.3	— 2.0	**1974**	— 29.7
— 6.8	— 2.1	— 3.5	6.2	2.5	— 1.2	**1975**	31.5
— 0.8	— 0.5	2.3	— 2.2	— 0.8	5.2	**1976**	19.1
— 1.6	— 2.1	— 0.2	— 4.3	2.7	0.3	**1977**	— 11.5
5.4	2.6	— 0.7	— 9.2	1.7	1.5	**1978**	1.1
0.9	5.3	0.0	— 6.9	4.3	1.7	**1979**	12.3
6.5	0.6	2.5	1.6	10.2	— 3.4	**1980**	25.8
— 0.2	— 6.2	— 5.4	4.9	3.7	— 3.0	**1981**	— 9.7
— 2.3	11.6	0.8	11.0	3.6	1.5	**1982**	14.8
— 3.0	1.1	1.0	— 1.5	1.7	— 0.9	**1983**	17.3
— 1.6	10.6	— 0.3	0.0	— 1.5	2.2	**1984**	1.4
— 0.5	— 1.2	— 3.5	4.3	6.5	4.5	**1985**	26.3
— 5.9	7.1	— 8.5	5.5	2.1	— 2.8	**1986**	14.6
4.8	3.5	— 2.4	— 21.8	— 8.5	7.3	**1987**	2.0
— 0.5	— 3.9	4.0	2.6	— 1.9	1.5	**1988**	12.4
8.8	1.6	— 0.7	— 2.5	1.7	2.1	**1989**	27.3
— 0.5	— 9.4	— 5.1	— 0.7	6.0	2.5	**1990**	— 6.6
4.5	2.0	— 1.9	1.2	— 4.4	11.2	**1991**	26.3
3.9	— 2.4	0.9	0.2	3.0	1.0	**1992**	4.5
— 0.5	3.4	— 1.0	1.9	— 1.3	1.0	**1993**	7.1
3.1	3.8	— 2.7	2.1	— 4.0	1.2	**1994**	— 1.5
3.2	0.0	4.0	— 0.5	4.1	1.7	**1995**	34.1
— 4.6	1.9	5.4	2.6	7.3	— 2.2	**1996**	20.3
7.8	— 5.7	5.3	— 3.4	4.5	1.6	**1997**	31.0
— 1.2	— 14.6	6.2	8.0	5.9	5.6	**1998**	26.7
— 3.2	— 0.6	— 2.9	6.3	1.9	5.8	**1999**	19.5
— 1.6	6.1	— 5.3	— 0.5	— 8.0	0.4	**2000**	— 10.1
— 1.1	— 6.4	— 8.2	1.8	7.5	0.8	**2001**	— 13.0
— 7.9	0.5	— 11.0	8.6	5.7	— 6.0	**2002**	— 23.4
1.6	1.8	— 1.2	5.5	0.7	5.1	**2003**	26.4
-3.4	0.2	0.9	1.4	3.9	3.2	**2004**	9.0
3.6	— 1.1	0.7	— 1.8	3.5	— 0.1	**2005**	3.0
0.5	2.1	2.5	3.2	1.6	1.3	**2006**	13.6
— 3.2	1.3	3.6	1.5	— 4.4	— 0.9	**2007**	3.5
— 1.0	1.2	— 9.2	— 16.8	— 7.5	0.8	**2008**	-38.5
7.4	3.4	3.6	— 2.0	5.7	1.8	**2009**	23.5
6.9	— 4.7	8.8	3.7	— 0.2	6.5	**2010**	12.8
— 2.1	— 5.7	— 7.2	10.8	— 0.5	0.9	**2011**	0.0
1.3	2.0	2.4	— 2.0	0.3	0.7	**2012**	13.4
4.9	— 3.1	3.0	4.5	2.8	2.4	**2013**	29.6
— 1.5	3.8	— 1.6	2.3	2.5	— 0.4	**2014**	11.4
35 / 65	36 / 65	29 / 65	39 / 65	43/ 65	49 / 65		48 / 65
54 %	55 %	45 %	60 %	66 %	75 %		74 %
1.0 %	0.0 %	— 0.5 %	0.8 %	1.5 %	1.7 %		9.1 %
6	9	12	7	2	1		

S&P 500 MONTH CLOSING VALUES

	JAN	FEB	MAR	APR	MAY	JUN
1950	17	17	17	18	19	18
1951	22	22	21	22	22	21
1952	24	23	24	23	24	25
1953	26	26	25	25	25	24
1954	26	26	27	28	29	29
1955	37	37	37	38	38	41
1956	44	45	48	48	45	47
1957	45	43	44	46	47	47
1958	42	41	42	43	44	45
1959	55	55	55	58	59	58
1960	56	56	55	54	56	57
1961	62	63	65	65	67	65
1962	69	70	70	65	60	55
1963	66	64	67	70	71	69
1964	77	78	79	79	80	82
1965	88	87	86	89	88	84
1966	93	91	89	91	86	85
1967	87	87	90	94	89	91
1968	92	89	90	97	99	100
1969	103	98	102	104	103	98
1970	85	90	90	82	77	73
1971	96	97	100	104	100	99
1972	104	107	107	108	110	107
1973	116	112	112	107	105	104
1974	97	96	94	90	87	86
1975	77	82	83	87	91	95
1976	101	100	103	102	100	104
1977	102	100	98	98	96	100
1978	89	87	89	97	97	96
1979	100	96	102	102	99	103
1980	114	114	102	106	111	114
1981	130	131	136	133	133	131
1982	120	113	112	116	112	110
1983	145	148	153	164	162	168
1984	163	157	159	160	151	153
1985	180	181	181	180	190	192
1986	212	227	239	236	247	251
1987	274	284	292	288	290	304
1988	257	268	259	261	262	274
1989	297	289	295	310	321	318
1990	329	332	340	331	361	358
1991	344	367	375	375	390	371
1992	409	413	404	415	415	408
1993	439	443	452	440	450	451
1994	482	467	446	451	457	444
1995	470	487	501	515	533	545
1996	636	640	646	654	669	671
1997	786	791	757	801	848	885
1998	980	1049	1102	1112	1091	1134
1999	1280	1238	1286	1335	1302	1373
2000	1394	1366	1499	1452	1421	1455
2001	1366	1240	1160	1249	1256	1224
2002	1130	1107	1147	1077	1067	990
2003	856	841	848	917	964	975
2004	1131	1145	1126	1107	1121	1141
2005	1181	1204	1181	1157	1192	1191
2006	1280	1281	1295	1311	1270	1270
2007	1438	1407	1421	1482	1531	1503
2008	1379	1331	1323	1386	1400	1280
2009	826	735	798	873	919	919
2010	1074	1104	1169	1187	1089	1031
2011	1286	1327	1326	1364	1345	1321
2012	1312	1366	1408	1398	1310	1362
2013	1498	1515	1569	1598	1631	1606
2014	1783	1869	1872	1884	1924	1960

S&P 500 MONTH CLOSING VALUES 🇺🇸 STOCK MKT

JUL	AUG	SEP	OCT	NOV	DEC	
18	18	19	20	20	20	**1950**
22	23	23	23	23	24	**1951**
25	25	25	25	26	27	**1952**
25	23	23	25	25	25	**1953**
31	30	32	32	34	36	**1954**
44	43	44	42	46	45	**1955**
49	48	45	46	45	47	**1956**
48	45	42	41	42	40	**1957**
47	48	50	51	52	55	**1958**
61	60	57	58	58	60	**1959**
56	57	54	53	56	58	**1960**
67	68	67	69	71	72	**1961**
58	59	56	57	62	63	**1962**
69	73	72	74	73	75	**1963**
83	82	84	85	84	85	**1964**
85	87	90	92	92	92	**1965**
84	77	77	80	80	80	**1966**
95	94	97	93	94	96	**1967**
98	99	103	103	108	104	**1968**
92	96	93	97	94	92	**1969**
78	82	84	83	87	92	**1970**
96	99	98	94	94	102	**1971**
107	111	111	112	117	118	**1972**
108	104	108	108	96	98	**1973**
79	72	64	74	70	69	**1974**
89	87	84	89	91	90	**1975**
103	103	105	103	102	107	**1976**
99	97	97	92	95	95	**1977**
101	103	103	93	95	96	**1978**
104	109	109	102	106	108	**1979**
122	122	125	127	141	136	**1980**
131	123	116	122	126	123	**1981**
107	120	120	134	139	141	**1982**
163	164	166	164	166	165	**1983**
151	167	166	166	164	167	**1984**
191	189	182	190	202	211	**1985**
236	253	231	244	249	242	**1986**
319	330	322	252	230	247	**1987**
272	262	272	279	274	278	**1988**
346	351	349	340	346	353	**1989**
356	323	306	304	322	330	**1990**
388	395	388	392	375	417	**1991**
424	414	418	419	431	436	**1992**
448	464	459	468	462	466	**1993**
458	475	463	472	454	459	**1994**
562	562	584	582	605	616	**1995**
640	652	687	705	757	741	**1996**
954	899	947	915	955	970	**1997**
1121	957	1017	1099	1164	1229	**1998**
1329	1320	1283	1363	1389	1469	**1999**
1431	1518	1437	1429	1315	1320	**2000**
1211	1134	1041	1060	1139	1148	**2001**
912	916	815	886	936	880	**2002**
990	1008	996	1051	1058	1112	**2003**
1102	1104	1115	1130	1174	1212	**2004**
1234	1220	1229	1207	1249	1248	**2005**
1277	1304	1336	1378	1401	1418	**2006**
1455	1474	1527	1549	1481	1468	**2007**
1267	1283	1165	969	896	903	**2008**
987	1021	1057	1036	1096	1115	**2009**
1102	1049	1141	1183	1181	1258	**2010**
1292	1219	1131	1253	1247	1258	**2011**
1379	1407	1441	1412	1416	1426	**2012**
1686	1633	1682	1757	1806	1848	**2013**
1931	2003	1972	2018	2068	2059	**2014**

DOW JONES PERCENT MONTH CHANGES

	JAN	FEB	MAR	APR	MAY	JUN
1950	0.8 %	0.8 %	1.3 %	4.0 %	4.2 %	— 6.4 %
1951	5.7	1.3	— 1.7	4.5	— 3.6	— 2.8
1952	0.6	— 3.9	3.6	— 4.4	2.1	4.3
1953	— 0.7	— 2.0	1.5	— 1.8	— 0.9	— 1.5
1954	4.1	0.7	3.1	5.2	2.6	1.8
1955	1.1	0.8	— 0.5	3.9	— 0.2	6.2
1956	— 3.6	2.8	5.8	0.8	— 7.4	3.1
1957	— 4.1	— 3.0	2.2	4.1	2.1	— 0.3
1958	3.3	— 2.2	1.6	2.0	1.5	3.3
1959	1.8	1.6	— 0.3	3.7	3.2	0.0
1960	— 8.4	1.2	— 2.1	— 2.4	4.0	2.4
1961	5.2	2.1	2.2	0.3	2.7	— 1.8
1962	— 4.3	1.2	— 0.2	— 5.9	— 7.8	— 8.5
1963	4.7	— 2.9	3.0	5.2	1.3	— 2.8
1964	2.9	1.9	1.6	— 0.3	1.2	1.3
1965	3.3	0.1	— 1.6	3.7	— 0.5	— 5.4
1966	1.5	— 3.2	— 2.8	1.0	— 5.3	— 1.6
1967	8.2	— 1.2	3.2	3.6	— 5.0	0.9
1968	— 5.5	— 1.8	0.0	8.5	— 1.4	— 0.1
1969	0.2	— 4.3	3.3	1.6	— 1.3	— 6.9
1970	— 7.0	4.5	1.0	— 6.3	— 4.8	— 2.4
1971	3.5	1.2	2.9	4.1	— 3.6	— 1.8
1972	1.3	2.9	1.4	1.4	0.7	— 3.3
1973	— 2.1	— 4.4	— 0.4	— 3.1	— 2.2	— 1.1
1974	0.6	0.6	— 1.6	— 1.2	— 4.1	0.0
1975	14.2	5.0	3.9	6.9	1.3	5.6
1976	14.4	— 0.3	2.8	— 0.3	— 2.2	2.8
1977	— 5.0	— 1.9	— 1.8	0.8	— 3.0	2.0
1978	— 7.4	— 3.6	2.1	10.5	0.4	— 2.6
1979	4.2	— 3.6	6.6	— 0.8	— 3.8	2.4
1980	4.4	— 1.5	— 9.0	4.0	4.1	2.0
1981	— 1.7	2.9	3.0	— 0.6	— 0.6	— 1.5
1982	— 0.4	— 5.4	— 0.2	3.1	— 3.4	— 0.9
1983	2.8	3.4	1.6	8.5	— 2.1	1.8
1984	— 3.0	— 5.4	0.9	0.5	— 5.6	2.5
1985	6.2	— 0.2	— 1.3	— 0.7	4.6	1.5
1986	1.6	8.8	6.4	— 1.9	5.2	0.9
1987	13.8	3.1	3.6	— 0.8	0.2	5.5
1988	1.0	5.8	— 4.0	2.2	— 0.1	5.4
1989	8.0	— 3.6	1.6	5.5	2.5	— 1.6
1990	— 5.9	1.4	3.0	— 1.9	8.3	0.1
1991	3.9	5.3	1.1	— 0.9	4.8	— 4.0
1992	1.7	1.4	— 1.0	3.8	1.1	— 2.3
1993	0.3	1.8	1.9	— 0.2	2.9	— 0.3
1994	6.0	— 3.7	— 5.1	1.3	2.1	— 3.5
1995	0.2	4.3	3.7	3.9	3.3	2.0
1996	5.4	1.7	1.9	— 0.3	1.3	0.2
1997	5.7	0.9	— 4.3	6.5	4.6	4.7
1998	0.0	8.1	3.0	3.0	— 1.8	0.6
1999	1.9	— 0.6	5.2	10.2	— 2.1	3.9
2000	— 4.5	— 7.4	7.8	— 1.7	— 2.0	— 0.7
2001	0.9	— 3.6	— 5.9	8.7	1.6	— 3.8
2002	— 1.0	1.9	2.9	— 4.4	— 0.2	— 6.9
2003	— 3.5	— 2.0	1.3	6.1	4.4	1.5
2004	0.3	0.9	— 2.1	— 1.3	— 0.4	2.4
2005	— 2.7	2.6	— 2.4	— 3.0	2.7	— 1.8
2006	1.4	1.2	1.1	2.3	— 1.7	— 0.2
2007	1.3	— 2.8	0.7	5.7	4.3	— 1.6
2008	— 4.6	— 3.0	0.0	4.5	— 1.4	— 10.2
2009	— 8.8	— 11.7	7.7	7.3	4.1	— 0.6
2010	— 3.5	2.6	5.1	1.4	— 7.9	— 3.6
2011	2.7	2.8	0.8	4.0	— 1.9	— 1.2
2012	3.4	3.8	2.0	0.0	— 6.2	3.9
2013	5.8	4.8	3.7	1.8	1.9	— 1.4
2014	— 5.3	5.8	0.8	0.7	0.8	0.7
FQ POS	42 / 65	37 / 65	43 / 65	43 / 65	33 / 65	30 / 65
% FQ POS	65 %	57 %	66 %	66 %	51 %	46 %
AVG GAIN	1.0 %	0.2 %	1.1 %	2.0 %	0.0 %	— 0.3 %
RANK GAIN	6	8	5	1	9	11

JUL	AUG	SEP	OCT	NOV	DEC		YEAR
0.1 %	3.6 %	4.4 %	− 0.6 %	1.2 %	3.4 %	**1950**	17.6 %
6.3	4.8	0.3	− 3.2	− 0.4	3.0	**1951**	14.4
1.9	− 1.6	− 1.6	− 0.5	5.4	2.9	**1952**	8.4
2.6	− 5.2	1.1	4.5	2.0	− 0.2	**1953**	− 3.8
4.3	− 3.5	7.4	− 2.3	9.9	4.6	**1954**	44.0
3.2	0.5	− 0.3	− 2.5	6.2	1.1	**1955**	20.8
5.1	− 3.1	− 5.3	1.0	− 1.5	5.6	**1956**	2.3
1.0	− 4.7	− 5.8	− 3.4	2.0	− 3.2	**1957**	− 12.8
5.2	1.1	4.6	2.1	2.6	4.7	**1958**	34.0
4.9	− 1.6	− 4.9	2.4	1.9	3.1	**1959**	16.4
− 3.7	1.5	− 7.3	0.1	2.9	3.1	**1960**	− 9.3
3.1	2.1	− 2.6	0.4	2.5	1.3	**1961**	18.7
6.5	1.9	− 5.0	1.9	10.1	0.4	**1962**	− 10.8
− 1.6	4.9	0.5	3.1	− 0.6	1.7	**1963**	17.0
1.2	− 0.3	4.4	− 0.3	0.3	− 0.1	**1964**	14.6
1.6	1.3	4.2	3.2	− 1.5	2.4	**1965**	10.9
− 2.6	− 7.0	− 1.8	4.2	− 1.9	− 0.7	**1966**	− 18.9
5.1	− 0.3	2.8	− 5.1	− 0.4	3.3	**1967**	15.2
− 1.6	1.5	4.4	1.8	3.4	− 4.2	**1968**	4.3
6.6	2.6	− 2.8	5.3	− 5.1	− 1.5	**1969**	− 15.2
7.4	4.2	− 0.5	− 0.7	5.1	5.6	**1970**	4.8
− 3.7	4.6	− 1.2	− 5.4	− 0.9	7.1	**1971**	6.1
− 0.5	4.2	− 1.1	0.2	6.6	0.2	**1972**	14.6
3.9	− 4.2	6.7	1.0	− 14.0	3.5	**1973**	− 16.6
− 5.6	− 10.4	− 10.4	9.5	− 7.0	− 0.4	**1974**	− 27.6
− 5.4	0.5	− 5.0	5.3	3.0	− 1.0	**1975**	38.3
− 1.8	− 1.1	1.7	− 2.6	− 1.8	6.1	**1976**	17.9
− 2.9	− 3.2	− 1.7	− 3.4	1.4	0.2	**1977**	− 17.3
5.3	1.7	− 1.3	− 8.5	0.8	0.8	**1978**	− 3.2
0.5	4.9	− 1.0	− 7.2	0.8	2.0	**1979**	4.2
7.8	− 0.3	0.0	− 0.8	7.4	− 2.9	**1980**	14.9
2.5	− 7.4	− 3.6	0.3	4.3	− 1.6	**1981**	− 9.2
− 0.4	11.5	− 0.6	10.6	4.8	0.7	**1982**	19.6
− 1.9	1.4	1.4	− 0.6	4.1	− 1.4	**1983**	20.3
− 1.5	9.8	− 1.4	0.1	− 1.5	1.9	**1984**	− 3.7
0.9	− 1.0	− 0.4	3.4	7.1	5.1	**1985**	27.7
− 6.2	6.9	− 6.9	6.2	1.9	− 1.0	**1986**	22.6
6.4	3.5	− 2.5	− 23.2	− 8.0	5.7	**1987**	2.3
− 0.6	− 4.6	4.0	1.7	− 1.6	2.6	**1988**	11.9
9.0	2.9	− 1.6	− 1.8	2.3	1.7	**1989**	27.0
0.9	− 10.0	− 6.2	− 0.4	4.8	2.9	**1990**	− 4.3
4.1	0.6	− 0.9	1.7	− 5.7	9.5	**1991**	20.3
2.3	− 4.0	0.4	− 1.4	2.4	− 0.1	**1992**	4.2
0.7	3.2	− 2.6	3.5	0.1	1.9	**1993**	13.7
3.8	4.0	− 1.8	1.7	− 4.3	2.5	**1994**	2.1
3.3	− 2.1	3.9	− 0.7	6.7	0.8	**1995**	33.5
− 2.2	1.6	4.7	2.5	8.2	− 1.1	**1996**	26.0
7.2	− 7.3	4.2	− 6.3	5.1	1.1	**1997**	22.6
− 0.8	− 15.1	4.0	9.6	6.1	0.7	**1998**	16.1
− 2.9	1.6	− 4.5	3.8	1.4	5.3	**1999**	24.7
0.7	6.6	− 5.0	3.0	− 5.1	3.6	**2000**	− 5.8
0.2	− 5.4	− 11.1	2.6	8.6	1.7	**2001**	− 7.1
− 5.5	− 0.8	− 12.4	10.6	5.9	− 6.2	**2002**	− 16.8
2.8	2.0	− 1.5	5.7	− 0.2	6.9	**2003**	25.3
− 2.8	0.3	− 0.9	− 0.5	4.0	3.4	**2004**	3.1
3.6	− 1.5	0.8	− 1.2	3.5	− 0.8	**2005**	− 0.6
0.3	1.7	2.6	3.4	1.2	2.0	**2006**	16.3
− 1.5	1.1	4.0	0.2	− 4.0	− 0.8	**2007**	6.4
0.2	1.5	− 6.0	− 14.1	− 5.3	− 0.6	**2008**	− 33.8
8.6	3.5	2.3	0.0	6.5	0.8	**2009**	18.8
7.1	− 4.3	7.7	3.1	− 1.0	5.2	**2010**	11.0
− 2.2	− 4.4	− 6.0	9.5	0.8	1.4	**2011**	5.5
1.0	0.6	2.6	− 2.5	− 0.5	0.6	**2012**	7.3
4.0	− 4.4	2.2	2.8	3.5	3.0	**2013**	26.5
− 1.6	3.2	− 0.3	2.0	2.5	0.0	**2014**	7.5
40 / 65	37 / 65	26 / 65	39/ 65	44/ 65	46 / 65		47 / 65
62 %	57 %	40 %	60 %	68 %	71 %		72 %
1.1 %	− 0.1 %	− 0.8 %	0.5 %	1.5 %	1.7 %		8.4 %
4	10	12	7	3	2		

DOW JONES
MONTH CLOSING VALUES

	JAN	FEB	MAR	APR	MAY	JUN
1950	202	203	206	214	223	209
1951	249	252	248	259	250	243
1952	271	260	270	258	263	274
1953	290	284	280	275	272	268
1954	292	295	304	319	328	334
1955	409	412	410	426	425	451
1956	471	484	512	516	478	493
1957	479	465	475	494	505	503
1958	450	440	447	456	463	478
1959	594	604	602	624	644	644
1960	623	630	617	602	626	641
1961	648	662	677	679	697	684
1962	700	708	707	665	613	561
1963	683	663	683	718	727	707
1964	785	800	813	811	821	832
1965	903	904	889	922	918	868
1966	984	952	925	934	884	870
1967	850	839	866	897	853	860
1968	856	841	841	912	899	898
1969	946	905	936	950	938	873
1970	744	778	786	736	700	684
1971	869	879	904	942	908	891
1972	902	928	941	954	961	929
1973	999	955	951	921	901	892
1974	856	861	847	837	802	802
1975	704	739	768	821	832	879
1976	975	973	1000	997	975	1003
1977	954	936	919	927	899	916
1978	770	742	757	837	841	819
1979	839	809	862	855	822	842
1980	876	863	786	817	851	868
1981	947	975	1004	998	992	977
1982	871	824	823	848	820	812
1983	1076	1113	1130	1226	1200	1222
1984	1221	1155	1165	1171	1105	1132
1985	1287	1284	1267	1258	1315	1336
1986	1571	1709	1819	1784	1877	1893
1987	2158	2224	2305	2286	2292	2419
1988	1958	2072	1988	2032	2031	2142
1989	2342	2258	2294	2419	2480	2440
1990	2591	2627	2707	2657	2877	2881
1991	2736	2882	2914	2888	3028	2907
1992	3223	3268	3236	3359	3397	3319
1993	3310	3371	3435	3428	3527	3516
1994	3978	3832	3636	3682	3758	3625
1995	3844	4011	4158	4321	4465	4556
1996	5395	5486	5587	5569	5643	5655
1997	6813	6878	6584	7009	7331	7673
1998	7907	8546	8800	9063	8900	8952
1999	9359	9307	9786	10789	10560	10971
2000	10941	10128	10922	10734	10522	10448
2001	10887	10495	9879	10735	10912	10502
2002	9920	10106	10404	9946	9925	9243
2003	8054	7891	7992	8480	8850	8985
2004	10488	10584	10358	10226	10188	10435
2005	10490	10766	10504	10193	10467	10275
2006	10865	10993	11109	11367	11168	11150
2007	12622	12269	12354	13063	13628	13409
2008	12650	12266	12263	12820	12638	11350
2009	8001	7063	7609	8168	8500	8447
2010	10067	10325	10857	11009	10137	9774
2011	11892	12226	12320	12811	12570	12414
2012	12633	12952	13212	13214	12393	12880
2013	13861	14054	14579	14840	15116	14910
2014	15699	16322	16458	16581	16717	16827

JUL	AUG	SEP	OCT	NOV	DEC	
209	217	226	225	228	235	**1950**
258	270	271	262	261	269	**1951**
280	275	271	269	284	292	**1952**
275	261	264	276	281	281	**1953**
348	336	361	352	387	404	**1954**
466	468	467	455	483	488	**1955**
518	502	475	480	473	500	**1956**
509	484	456	441	450	436	**1957**
503	509	532	543	558	584	**1958**
675	664	632	647	659	679	**1959**
617	626	580	580	597	616	**1960**
705	720	701	704	722	731	**1961**
598	609	579	590	649	652	**1962**
695	729	733	755	751	763	**1963**
841	839	875	873	875	874	**1964**
882	893	931	961	947	969	**1965**
847	788	774	807	792	786	**1966**
904	901	927	880	876	905	**1967**
883	896	936	952	985	944	**1968**
816	837	813	856	812	800	**1969**
734	765	761	756	794	839	**1970**
858	898	887	839	831	890	**1971**
925	964	953	956	1018	1020	**1972**
926	888	947	957	822	851	**1973**
757	679	608	666	619	616	**1974**
832	835	794	836	861	852	**1975**
985	974	990	965	947	1005	**1976**
890	862	847	818	830	831	**1977**
862	877	866	793	799	805	**1978**
846	888	879	816	822	839	**1979**
935	933	932	925	993	964	**1980**
952	882	850	853	889	875	**1981**
809	901	896	992	1039	1047	**1982**
1199	1216	1233	1225	1276	1259	**1983**
1115	1224	1207	1207	1189	1212	**1984**
1348	1334	1329	1374	1472	1547	**1985**
1775	1898	1768	1878	1914	1896	**1986**
2572	2663	2596	1994	1834	1939	**1987**
2129	2032	2113	2149	2115	2169	**1988**
2661	2737	2693	2645	2706	2753	**1989**
2905	2614	2453	2442	2560	2634	**1990**
3025	3044	3017	3069	2895	3169	**1991**
3394	3257	3272	3226	3305	3301	**1992**
3540	3651	3555	3681	3684	3754	**1993**
3765	3913	3843	3908	3739	3834	**1994**
4709	4611	4789	4756	5075	5117	**1995**
5529	5616	5882	6029	6522	6448	**1996**
8223	7622	7945	7442	7823	7908	**1997**
8883	7539	7843	8592	9117	9181	**1998**
10655	10829	10337	10730	10878	11453	**1999**
10522	11215	10651	10971	10415	10788	**2000**
10523	9950	8848	9075	9852	10022	**2001**
8737	8664	7592	8397	8896	8342	**2002**
9234	9416	9275	9801	9782	10454	**2003**
10140	10174	10080	10027	10428	10783	**2004**
10641	10482	10569	10440	10806	10718	**2005**
11186	11381	11679	12801	12222	12463	**2006**
13212	13358	13896	13930	13372	13265	**2007**
11378	11544	10851	9325	8829	8776	**2008**
9172	9496	9712	9713	10345	10428	**2009**
10466	10015	10788	11118	11006	11578	**2010**
12143	11614	10913	11955	12046	12218	**2011**
13009	13091	13437	13096	13026	13104	**2012**
15500	14810	15130	15546	16086	16577	**2013**
16563	17098	17043	17391	17828	17823	**2014**

NASDAQ PERCENT MONTH CHANGES

	JAN	FEB	MAR	APR	MAY	JUN
1972	4.2	5.5	2.2	2.5	0.9	— 1.8
1973	— 4.0	— 6.2	— 2.4	— 8.2	— 4.8	— 1.6
1974	3.0	— 0.6	— 2.2	— 5.9	— 7.7	— 5.3
1975	16.6	4.6	3.6	3.8	5.8	4.7
1976	12.1	3.7	0.4	— 0.6	— 2.3	2.6
1977	— 2.4	— 1.0	— 0.5	1.4	0.1	4.3
1978	— 4.0	0.6	4.7	8.5	4.4	0.0
1979	6.6	— 2.6	7.5	1.6	— 1.8	5.1
1980	7.0	— 2.3	— 17.1	6.9	7.5	4.9
1981	— 2.2	0.1	6.1	3.1	3.1	— 3.5
1982	— 3.8	— 4.8	— 2.1	5.2	— 3.3	— 4.1
1983	6.9	5.0	3.9	8.2	5.3	3.2
1984	— 3.7	— 5.9	— 0.7	— 1.3	— 5.9	2.9
1985	12.8	2.0	— 1.8	0.5	3.6	1.9
1986	3.4	7.1	4.2	2.3	4.4	1.3
1987	12.4	8.4	1.2	— 2.9	— 0.3	2.0
1988	4.3	6.5	2.1	1.2	— 2.3	6.6
1989	5.2	— 0.4	1.8	5.1	4.3	— 2.4
1990	— 8.6	2.4	2.3	— 3.5	9.3	0.7
1991	10.8	9.4	6.4	0.5	4.4	— 6.0
1992	5.8	2.1	— 4.7	— 4.2	1.1	— 3.7
1993	2.9	— 3.7	2.9	— 4.2	5.9	0.5
1994	3.0	— 1.0	— 6.2	— 1.3	0.2	— 4.0
1995	0.4	5.1	3.0	3.3	2.4	8.0
1996	0.7	3.8	0.1	8.1	4.4	— 4.7
1997	6.9	— 5.1	— 6.7	3.2	11.1	3.0
1998	3.1	9.3	3.7	1.8	— 4.8	6.5
1999	14.3	— 8.7	7.6	3.3	— 2.8	8.7
2000	— 3.2	19.2	— 2.6	— 15.6	— 11.9	16.6
2001	12.2	— 22.4	— 14.5	15.0	— 0.3	2.4
2002	— 0.8	— 10.5	6.6	— 8.5	— 4.3	— 9.4
2003	— 1.1	1.3	0.3	9.2	9.0	1.7
2004	3.1	— 1.8	— 1.8	— 3.7	3.5	3.1
2005	— 5.2	— 0.5	— 2.6	— 3.9	7.6	— 0.5
2006	4.6	— 1.1	2.6	— 0.7	— 6.2	— 0.3
2007	2.0	— 1.9	0.2	4.3	3.1	0.0
2008	— 9.9	— 5.0	0.3	5.9	4.6	— 9.1
2009	— 6.4	— 6.7	10.9	12.3	3.3	3.4
2010	— 5.4	4.2	7.1	2.6	— 8.3	— 6.5
2011	1.8	3.0	0.0	3.3	— 1.3	— 2.2
2012	8.0	5.4	4.2	— 1.5	— 7.2	3.8
2013	4.1	0.6	3.4	1.9	3.8	— 1.5
2014	— 1.7	5.0	— 2.5	— 2.0	3.1	3.9
FQ POS	28/43	23/43	27/43	27/43	26/43	25/43
% FQ POS	65 %	53 %	63 %	63 %	60 %	58 %
AVG GAIN	2.7 %	0.5 %	0.7 %	1.3 %	1.0 %	0.8 %
RANK GAIN	1	9	7	4	5	6

NASDAQ PERCENT MONTH CHANGES

STOCK MKT

JUL	AUG	SEP	OCT	NOV	DEC		YEAR
— 1.8	1.7	— 0.3	0.5	2.1	0.6	**1972**	17.2
7.6	— 3.5	6.0	— 0.9	— 15.1	— 1.4	**1973**	— 31.1
— 7.9	— 10.9	— 10.7	17.2	— 3.5	— 5.0	**1974**	— 35.1
— 4.4	— 5.0	— 5.9	3.6	2.4	— 1.5	**1975**	29.8
1.1	— 1.7	1.7	— 1.0	0.9	7.4	**1976**	26.1
0.9	— 0.5	0.7	— 3.3	5.8	1.8	**1977**	7.3
5.0	6.9	— 1.6	— 16.4	3.2	2.9	**1978**	12.3
2.3	6.4	— 0.3	— 9.6	6.4	4.8	**1979**	28.1
8.9	5.7	3.4	2.7	8.0	— 2.8	**1980**	33.9
— 1.9	— 7.5	— 8.0	8.4	3.1	— 2.7	**1981**	— 3.2
— 2.3	6.2	5.6	13.3	9.3	0.0	**1982**	18.7
— 4.6	— 3.8	1.4	— 7.4	4.1	— 2.5	**1983**	19.9
— 4.2	10.9	— 1.8	— 1.2	— 1.9	1.9	**1984**	— 11.3
1.7	— 1.2	— 5.8	4.4	7.4	3.5	**1985**	31.5
— 8.4	3.1	— 8.4	2.9	— 0.3	— 3.0	**1986**	7.4
2.4	4.6	— 2.4	— 27.2	— 5.6	8.3	**1987**	— 5.2
— 1.9	— 2.8	2.9	— 1.3	— 2.9	2.7	**1988**	15.4
4.2	3.4	0.8	— 3.7	0.1	— 0.3	**1989**	19.2
— 5.2	— 13.0	— 9.6	— 4.3	8.9	4.1	**1990**	— 17.8
5.5	4.7	0.2	3.1	— 3.5	11.9	**1991**	56.9
3.1	— 3.0	3.6	3.8	7.9	3.7	**1992**	15.5
0.1	5.4	2.7	2.2	— 3.2	3.0	**1993**	14.7
2.3	6.0	— 0.2	1.7	— 3.5	0.2	**1994**	— 3.2
7.3	1.9	2.3	— 0.7	2.2	— 0.7	**1995**	39.9
— 8.8	5.6	7.5	— 0.4	5.8	— 0.1	**1996**	22.7
10.5	— 0.4	6.2	— 5.5	0.4	— 1.9	**1997**	21.6
— 1.2	— 19.9	13.0	4.6	10.1	12.5	**1998**	39.6
— 1.8	3.8	0.2	8.0	12.5	22.0	**1999**	85.6
— 5.0	11.7	— 12.7	— 8.3	— 22.9	— 4.9	**2000**	— 39.3
— 6.2	— 10.9	— 17.0	12.8	14.2	1.0	**2001**	— 21.1
— 9.2	— 1.0	— 10.9	13.5	11.2	— 9.7	**2002**	— 31.5
6.9	4.3	— 1.3	8.1	1.5	2.2	**2003**	50.0
— 7.8	— 2.6	3.2	4.1	6.2	3.7	**2004**	8.6
6.2	— 1.5	0.0	— 1.5	5.3	— 1.2	**2005**	1.4
— 3.7	4.4	3.4	4.8	2.7	— 0.7	**2006**	9.5
— 2.2	2.0	4.0	5.8	— 6.9	— 0.3	**2007**	9.8
1.4	1.8	— 11.6	— 17.7	— 10.8	2.7	**2008**	— 40.5
7.8	1.5	5.6	— 3.6	4.9	5.8	**2009**	43.9
6.9	— 6.2	12.0	5.9	— 0.4	6.2	**2010**	16.9
— 0.6	— 6.4	— 6.4	11.1	— 2.4	— 0.6	**2011**	— 1.8
0.2	4.3	1.6	— 4.5	1.1	0.3	**2012**	15.9
6.6	— 1.0	5.1	3.9	3.6	2.9	**2013**	38.3
— 0.9	4.8	— 1.9	3.1	3.5	— 1.2	**2014**	13.4
22/43	23/43	23/43	24/43	29/43	25/43		31/43
51 %	53 %	53 %	56 %	67 %	58 %		72 %
0.2 %	0.2 %	— 0.5 %	0.7 %	1.7 %	1.8 %		12.3 %
10	11	12	8	3	2		

NASDAQ MONTH
CLOSING VALUES

	JAN	FEB	MAR	APR	MAY	JUN
1972	119	125	128	131	133	130
1973	128	120	117	108	103	101
1974	95	94	92	87	80	76
1975	70	73	76	79	83	87
1976	87	90	91	90	88	90
1977	96	95	94	95	96	100
1978	101	101	106	115	120	120
1979	126	123	132	134	131	138
1980	162	158	131	140	150	158
1981	198	198	210	217	223	216
1982	188	179	176	185	179	171
1983	248	261	271	293	309	319
1984	268	253	251	247	233	240
1985	279	284	279	281	291	296
1986	336	360	375	383	400	406
1987	392	425	430	418	417	425
1988	345	367	375	379	370	395
1989	401	400	407	428	446	435
1990	416	426	436	420	459	462
1991	414	453	482	485	506	476
1992	620	633	604	579	585	564
1993	696	671	690	661	701	704
1994	800	793	743	734	735	706
1995	755	794	817	844	865	933
1996	1060	1100	1101	1191	1243	1185
1997	1380	1309	1222	1261	1400	1442
1998	1619	1771	1836	1868	1779	1895
1999	2506	2288	2461	2543	2471	2686
2000	3940	4697	4573	3861	3401	3966
2001	2773	2152	1840	2116	2110	2161
2002	1934	1731	1845	1688	1616	1463
2003	1321	1338	1341	1464	1596	1623
2004	2066	2030	1994	1920	1987	2048
2005	2062	2052	1999	1922	2068	2057
2006	2306	2281	2340	2323	2179	2172
2007	2464	2416	2422	2525	2605	2603
2008	2390	2271	2279	2413	2523	2293
2009	1476	1378	1529	1717	1774	1835
2010	2147	2238	2398	2461	2257	2109
2011	2700	2782	2781	2874	2835	2774
2012	2814	2967	3092	3046	2827	2935
2013	3142	3160	3268	3329	3456	3403
2014	4104	4308	4199	4115	4243	4408

NASDAQ MONTH CLOSING VALUES

STOCK MKT

JUL	AUG	SEP	OCT	NOV	DEC	
128	130	130	130	133	134	**1972**
109	105	111	110	94	92	**1973**
70	62	56	65	63	60	**1974**
83	79	74	77	79	78	**1975**
91	90	91	90	91	98	**1976**
101	100	101	98	103	105	**1977**
126	135	133	111	115	118	**1978**
141	150	150	136	144	151	**1979**
172	182	188	193	208	202	**1980**
212	196	180	195	201	196	**1981**
167	178	188	213	232	232	**1982**
304	292	297	275	286	279	**1983**
230	255	250	247	242	247	**1984**
301	298	280	293	314	325	**1985**
371	383	351	361	360	349	**1986**
435	455	444	323	305	331	**1987**
387	377	388	383	372	381	**1988**
454	469	473	456	456	455	**1989**
438	381	345	330	359	374	**1990**
502	526	527	543	524	586	**1991**
581	563	583	605	653	677	**1992**
705	743	763	779	754	777	**1993**
722	766	764	777	750	752	**1994**
1001	1020	1044	1036	1059	1052	**1995**
1081	1142	1227	1222	1293	1291	**1996**
1594	1587	1686	1594	1601	1570	**1997**
1872	1499	1694	1771	1950	2193	**1998**
2638	2739	2746	2966	3336	4069	**1999**
3767	4206	3673	3370	2598	2471	**2000**
2027	1805	1499	1690	1931	1950	**2001**
1328	1315	1172	1330	1479	1336	**2002**
1735	1810	1787	1932	1960	2003	**2003**
1887	1838	1897	1975	2097	2175	**2004**
2185	2152	2152	2120	2233	2205	**2005**
2091	2184	2258	2367	2432	2415	**2006**
2546	2596	2702	2859	2661	2652	**2007**
2326	2368	2092	1721	1536	1577	**2008**
1979	2009	2122	2045	2145	2269	**2009**
2255	2114	2369	2507	2498	2653	**2010**
2756	2579	2415	2684	2620	2605	**2011**
2940	3067	3116	2977	3010	3020	**2012**
3626	3590	3771	3920	4060	4177	**2013**
4370	4580	4493	4631	4792	4736	**2014**

S&P/TSX MONTH PERCENT CHANGES

	JAN	FEB	MAR	APR	MAY	JUN
1985	8.1	0.0	0.7	0.8	3.8	— 0.8
1986	— 1.7	0.5	6.7	1.1	1.4	— 1.2
1987	9.2	4.5	6.9	— 0.6	— 0.9	1.5
1988	— 3.3	4.8	3.4	0.8	— 2.7	5.9
1989	6.7	— 1.2	0.2	1.4	2.2	1.5
1990	— 6.7	— 0.5	— 1.3	— 8.2	6.7	— 0.6
1991	0.5	5.8	1.0	-0.8	2.2	— 2.3
1992	2.4	— 0.4	— 4.7	— 1.7	1.0	0.0
1993	— 1.3	4.4	4.4	5.2	2.5	2.2
1994	5.4	— 2.9	— 2.1	— 1.4	1.4	— 7.0
1995	— 4.7	2.7	4.6	— -0.8	4.0	1.8
1996	5.4	— 0.7	0.8	3.5	1.9	— 3.9
1997	3.1	0.8	— 5.0	2.2	6.8	0.9
1998	0.0	5.9	6.6	1.4	— 1.0	— 2.9
1999	3.8	— 6.2	4.5	6.3	— 2.5	2.5
2000	0.8	7.6	3.7	— 1.2	— 1.0	10.2
2001	4.3	— 13.3	— 5.8	4.5	2.7	— 5.2
2002	— 0.5	— 0.1	2.8	— 2.4	— 0.1	— 6.7
2003	— 0.7	— 0.2	— 3.2	3.8	4.2	1.8
2004	3.7	3.1	— 2.3	— 4.0	2.1	1.5
2005	— 0.5	5.0	— 0.6	— 3.5	3.6	3.1
2006	6.0	— 2.2	3.6	0.8	— 3.8	— 1.1
2007	1.0	0.1	0.9	1.9	4.8	— 1.1
2008	— 4.9	3.3	— 1.7	4.4	5.6	— 1.7
2009	— 3.3	— 6.6	7.4	6.9	11.2	0.0
2010	— 5.5	4.8	3.5	1.4	— 3.7	— 4.0
2011	0.8	4.3	— 0.1	— 1.2	— 1.0	— 3.6
2012	4.2	1.5	— 2.0	— 0.8	— 6.3	0.7
2013	2.0	1.1	— 0.6	— 2.3	1.6	— 4.1
2014	0.5	3.8	0.9	2.2	— 0.3	3.7
FQ POS	19/30	18/30	18/30	17/30	19/30	14/30
% FQ POS	63 %	60 %	60 %	57 %	63 %	47 %
AVG GAIN	1.2 %	1.0 %	1.1 %	0.7 %	1.5 %	-0.3 %
RANK GAIN	3	5	4	7	2	11

S&P/TSX MONTH PERCENT CHANGES

STOCK MKT

JUL	AUG	SEP	OCT	NOV	DEC	YEAR	
2.4	1.5	— 6.7	1.6	6.8	1.3	1985	20.5
— 4.9	3.2	— 1.6	1.6	0.7	0.6	1986	6.0
7.8	— 0.9	— 2.3	— 22.6	— 1.4	6.1	1987	3.1
— 1.9	— 2.7	— 0.1	3.4	— 3.0	2.9	1988	7.3
5.6	1.0	— 1.7	— 0.6	0.6	0.7	1989	17.1
0.5	— 6.0	— 5.6	— 2.5	2.3	3.4	1990	— 18.0
2.1	— 0.6	— 3.7	3.8	— 1.9	1.9	1991	7.8
1.6	— 1.2	— 3.1	1.2	— 1.6	2.1	1992	— 4.6
0.0	4.3	— 3.6	6.6	— 1.8	3.4	1993	29.0
3.8	4.1	0.1	— 1.4	— 4.6	2.9	1994	— 2.5
1.9	— 2.1	0.3	— 1.6	4.5	1.1	1995	11.9
— 2.3	4.3	2.9	5.8	7.5	— 1.5	1996	25.7
6.8	— 3.9	6.5	— 2.8	— 4.8	2.9	1997	13.0
— 5.9	— 20.2	1.5	10.6	2.2	2.2	1998	— 3.2
1.0	— 1.6	— 0.2	4.3	3.6	11.9	1999	29.7
2.1	8.1	— 7.7	— 7.1	— 8.5	1.3	2000	6.2
— 0.6	— 3.8	— 7.6	0.7	7.8	3.5	2001	— 13.9
— 7.6	0.1	— 6.5	1.1	5.1	0.7	2002	— 14.0
3.9	3.6	— 1.3	4.7	1.1	4.6	2003	24.3
— 1.0	— 1.0	3.5	2.3	1.8	2.4	2004	12.5
5.3	2.4	3.2	— 5.7	4.2	4.1	2005	21.9
1.9	2.1	— 2.6	5.0	3.3	1.2	2006	14.5
— 0.3	— 1.5	3.2	3.7	— 6.4	1.1	2007	7.2
— 6.0	1.3	— 14.7	— 16.9	— 5.0	— 3.1	2008	— 35.0
4.0	0.8	4.8	— 4.2	4.9	2.6	2009	30.7
3.7	1.7	3.8	2.5	2.2	3.8	2010	14.4
— 2.7	— 1.4	— 9.0	5.4	— 0.4	— 2.0	2011	— 11.1
0.6	2.4	3.1	0.9	— 1.5	1.6	2012	4.0
2.9	1.3	1.1	4.5	0.3	1.7	2013	9.6
1.2	1.9	— 4.3	— 2.3	0.9	— 0.8	2014	7.4
20/30	17/30	12/30	19/30	18/30	26/30		22/30
67 %	57 %	40 %	66 %	60 %	87 %		73 %
0.9 %	— 0.1 %	— 1.6 %	0.1 %	0.6 %	2.2 %		7.4 %
6	10	12	9	8	1		

S&P/TSX MONTH CLOSING VALUES

	JAN	FEB	MAR	APR	MAY	JUN
1985	2595	2595	2613	2635	2736	2713
1986	2843	2856	3047	3079	3122	3086
1987	3349	3499	3739	3717	3685	3740
1988	3057	3205	3314	3340	3249	3441
1989	3617	3572	3578	3628	3707	3761
1990	3704	3687	3640	3341	3565	3544
1991	3273	3462	3496	3469	3546	3466
1992	3596	3582	3412	3356	3388	3388
1993	3305	3452	3602	3789	3883	3966
1994	4555	4424	4330	4267	4327	4025
1995	4018	4125	4314	4280	4449	4527
1996	4968	4934	4971	5147	5246	5044
1997	6110	6158	5850	5977	6382	6438
1998	6700	7093	7559	7665	7590	7367
1999	6730	6313	6598	7015	6842	7010
2000	8481	9129	9462	9348	9252	10196
2001	9322	8079	7608	7947	8162	7736
2002	7649	7638	7852	7663	7656	7146
2003	6570	6555	6343	6586	6860	6983
2004	8521	8789	8586	8244	8417	8546
2005	9204	9668	9612	9275	9607	9903
2006	11946	11688	12111	12204	11745	11613
2007	13034	13045	13166	13417	14057	13907
2008	13155	13583	13350	13937	14715	14467
2009	8695	8123	8720	9325	10370	10375
2010	11094	11630	12038	12211	11763	11294
2011	13552	14137	14116	13945	13803	13301
2012	12452	12644	12392	12293	11513	11597
2013	12685	12822	12750	12457	12650	12129
2014	13695	14210	14335	14652	14604	15146

JUL	AUG	SEP	OCT	NOV	DEC	
2779	2820	2632	2675	2857	2893	1985
2935	3028	2979	3027	3047	3066	1986
4030	3994	3902	3019	2978	3160	1987
3377	3286	3284	3396	3295	3390	1988
3971	4010	3943	3919	3943	3970	1989
3561	3346	3159	3081	3151	3257	1990
3540	3518	3388	3516	3449	3512	1991
3443	3403	3298	3336	3283	3350	1992
3967	4138	3991	4256	4180	4321	1993
4179	4350	4354	4292	4093	4214	1994
4615	4517	4530	4459	4661	4714	1995
4929	5143	5291	5599	6017	5927	1996
6878	6612	7040	6842	6513	6699	1997
6931	5531	5614	6208	6344	6486	1998
7081	6971	6958	7256	7520	8414	1999
10406	11248	10378	9640	8820	8934	2000
7690	7399	6839	6886	7426	7688	2001
6605	6612	6180	6249	6570	6615	2002
7258	7517	7421	7773	7859	8221	2003
8458	8377	8668	8871	9030	9247	2004
10423	10669	11012	10383	10824	11272	2005
11831	12074	11761	12345	12752	12908	2006
13869	13660	14099	14625	13689	13833	2007
13593	13771	11753	9763	9271	8988	2008
10787	10868	11935	10911	11447	11746	2009
11713	11914	12369	12676	12953	13443	2010
12946	12769	11624	12252	12204	11955	2011
11665	11949	12317	12423	12239	12434	2012
12487	12654	12787	13361	13395	13622	2013
15331	15626	14961	14613	14745	14632	2014

10 BEST

10 WORST

YEARS

	Close	Change	Change
1954	36	11 pt	45.0 %
1958	55	15	38.1
1995	616	157	34.1
1975	90	22	31.5
1997	970	230	31.0
2013	1848	422	29.6
1989	353	76	27.3
1998	1229	259	26.7
1955	45	10	26.4
2003	1112	232	26.4

YEARS

	Close	Change	Change
2008	903	− 566 pt	− 38.5 %
1974	69	− 29	− 29.7
2002	880	− 268	− 23.4
1973	98	− 21	− 17.4
1957	40	− 7	− 14.3
1966	80	− 12	− 13.1
2001	1148	− 172	− 13.0
1962	63	− 8	− 11.8
1977	95	− 12	− 11.5
1969	92	− 12	− 11.4

MONTHS

	Close	Change	Change
Oct 1974	74	10 pt	16.3 %
Aug 1982	120	12	11.6
Dec 1991	417	42	11.2
Oct 1982	134	13	11.0
Oct 2011	1253	122	10.8
Aug 1984	167	16	10.6
Nov 1980	141	13	10.2
Nov 1962	62	6	10.2
Mar 2000	1499	132	9.7
Apr 2009	798	75	9.4

MONTHS

	Close	Change	Change
Oct 1987	252	− 70 pt	− 21.8 %
Oct 2008	969	− 196	− 16.8
Aug 1998	957	− 163	− 14.6
Sep 1974	64	− 9	− 11.9
Nov 1973	96	− 12	− 11.4
Sep 2002	815	− 101	− 11.0
Feb 2009	735	− 91	− 11.0
Mar 1980	102	− 12	− 10.2
Aug 1990	323	− 34	− 9.4
Feb 2001	1240	− 126	− 9.2

DAYS

		Close	Change	Change
Mon	2008 Oct 13	1003	104 pt	11.6 %
Tue	2008 Oct 28	941	92	10.8
Wed	1987 Oct 21	258	22	9.1
Mon	2009 Mar 23	883	54	7.1
Thu	2008 Nov 13	911	59	6.9
Mon	2008 Nov 24	852	52	6.5
Tues	2009 Mar 10	720	43	6.4
Fri	2008 Nov 21	800	48	6.3
Wed	2002 Jul 24	843	46	5.7
Tue	2008 Sep 30	1166	60	5.4

DAYS

		Close	Change	Change
Mon	1987 Oct 19	225	− 58 pt	− 20.5 %
Wed	2008 Oct 15	908	− 90	− 9.0
Mon	2008 Dec 01	816	− 80	− 8.9
Mon	2008 Sep 29	1106	− 107	− 8.8
Mon	1987 Oct 26	228	− 21	− 8.3
Thu	2008 Oct 09	910	− 75	− 7.6
Mon	1997 Oct 27	877	− 65	− 6.9
Mon	1998 Aug 31	957	− 70	− 6.8
Fri	1988 Jan 8	243	− 18	− 6.8
Thu	2008 Nov 20	752	− 54	− 6.7

10 BEST

10 WORST

YEARS

	Close	Change	Change
1954	404	124 pt	44.0 %
1975	852	236	38.3
1958	584	148	34.0
1995	5117	1283	33.5
1985	1547	335	27.7
1989	2753	585	27.0
2013	16577	3473	26.5
1996	6448	1331	26.0
2003	10454	2112	25.3
1999	11453	2272	25.2

YEARS

	Close	Change	Change
2008	8776	– 4488 pt	– 33.8 %
1974	616	– 235	– 27.6
1966	786	– 184	– 18.9
1977	831	– 174	– 17.3
2002	8342	– 1680	– 16.8
1973	851	– 169	– 16.6
1969	800	– 143	– 15.2
1957	436	– 64	– 12.8
1962	652	– 79	– 10.8
1960	616	– 64	– 9.3

MONTHS

	Close	Change	Change
Aug 1982	901	93 pt	11.5 %
Oct 1982	992	95	10.6
Oct 2002	8397	805	10.6
Apr 1978	837	80	10.5
Apr 1999	10789	1003	10.2
Nov 1962	649	60	10.1
Nov 1954	387	35	9.9
Aug 1984	1224	109	9.8
Oct 1998	8592	750	9.6
Oct 2011	11955	1042	9.5

MONTHS

	Close	Change	Change
Oct 1987	1994	– 603 pt	– 23.2 %
Aug 1998	7539	– 1344	– 15.1
Oct 2008	9325	– 1526	– 14.1
Nov 1973	822	– 134	– 14.0
Sep 2002	7592	– 1072	– 12.4
Feb 2009	7063	– 938	– 11.7
Sep 2001	8848	– 1102	– 11.1
Sep 1974	608	– 71	– 10.4
Aug 1974	679	– 79	– 10.4
Jun 2008	11350	– 1288	– 10.2

DAYS

		Close	Change	Change
Mon	2008 Oct 13	9388	936 pt	11.1 %
Tue	2008 Oct 28	9065	889	10.9
Wed	1987 Oct 21	2028	187	10.2
Mon	2009 Mar 23	7776	497	6.8
Thu	2008 Nov 13	8835	553	6.7
Fri	2008 Nov 21	8046	494	6.5
Wed	2002 Jul 24	8191	489	6.3
Tue	1987 Oct 20	1841	102	5.9
Tue	2009 Mar 10	6926	379	5.8
Mon	2002 Jul 29	8712	448	5.4

DAYS

		Close	Change	Change
Mon	1987 Oct 19	1739	– 508 pt	– 22.6 %
Mon	1987 Oct 26	1794	– 157	– 8.0
Wed	2008 Oct 15	8578	– 733	– 7.9
Mon	2008 Dec 01	8149	– 680	– 7.7
Thu	2008 Oct 09	8579	– 679	– 7.3
Mon	1997 Oct 27	8366	– 554	– 7.2
Mon	2001 Sep 17	8921	– 685	– 7.1
Mon	2008 Sep 29	10365	– 778	– 7.0
Fri	1989 Oct 13	2569	– 191	– 6.9
Fri	1988 Jan 8	1911	– 141	– 6.9

10 BEST

10 WORST

YEARS

	Close	Change	Change
1999	4069	1877 pt	85.6 %
1991	586	213	56.9
2003	2003	668	50.0
2009	2269	692	43.9
1995	1052	300	39.9
1998	2193	622	39.6
2013	4161	1157	38.3
1980	202	51	33.9
1985	325	78	31.5
1975	78	18	29.8

YEARS

	Close	Change	Change
2008	1577	− 1075 pt	− 40.5 %
2000	2471	− 1599	− 39.3
1974	60	− 32	− 35.1
2002	1336	− 615	− 31.5
1973	92	− 42	− 31.1
2001	1950	− 520	− 21.1
1990	374	− 81	− 17.8
1984	247	− 32	− 11.3
1987	331	− 18	− 5.2
1981	196	− 7	− 3.2

MONTHS

	Close	Change	Change
Dec 1999	4069	733 pt	22.0 %
Feb 2000	4697	756	19.2
Oct 1974	65	10	17.2
Jun 2000	3966	565	16.6
Apr 2001	2116	276	15.0
Nov 2001	1931	240	14.2
Oct 2002	1330	158	13.5
Oct 1982	1771	25	13.3
Sep 1998	1694	195	13.0
Oct 2001	1690	191	12.8

MONTHS

	Close	Change	Change
Oct 1987	323	− 121 pt	− 27.2 %
Nov 2000	2598	− 772	− 22.9
Feb 2001	2152	− 621	− 22.4
Aug 1998	1499	− 373	− 19.9
Oct 2008	1721	− 371	− 17.7
Mar 1980	131	− 27	− 17.1
Sep 2001	1499	− 307	− 17.0
Oct 1978	111	− 22	− 16.4
Apr 2000	3861	− 712	− 15.6
Nov 1973	94	− 17	− 15.1

DAYS

		Close	Change	Change
Wed	2001 Jan 3	2617	325 pt	14.2 %
Mon	2008 Oct 13	1844	195	11.8
Tue	2000 Dec 5	2890	274	10.5
Tue	2008 Oct 28	1649	144	9.5
Thu	2001 Apr 5	1785	146	8.9
Wed	2001 Apr 18	2079	156	8.1
Tue	2000 May 30	3459	254	7.9
Fri	2000 Oct 13	3317	242	7.9
Thu	2000 Oct 19	3419	247	7.8
Wed	2002 May 8	1696	122	7.8

DAYS

		Close	Change	Change
Mon	1987 Oct 19	360	− 46 pt	− 11.3 %
Fri	2000 Apr 14	3321	− 355	− 9.7
Mon	2008 Sep 29	1984	− 200	− 9.1
Mon	1987 Oct 26	299	− 30	− 9.0
Tue	1987 Oct 20	328	− 32	− 9.0
Mon	2008 Dec 01	1398	− 138	− 9.0
Mon	1998 Aug 31	1499	− 140	− 8.6
Wed	2008 Oct 15	1628	− 151	− 8.5
Mon	2000 Apr 03	4224	− 349	− 7.6
Tue	2001 Jan 02	2292	− 179	− 7.2

10 BEST

10 WORST

YEARS

	Close	Change	Change
2009	8414	2758 pt	30.7 %
1999	4321	1928	29.7
1993	5927	971	29.0
1996	8221	1213	25.7
2003	11272	1606	24.3
2005	2893	2026	21.9
1985	3970	500	20.8
1989	12908	580	17.1
2006	6699	1636	14.5
2010	13433	1697	14.4

YEARS

	Close	Change	Change
2008	8988	− 4845 pt	− 35.0 %
1990	3257	− 713	− 18.0
2002	6615	− 1074	− 14.0
2001	7688	− 1245	− 13.9
2011	11955	− 1488	− 11.1
1992	3350	− 162	− 4.6
1998	6486	− 214	− 3.2
1994	4214	− 108	− 2.5
1987	3160	94	3.1
2012	12434	479	4.0

MONTHS

	Close	Change	Change
Dec 1999	8414	891 pt	11.8 %
May 2009	8500	1045	11.2
Oct 1998	6208	594	10.6
Jun 2000	10196	943	10.2
Jan 1985	2595	195	8.1
Aug 2000	11248	842	8.1
Nov 2001	7426	540	7.8
Jul 1987	4030	290	7.8
Feb 2000	9129	648	7.6
Nov 1996	6017	418	7.5

MONTHS

	Close	Change	Change
Oct 1987	3019	− 883 pt	− 22.6 %
Aug 1998	5531	− 1401	− 20.2
Oct 2008	9763	− 1990	− 16.9
Sep 2008	11753	− 2018	− 14.7
Feb 2001	8079	− 1243	− 13.3
Sep 2011	11624	− 1145	− 9.0
Nov 2000	8820	− 820	− 8.5
Apr 1990	3341	− 299	− 8.2
Sep 2000	10378	− 870	− 7.7
Sep 2001	6839	− 561	− 7.6

DAYS

		Close	Change	Change
Tue	2008 Oct 14	9956	891 pt	9.8 %
Wed	1987 Oct 21	3246	269	9.0
Mon	2008 Oct 20	10251	689	7.2
Tue	2008 Oct 28	9152	614	7.2
Fri	2008 Sep 19	12913	848	7.0
Fri	2008 Nov 28	9271	517	5.9
Fri	2008 Nov 21	8155	431	5.6
Mon	2008 Dec 08	8567	450	5.5
Mon	2009 Mar 23	8959	452	5.3
Fri	1987 Oct 30	3019	147	5.1

DAYS

		Close	Change	Change
Mon	1987 Oct 19	3192	− 407 pt	− 11.3 %
Mon	2008 Dec 01	8406	− 864	− 9.3
Thu	2008 Nov 20	7725	− 766	− 9.0
Mon	2008 Oct 27	8537	− 757	− 8.1
Wed	2000 Oct 25	9512	− 840	− 8.1
Mon	1987 Oct 26	2846	− 233	− 7.6
Thu	2008 Oct 02	10901	− 814	− 6.9
Mon	2008 Sep 29	11285	− 841	− 6.9
Tue	1987 Oct 20	2977	− 215	− 6.7
Fri	2001 Feb 16	8393	− 574	− 6.4

BOND YIELDS

BOND YIELDS 🇺🇸 10 YEAR TREASURY*

	JAN	FEB	MAR	APR	MAY	JUN
1954	2.48	2.47	2.37	2.29	2.37	2.38
1955	2.61	2.65	2.68	2.75	2.76	2.78
1956	2.9	2.84	2.96	3.18	3.07	3
1957	3.46	3.34	3.41	3.48	3.6	3.8
1958	3.09	3.05	2.98	2.88	2.92	2.97
1959	4.02	3.96	3.99	4.12	4.31	4.34
1960	4.72	4.49	4.25	4.28	4.35	4.15
1961	3.84	3.78	3.74	3.78	3.71	3.88
1962	4.08	4.04	3.93	3.84	3.87	3.91
1963	3.83	3.92	3.93	3.97	3.93	3.99
1964	4.17	4.15	4.22	4.23	4.2	4.17
1965	4.19	4.21	4.21	4.2	4.21	4.21
1966	4.61	4.83	4.87	4.75	4.78	4.81
1967	4.58	4.63	4.54	4.59	4.85	5.02
1968	5.53	5.56	5.74	5.64	5.87	5.72
1969	6.04	6.19	6.3	6.17	6.32	6.57
1970	7.79	7.24	7.07	7.39	7.91	7.84
1971	6.24	6.11	5.7	5.83	6.39	6.52
1972	5.95	6.08	6.07	6.19	6.13	6.11
1973	6.46	6.64	6.71	6.67	6.85	6.9
1974	6.99	6.96	7.21	7.51	7.58	7.54
1975	7.5	7.39	7.73	8.23	8.06	7.86
1976	7.74	7.79	7.73	7.56	7.9	7.86
1977	7.21	7.39	7.46	7.37	7.46	7.28
1978	7.96	8.03	8.04	8.15	8.35	8.46
1979	9.1	9.1	9.12	9.18	9.25	8.91
1980	10.8	12.41	12.75	11.47	10.18	9.78
1981	12.57	13.19	13.12	13.68	14.1	13.47
1982	14.59	14.43	13.86	13.87	13.62	14.3
1983	10.46	10.72	10.51	10.4	10.38	10.85
1984	11.67	11.84	12.32	12.63	13.41	13.56
1985	11.38	11.51	11.86	11.43	10.85	10.16
1986	9.19	8.7	7.78	7.3	7.71	7.8
1987	7.08	7.25	7.25	8.02	8.61	8.4
1988	8.67	8.21	8.37	8.72	9.09	8.92
1989	9.09	9.17	9.36	9.18	8.86	8.28
1990	8.21	8.47	8.59	8.79	8.76	8.48
1991	8.09	7.85	8.11	8.04	8.07	8.28
1992	7.03	7.34	7.54	7.48	7.39	7.26
1993	6.6	6.26	5.98	5.97	6.04	5.96
1994	5.75	5.97	6.48	6.97	7.18	7.1
1995	7.78	7.47	7.2	7.06	6.63	6.17
1996	5.65	5.81	6.27	6.51	6.74	6.91
1997	6.58	6.42	6.69	6.89	6.71	6.49
1998	5.54	5.57	5.65	5.64	5.65	5.5
1999	4.72	5	5.23	5.18	5.54	5.9
2000	6.66	6.52	6.26	5.99	6.44	6.1
2001	5.16	5.1	4.89	5.14	5.39	5.28
2002	5.04	4.91	5.28	5.21	5.16	4.93
2003	4.05	3.9	3.81	3.96	3.57	3.33
2004	4.15	4.08	3.83	4.35	4.72	4.73
2005	4.22	4.17	4.5	4.34	4.14	4.00
2006	4.42	4.57	4.72	4.99	5.11	5.11
2007	4.76	4.72	4.56	4.69	4.75	5.10
2008	3.74	3.74	3.51	3.68	3.88	4.10
2009	2.52	2.87	2.82	2.93	3.29	3.72
2010	3.73	3.69	3.73	3.85	3.42	3.20
2011	3.39	3.58	3.41	3.46	3.17	3.00
2012	1.97	1.97	2.17	2.05	1.80	1.62
2013	1.91	1.98	1.96	1.76	1.93	2.30
2014	2.86	2.71	2.72	2.71	2.56	2.60

* Source: Federal Reserve Bank of St. Louis, monthly data calculated as average of business days

10 YEAR TREASURY BOND YIELDS

JUL	AUG	SEP	OCT	NOV	DEC	
2.3	2.36	2.38	2.43	2.48	2.51	**1954**
2.9	2.97	2.97	2.88	2.89	2.96	**1955**
3.11	3.33	3.38	3.34	3.49	3.59	**1956**
3.93	3.93	3.92	3.97	3.72	3.21	**1957**
3.2	3.54	3.76	3.8	3.74	3.86	**1958**
4.4	4.43	4.68	4.53	4.53	4.69	**1959**
3.9	3.8	3.8	3.89	3.93	3.84	**1960**
3.92	4.04	3.98	3.92	3.94	4.06	**1961**
4.01	3.98	3.98	3.93	3.92	3.86	**1962**
4.02	4	4.08	4.11	4.12	4.13	**1963**
4.19	4.19	4.2	4.19	4.15	4.18	**1964**
4.2	4.25	4.29	4.35	4.45	4.62	**1965**
5.02	5.22	5.18	5.01	5.16	4.84	**1966**
5.16	5.28	5.3	5.48	5.75	5.7	**1967**
5.5	5.42	5.46	5.58	5.7	6.03	**1968**
6.72	6.69	7.16	7.1	7.14	7.65	**1969**
7.46	7.53	7.39	7.33	6.84	6.39	**1970**
6.73	6.58	6.14	5.93	5.81	5.93	**1971**
6.11	6.21	6.55	6.48	6.28	6.36	**1972**
7.13	7.4	7.09	6.79	6.73	6.74	**1973**
7.81	8.04	8.04	7.9	7.68	7.43	**1974**
8.06	8.4	8.43	8.14	8.05	8	**1975**
7.83	7.77	7.59	7.41	7.29	6.87	**1976**
7.33	7.4	7.34	7.52	7.58	7.69	**1977**
8.64	8.41	8.42	8.64	8.81	9.01	**1978**
8.95	9.03	9.33	10.3	10.65	10.39	**1979**
10.25	11.1	11.51	11.75	12.68	12.84	**1980**
14.28	14.94	15.32	15.15	13.39	13.72	**1981**
13.95	13.06	12.34	10.91	10.55	10.54	**1982**
11.38	11.85	11.65	11.54	11.69	11.83	**1983**
13.36	12.72	12.52	12.16	11.57	11.5	**1984**
10.31	10.33	10.37	10.24	9.78	9.26	**1985**
7.3	7.17	7.45	7.43	7.25	7.11	**1986**
8.45	8.76	9.42	9.52	8.86	8.99	**1987**
9.06	9.26	8.98	8.8	8.96	9.11	**1988**
8.02	8.11	8.19	8.01	7.87	7.84	**1989**
8.47	8.75	8.89	8.72	8.39	8.08	**1990**
8.27	7.9	7.65	7.53	7.42	7.09	**1991**
6.84	6.59	6.42	6.59	6.87	6.77	**1992**
5.81	5.68	5.36	5.33	5.72	5.77	**1993**
7.3	7.24	7.46	7.74	7.96	7.81	**1994**
6.28	6.49	6.2	6.04	5.93	5.71	**1995**
6.87	6.64	6.83	6.53	6.2	6.3	**1996**
6.22	6.3	6.21	6.03	5.88	5.81	**1997**
5.46	5.34	4.81	4.53	4.83	4.65	**1998**
5.79	5.94	5.92	6.11	6.03	6.28	**1999**
6.05	5.83	5.8	5.74	5.72	5.24	**2000**
5.24	4.97	4.73	4.57	4.65	5.09	**2001**
4.65	4.26	3.87	3.94	4.05	4.03	**2002**
3.98	4.45	4.27	4.29	4.3	4.27	**2003**
4.5	4.28	4.13	4.1	4.19	4.23	**2004**
4.18	4.26	4.20	4.46	4.54	4.47	**2005**
5.09	4.88	4.72	4.73	4.60	4.56	**2006**
5.00	4.67	4.52	4.53	4.15	4.10	**2007**
4.01	3.89	3.69	3.81	3.53	2.42	**2008**
3.56	3.59	3.40	3.39	3.40	3.59	**2009**
3.01	2.70	2.65	2.54	2.76	3.29	**2010**
3.00	2.30	1.98	2.15	2.01	1.98	**2011**
1.53	1.68	1.72	1.75	1.65	1.72	**2012**
2.58	2.74	2.81	2.62	2.72	2.90	**2013**
2.54	2.42	2.53	2.30	2.33	2.21	**2014**

BOND YIELDS ≣≣5 YEAR TREASURY*

	JAN	FEB	MAR	APR	MAY	JUN
1954	2.17	2.04	1.93	1.87	1.92	1.92
1955	2.32	2.38	2.48	2.55	2.56	2.59
1956	2.84	2.74	2.93	3.20	3.08	2.97
1957	3.47	3.39	3.46	3.53	3.64	3.83
1958	2.88	2.78	2.64	2.46	2.41	2.46
1959	4.01	3.96	3.99	4.12	4.35	4.50
1960	4.92	4.69	4.31	4.29	4.49	4.12
1961	3.67	3.66	3.60	3.57	3.47	3.81
1962	3.94	3.89	3.68	3.60	3.66	3.64
1963	3.58	3.66	3.68	3.74	3.72	3.81
1964	4.07	4.03	4.14	4.15	4.05	4.02
1965	4.10	4.15	4.15	4.15	4.15	4.15
1966	4.86	4.98	4.92	4.83	4.89	4.97
1967	4.70	4.74	4.54	4.51	4.75	5.01
1968	5.54	5.59	5.76	5.69	6.04	5.85
1969	6.25	6.34	6.41	6.30	6.54	6.75
1970	8.17	7.82	7.21	7.50	7.97	7.85
1971	5.89	5.56	5.00	5.65	6.28	6.53
1972	5.59	5.69	5.87	6.17	5.85	5.91
1973	6.34	6.60	6.80	6.67	6.80	6.69
1974	6.95	6.82	7.31	7.92	8.18	8.10
1975	7.41	7.11	7.30	7.99	7.72	7.51
1976	7.46	7.45	7.49	7.25	7.59	7.61
1977	6.58	6.83	6.93	6.79	6.94	6.76
1978	7.77	7.83	7.86	7.98	8.18	8.36
1979	9.20	9.13	9.20	9.25	9.24	8.85
1980	10.74	12.60	13.47	11.84	9.95	9.21
1981	12.77	13.41	13.41	13.99	14.63	13.95
1982	14.65	14.54	13.98	14.00	13.75	14.43
1983	10.03	10.26	10.08	10.02	10.03	10.63
1984	11.37	11.54	12.02	12.37	13.17	13.48
1985	10.93	11.13	11.52	11.01	10.34	9.60
1986	8.68	8.34	7.46	7.05	7.52	7.64
1987	6.64	6.79	6.79	7.57	8.26	8.02
1988	8.18	7.71	7.83	8.19	8.58	8.49
1989	9.15	9.27	9.51	9.30	8.91	8.29
1990	8.12	8.42	8.60	8.77	8.74	8.43
1991	7.70	7.47	7.77	7.70	7.70	7.94
1992	6.24	6.58	6.95	6.78	6.69	6.48
1993	5.83	5.43	5.19	5.13	5.20	5.22
1994	5.09	5.40	5.94	6.52	6.78	6.70
1995	7.76	7.37	7.05	6.86	6.41	5.93
1996	5.36	5.38	5.97	6.30	6.48	6.69
1997	6.33	6.20	6.54	6.76	6.57	6.38
1998	5.42	5.49	5.61	5.61	5.63	5.52
1999	4.60	4.91	5.14	5.08	5.44	5.81
2000	6.58	6.68	6.50	6.26	6.69	6.30
2001	4.86	4.89	4.64	4.76	4.93	4.81
2002	4.34	4.30	4.74	4.65	4.49	4.19
2003	3.05	2.90	2.78	2.93	2.52	2.27
2004	3.12	3.07	2.79	3.39	3.85	3.93
2005	3.71	3.77	4.17	4.00	3.85	3.77
2006	4.35	4.57	4.72	4.90	5.00	5.07
2007	4.75	4.71	4.48	4.59	4.67	5.03
2008	2.98	2.78	2.48	2.84	3.15	3.49
2009	1.60	1.87	1.82	1.86	2.13	2.71
2010	2.48	2.36	2.43	2.58	2.18	2.00
2011	1.99	2.26	2.11	2.17	1.84	1.58
2012	0.84	0.83	1.02	0.89	0.76	0.71
2013	0.81	0.85	0.82	0.71	0.84	1.20
2014	1.65	1.52	1.64	1.70	1.59	1.68

* Source: Federal Reserve Bank of St. Louis, monthly data calculated as average of business days

5 YEAR TREASURY BOND YIELDS

JUL	AUG	SEP	OCT	NOV	DEC	
1.85	1.90	1.96	2.02	2.09	2.16	1954
2.72	2.86	2.85	2.76	2.81	2.93	1955
3.12	3.41	3.47	3.40	3.56	3.70	1956
4.00	4.00	4.03	4.08	3.72	3.08	1957
2.77	3.29	3.69	3.78	3.70	3.82	1958
4.58	4.57	4.90	4.72	4.75	5.01	1959
3.79	3.62	3.61	3.76	3.81	3.67	1960
3.84	3.96	3.90	3.80	3.82	3.91	1961
3.80	3.71	3.70	3.64	3.60	3.56	1962
3.89	3.89	3.96	3.97	4.01	4.04	1963
4.03	4.05	4.08	4.07	4.04	4.09	1964
4.15	4.20	4.25	4.34	4.46	4.72	1965
5.17	5.50	5.50	5.27	5.36	5.00	1966
5.23	5.31	5.40	5.57	5.78	5.75	1967
5.60	5.50	5.48	5.55	5.66	6.12	1968
7.01	7.03	7.57	7.51	7.53	7.96	1969
7.59	7.57	7.29	7.12	6.47	5.95	1970
6.85	6.55	6.14	5.93	5.78	5.69	1971
5.97	6.02	6.25	6.18	6.12	6.16	1972
7.33	7.63	7.05	6.77	6.92	6.80	1973
8.38	8.63	8.37	7.97	7.68	7.31	1974
7.92	8.33	8.37	7.97	7.80	7.76	1975
7.49	7.31	7.13	6.75	6.52	6.10	1976
6.84	7.03	7.04	7.32	7.34	7.48	1977
8.54	8.33	8.43	8.61	8.84	9.08	1978
8.90	9.06	9.41	10.63	10.93	10.42	1979
9.53	10.84	11.62	11.86	12.83	13.25	1980
14.79	15.56	15.93	15.41	13.38	13.60	1981
14.07	13.00	12.25	10.80	10.38	10.22	1982
11.21	11.63	11.43	11.28	11.41	11.54	1983
13.27	12.68	12.53	12.06	11.33	11.07	1984
9.70	9.81	9.81	9.69	9.28	8.73	1985
7.06	6.80	6.92	6.83	6.76	6.67	1986
8.01	8.32	8.94	9.08	8.35	8.45	1987
8.66	8.94	8.69	8.51	8.79	9.09	1988
7.83	8.09	8.17	7.97	7.81	7.75	1989
8.33	8.44	8.51	8.33	8.02	7.73	1990
7.91	7.43	7.14	6.87	6.62	6.19	1991
5.84	5.60	5.38	5.60	6.04	6.08	1992
5.09	5.03	4.73	4.71	5.06	5.15	1993
6.91	6.88	7.08	7.40	7.72	7.78	1994
6.01	6.24	6.00	5.86	5.69	5.51	1995
6.64	6.39	6.60	6.27	5.97	6.07	1996
6.12	6.16	6.11	5.93	5.80	5.77	1997
5.46	5.27	4.62	4.18	4.54	4.45	1998
5.68	5.84	5.80	6.03	5.97	6.19	1999
6.18	6.06	5.93	5.78	5.70	5.17	2000
4.76	4.57	4.12	3.91	3.97	4.39	2001
3.81	3.29	2.94	2.95	3.05	3.03	2002
2.87	3.37	3.18	3.19	3.29	3.27	2003
3.69	3.47	3.36	3.35	3.53	3.60	2004
3.98	4.12	4.01	4.33	4.45	4.39	2005
5.04	4.82	4.67	4.69	4.58	4.53	2006
4.88	4.43	4.20	4.20	3.67	3.49	2007
3.30	3.14	2.88	2.73	2.29	1.52	2008
2.46	2.57	2.37	2.33	2.23	2.34	2009
1.76	1.47	1.41	1.18	1.35	1.93	2010
1.54	1.02	0.90	1.06	0.91	0.89	2011
0.62	0.71	0.67	0.71	0.67	0.70	2012
1.40	1.52	1.60	1.37	1.37	1.58	2013
1.70	1.63	1.77	1.55	1.62	1.64	2014

BOND YIELDS 3 MONTH TREASURY

	JAN	FEB	MAR	APR	MAY	JUN
1982	12.92	14.28	13.31	13.34	12.71	13.08
1983	8.12	8.39	8.66	8.51	8.50	9.14
1984	9.26	9.46	9.89	10.07	10.22	10.26
1985	8.02	8.56	8.83	8.22	7.73	7.18
1986	7.30	7.29	6.76	6.24	6.33	6.40
1987	5.58	5.75	5.77	5.82	5.85	5.85
1988	6.00	5.84	5.87	6.08	6.45	6.66
1999	8.56	8.84	9.14	8.96	8.74	8.43
1990	7.90	8.00	8.17	8.04	8.01	7.99
1991	6.41	6.12	6.09	5.83	5.63	5.75
1992	3.91	3.95	4.14	3.84	3.72	3.75
1993	3.07	2.99	3.01	2.93	3.03	3.14
1994	3.04	3.33	3.59	3.78	4.27	4.25
1995	5.90	5.94	5.91	5.84	5.85	5.64
1996	5.15	4.96	5.10	5.09	5.15	5.23
1997	5.17	5.14	5.28	5.30	5.20	5.07
1998	5.18	5.23	5.16	5.08	5.14	5.12
1999	4.45	4.56	4.57	4.41	4.63	4.72
2000	5.50	5.73	5.86	5.82	5.99	5.86
2001	5.29	5.01	4.54	3.97	3.70	3.57
2002	1.68	1.76	1.83	1.75	1.76	1.73
2003	1.19	1.19	1.15	1.15	1.09	0.94
2004	0.90	0.94	0.95	0.96	1.04	1.29
2005	2.37	2.58	2.80	2.84	2.90	3.04
2006	4.34	4.54	4.63	4.72	4.84	4.92
2007	5.11	5.16	5.08	5.01	4.87	4.74
2008	2.82	2.17	1.28	1.31	1.76	1.89
2009	0.13	0.30	0.22	0.16	0.18	0.18
2010	0.06	0.11	0.15	0.16	0.16	0.12
2011	0.15	0.13	0.10	0.06	0.04	0.04
2012	0.03	0.09	0.08	0.08	0.09	0.09
2013	0.07	0.10	0.09	0.06	0.04	0.05
2014	0.04	0.05	0.05	0.03	0.03	0.04

* Source: Federal Reserve Bank of St. Louis, monthly data calculated as average of business days

3 MONTH TREASURY  BOND YIELDS

JUL	AUG	SEP	OCT	NOV	DEC	
11.86	9.00	8.19	7.97	8.35	8.20	**1982**
9.45	9.74	9.36	8.99	9.11	9.36	**1983**
10.53	10.90	10.80	10.12	8.92	8.34	**1984**
7.32	7.37	7.33	7.40	7.48	7.33	**1985**
6.00	5.69	5.35	5.32	5.50	5.68	**1986**
5.88	6.23	6.62	6.35	5.89	5.96	**1987**
6.95	7.30	7.48	7.60	8.03	8.35	**1988**
8.15	8.17	8.01	7.90	7.94	7.88	**1999**
7.87	7.69	7.60	7.40	7.29	6.95	**1990**
5.75	5.50	5.37	5.14	4.69	4.18	**1991**
3.28	3.20	2.97	2.93 ·	3.21	3.29	**1992**
3.11	3.09	3.01	3.09	3.18	3.13	**1993**
4.46	4.61	4.75	5.10	5.45	5.76	**1994**
5.59	5.57	5.43	5.44	5.52	5.29	**1995**
5.30	5.19	5.24	5.12	5.17	5.04	**1996**
5.19	5.28	5.08	5.11	5.28	5.30	**1997**
5.09	5.04	4.74	4.07	4.53	4.50	**1998**
4.69	4.87	4.82	5.02	5.23	5.36	**1999**
6.14	6.28	6.18	6.29	6.36	5.94	**2000**
3.59	3.44	2.69	2.20	1.91	1.72	**2001**
1.71	1.65	1.66	1.61	1.25	1.21	**2002**
0.92	0.97	0.96	0.94	0.95	0.91	**2003**
1.36	1.50	1.68	1.79	2.11	2.22	**2004**
3.29	3.52	3.49	3.79	3.97	3.97	**2005**
5.08	5.09	4.93	5.05	5.07	4.97	**2006**
4.96	4.32	3.99	4.00	3.35	3.07	**2007**
1.66	1.75	1.15	0.69	0.19	0.03	**2008**
0.18	0.17	0.12	0.07	0.05	0.05	**2009**
0.16	0.16	0.15	0.13	0.14	0.14	**2010**
0.04	0.02	0.01	0.02	0.01	0.01	**2011**
0.10	0.10	0.11	0.10	0.09	0.07	**2012**
0.04	0.04	0.02	0.05	0.07	0.07	**2013**
0.03	0.03	0.02	0.02	0.02	0.03	**2014**

BOND YIELDS — MOODY'S SEASONED CORPORATE Aaa*

	JAN	FEB	MAR	APR	MAY	JUN
1950	2.57	2.58	2.58	2.60	2.61	2.62
1951	2.66	2.66	2.78	2.87	2.89	2.94
1952	2.98	2.93	2.96	2.93	2.93	2.94
1953	3.02	3.07	3.12	3.23	3.34	3.40
1954	3.06	2.95	2.86	2.85	2.88	2.90
1955	2.93	2.93	3.02	3.01	3.04	3.05
1956	3.11	3.08	3.10	3.24	3.28	3.26
1957	3.77	3.67	3.66	3.67	3.74	3.91
1958	3.60	3.59	3.63	3.60	3.57	3.57
1959	4.12	4.14	4.13	4.23	4.37	4.46
1960	4.61	4.56	4.49	4.45	4.46	4.45
1961	4.32	4.27	4.22	4.25	4.27	4.33
1962	4.42	4.42	4.39	4.33	4.28	4.28
1963	4.21	4.19	4.19	4.21	4.22	4.23
1964	4.39	4.36	4.38	4.40	4.41	4.41
1965	4.43	4.41	4.42	4.43	4.44	4.46
1966	4.74	4.78	4.92	4.96	4.98	5.07
1967	5.20	5.03	5.13	5.11	5.24	5.44
1968	6.17	6.10	6.11	6.21	6.27	6.28
1969	6.59	6.66	6.85	6.89	6.79	6.98
1970	7.91	7.93	7.84	7.83	8.11	8.48
1971	7.36	7.08	7.21	7.25	7.53	7.64
1972	7.19	7.27	7.24	7.30	7.30	7.23
1973	7.15	7.22	7.29	7.26	7.29	7.37
1974	7.83	7.85	8.01	8.25	8.37	8.47
1975	8.83	8.62	8.67	8.95	8.90	8.77
1976	8.60	8.55	8.52	8.40	8.58	8.62
1977	7.96	8.04	8.10	8.04	8.05	7.95
1978	8.41	8.47	8.47	8.56	8.69	8.76
1979	9.25	9.26	9.37	9.38	9.50	9.29
1980	11.09	12.38	12.96	12.04	10.99	10.58
1981	12.81	13.35	13.33	13.88	14.32	13.75
1982	15.18	15.27	14.58	14.46	14.26	14.81
1983	11.79	12.01	11.73	11.51	11.46	11.74
1984	12.20	12.08	12.57	12.81	13.28	13.55
1985	12.08	12.13	12.56	12.23	11.72	10.94
1986	10.05	9.67	9.00	8.79	9.09	9.13
1987	8.36	8.38	8.36	8.85	9.33	9.32
1988	9.88	9.40	9.39	9.67	9.90	9.86
1989	9.62	9.64	9.80	9.79	9.57	9.10
1990	8.99	9.22	9.37	9.46	9.47	9.26
1991	9.04	8.83	8.93	8.86	8.86	9.01
1992	8.20	8.29	8.35	8.33	8.28	8.22
1993	7.91	7.71	7.58	7.46	7.43	7.33
1994	6.92	7.08	7.48	7.88	7.99	7.97
1995	8.46	8.26	8.12	8.03	7.65	7.30
1996	6.81	6.99	7.35	7.50	7.62	7.71
1997	7.42	7.31	7.55	7.73	7.58	7.41
1998	6.61	6.67	6.72	6.69	6.69	6.53
1999	6.24	6.40	6.62	6.64	6.93	7.23
2000	7.78	7.68	7.68	7.64	7.99	7.67
2001	7.15	7.10	6.98	7.20	7.29	7.18
2002	6.55	6.51	6.81	6.76	6.75	6.63
2003	6.17	5.95	5.89	5.74	5.22	4.97
2004	5.54	5.50	5.33	5.73	6.04	6.01
2005	5.36	5.20	5.40	5.33	5.15	4.96
2006	5.29	5.35	5.53	5.84	5.95	5.89
2007	5.40	5.39	5.30	5.47	5.47	5.79
2008	5.33	5.53	5.51	5.55	5.57	5.68
2009	5.05	5.27	5.50	5.39	5.54	5.61
2010	5.26	5.35	5.27	5.29	4.96	4.88
2011	5.04	5.22	5.13	5.16	4.96	4.99
2012	3.85	3.85	3.99	3.96	3.80	3.64
2013	3.80	3.90	3.93	3.73	3.89	4.27
2014	4.49	4.45	4.38	4.24	4.16	4.25

* Source: Federal Reserve Bank of St. Louis, monthly data calculated as average of business days

MOODY'S SEASONED CORPORATE Aaa ≣ BOND YIELDS

JUL	AUG	SEP	OCT	NOV	DEC	
2.65	2.61	2.64	2.67	2.67	2.67	**1950**
2.94	2.88	2.84	2.89	2.96	3.01	**1951**
2.95	2.94	2.95	3.01	2.98	2.97	**1952**
3.28	3.24	3.29	3.16	3.11	3.13	**1953**
2.89	2.87	2.89	2.87	2.89	2.90	**1954**
3.06	3.11	3.13	3.10	3.10	3.15	**1955**
3.28	3.43	3.56	3.59	3.69	3.75	**1956**
3.99	4.10	4.12	4.10	4.08	3.81	**1957**
3.67	3.85	4.09	4.11	4.09	4.08	**1958**
4.47	4.43	4.52	4.57	4.56	4.58	**1959**
4.41	4.28	4.25	4.30	4.31	4.35	**1960**
4.41	4.45	4.45	4.42	4.39	4.42	**1961**
4.34	4.35	4.32	4.28	4.25	4.24	**1962**
4.26	4.29	4.31	4.32	4.33	4.35	**1963**
4.40	4.41	4.42	4.42	4.43	4.44	**1964**
4.48	4.49	4.52	4.56	4.60	4.68	**1965**
5.16	5.31	5.49	5.41	5.35	5.39	**1966**
5.58	5.62	5.65	5.82	6.07	6.19	**1967**
6.24	6.02	5.97	6.09	6.19	6.45	**1968**
7.08	6.97	7.14	7.33	7.35	7.72	**1969**
8.44	8.13	8.09	8.03	8.05	7.64	**1970**
7.64	7.59	7.44	7.39	7.26	7.25	**1971**
7.21	7.19	7.22	7.21	7.12	7.08	**1972**
7.45	7.68	7.63	7.60	7.67	7.68	**1973**
8.72	9.00	9.24	9.27	8.89	8.89	**1974**
8.84	8.95	8.95	8.86	8.78	8.79	**1975**
8.56	8.45	8.38	8.32	8.25	7.98	**1976**
7.94	7.98	7.92	8.04	8.08	8.19	**1977**
8.88	8.69	8.69	8.89	9.03	9.16	**1978**
9.20	9.23	9.44	10.13	10.76	10.74	**1979**
11.07	11.64	12.02	12.31	12.97	13.21	**1980**
14.38	14.89	15.49	15.40	14.22	14.23	**1981**
14.61	13.71	12.94	12.12	11.68	11.83	**1982**
12.15	12.51	12.37	12.25	12.41	12.57	**1983**
13.44	12.87	12.66	12.63	12.29	12.13	**1984**
10.97	11.05	11.07	11.02	10.55	10.16	**1985**
8.88	8.72	8.89	8.86	8.68	8.49	**1986**
9.42	9.67	10.18	10.52	10.01	10.11	**1987**
9.96	10.11	9.82	9.51	9.45	9.57	**1988**
8.93	8.96	9.01	8.92	8.89	8.86	**1989**
9.24	9.41	9.56	9.53	9.30	9.05	**1990**
9.00	8.75	8.61	8.55	8.48	8.31	**1991**
8.07	7.95	7.92	7.99	8.10	7.98	**1992**
7.17	6.85	6.66	6.67	6.93	6.93	**1993**
8.11	8.07	8.34	8.57	8.68	8.46	**1994**
7.41	7.57	7.32	7.12	7.02	6.82	**1995**
7.65	7.46	7.66	7.39	7.10	7.20	**1996**
7.14	7.22	7.15	7.00	6.87	6.76	**1997**
6.55	6.52	6.40	6.37	6.41	6.22	**1998**
7.19	7.40	7.39	7.55	7.36	7.55	**1999**
7.65	7.55	7.62	7.55	7.45	7.21	**2000**
7.13	7.02	7.17	7.03	6.97	6.77	**2001**
6.53	6.37	6.15	6.32	6.31	6.21	**2002**
5.49	5.88	5.72	5.70	5.65	5.62	**2003**
5.82	5.65	5.46	5.47	5.52	5.47	**2004**
5.06	5.09	5.13	5.35	5.42	5.37	**2005**
5.85	5.68	5.51	5.51	5.33	5.32	**2006**
5.73	5.79	5.74	5.66	5.44	5.49	**2007**
5.67	5.64	5.65	6.28	6.12	5.05	**2008**
5.41	5.26	5.13	5.15	5.19	5.26	**2009**
4.72	4.49	4.53	4.68	4.87	5.02	**2010**
4.93	4.37	4.09	3.98	3.87	3.93	**2011**
3.40	3.48	3.49	3.47	3.50	3.65	**2012**
4.34	4.54	4.64	4.53	4.63	4.62	**2013**
4.16	4.08	4.11	3.92	3.92	3.79	**2014**

MOODY'S SEASONED
CORPORATE Baa*

	JAN	FEB	MAR	APR	MAY	JUN
1950	3.24	3.24	3.24	3.23	3.25	3.28
1951	3.17	3.16	3.23	3.35	3.40	3.49
1952	3.59	3.53	3.51	3.50	3.49	3.50
1953	3.51	3.53	3.57	3.65	3.78	3.86
1954	3.71	3.61	3.51	3.47	3.47	3.49
1955	3.45	3.47	3.48	3.49	3.50	3.51
1956	3.60	3.58	3.60	3.68	3.73	3.76
1957	4.49	4.47	4.43	4.44	4.52	4.63
1958	4.83	4.66	4.68	4.67	4.62	4.55
1959	4.87	4.89	4.85	4.86	4.96	5.04
1960	5.34	5.34	5.25	5.20	5.28	5.26
1961	5.10	5.07	5.02	5.01	5.01	5.03
1962	5.08	5.07	5.04	5.02	5.00	5.02
1963	4.91	4.89	4.88	4.87	4.85	4.84
1964	4.83	4.83	4.83	4.85	4.85	4.85
1965	4.80	4.78	4.78	4.80	4.81	4.85
1966	5.06	5.12	5.32	5.41	5.48	5.58
1967	5.97	5.82	5.85	5.83	5.96	6.15
1968	6.84	6.80	6.85	6.97	7.03	7.07
1969	7.32	7.30	7.51	7.54	7.52	7.70
1970	8.86	8.78	8.63	8.70	8.98	9.25
1971	8.74	8.39	8.46	8.45	8.62	8.75
1972	8.23	8.23	8.24	8.24	8.23	8.20
1973	7.90	7.97	8.03	8.09	8.06	8.13
1974	8.48	8.53	8.62	8.87	9.05	9.27
1975	10.81	10.65	10.48	10.58	10.69	10.62
1976	10.41	10.24	10.12	9.94	9.86	9.89
1977	9.08	9.12	9.12	9.07	9.01	8.91
1978	9.17	9.20	9.22	9.32	9.49	9.60
1979	10.13	10.08	10.26	10.33	10.47	10.38
1980	12.42	13.57	14.45	14.19	13.17	12.71
1981	15.03	15.37	15.34	15.56	15.95	15.80
1982	17.10	17.18	16.82	16.78	16.64	16.92
1983	13.94	13.95	13.61	13.29	13.09	13.37
1984	13.65	13.59	13.99	14.31	14.74	15.05
1985	13.26	13.23	13.69	13.51	13.15	12.40
1986	11.44	11.11	10.50	10.19	10.29	10.34
1987	9.72	9.65	9.61	10.04	10.51	10.52
1988	11.07	10.62	10.57	10.90	11.04	11.00
1989	10.65	10.61	10.67	10.61	10.46	10.03
1990	9.94	10.14	10.21	10.30	10.41	10.22
1991	10.45	10.07	10.09	9.94	9.86	9.96
1992	9.13	9.23	9.25	9.21	9.13	9.05
1993	8.67	8.39	8.15	8.14	8.21	8.07
1994	7.65	7.76	8.13	8.52	8.62	8.65
1995	9.08	8.85	8.70	8.60	8.20	7.90
1996	7.47	7.63	8.03	8.19	8.30	8.40
1997	8.09	7.94	8.18	8.34	8.20	8.02
1998	7.19	7.25	7.32	7.33	7.30	7.13
1999	7.29	7.39	7.53	7.48	7.72	8.02
2000	8.33	8.29	8.37	8.40	8.90	8.48
2001	7.93	7.87	7.84	8.07	8.07	7.97
2002	7.87	7.89	8.11	8.03	8.09	7.95
2003	7.35	7.06	6.95	6.85	6.38	6.19
2004	6.44	6.27	6.11	6.46	6.75	6.78
2005	6.02	5.82	6.06	6.05	6.01	5.86
2006	6.24	6.27	6.41	6.68	6.75	6.78
2007	6.34	6.28	6.27	6.39	6.39	6.70
2008	6.54	6.82	6.89	6.97	6.93	7.07
2009	8.14	8.08	8.42	8.39	8.06	7.50
2010	6.25	6.34	6.27	6.25	6.05	6.23
2011	6.09	6.15	6.03	6.02	5.78	5.75
2012	5.23	5.14	5.23	5.19	5.07	5.02
2013	4.73	4.85	4.85	4.59	4.73	5.19
2014	5.19	5.10	5.06	4.90	4.76	4.80

* Source: Federal Reserve Bank of St. Louis, monthly data calculated as average of business days

MOODY'S SEASONED CORPORATE Baa* BOND YIELDS

JUL	AUG	SEP	OCT	NOV	DEC	
3.32	3.23	3.21	3.22	3.22	3.20	1950
3.53	3.50	3.46	3.50	3.56	3.61	1951
3.50	3.51	3.52	3.54	3.53	3.51	1952
3.86	3.85	3.88	3.82	3.75	3.74	1953
3.50	3.49	3.47	3.46	3.45	3.45	1954
3.52	3.56	3.59	3.59	3.58	3.62	1955
3.80	3.93	4.07	4.17	4.24	4.37	1956
4.73	4.82	4.93	4.99	5.09	5.03	1957
4.53	4.67	4.87	4.92	4.87	4.85	1958
5.08	5.09	5.18	5.28	5.26	5.28	1959
5.22	5.08	5.01	5.11	5.08	5.10	1960
5.09	5.11	5.12	5.13	5.11	5.10	1961
5.05	5.06	5.03	4.99	4.96	4.92	1962
4.84	4.83	4.84	4.83	4.84	4.85	1963
4.83	4.82	4.82	4.81	4.81	4.81	1964
4.88	4.88	4.91	4.93	4.95	5.02	1965
5.68	5.83	6.09	6.10	6.13	6.18	1966
6.26	6.33	6.40	6.52	6.72	6.93	1967
6.98	6.82	6.79	6.84	7.01	7.23	1968
7.84	7.86	8.05	8.22	8.25	8.65	1969
9.40	9.44	9.39	9.33	9.38	9.12	1970
8.76	8.76	8.59	8.48	8.38	8.38	1971
8.23	8.19	8.09	8.06	7.99	7.93	1972
8.24	8.53	8.63	8.41	8.42	8.48	1973
9.48	9.77	10.18	10.48	10.60	10.63	1974
10.55	10.59	10.61	10.62	10.56	10.56	1975
9.82	9.64	9.40	9.29	9.23	9.12	1976
8.87	8.82	8.80	8.89	8.95	8.99	1977
9.60	9.48	9.42	9.59	9.83	9.94	1978
10.29	10.35	10.54	11.40	11.99	12.06	1979
12.65	13.15	13.70	14.23	14.64	15.14	1980
16.17	16.34	16.92	17.11	16.39	16.55	1981
16.80	16.32	15.63	14.73	14.30	14.14	1982
13.39	13.64	13.55	13.46	13.61	13.75	1983
15.15	14.63	14.35	13.94	13.48	13.40	1984
12.43	12.50	12.48	12.36	11.99	11.58	1985
10.16	10.18	10.20	10.24	10.07	9.97	1986
10.61	10.80	11.31	11.62	11.23	11.29	1987
11.11	11.21	10.90	10.41	10.48	10.65	1988
9.87	9.88	9.91	9.81	9.81	9.82	1989
10.20	10.41	10.64	10.74	10.62	10.43	1990
9.89	9.65	9.51	9.49	9.45	9.26	1991
8.84	8.65	8.62	8.84	8.96	8.81	1992
7.93	7.60	7.34	7.31	7.66	7.69	1993
8.80	8.74	8.98	9.20	9.32	9.10	1994
8.04	8.19	7.93	7.75	7.68	7.49	1995
8.35	8.18	8.35	8.07	7.79	7.89	1996
7.75	7.82	7.70	7.57	7.42	7.32	1997
7.15	7.14	7.09	7.18	7.34	7.23	1998
7.95	8.15	8.20	8.38	8.15	8.19	1999
8.35	8.26	8.35	8.34	8.28	8.02	2000
7.97	7.85	8.03	7.91	7.81	8.05	2001
7.90	7.58	7.40	7.73	7.62	7.45	2002
6.62	7.01	6.79	6.73	6.66	6.60	2003
6.62	6.46	6.27	6.21	6.20	6.15	2004
5.95	5.96	6.03	6.30	6.39	6.32	2005
6.76	6.59	6.43	6.42	6.20	6.22	2006
6.65	6.65	6.59	6.48	6.40	6.65	2007
7.16	7.15	7.31	8.88	9.21	8.43	2008
7.09	6.58	6.31	6.29	6.32	6.37	2009
6.01	5.66	5.66	5.72	5.92	6.10	2010
5.76	5.36	5.27	5.37	5.14	5.25	2011
4.87	4.91	4.84	4.58	4.51	4.63	2012
5.32	5.42	5.47	5.31	5.38	5.38	2013
4.73	4.69	4.80	4.69	4.79	4.74	2014

COMMODITIES

OIL - WEST TEXAS INTERMEDIATE
CLOSING VALUES $ / bbl

	JAN	FEB	MAR	APR	MAY	JUN
1950	2.6	2.6	2.6	2.6	2.6	2.6
1951	2.6	2.6	2.6	2.6	2.6	2.6
1952	2.6	2.6	2.6	2.6	2.6	2.6
1953	2.6	2.6	2.6	2.6	2.6	2.8
1954	2.8	2.8	2.8	2.8	2.8	2.8
1955	2.8	2.8	2.8	2.8	2.8	2.8
1956	2.8	2.8	2.8	2.8	2.8	2.8
1957	2.8	3.1	3.1	3.1	3.1	3.1
1958	3.1	3.1	3.1	3.1	3.1	3.1
1959	3.0	3.0	3.0	3.0	3.0	3.0
1960	3.0	3.0	3.0	3.0	3.0	3.0
1961	3.0	3.0	3.0	3.0	3.0	3.0
1962	3.0	3.0	3.0	3.0	3.0	3.0
1963	3.0	3.0	3.0	3.0	3.0	3.0
1964	3.0	3.0	3.0	3.0	3.0	3.0
1965	2.9	2.9	2.9	2.9	2.9	2.9
1966	2.9	2.9	2.9	2.9	2.9	2.9
1967	3.0	3.0	3.0	3.0	3.0	3.0
1968	3.1	3.1	3.1	3.1	3.1	3.1
1969	3.1	3.1	3.3	3.4	3.4	3.4
1970	3.4	3.4	3.4	3.4	3.4	3.4
1971	3.6	3.6	3.6	3.6	3.6	3.6
1972	3.6	3.6	3.6	3.6	3.6	3.6
1973	3.6	3.6	3.6	3.6	3.6	3.6
1974	10.1	10.1	10.1	10.1	10.1	10.1
1975	11.2	11.2	11.2	11.2	11.2	11.2
1976	11.2	12.0	12.1	12.2	12.2	12.2
1977	13.9	13.9	13.9	13.9	13.9	13.9
1978	14.9	14.9	14.9	14.9	14.9	14.9
1979	14.9	15.9	15.9	15.9	18.1	19.1
1980	32.5	37.0	38.0	39.5	39.5	39.5
1981	38.0	38.0	38.0	38.0	38.0	36.0
1982	33.9	31.6	28.5	33.5	35.9	35.1
1983	31.2	29.0	28.8	30.6	30.0	31.0
1984	29.7	30.1	30.8	30.6	30.5	30.0
1985	25.6	27.3	28.2	28.8	27.6	27.1
1986	22.9	15.4	12.6	12.8	15.4	13.5
1987	18.7	17.7	18.3	18.6	19.4	20.0
1988	17.2	16.8	16.2	17.9	17.4	16.5
1989	18.0	17.8	19.4	21.0	20.0	20.0
1990	22.6	22.1	20.4	18.6	18.2	16.9
1991	25.0	20.5	19.9	20.8	21.2	20.2
1992	18.8	19.0	18.9	20.2	20.9	22.4
1993	19.1	20.1	20.3	20.3	19.9	19.1
1994	15.0	14.8	14.7	16.4	17.9	19.1
1995	18.0	18.5	18.6	19.9	19.7	18.4
1996	18.9	19.1	21.4	23.6	21.3	20.5
1997	25.2	22.2	21.0	19.7	20.8	19.2
1998	16.7	16.1	15.0	15.4	14.9	13.7
1999	12.5	12.0	14.7	17.3	17.8	17.9
2000	27.2	29.4	29.9	25.7	28.8	31.8
2001	29.6	29.6	27.2	27.4	28.6	27.6
2002	19.7	20.7	24.4	26.3	27.0	25.5
2003	32.9	35.9	33.6	28.3	28.1	30.7
2004	34.3	34.7	36.8	36.7	40.3	38.0
2005	46.8	48.0	54.3	53.0	49.8	56.3
2006	65.5	61.6	62.9	69.7	70.9	71.0
2007	54.6	59.3	60.6	64.0	63.5	67.5
2008	93.0	95.4	105.6	112.6	125.4	133.9
2009	41.7	39.2	48.0	49.8	59.2	69.7
2010	78.2	76.4	81.2	84.5	73.8	75.4
2011	89.4	89.6	102.9	110.0	101.3	96.3
2012	100.3	102.3	106.2	103.3	94.7	82.3
2013	94.8	95.3	92.9	92.0	94.5	95.8
2014	94.6	100.8	100.8	102.1	102.2	105.8

* Source: Federal Reserve

OIL - WEST TEXAS INTERMEDIATE CLOSING VALUES $ / bbl

COMMODITIES

JUL	AUG	SEP	OCT	NOV	DEC	
2.6	2.6	2.6	2.6	2.6	2.6	1950
2.6	2.6	2.6	2.6	2.6	2.6	1951
2.6	2.6	2.6	2.6	2.6	2.6	1952
2.8	2.8	2.8	2.8	2.8	2.8	1953
2.8	2.8	2.8	2.8	2.8	2.8	1954
2.8	2.8	2.8	2.8	2.8	2.8	1955
2.8	2.8	2.8	2.8	2.8	2.8	1956
3.1	3.1	3.1	3.1	3.1	3.0	1957
3.1	3.1	3.1	3.1	3.0	3.0	1958
3.0	3.0	3.0	3.0	3.0	3.0	1959
3.0	3.0	3.0	3.0	3.0	3.0	1960
3.0	3.0	3.0	3.0	3.0	3.0	1961
3.0	3.0	3.0	3.0	3.0	3.0	1962
3.0	3.0	3.0	3.0	3.0	3.0	1963
2.9	2.9	2.9	2.9	2.9	2.9	1964
2.9	2.9	2.9	2.9	2.9	2.9	1965
2.9	2.9	3.0	3.0	3.0	3.0	1966
3.0	3.1	3.1	3.1	3.1	3.1	1967
3.1	3.1	3.1	3.1	3.1	3.1	1968
3.4	3.4	3.4	3.4	3.4	3.4	1969
3.3	3.3	3.3	3.3	3.3	3.6	1970
3.6	3.6	3.6	3.6	3.6	3.6	1971
3.6	3.6	3.6	3.6	3.6	3.6	1972
3.6	4.3	4.3	4.3	4.3	4.3	1973
10.1	10.1	10.1	11.2	11.2	11.2	1974
11.2	11.2	11.2	11.2	11.2	11.2	1975
12.2	12.2	13.9	13.9	13.9	13.9	1976
13.9	14.9	14.9	14.9	14.9	14.9	1977
14.9	14.9	14.9	14.9	14.9	14.9	1978
21.8	26.5	28.5	29.0	31.0	32.5	1979
39.5	38.0	36.0	36.0	36.0	37.0	1980
36.0	36.0	36.0	35.0	36.0	35.0	1981
34.2	34.0	35.6	35.7	34.2	31.7	1982
31.7	31.9	31.1	30.4	29.8	29.2	1983
28.8	29.3	29.3	28.8	28.1	25.4	1984
27.3	27.8	28.3	29.5	30.8	27.2	1985
11.6	15.1	14.9	14.9	15.2	16.1	1986
21.4	20.3	19.5	19.8	18.9	17.2	1987
15.5	15.5	14.5	13.8	14.0	16.3	1988
19.6	18.5	19.6	20.1	19.8	21.1	1989
18.6	27.2	33.7	35.9	32.3	27.3	1990
21.4	21.7	21.9	23.2	22.5	19.5	1991
21.8	21.4	21.9	21.7	20.3	19.4	1992
17.9	18.0	17.5	18.1	16.7	14.5	1993
19.7	18.4	17.5	17.7	18.1	17.2	1994
17.3	18.0	18.2	17.4	18.0	19.0	1995
21.3	22.0	24.0	24.9	23.7	25.4	1996
19.6	19.9	19.8	21.3	20.2	18.3	1997
14.1	13.4	15.0	14.4	12.9	11.3	1998
20.1	21.3	23.9	22.6	25.0	26.1	1999
29.8	31.2	33.9	33.1	34.4	28.5	2000
26.5	27.5	25.9	22.2	19.7	19.3	2001
26.9	28.4	29.7	28.9	26.3	29.4	2002
30.8	31.6	28.3	30.3	31.1	32.2	2003
40.7	44.9	46.0	53.1	48.5	43.3	2004
58.7	65.0	65.6	62.4	58.3	59.4	2005
74.4	73.1	63.9	58.9	59.4	62.0	2006
74.2	72.4	79.9	86.2	94.6	91.7	2007
133.4	116.6	103.9	76.7	57.4	41.0	2008
64.1	71.1	69.5	75.6	78.1	74.3	2009
76.4	76.8	75.3	81.9	84.1	89.0	2010
97.2	86.3	85.6	86.4	97.2	98.6	2011
87.9	94.2	94.7	89.6	86.7	88.3	2012
104.7	106.6	106.3	100.5	93.9	97.6	2013
103.6	96.5	93.2	84.4	75.8	59.3	2014

GOLD $US/OZ LONDON PM
MONTH CLOSE

	JAN	FEB	MAR	APR	MAY	JUN
1970	34.9	35.0	35.1	35.6	36.0	35.4
1971	37.9	38.7	38.9	39.0	40.5	40.1
1972	45.8	48.3	48.3	49.0	54.6	62.1
1973	65.1	74.2	84.4	90.5	102.0	120.1
1974	129.2	150.2	168.4	172.2	163.3	154.1
1975	175.8	181.8	178.2	167.0	167.0	166.3
1976	128.2	132.3	129.6	128.4	125.5	123.8
1977	132.3	142.8	148.9	147.3	143.0	143.0
1978	175.8	182.3	181.6	170.9	184.2	183.1
1979	233.7	251.3	240.1	245.3	274.6	277.5
1980	653.0	637.0	494.5	518.0	535.5	653.5
1981	506.5	489.0	513.8	482.8	479.3	426.0
1982	387.0	362.6	320.0	361.3	325.3	317.5
1983	499.5	408.5	414.8	429.3	437.5	416.0
1984	373.8	394.3	388.5	375.8	384.3	373.1
1985	306.7	287.8	329.3	321.4	314.0	317.8
1986	350.5	338.2	344.0	345.8	343.2	345.5
1987	400.5	405.9	405.9	453.3	451.0	447.3
1988	458.0	426.2	457.0	449.0	455.5	436.6
1989	394.0	387.0	383.2	377.6	361.8	373.0
1990	415.1	407.7	368.5	367.8	363.1	352.2
1991	366.0	362.7	355.7	357.8	360.4	368.4
1992	354.1	353.1	341.7	336.4	337.5	343.4
1993	330.5	327.6	337.8	354.3	374.8	378.5
1994	377.9	381.6	389.2	376.5	387.6	388.3
1995	374.9	376.4	392.0	389.8	384.3	387.1
1996	405.6	400.7	396.4	391.3	390.6	382.0
1997	345.5	358.6	348.2	340.2	345.6	334.6
1998	304.9	297.4	301.0	310.7	293.6	296.3
1999	285.4	287.1	279.5	286.6	268.6	261.0
2000	283.3	293.7	276.8	275.1	272.3	288.2
2001	264.5	266.7	257.7	263.2	267.5	270.6
2002	282.3	296.9	301.4	308.2	326.6	318.5
2003	367.5	347.5	334.9	336.8	361.4	346.0
2004	399.8	395.9	423.7	388.5	393.3	395.8
2005	422.2	435.5	427.5	435.7	414.5	437.1
2006	568.8	556.0	582.0	644.0	653.0	613.5
2007	650.5	664.2	661.8	677.0	659.1	650.5
2008	923.3	971.5	933.5	871.0	885.8	930.3
2009	919.5	952.0	916.5	883.3	975.5	934.5
2010	1078.5	1108.3	1115.5	1179.3	1207.5	1244.0
2011	1327.0	1411.0	1439.0	1535.5	1536.5	1505.5
2012	1744.0	1770.0	1662.5	1651.3	1558.0	1598.5
2013	1664.8	1588.5	1598.3	1469.0	1394.5	1192.0
2014	1251.0	1326.5	1291.75	1288.5	1250.5	1315.0

* Source: Bank of England

GOLD $US/OZ LONDON PM MONTH CLOSE

COMMODITIES

JUL	AUG	SEP	OCT	NOV	DEC	
35.3	35.4	36.2	37.5	37.4	37.4	**1970**
41.0	42.7	42.0	42.5	42.9	43.5	**1971**
65.7	67.0	65.5	64.9	62.9	63.9	**1972**
120.2	106.8	103.0	100.1	94.8	106.7	**1973**
143.0	154.6	151.8	158.8	181.7	183.9	**1974**
166.7	159.8	141.3	142.9	138.2	140.3	**1975**
112.5	104.0	116.0	123.2	130.3	134.5	**1976**
144.1	146.0	154.1	161.5	160.1	165.0	**1977**
200.3	208.7	217.1	242.6	193.4	226.0	**1978**
296.5	315.1	397.3	382.0	415.7	512.0	**1979**
614.3	631.3	666.8	629.0	619.8	589.8	**1980**
406.0	425.5	428.8	427.0	414.5	397.5	**1981**
342.9	411.5	397.0	423.3	436.0	456.9	**1982**
422.0	414.3	405.0	382.0	405.0	382.4	**1983**
342.4	348.3	343.8	333.5	329.0	309.0	**1984**
327.5	333.3	326.5	325.1	325.3	326.8	**1985**
357.5	384.7	423.2	401.0	383.5	388.8	**1986**
462.5	453.4	459.5	468.8	492.5	484.1	**1987**
436.8	427.8	397.7	412.4	422.6	410.3	**1988**
368.3	359.8	366.5	375.3	408.2	398.6	**1989**
372.3	387.8	408.4	379.5	384.9	386.2	**1990**
362.9	347.4	354.9	357.5	366.3	353.2	**1991**
357.9	340.0	349.0	339.3	334.2	332.9	**1992**
401.8	371.6	355.5	369.6	370.9	391.8	**1993**
384.0	385.8	394.9	383.9	383.1	383.3	**1994**
383.4	382.4	384.0	382.7	387.8	387.0	**1995**
385.3	386.5	379.0	379.5	371.3	369.3	**1996**
326.4	325.4	332.1	311.4	296.8	290.2	**1997**
288.9	273.4	293.9	292.3	294.7	287.8	**1998**
255.6	254.8	299.0	299.1	291.4	290.3	**1999**
276.8	277.0	273.7	264.5	269.1	274.5	**2000**
265.9	273.0	293.1	278.8	275.5	276.5	**2001**
304.7	312.8	323.7	316.9	319.1	347.2	**2002**
354.8	375.6	388.0	386.3	398.4	416.3	**2003**
391.4	407.3	415.7	425.6	453.4	435.6	**2004**
429.0	433.3	473.3	470.8	495.7	513.0	**2005**
632.5	623.5	599.3	603.8	646.7	632.0	**2006**
665.5	672.0	743.0	789.5	783.5	833.8	**2007**
918.0	833.0	884.5	730.8	814.5	869.8	**2008**
939.0	955.5	995.8	1040.0	1175.8	1087.5	**2009**
1169.0	1246.0	1307.0	1346.8	1383.5	1405.5	**2010**
1628.5	1813.5	1620.0	1722.0	1746.0	1531.0	**2011**
1622.0	1648.5	1776.0	1719.0	1726.0	1657.5	**2012**
1314.5	1394.8	1326.5	1324.0	1253.0	1204.5	**2013**
1285.3	1285.8	1216.5	1164.8	1282.8	1206.0	**2014**

FOREIGN EXCHANGE

US DOLLAR vs CDN DOLLAR
MONTHLY AVG. VALUES*

	JAN US / CDN	JAN CDN / US	FEB US / CDN	FEB CDN / US	MAR US / CDN	MAR CDN /US	APR US / CDN	APR CDN / US	MAY US / CDN	MAY CDN / US	JUN US / CDN	JUN CDN / US
1971	1.01	0.99	1.01	0.99	1.01	0.99	1.01	0.99	1.01	0.99	1.02	0.98
1972	1.01	0.99	1.00	1.00	1.00	1.00	1.00	1.00	0.99	1.01	0.98	1.02
1973	1.00	1.00	1.00	1.00	1.00	1.00	1.00	1.00	1.00	1.00	1.00	1.00
1974	0.99	1.01	0.98	1.02	0.97	1.03	0.97	1.03	0.96	1.04	0.97	1.03
1975	0.99	1.01	1.00	1.00	1.00	1.00	1.01	0.99	1.03	0.97	1.03	0.97
1976	1.01	0.99	0.99	1.01	0.99	1.01	0.98	1.02	0.98	1.02	0.97	1.03
1977	1.01	0.99	1.03	0.97	1.05	0.95	1.05	0.95	1.05	0.95	1.06	0.95
1978	1.10	0.91	1.11	0.90	1.13	0.89	1.14	0.88	1.12	0.89	1.12	0.89
1979	1.19	0.84	1.20	0.84	1.17	0.85	1.15	0.87	1.16	0.87	1.17	0.85
1980	1.16	0.86	1.16	0.87	1.17	0.85	1.19	0.84	1.17	0.85	1.15	0.87
1981	1.19	0.84	1.20	0.83	1.19	0.84	1.19	0.84	1.20	0.83	1.20	0.83
1982	1.19	0.84	1.21	0.82	1.22	0.82	1.23	0.82	1.23	0.81	1.28	0.78
1983	1.23	0.81	1.23	0.81	1.23	0.82	1.23	0.81	1.23	0.81	1.23	0.81
1984	1.25	0.80	1.25	0.80	1.27	0.79	1.28	0.78	1.29	0.77	1.30	0.77
1985	1.32	0.76	1.35	0.74	1.38	0.72	1.37	0.73	1.38	0.73	1.37	0.73
1986	1.41	0.71	1.40	0.71	1.40	0.71	1.39	0.72	1.38	0.73	1.39	0.72
1987	1.36	0.73	1.33	0.75	1.32	0.76	1.32	0.76	1.34	0.75	1.34	0.75
1988	1.29	0.78	1.27	0.79	1.25	0.80	1.24	0.81	1.24	0.81	1.22	0.82
1989	1.19	0.84	1.19	0.84	1.20	0.84	1.19	0.84	1.19	0.84	1.20	0.83
1990	1.17	0.85	1.20	0.84	1.18	0.85	1.16	0.86	1.17	0.85	1.17	0.85
1991	1.16	0.87	1.15	0.87	1.16	0.86	1.15	0.87	1.15	0.87	1.14	0.87
1992	1.16	0.86	1.18	0.85	1.19	0.84	1.19	0.84	1.20	0.83	1.20	0.84
1993	1.28	0.78	1.26	0.79	1.25	0.80	1.26	0.79	1.27	0.79	1.28	0.78
1994	1.32	0.76	1.34	0.74	1.36	0.73	1.38	0.72	1.38	0.72	1.38	0.72
1995	1.41	0.71	1.40	0.71	1.41	0.71	1.38	0.73	1.36	0.73	1.38	0.73
1996	1.37	0.73	1.38	0.73	1.37	0.73	1.36	0.74	1.37	0.73	1.37	0.73
1997	1.35	0.74	1.36	0.74	1.37	0.73	1.39	0.72	1.38	0.72	1.38	0.72
1998	1.44	0.69	1.43	0.70	1.42	0.71	1.43	0.70	1.45	0.69	1.47	0.68
1999	1.52	0.66	1.50	0.67	1.52	0.66	1.49	0.67	1.46	0.68	1.47	0.68
2000	1.45	0.69	1.45	0.69	1.46	0.68	1.47	0.68	1.50	0.67	1.48	0.68
2001	1.50	0.67	1.52	0.66	1.56	0.64	1.56	0.64	1.54	0.65	1.52	0.66
2002	1.60	0.63	1.60	0.63	1.59	0.63	1.58	0.63	1.55	0.65	1.53	0.65
2003	1.54	0.65	1.51	0.66	1.48	0.68	1.46	0.69	1.38	0.72	1.35	0.74
2004	1.30	0.77	1.33	0.75	1.33	0.75	1.34	0.75	1.38	0.73	1.36	0.74
2005	1.22	0.82	1.24	0.81	1.22	0.82	1.24	0.81	1.26	0.80	1.24	0.81
2006	1.16	0.86	1.15	0.87	1.16	0.86	1.14	0.87	1.11	0.90	1.11	0.90
2007	1.18	0.85	1.17	0.85	1.17	0.86	1.14	0.88	1.10	0.91	1.07	0.94
2008	1.01	0.99	1.00	1.00	1.00	1.00	1.01	0.99	1.00	1.00	1.02	0.98
2009	1.22	0.82	1.25	0.80	1.26	0.79	1.22	0.82	1.15	0.87	1.13	0.89
2010	1.04	0.96	1.06	0.95	1.02	0.98	1.01	0.99	1.04	0.96	1.04	0.96
2011	0.99	1.01	0.99	1.01	0.98	1.02	0.96	1.04	0.97	1.03	0.98	1.02
2012	1.01	0.99	1.00	1.00	0.99	1.01	0.99	1.01	1.01	0.99	1.03	0.97
2013	0.99	1.01	1.01	0.99	1.02	.098	1.02	0.98	1.02	0.98	1.03	0.97
2014	1.09	0.91	1.11	0.90	1.11	0.90	1.10	0.91	1.09	0.92	1.08	0.92

Source: Federal Reserve: Avg of daily rates, noon buying rates in New York City for cable transfers payable in foreign currencies

US DOLLAR vs CDN DOLLAR
MONTHLY AVG. VALUES

JUL		AUG		SEP		OCT		NOV		DEC		
US / CDN		US / CDN		US / CDN		US / CDN		US / CDN		US / CDN		
CDN / US		CDN / US		CDN / US		CDN / US		CDN / US		CDN / US		
1.02	0.98	1.01	0.99	1.01	0.99	1.00	1.00	1.00	1.00	1.00	1.00	**1971**
0.98	1.02	0.98	1.02	0.98	1.02	0.98	1.02	0.99	1.01	1.00	1.00	**1972**
1.00	1.00	1.00	1.00	1.01	0.99	1.00	1.00	1.00	1.00	1.00	1.00	**1973**
0.98	1.02	0.98	1.02	0.99	1.01	0.98	1.02	0.99	1.01	0.99	1.01	**1974**
1.03	0.97	1.04	0.97	1.03	0.97	1.03	0.98	1.01	0.99	1.01	0.99	**1975**
0.97	1.03	0.99	1.01	0.98	1.03	0.97	1.03	0.99	1.01	1.02	0.98	**1976**
1.06	0.94	1.08	0.93	1.07	0.93	1.10	0.91	1.11	0.90	1.10	0.91	**1977**
1.12	0.89	1.14	0.88	1.17	0.86	1.18	0.85	1.17	0.85	1.18	0.85	**1978**
1.16	0.86	1.17	0.85	1.17	0.86	1.18	0.85	1.18	0.85	1.17	0.85	**1979**
1.15	0.87	1.16	0.86	1.16	0.86	1.17	0.86	1.19	0.84	1.20	0.84	**1980**
1.21	0.83	1.22	0.82	1.20	0.83	1.20	0.83	1.19	0.84	1.19	0.84	**1981**
1.27	0.79	1.25	0.80	1.23	0.81	1.23	0.81	1.23	0.82	1.24	0.81	**1982**
1.23	0.81	1.23	0.81	1.23	0.81	1.23	0.81	1.24	0.81	1.25	0.80	**1983**
1.32	0.76	1.30	0.77	1.31	0.76	1.32	0.76	1.32	0.76	1.32	0.76	**1984**
1.35	0.74	1.36	0.74	1.37	0.73	1.37	0.73	1.38	0.73	1.40	0.72	**1985**
1.38	0.72	1.39	0.72	1.39	0.72	1.39	0.72	1.39	0.72	1.38	0.72	**1986**
1.33	0.75	1.33	0.75	1.32	0.76	1.31	0.76	1.32	0.76	1.31	0.76	**1987**
1.21	0.83	1.22	0.82	1.23	0.82	1.21	0.83	1.22	0.82	1.20	0.84	**1988**
1.19	0.84	1.18	0.85	1.18	0.85	1.17	0.85	1.17	0.85	1.16	0.86	**1989**
1.16	0.86	1.14	0.87	1.16	0.86	1.16	0.86	1.16	0.86	1.16	0.86	**1990**
1.15	0.87	1.15	0.87	1.14	0.88	1.13	0.89	1.13	0.88	1.15	0.87	**1991**
1.19	0.84	1.19	0.84	1.22	0.82	1.25	0.80	1.27	0.79	1.27	0.79	**1992**
1.28	0.78	1.31	0.76	1.32	0.76	1.33	0.75	1.32	0.76	1.33	0.75	**1993**
1.38	0.72	1.38	0.73	1.35	0.74	1.35	0.74	1.36	0.73	1.39	0.72	**1994**
1.36	0.73	1.36	0.74	1.35	0.74	1.35	0.74	1.35	0.74	1.37	0.73	**1995**
1.37	0.73	1.37	0.73	1.37	0.73	1.35	0.74	1.34	0.75	1.36	0.73	**1996**
1.38	0.73	1.39	0.72	1.39	0.72	1.39	0.72	1.41	0.71	1.43	0.70	**1997**
1.49	0.67	1.53	0.65	1.52	0.66	1.55	0.65	1.54	0.65	1.54	0.65	**1998**
1.49	0.67	1.49	0.67	1.48	0.68	1.48	0.68	1.47	0.68	1.47	0.68	**1999**
1.48	0.68	1.48	0.67	1.49	0.67	1.51	0.66	1.54	0.65	1.52	0.66	**2000**
1.53	0.65	1.54	0.65	1.57	0.64	1.57	0.64	1.59	0.63	1.58	0.63	**2001**
1.55	0.65	1.57	0.64	1.58	0.63	1.58	0.63	1.57	0.64	1.56	0.64	**2002**
1.38	0.72	1.40	0.72	1.36	0.73	1.32	0.76	1.31	0.76	1.31	0.76	**2003**
1.32	0.76	1.31	0.76	1.29	0.78	1.25	0.80	1.20	0.84	1.22	0.82	**2004**
1.22	0.82	1.20	0.83	1.18	0.85	1.18	0.85	1.18	0.85	1.16	0.86	**2005**
1.13	0.89	1.12	0.89	1.12	0.90	1.13	0.89	1.14	0.88	1.15	0.87	**2006**
1.05	0.95	1.06	0.95	1.03	0.97	0.98	1.03	0.97	1.03	1.00	1.00	**2007**
1.01	0.99	1.05	0.95	1.06	0.95	1.18	0.84	1.22	0.82	1.23	0.81	**2008**
1.12	0.89	1.09	0.92	1.08	0.92	1.05	0.95	1.06	0.94	1.05	0.95	**2009**
1.04	0.96	1.04	0.96	1.03	0.97	1.02	0.98	1.01	0.99	1.01	0.99	**2010**
0.96	1.05	0.98	1.02	1.00	1.00	1.02	0.98	1.02	0.98	1.02	0.98	**2011**
1.01	0.99	0.99	1.01	.098	1.02	0.99	1.01	1.00	1.00	0.99	1.01	**2012**
1.04	0.96	1.04	0.96	1.03	0.97	1.04	0.96	1.05	0.95	1.06	0.94	**2013**
1.07	0.93	1.09	0.92	1.10	0.91	1.12	0.89	1.13	0.88	1.15	0.87	**2014**

	JAN		FEB		MAR		APR		MAY		JUN	
	EUR / US	US / EUR	EUR / US	US / EUR	EUR / US	US / EUR	EUR / US	US / EUR	EUR / US	US / EUR	EUR / US	US / EUR
1999	1.16	0.86	1.12	0.89	1.09	0.92	1.07	0.93	1.06	0.94	1.04	0.96
2000	1.01	0.99	0.98	1.02	0.96	1.04	0.94	1.06	0.91	1.10	0.95	1.05
2001	0.94	1.07	0.92	1.09	0.91	1.10	0.89	1.12	0.88	1.14	0.85	1.17
2002	0.88	1.13	0.87	1.15	0.88	1.14	0.89	1.13	0.92	1.09	0.96	1.05
2003	1.06	0.94	1.08	0.93	1.08	0.93	1.09	0.92	1.16	0.87	1.17	0.86
2004	1.26	0.79	1.26	0.79	1.23	0.82	1.20	0.83	1.20	0.83	1.21	0.82
2005	1.31	0.76	1.30	0.77	1.32	0.76	1.29	0.77	1.27	0.79	1.22	0.82
2006	1.21	0.82	1.19	0.84	1.20	0.83	1.23	0.81	1.28	0.78	1.27	0.79
2007	1.30	0.77	1.31	0.76	1.32	0.75	1.35	0.74	1.35	0.74	1.34	0.75
2008	1.47	0.68	1.48	0.68	1.55	0.64	1.58	0.63	1.56	0.64	1.56	0.64
2009	1.32	0.76	1.28	0.78	1.31	0.77	1.32	0.76	1.36	0.73	1.40	0.71
2010	1.43	0.70	1.37	0.73	1.36	0.74	1.34	0.75	1.26	0.80	1.22	0.82
2011	1.34	0.75	1.37	0.73	1.40	0.71	1.45	0.69	1.43	0.70	1.44	0.69
2012	1.29	0.77	1.32	0.76	1.32	0.76	1.32	0.76	1.28	0.78	1.25	0.80
2013	1.33	0.75	1.33	0.75	1.30	0.77	1.30	0.77	1.30	0.77	1.32	0.76
2014	1.36	0.73	1.37	0.73	1.38	0.72	1.38	0.72	1.37	0.73	1.36	0.74

Source: Federal Reserve: Avg of daily rates, noon buying rates in New York City for cable transfers payable in foreign currencies